The Columbia Guide to the Vietnam War

COLUMBIA GUIDES TO AMERICAN HISTORY AND CULTURES

Columbia Guides to American History and Cultures

Michael Kort,
The Columbia Guide to the Cold War

Catherine Clinton and Christine Lunardini,
The Columbia Guide to American Women in the Nineteenth Century

David Farber and Beth Bailey, editors,
The Columbia Guide to America in the 1960s

The Columbia Guide to the Vietnam War

David L. Anderson

COLUMBIA UNIVERSITY PRESS

NEW YORK

Columbia University Press
Publishers Since 1893
New York   Chichester, West Sussex

Copyright © 2002 Columbia University Press
All rights reserved

Library of Congress Cataloging-in-Publication Data

Anderson, David L., 1946–
    The Columbia guide to the Vietnam War / David L. Anderson.
        p.   cm. — (Columbia guides to American history and cultures)
    Includes bibliographical references and index.
    ISBN 0–231–11492–3
    1. Vietnamese Conflict, 1961–1975.   I. Title.   II. Series.

DS557.5 .A54 2002
959.704′3—dc21

                                                           2002020143

                    ∞

Columbia University Press books are printed
on permanent and durable acid-free paper.
Printed in the United States of America
10 9 8 7 6 5 4 3 2 1

CONTENTS

INTRODUCTION

This guide is intended to make the history of the Vietnam War accessible to contemporary readers and applicable to their concerns. The guide is divided into five parts. Part I, "Historical Narrative," offers an overview of the Vietnam War that provides a chronological frame of reference. Within that chronicle, key issues and questions for each period are articulated, and often these issues have produced arguments that comprise both the historical and continuing debate over the war. In chapter 7 of part I, the "Theories of Causation" section summarizes various schools of historical interpretation of the war. Names and terms that appear in boldface upon first reference in part I are more fully identified and discussed in part II. There are also cross-references in part I to document excerpts found in appendix 1. Part II, "The Vietnam War from A to Z," is a mini-encyclopedia with descriptions and analyses of individuals, events, units and groups, military operations, and specialized terms. Part III is a chronology of key events listed by year, and also by month and day where appropriate. Part IV is an annotated guide to resources for studying the war. It is arranged topically. In addition to various kinds of printed works, the resources include theatrical films, documentaries, CD-ROMs, and Internet URLs. The Internet sources are primarily government and university sites that are reliable and likely to remain online. Part V contains two appendices. Appendix 1 presents a collection of excerpts from historical documents, and appendix 2 lists statistical data on such things as troop levels, casualties, bombing tonnage, and expenditures.

Readers may use this guide in several ways. The historical overview in part I can be read as a brief, interpretive history of the entire war. If there is interest in one particular aspect of the war, the reader can consult the relevant subsections of the narrative. Additional details on subjects discussed in the narrative can be found in part II, "The Vietnam War from A to Z." The chronology in part III provides another way to place events in historical perspective or to focus on a particular point in time. The topical arrangement of the resources in part IV basically parallels the organization of the subheadings in part I, and hence further reading on the issues raised in part I can be found in the corresponding section of part IV. The documents and statistics in part V supplement the information in the other sections. Since the information in parts II, III, IV, and V is arranged in standard alphabetical, bibliographical, and tabular form, the reader may use the book as a dictionary or almanac to look up isolated facts. The index also directs the reader to main entries and to many additional items mentioned briefly in the narrative and mini-encyclopedia.

This guide is intended to be both a reference resource and an aid to unraveling the tangled web of the Vietnam War. The goal is to provide the reader with a versatile, objective, and reliable way to understand the intense and significant debate over the war.

ABBREVIATIONS

AFV	American Friends of Vietnam
APC	Armored Personnel Carrier
ARVN	Army of the Republic of Vietnam
CALCAV	Clergy and Laity Concerned About Vietnam
CIA	Central Intelligence Agency
CIDG	Civilian Irregular Defense Groups
CORDS	Civilian Operations and Revolutionary Development Support
COSVN	Central Office for South Vietnam
CPK	Communist Party of Kampuchea
DMZ	Demilitarized Zone
DRV	Democratic Republic of Vietnam
ICP	Indochinese Communist Party
JCS	Joint Chiefs of Staff
MAAG	Military Assistance Advisory Group
MACV	Military Assistance Command, Vietnam
NLF	National Liberation Front
NVA	North Vietnamese Army
PAVN	People's Army of Vietnam
PLAF	People's Liberation Armed Forces
POW/MIA	Prisoner of War/Missing in Action

PRC	People's Republic of China
PRG	Provisional Revolutionary Government
PTSD	Post-traumatic Stress Disorder
RF/PF	Regional Forces/Popular Forces
RVN	Republic of Vietnam
SEATO	Southeast Asia Treaty Organization
SRV	Socialist Republic of Vietnam
SDS	Students for a Democratic Society
VCI	Vietcong Infrastructure
VNQDD	Vietnam Quoc Dan Dang (Vietnam Nationalist Party)
VVAW	Vietnam Veterans Against the War

CHINA

Red River

Mekong River

Black River

BURMA

TONKIN

Cao Bang

Dienbienphu

Hanoi

Haiphong

Gulf of Tonkin

HAINAN

Luang Prabang

L A O S

V I E T

Vientiane

Hue

Tourane

THAILAND

A N N A M

Bangkok

Mekong R.

Tonle Sap

C A M B O D I A

Gulf of Thailand

Phnom Penh

COCHINCHINA

Saigon

✪ French Colonial
Administrative Centers

0   100 km

0   100 mi

N

SOUTH CHINA SEA

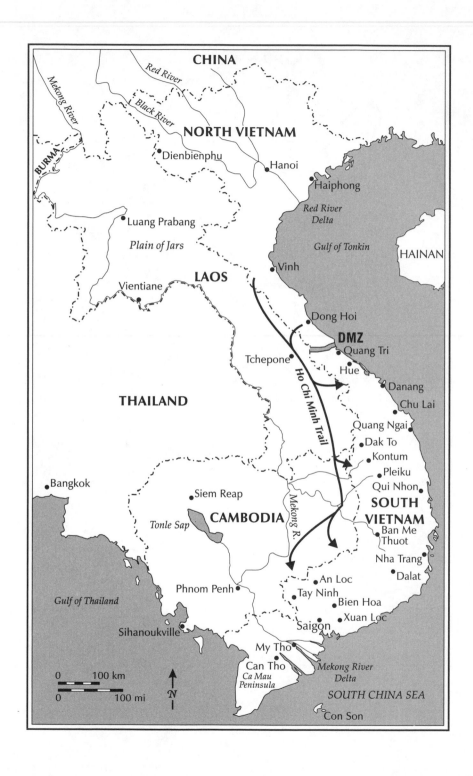

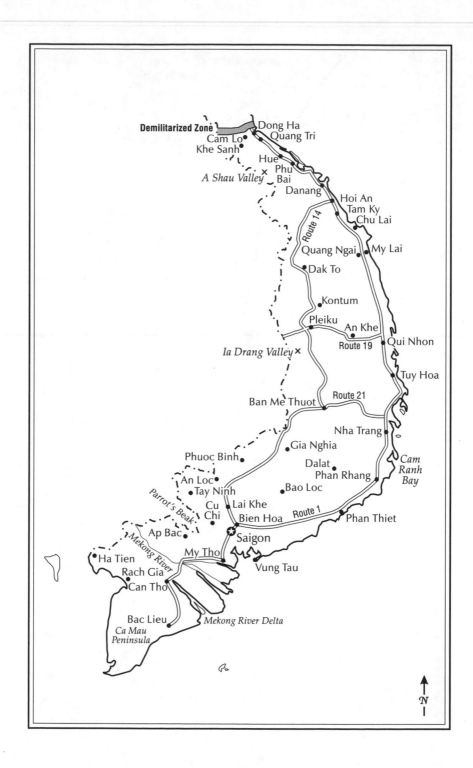

The Columbia Guide to the Vietnam War

PART I

Historical Narrative

Chapter 1

STUDYING THE VIETNAM WAR

To study the Vietnam War one must be prepared to struggle with ambiguity. The war was and continues to be divisive and confusing because both its general outlines and its specific details have been the subject of so much intense debate. There are even arguments over what the war should be called—the Vietnam War, the Indochina War, the American War in Vietnam, and other variations. The name "Vietnam War" is the term most Americans use to denote the conflict that involved the United States in Indochina from about 1950 to 1975. Like the name, the dates are approximate. The French War in Indochina, or the First Indochina War as it is also called, began at the end of World War II and continued until a cease-fire was arranged at the **Geneva Conference** of 1954. The Second Indochina War, or what the Vietnamese term the American War, began around 1960 and continued until the last American civil and military officials departed Saigon in April 1975. Direct U.S. involvement in the Indochina Wars stretched from the middle of the French War until the evacuation of Americans from Saigon in 1975. To understand fully American involvement over that period, however, it is also necessary to consider the history of Vietnam and the United States before 1950 and after 1975. In addition, the Vietnam War has to be understood as a Southeast Asian conflict that spread beyond the borders of Vietnam.

For Americans the Vietnam War was long, costly, and divisive. It was even longer and more costly for the Vietnamese, but that fact made the war only more controversial for Americans. As American casualties mounted and ultimately totaled over 58,000 killed or missing, citizens went beyond simply asking why the United States was in Vietnam to demanding some justification for such sacrifices. As the level of U.S. destruction of the Vietnamese also grew into the hundreds of thousands, some Americans questioned what such ruthlessness revealed about their country's values. World War II had been long and destructive but had united Americans. In sharp contrast, the Vietnam War polarized Americans. Some citizens accepted their losses and the violence of the war as necessary and justified. Others felt that their own grievous losses were without purpose and that the American military intervention in Vietnam was excessive and unjust. These differing perceptions at the time, and ever since, were filtered through ideological and cultural lenses. Hence the events took on different appearances and different meanings, creating the ambiguity that still clouds the understanding of the Vietnam War.

The nature of American historical analysis of the war has changed over time, and the changes reveal the challenges inherent in explaining the Vietnam experience. Prior to the 1960s few American scholars had written about Vietnam. During the war most American scholarly studies were critical of U.S. involvement. Such disagreement with official U.S. policy reversed the pattern of historical works during World War II and the early Cold War. In the so-called orthodox histories of those previous wars, scholars defended or sought to justify U.S. actions. It was not until later that so-called revisionists began to fault U.S. policy in various ways. During the Vietnam War a variety of criticisms appeared as the size of the U.S. commitment grew. Thus the initial, conventional interpretations were negative assessments and included, in particular, the quagmire theory that American leaders blundered into Vietnam or the stalemate theory that leaders lacked the political courage to end what they knew was a losing venture. The most frequently encountered orthodox critique was a liberal-realist interpretation that policymakers had misapplied to Vietnam the containment strategy intended to counter Soviet power in Europe. More extreme than these orthodox complaints was a radical analysis that attacked the American military campaign as imperialist. After the war ended, a revisionist, or "win," school appeared. Its proponents argued that American intervention in Vietnam was merited and that the United States could have won the war if it had used more military force. This contention sparked a number of postrevisionist rebuttals, which were generally reaffirmations (often with more evidence available) of one of the earlier orthodox critiques.

Regardless of whether they viewed the war as just or unjust, the overwhelming majority of Americans polled in various surveys in the years after the war labeled it a mistake. Without question, this negative assessment was an acknowledgment that the United States had lost the war. Despite enormous effort and sacrifice, the U.S. military had not been able to preserve the independence of

South Vietnam and sustain it as a noncommunist bastion against Asian communism, which had been the stated objectives of U.S. policy. While not surprising that Americans understood that mistakes and failures had occurred, the same opinion polls revealed that most respondents could not specifically identify the errors. They did not know whether the United States had done too much or too little. They could not identify specific policies, and, in fact, many could not correctly identify the opposing sides or which side the United States supported. In one 1989 sampling of entering college students, almost one-fourth thought that the opposing sides were North and South *Korea*.

There is more of an imperative to learning about the Vietnam War than just the often repeated adage that those who do not learn from history are condemned to repeat it. The memory of Vietnam is painful for Americans and not one that the society wishes to recall in its entirety, if even at all. A number of writers have characterized the Vietnam experience as a wound, both physical and psychological, on American society. There are parallel legacies of America in Vietnam and Vietnam in America, and it is the latter, the wound within, that tore at the United States then and continues to haunt the national psyche. During the war the wound was open and bleeding as Americans turned on each other in acrimonious debate. The tension of the era went beyond the war itself and included generational, racial, and ideological confrontations.

When the fighting ended and the U.S. troops left Vietnam, the trauma began to recede. There was, in fact, an unwillingness throughout the 1970s to examine carefully what Vietnam had done to America. The wound scabbed over but did not heal. Eventually, in the 1980s, often through the efforts of anguished veterans who needed to resolve their own personal torment, the Vietnam War began to be reexamined. Construction of the **Vietnam Veterans Memorial** ("The Wall") in Washington, D.C., poetry and fiction by veterans, movies, memoirs, and historical research started to dress the wound. This process continued into the 1990s, as more information about what had been secret wartime decision making became known. With more knowledge and more open dialogue, some understanding began to develop about how a great nation like the United States could go so wrong. At the same time, however, the process was more like picking at the scab rather than healing the wound. Cynicism and distrust of leaders still abounded. Old wartime polarities continued to echo in the debates. In 1991 President **George H. W. Bush** led the United States into war against Iraq with broad popular support. Although Bush proclaimed that the Gulf War had finally put the ghost of Vietnam to rest, his own eagerness to end the war quickly and to avoid a protracted and costly engagement demonstrated how strong the memory of Vietnam remained.

As the Gulf War recalled old images of Vietnam, the Cold War that had provided much of the rationale for initial U.S. involvement in Southeast Asia was coming to an end. The Soviet Union and its ruling Communist Party Central

Committee formally dissolved in 1991. This historic turn of events, like Bush's bravura pronouncements about the Gulf War, seemed to have made Vietnam less relevant to the present. In fact, the opposite has been the case. Dissent over the Vietnam War had so disrupted the fiber of American life that the public was skeptical of the national leadership's declarations of purpose and calls for sacrifice. Without the Soviet threat and with bitter memories of Vietnam still lingering, the role of the United States, as the world's lone superpower, was difficult to define in genocidal regional conflicts in the Balkans and in Africa during the 1990s.

As with any major historical event, the Vietnam War does not provide a precise blueprint for present and future actions. Iraq in 1991 or Serbia in 1995 was not Vietnam in 1965 anymore than Vietnam in 1965 was Czechoslovakia in 1938 or Korea in 1950. The meaningful application of history in contemporary life requires a disciplined study of the past with the twin goals of a faithful rendering of past events and a judicious use of analytical principles that transcend time and place. Were there any redeeming features of the Vietnam War for the United States? What do Americans need to understand about the war from Vietnam's perspective? What did the Vietnam War reveal about American culture, history, and values, and what effect did the war have on them? Given its especially contentious nature, the Vietnam War must be approached with extreme caution before making sweeping claims of its relevance or irrelevance today. Care is in order, but avoidance of the study of the war is not.

Chapter 2

VIETNAM: HISTORICAL BACKGROUND

For most Americans the word "Vietnam" refers to a war, but Vietnam was a country with a distinctive history long before it was a war. A Chinese history from 208 B.C. provided the first recorded reference to a non-Chinese people living to the south, in a kingdom called Nam Viet (or Nan Yue in Chinese). From that date two thousand years of recorded history led up to the tumultuous wars in twentieth-century Vietnam.

ROOTS OF THE VIETNAMESE
CULTURE AND STATE

Two historical characteristics of the Vietnamese people emerged from their past. One was a sense of separate ethnic identity and resistance to outside domination derived from a millennium of resistance to control by their powerful Chinese neighbors. The other was a repeated inability to achieve lasting unity among themselves. These two powerful patterns of struggle against external threat and for internal cohesion were clearly visible throughout Vietnam's history into and including the wars with the French and Americans in the second half of the twentieth century. The Vietnamese have fought many times for home rule and over who will rule at home.

WHAT ARE THE CULTURAL ROOTS
OF THE VIETNAMESE NATION?

In 111 B.C. China's powerful Han dynasty extended political control over the Vietnamese people, then centered in the **Red River Delta**. Although China's ability to manage its southern province ebbed and flowed over the centuries, it was not until a decisive naval engagement in A.D. 938 that the Vietnamese fully regained political independence. Although Vietnam's leaders had always preserved considerable political autonomy from China, Vietnamese culture became heavily sinicized by the influence of the vigorous Han and Tang dynasties. Chinese language, arts, and Confucian philosophy shaped Vietnam's culture. In fact, the Vietnamese ability to adopt China's bureaucratic system of administration may have been what helped the always recalcitrant province to ultimately grow strong enough to break China's grasp. In some ways, Vietnam became a defiant replica of China—a smaller version of China's large dragon.

The end of Chinese authority did not mean that a unified Vietnamese state came into being, and for the next thousand years the Vietnamese faced the challenge of establishing a stable political structure in their own country. Power in Vietnam was hereditary, and the right to rule was contested by various families. After about a century of internal conflict following the victory over the Chinese, the Ly dynasty emerged to establish a stable central government that administered the country in the Chinese style through gentry officials chosen by examinations on the Chinese classics. In the thirteenth century, owing to the lack of a male heir, the Ly gave way to the Tran family in a peaceful transition, and internal order continued under the gentry (or what Westerners later called "mandarin") system. This stability was undermined, however, by continued external threats to Vietnam.

In several major military engagements, the Vietnamese repulsed Mongol forces from the north in the 1280s, and then in the fourteenth century they fought a series of successful campaigns against invaders from **Champa**, the area that is now central Vietnam. The military leader of the victory over the Chams then overthrew the Tran dynasty and set off turmoil in Vietnam that tempted the strong Ming dynasty of China once again to attempt to reclaim the former Chinese province. In 1428, however, Le Loi, a great hero of Vietnamese history and founder of the Le dynasty, forced China to recognize Vietnam's autonomy.

With the northern border secure, the Le dynasty began what is known as the March to the South in 1471. Initially aimed at removing the remaining vestiges of threat from Champa, this southern expansion continued for three hundred years until the Vietnamese claimed all the territory along the Southeast Asian coast down to the tip of the Cau Mau Peninsula. This geographic expansion brought with it a breakdown of the Le's central authority and led to a regional division of power among three rival families. A number of bloody wars finally eliminated the Mac family and brought a stalemate between the Trinh and Nguyen families. The line of demarcation between their areas of control was a wall built by the Nguyen. Located north of **Hue**, the wall was very near the line drawn at the Geneva Conference in 1954 to divide North and South Vietnam.

HOW HAVE THE CONCEPTS OF THE NATION, THE REGION, AND THE VILLAGE SHAPED VIETNAMESE HISTORY?

As rival families fought to consolidate power and form a unified Vietnamese nation, strong forces of regionalism and rebellion against the central authority persisted. The geography of Vietnam was a major obstacle to national unity. The area populated by the Vietnamese consisted of a strip of fertile land hugging the coast of the South China Sea, from the agriculturally rich Red River Delta in the north to the similarly productive **Mekong River Delta** in the south. Mountains to the west confined the population to the coast, and ridges from this mountain range extended to the shore, effectively isolating the country's disparate regions. Distance and topography hampered central authority and gave protection to rebels.

In these settlements, scattered along Vietnam's thousand-mile length and economically based on patty rice cultivation, the local village, not the courts of emperors or powerful families, became the locus of authority. The villagers shared a common Confucian culture but retained their autonomy over their own affairs in a deeply rooted pattern of family, property, and tradition. This fragmentation of political authority was one reason why the Trinh and Nguyen had not been able to break their stalemate. The villages were also fertile ground for the emergence of rebel movements that challenged regional and central authority. It was, in fact, a village-based rebellion that erupted in 1777, in Nguyen territory near Hue, that broke the stalemate and produced the unity that Vietnam had been struggling for centuries to achieve.

This **Tay Son Rebellion** took its name from the village of its leaders, three brothers. Directed at first against local corruption, the rebellion spread to ignite a series of battles that ended with defeat of both the Nguyen and Trinh families. It was not the Tay Son rebels who emerged victorious, however. With fighting concentrated in the north against the Trinh, a surviving Nguyen heir, Nguyen Anh, seized the Mekong Delta with military aid provided by a French priest, Pigneau de Béhaine (see **Catholics**). To protect French missionaries, whose predecessors had first come to the region in the seventeenth century, Pigneau arranged for French merchants to pay European mercenaries and arm them with modern weapons. With this help, Nguyen Anh's forces moved north and took the Tay Son strongholds. In 1802 Nguyen Anh proclaimed himself Emperor Gia Long over a united Vietnam that stretched from the border with

China to the Gulf of Siam. Although regional authorities throughout the country agreed to recognize Gia Long as emperor, much real power still remained in the hands of village and regional leaders.

THE IMPACT OF FRENCH COLONIALISM

The **Nguyen dynasty** that Gia Long founded, with its capital at Hue, was Vietnam's last dynasty. The traditional Confucian political and social structure that it represented collapsed under the colonial rule of the French, who rose to dominate Vietnam and neighboring Cambodia and Laos in the nineteenth and twentieth centuries. An empty shell of the monarchy remained until both it and French colonialism fell victim in the 1950s to revolutionary changes.

Because of Pigneau's help and because he was aware of the strength of Western power, Gia Long tolerated the presence of French missionaries in his country, but he and, especially, his successors were hostile to Christianity. Increasing persecution of missionaries and the West's growing appetite for markets and resources in the nineteenth century caused France to send a naval force to Tourane (**Danang**) in 1858. From then until 1897, in a piecemeal fashion, France used military force to create what it called the Indochina Union, headed by a French governor-general in **Hanoi**. French Indochina consisted of five parts. In 1862 Emperor Tu Duc ceded **Cochinchina**, the area around Saigon, to France as a colony. **Annam** (central Vietnam around Hue) and **Tonkin** (northern Vietnam around Hanoi) became French protectorates in 1883. Paris also established protectorates in Cambodia in 1862 and Laos in 1893.

IN WHAT WAYS DID FRENCH COLONIALISM ALTER VIETNAMESE SOCIETY?

French colonial rule in Vietnam was incredibly illiberal, narrow-minded, and destructive. The partitioning of Vietnam into three *pays* (countries), as the French called Tonkin, Annam, and Cochinchina, reversed centuries of Vietnamese efforts to create national unity. The Nguyen emperors had themselves administered their elongated country through three *ky* (regions) that were roughly analogous to the *pays*, but where the emperors sought to use this structure to promote unity, the French desired division. The colonial authorities even outlawed the use of the name "Vietnam." This colonial-enforced regionalism magnified cultural differences that had already existed from the March to the South, which brought Chams, Khmers, and others into Vietnam's borders. Vietnam's difficulty in achieving internal unity in the face of external threats was once again manifest.

The French governors sought to protect their authority by depriving the country of its native leadership. Giving their program the high sounding name *mission civilisatrice* (civilizing mission), they not only sought to replace Vietnam's political leadership but also Vietnam's literature, thought, and culture. The social order in Vietnam was decapitated. The mandarin class was either compromised by collaboration with the French or isolated in hopeless efforts to revive Confucianism as an antidote to Western wealth and power. Colonial bureaucracy took over much of the administrative role of the village gentry and chiefs, thereby removing the legal autonomy of the villages and debilitating the Vietnamese social system. Vietnamese attempts to organize modern alternatives, such as political parties or labor organizations, were stamped out by police control over travel, mail, and publications that effectively repressed any type of indigenous movement for collective action.

French colonialism aimed to make a mercantilist profit out of what was largely a subsistence economy. Economic exploitation of Indochina gave no opportunity for a broad-based system of capitalism to develop among the Vietnamese. In fact, capitalism had a very bad image in Vietnam. French taxes and low wages in the Red River Delta added to the poverty and insecurity that already existed in that overcrowded area. In the Mekong River Delta, where open land had been available for landless peasants, a plantation economy put that land in the hands of an elite minority of Vietnamese collaborators. Economic conditions worsened for peasants, while plantation owners, exporters, the Banque de l'Indochine, money lenders, and rice traders got rich. Colonialism was breeding revolutionary attitudes among the people (see document 1, appendix 1).

THE RISE OF VIETNAMESE NATIONALISM

The harsh French colonial policies violently uprooted Vietnamese society, but they did not extinguish the centuries-old passion for independence and national unity. From the outset of French conquest, Vietnamese resisted in various ways. From indecision and miscalculation, the imperial court failed to provide leadership, and the Vietnamese gentry was on its own on how to respond. Some collaborated with the colonialists, some simply dropped out of public life, and some openly fought back only to be soundly defeated by a superior force. By the 1890s, however, some Vietnamese were examining how other Asian peoples were responding to Western imperialism. Out of that examination came a modern sense of Vietnamese nationalism. How best to combat the powerful intruders remained much debated, however.

The representative figure of this Vietnamese resistance to colonialism was **Phan Boi Chau**. Educated in both Confucian and Western thought, he looked for lessons from China's efforts at self-strengthening, Japan's Meiji Restoration, and finally Sun Yat-sen's republican movement in China. Strongly anti-French, he and his Modernization Society at first advocated a constitutional monarchy and then, inspired by China's Revolution of 1911, a Vietnamese republic. An organizer and propagandist who often lived outside Vietnam, Chau was seized by French agents in China in 1925. Sentenced to death for sedition, he was paroled to home confinement in Hue and died in obscurity in 1940. His work represented a significant shift in the goals of the anti-French activists, away from efforts to restore the monarchy toward a focus on the Vietnamese nation and a government representative of people of all social classes. His ambiguous combination of tradition and modernization, and disagreements among his adherents over confrontation versus cooperation with the French masters, however, made Chau's nationalist program too moderate to contest French power. By the time of his death, he was an anachronism.

Other moderate nationalists fared no better. There were several attempts by urban intellectuals to create political parties that would challenge the colonial government. One of the most significant was the **Vietnam Quoc Dan Dang** (VNQDD), or Vietnam Nationalist Party. Created in 1927, it sought to emulate China's Guomindang, or Nationalist Party. Since the French governors outlawed all Vietnamese political parties (except for the nonthreatening Constitutionalist Party of the Francophile elite), the VNQDD functioned secretly. It recruited members who were students, soldiers, low-level bureaucrats, women, and small-business owners. It had no rural or broad popular base. In 1930 the VNQDD attempted to spark an armed rebellion, which was quickly and ruthlessly crushed by the authorities. Hundreds of party members were arrested, and many were executed (some leaders were beheaded) or sentenced to harsh imprisonment and forced labor. For Vietnamese patriots to hope to break French control of the country, they were going to have to enlist a broad segment of the population in a more disciplined effort.

THE ORIGINS OF VIETNAMESE COMMUNISM

Revolution seemed to be the only answer to the economic exploitation, political repression, and cultural arrogance of French colonialism, and in 1925 an embryonic revolutionary party appeared. A secret group, Vietnam Thanh Nien Cach Mang Dong Chi Hoi, or Vietnamese Revolutionary Youth League, was formed in south China by a man calling himself Nguyen Ai Quoc. Its goals were simply stated as national independence and social equality for Vietnamese. In 1930 the Thanh Nien became the basis for the creation of the **Indochinese Communist Party** (ICP) (see document 2, appendix 1). In the early 1940s Nguyen Ai Quoc changed his name to **Ho Chi Minh**. This singular individual was the leader of the Vietnamese communist movement from its inception until his death in 1969.

WHAT ARE THE NATURE OF AND THE RELATIONSHIP BETWEEN NATIONALISM AND COMMUNISM IN VIETNAM?

This question is central to the twentieth-century history of Vietnam and often has been posed specifically with regard to Ho Chi Minh. Ho was a Vietnamese nationalist who became a communist, and who then combined both identities in his own charismatic leadership and in the movement that he not only headed but symbolized.

Ho's father was a mandarin who had to struggle to provide for his family after losing his government post for refusing to enforce French colonial laws. His father was also a friend of Phan Boi Chau. From an early age, Ho was filled with a sense of the injustice and hardship caused by French rule and of the lessons imparted by Chau of the importance of political organization to counter European dominance. Under the colonial education system, he learned French and was exposed to Western literature and ideas. He was, in fact, a student in France during World War I and tried unsuccessfully to present a petition for Vietnamese independence to the Versailles Peace Conference. This rebuff starkly contradicted the self-determination rhetoric of Woodrow Wilson at Versailles and had a formative impact on the young Nguyen Ai Quoc. He had also discovered the writings of Vladimir Lenin, which to him explained the theory behind the successful Bolshevik Revolution in Russia and provided a blueprint for successful social and political revolution for victims of imperialism like the Vietnamese. In 1920 Ho became a founding member of the French Communist Party.

Ho embarked on a career as a communist party organizer. He lived in the Soviet Union, China, and elsewhere outside Vietnam but was always committed to Vietnamese independence through the vehicle of Marxist-Leninist revolution. The Vietnamese communists embraced ideals of national self-determination, revolutionary class struggle, and party dictatorship similar to those that also shaped the Chinese Communist Party, which was founded in 1921. Asian Marxists like Ho and China's **Mao Zedong** understood that there was no proletariat and bourgeoisie of sufficient size in their countries to fit the model of industrialized Europe. The masses were predominantly rural peasants, and they were farmers whose social and economic security had been uprooted by Western imperialism. The Vietnamese communists considered Marxism to be a new form of social community, something like what the old village community had been in the peasant mind.

Shortly after creation of the ICP, a major peasant revolt against the local authorities broke out in Nghe-Tinh Province in Annam. Near starvation conditions in the region sparked the outbreak, and communist organizers tried to help the peasants form "soviets" to take control, reduce rents, and even break up some large land holdings. By the spring of 1931 the French governors had restored order and had arrested and executed hundreds of communist cadres. Ho reflected that these events demonstrated the revolutionary potential of the peasants but also the importance of proper preparation and broad national support before attempting direct action.

Although forced to lie low in Vietnam and to operate largely from China and Thailand, the party leadership survived the crackdown. Ho was arrested in Hong Kong by British police for suspicious activities. Released from jail in 1933, he went to Moscow on orders from the Comintern, which had concerns about his nationalist inclinations and variant, agrarian interpretation of Marxist doctrine. With the rise of Adolph Hitler in Germany and Japanese aggression in China, the Comintern directed Asian communists to undertake united front strategies with bourgeois and progressive opponents of fascism. Ho had favored patriotic fronts since his creation of the Revolutionary Youth League. France itself formed a Popular Front government in 1936 and legalized such groups in its colonies. Without revealing their communist identities, ICP members established the Indochina Democratic Front in Tonkin. The Central Committee of the ICP sent two of the front's young and talented members, **Pham Van Dong** and **Vo Nguyen Giap**, to China in the spring of 1940 to work with Ho, who had left Moscow and was working with the Chinese Communist Party. In September 1940 Japanese forces, with the acquiescence of the Vichy French government that was collaborating with Germany, took over bases in Indochina for the war against China. Ho and his comrades began immediately to try to forge alliances with all Vietnamese nationalists who opposed the French and the Japanese. World War II had come to Southeast Asia, and it started a process that would end French colonialism.

Chapter 3

UNITED STATES: HISTORICAL BACKGROUND

The American War in Vietnam is filled with ironies. There are, for example, some striking parallels in the histories of the two countries. In the eighteenth century, the United States fought for and gained its independence in an anti-colonial war against a European mercantilist power. The United States struggled both before and after its independence to achieve national unity and went through a bloody civil war between North and South. Such similarities with Vietnam's quest for independence and unity can be carried only to a point, of course. Many differences of time, place, and culture make for important distinctions between the two countries. To understand how the United States came to be so immersed in Vietnam after World War II, however, historical patterns and traditions of United States involvement in world affairs must be examined. To use a term popular with cultural theorists, American historical experience "foregrounds" the Vietnam War.

IDEALISM AND REALISM IN U.S. FOREIGN POLICY

WHAT IS THE RELATIONSHIP BETWEEN THE EMERGENCE OF THE UNITED STATES AS A WORLD POWER AND THE AMERICAN SELF-IMAGE AS A GLOBAL GUARDIAN OF DEMOCRACY?

From its birth, the American nation experienced tension between its democratic ideals and national self-interest. The earliest English settlers self-consciously

proclaimed America to be "a City upon a Hill," that is, a model of self-government and economic opportunity for the world. These idealists were also realists
who faced harsh conditions and hostile foes in the New World. They could be
eminently pragmatic and even ruthless to ensure their survival and pursue their
ambitions. Out of a wilderness they built farms, communities, and, eventually, a
thriving nation, and they emerged with a sense of self-satisfaction and moral rec-
titude.

The American self-image at home and abroad came to be shaped by aggrandizement and altruism, motives that can both clash and complement each other.
This ambiguity produced, in turn, some ambivalent attitudes. Americans had a
vast continent stretching before them and a seemingly safe distance separating
them from the dangers of European conflicts in the nineteenth century. These
circumstances produced a desire among some for isolation from the rest of the
world. Americans were never divorced commercially from the world, however,
and they also possessed a powerful national myth that the American Revolution
and the effective U.S. Constitution that emerged afterward had made the United
States the freest, most democratic, most republican, and most progressive political system ever created. Sometimes termed "exceptionalism" by historians, this
belief presumed that the United States was the closest any people had ever come
to a virtuous and equitable society. Exceptionalism also carried with it a sense of
responsibility to share this remarkable achievement with others. This sense of
mission combined with the sense of self-preservation formed a potent prescrip-
tion for the expansion of American global involvement. This version of America's worldview invited the nation to make the world a better place for the benefit of others and for the sake of American interests and ideals.

THE UNITED STATES
AND THE OPEN DOOR IN ASIA

The dilemma inherent in the American worldview was apparent in Asia at the
beginning of the twentieth century. Through most of the nineteenth century
the United States focused its expansive energies and sense of mission on North
America. Early in the century it followed its philosophy of benevolent and inevitable imperialist expansion, so called Manifest Destiny, to occupy the land
from the Atlantic to the Pacific, and after mid-century it utilized its great natural
resources and growing domestic market to create one of the strongest industrial
economies in the world. As the end of the century neared, the continental frontier had disappeared, and a major economic depression seemed to indicate that
growth of U.S. industrial production had exceeded the capacity of the home
market to absorb it. Some Americans began looking across the Pacific to Asia for
customers, but there they found the British, French, other Europeans, and the
rapidly modernizing Japanese already claiming colonies or threatening to seize

commercial control of key markets, especially regions in China. Like the early American settlers facing the wilderness—and influenced by popular Social Darwinist ideas about Western cultural supremacy—U.S. leaders pondered a leap into the imperialist scramble in Asia.

Despite sharing much of the European racial bias toward Asians and disdain for Asian culture, Americans were keenly aware that colonization, military interventionism, and even government action to protect private commercial interests were contrary to American national traditions. Officials in Washington and leaders in American business did not wish to emulate the French example in Indochina. Some were concerned about American democratic principles and others about the risks of military and economic burdens in distant places. In order to meet the challenge of creating an approach that would protect American interests and ideals, the administration of President William McKinley took three fateful steps: a war with Spain in 1898, assertion of an open door in China, and annexation of the Philippine Islands. Together, these actions initiated the American Open Door Policy in Asia.

DID THE OPEN DOOR POLICY IN ASIA INCLUDE ELEMENTS OF BOTH IMPERIALISM AND IDEALISM?

Historians have disagreed about the meaning of the Open Door Policy because of its ambiguous combination of imperialism and idealism, but most scholars agree that it marked a significant step in U.S. foreign policy. McKinley based his request for a congressional declaration of war against Spain on an abstract ideal, the defense of Cuba's right to self-determination and the elimination of Spanish colonial rule, but an independent Cuba also meant markets and resources for Americans. Hence the war began with dual objectives and quickly became more complicated when U.S. naval forces took possession of Manila Bay in the Spanish colony of the Philippines. The United States quickly broke Spain's weak grip on Cuba, but before the fate of the Philippines could be determined, a crisis developed in China.

It appeared that several European nations and Japan were about to divide China into spheres of influence. Rather than claim a U.S. sphere, McKinley's secretary of state, John Hay, asked the nations to allow others to have commercial access to their areas of economic interest in China. He obtained and announced qualified pledges to respect an open door for trade. In July 1900, when the Boxer Uprising in China threatened to renew foreign claims for economic and territorial concessions, Hay issued a second Open Door Note, which was a unilateral declaration that free trade could only be preserved if China remained a single entity.

While these events were occurring in 1899 and 1900, the U.S. Senate ratified a treaty with Spain making the Philippines a U.S. possession, which prompted an armed resistance to American rule from Philippine rebels led by Emilio Aguinaldo. The ensuing war was marked by savagery by both sides. In 1901 U.S. soldiers subdued the rebels, whom they called "**gooks**" (a racial epithet also used by U.S. soldiers later to refer to Vietnamese).

U.S. interest in an open door for trade in China and possession of the Philippines as a base for that trade revealed that the temptations of empire could overwhelm America's altruistic impulses. At the same time, American leaders rationalized these actions as being in the long-term best interests of China and the Philippines. Historians such as the scholar-diplomat George Kennan have argued that the Open Door Policy was not based on a realistic pursuit of U.S. interest but rather on confused and idealistic clichés about protecting China's sovereignty and tutoring the Filipinos. These abstract concepts did not provide clear guidance for U.S. policy. Conversely, William Appleman Williams and other historians have characterized the Open Door Policy as a rational attempt to preserve and use the strength of the U.S. economy. Williams terms it a tragedy, however, that this defense of U.S. material interests then and later led U.S. leaders to violate basic American ideals, such as the right of people to self-determination. Most historians today accept the idea of an American empire, but debate continues over how it compares to the imperialism of other Western nations (see documents 3 and 4, appendix 1).

THE WORLD WARS:
THE LEGACIES OF WILSON AND MUNICH

In the first half of the twentieth century, the United States fought and won, with its allies, two major world wars. The McKinley administration's forays into Cuba, China, and the Philippines were relatively painless for the United States and generated a false complacency about inherent risks in the nation's dual goals. It appeared to be within America's power to advance liberal democratic ideals in the world and to protect U.S. security and material interests. Indeed, American leaders conceived of the two objectives as mutually reinforcing. What was good for America was good for the world, and vice versa. In World War I and World War II, the success of American arms backed by the strength of the American economy seemed to give credence to this thinking.

In leading the United States into World War I, President Woodrow Wilson articulated an appealing national vision that equated American ideals and self-interest with the goal of a world free of power politics and aggression. At first reluctant to enter the conflict, Wilson eventually declared that the United States would join the fray with the purpose of making this "the war to end all wars." Although World War I failed to resolve forever all international conflict, Wilson's stirring rhetoric continued to shape the objectives of U.S. foreign policy in World War II and during the Cold War that followed.

WHAT WERE THE LEGACIES OF WILSONIAN COLLECTIVE SECURITY AND THE EXAMPLE OF APPEASEMENT AT MUNICH?

In his statement of war aims—his Fourteen Points, which included proposals for respecting the interests of colonial populations and for a league of nations—Wilson condemned aggression and argued that collective security was possible through the common interest in peace shared by all peoples (see document 5, appendix 1). This idealistic view of world order fell victim to the ambitions of Italy, Germany, and Japan in the 1930s, as those states revealed their willingness to choose aggression to gain national objectives. The symbol of the impotence of paper pledges of mutual respect was the Munich Agreement of September 1938, in which British and French leaders agreed to German annexation of part of Czechoslovakia in return for Adolph Hitler's promise of no additional aggression (see **Munich Analogy**). Six months later Hitler demanded the rest of Czechoslovakia, and the Munich Agreement forever became the example of the futility of appeasement. It took two more years before the United States entered World War II as a belligerent, but the challenge of the dictators led **Franklin D. Roosevelt** to renew the appeal to Wilson's ideals.

In the tradition of Wilson, Roosevelt defined U.S. war aims in World War II as the defense of freedom—the freedom of people to choose their own government, to be secure in their own territory, and to trade openly in a world without economic barriers (see document 6, appendix 1). As Hay's Open Door Notes had revealed, these altruistic-sounding objectives also meant the preservation of a stable world in which U.S. political and economic interests were not threatened. Unlike Wilson, who was a reluctant war leader, Roosevelt accepted the reality that American power had to be a balance to the forces of aggression. The failure of appeasement at Munich provided evidence that military defeat was the only message aggressors understood. For this reason, among others, Roosevelt rejected the Wilsonian hope for a war without victors and called for "absolute victory" in his address to Congress the day after Japan bombed Pearl Harbor.

DID WORLD WAR II CREATE A "VICTORY CULTURE" IN AMERICA?

When World War II ended in 1945, the United States was not only victorious, it was also the most powerful nation in the world. Britain and the Soviet Union were wartime allies of the United States and shared in the triumph over fascism, but both countries were themselves heavily damaged by the war. The losers—Germany, Italy, and Japan—were prostrate, and other major nations, such as France and China, were burdened by the weight of war, occupation, and their own internal divisions. In contrast, the United States stood triumphant with its fields and factories unscathed, its productivity—geared up for war—at an all-time high, and its military and technological dominance—symbolized by the

atomic bombs dropped on Japan—well beyond any potential rival. At that moment, the United States was the strongest nation the world had ever known.

The might of the nation blended in American thought with a sense of righ-
teousness. The cultural myth of American exceptionalism, of the goodness of
America vanquishing the evils of autocracy, dictatorship, and militarism,
seemed to have been realized. Even during the war and before victory was assured, Hollywood movies, government pronouncements, and public expressions of patriotism painted heroic images of the United States and its past.
America cast itself in the role of rescuer. As the Open Door Policy and Wilsonian internationalism had done, American attitudes at the end of World War II
equated U.S. ideals and interests with those of the world.

THE ORIGINS OF THE COLD WAR

Despite the glow of victory, the end of the war did not bring peace and security
for the United States and the rest of the world. Even as the war drew to a close
and then in the months immediately following, suspicion and hostility, which
eventually led to armed confrontations, frequently to the brink of war, developed between the United States and the Soviet Union. The origins of the Cold
War are complex, but the result was a division of the world into separate spheres
of influence around one or the other of the nations, with other areas outside
these spheres being contested by both. It was in the context of the Cold War that
U.S. history intersected with Vietnamese history.

WAS THE UNITED STATES ON THE OFFENSIVE OR DEFENSIVE
IN THE COLD WAR?

In the Open Door Policy, World War I, and World War II, American self-image
portrayed the nation as the defender of its own as well as others' rights. The of-
fenders were monarchists, imperialists, militarists, and fascists. As the annexation of the Philippines revealed, however, the line between altruism and ac-
quisitiveness could be easily blurred. The Open Door Policy used the rhetoric
of freedom to try to discourage economic barriers that worked against U.S. interests. Wilson and Roosevelt's condemnations of aggression were defenses of a
status quo that, at the time, favored the United States and not dissatisfied nations such as Germany and Japan. At the end of World War II, the American vision of the postwar world was not universally accepted.

Despite World War II's lessons of power politics, U.S. objectives still retained
the Wilsonian ideal that world affairs could be governed by abstract principles
of fairness. Conversely, Soviet leader Josef Stalin insisted that, regardless of what
the United States considered fair, his government would use its power to protect
its vital interests. One issue of clear concern to the Soviet Union was the future

of its border state Poland. In the American view, Poland had the right to free elections to choose its own government, but from Moscow's perspective, the security of the USSR required the Poles to choose a regime friendly to Russia.

Differences between the United States and the Soviet Union on a host of postwar issues, such as the government of Poland, pose profound questions about the causes of the Cold War. Stalin's demands (backed by the presence of the Red Army in Eastern Europe) for influence over Poland made him appear to be an aggressor like Hitler, and the lesson of Munich suggested that Soviet control over Poland should be countered by force if necessary. Further evidence of aggression could be found in the historic ambition of Russian leaders to possess Poland. Stalin's communist ideology also made Soviet power threatening. Stalin asserted that the capitalist West was intent upon the conquest of his country and economically vulnerable areas like Poland. Thus history, ideology, and Stalin's reputation for ruthlessness were used by American leaders to cast the USSR as aggressive and U.S. political, economic, and military opposition to Moscow as defensive.

On the other hand, the United States had a tremendous advantage in economic and military power over the Soviet Union in 1945. The question can be reasonably raised as to whether this strength tempted the United States to be more assertive and interventionist in areas that were of less interest to it than to Moscow. The United States had never had any historic interest in Poland, for example, whereas Russia did. Stalin's charge of capitalist imperialism in Eastern Europe was ideologically inspired but also logical from his perspective. Was the United States seeking an open door in Poland to defend self-determination or to keep open a market for Western European and American exploitation? If any of these motives were at work, then the United States could be characterized as being on the offensive in the Cold War.

Since U.S. and Soviet leaders both universalized their rationales for their Cold War conduct, the conflict spread throughout Europe and the world. Tension mounted with belligerent talk from both sides. In 1947, to gain an appropriation from Congress for aid to Greek and Turkish governments facing communist insurgencies, President **Harry Truman** enunciated his Truman Doctrine, which pledged U.S. help to any government in the world facing such a threat. This speech was the opening of the **containment policy**, of which the U.S. military intervention in Vietnam would ultimately be a part (see document 7, appendix 1).

When the president declared the Truman Doctrine, his concern was Europe not Asia, but he provided no such qualification of his statements. Already underway in Southeast Asia was a war between French colonialists and Vietnamese communists led by Ho Chi Minh. Very soon, the legacies of the Open Door Policy, Wilsonian internationalism, the failure of appeasement at Munich, victory in World War II, and the Truman Doctrine were to influence U.S. assessments of the strategic importance of the conflict in Vietnam to the United States.

Chapter 4

THE FRENCH WAR IN VIETNAM

After World War II France fought an eight-year war against the **Vietminh** in an ultimately futile effort to retain Indochina as a colony. The opportunity for the Vietnamese to rise against their colonial masters came from the Japanese invasion of Southeast Asia. By mid-1942 Japan's military controlled French Indochina, the Dutch East Indies, the American Philippines, Thailand, and the British colonies of Hong Kong, Burma, and Malaya. The broad sweep of Tokyo's forces spelled doom for Western colonialism, as the once seemingly invincible oppressors fell before an Asian onslaught. The Japanese promoted the idea of Asia for Asians in an effort to encourage support for themselves. Instead, they inspired local independence movements such as the Vietminh, who were both anti-French and anti-Japanese.

In contrast to the British, Dutch, and American commanders who resisted before eventually yielding to Japan's assault, the French governors in Indochina gave Tokyo access to resources and military base facilities in return for allowing the French to continue to administer their colony. Hence Ho Chi Minh and the Communist Party organized the Vietminh as a patriotic front of any Vietnamese determined to free their country from both the old European masters and the new Asian aggressors. By collaborating with the Japanese, French colonial officials isolated themselves from the Western governments and held their position at the mercy of Japan. Conversely, Ho Chi Minh actively sought contact with American intelligence officers in southern China and proposed cooperation in a common fight against the Japanese. Because Ho and his organization were virtually unknown to the world, they got little response at first. In 1945, however, as the Japanese retreated in the Pacific before advancing U.S. forces, the chance for Vietnamese independence, for which Ho had long been preparing, emerged.

THE AUGUST REVOLUTION

By the spring of 1945, Tokyo knew that collaboration with French colonialism in Vietnam had outlived its usefulness. On March 9 Japanese troops suddenly attacked and eliminated French troops and officials in Indochina. With France already liberated from German occupation and U.S. military power within striking distance of Japan, the surprise move in Indochina was part of a new Japanese effort to protect its interests there. Tokyo immediately recognized an independent Vietnam under Emperor **Bao Dai**, the heir of the Nguyen dynasty. There had been no real royal government for almost a century, but Bao Dai went through the motions of setting up a cabinet in the old capital of Hue. This government had no chance of survival without Japanese support, but on August 14 Japan surrendered to the Allies. Vietnam was a political vacuum into which the Vietminh rushed.

Using the name Nguyen Ai Quoc for the last time, Ho Chi Minh called upon the people of Vietnam to rise up and take control of the country. From their base areas near the Chinese border, Vietminh cadre quickly orchestrated the seizure of power in villages and towns in north and central Vietnam. Under this pressure, Bao Dai abdicated his impotent throne. This **August Revolution** took only a few days, and on September 2, 1945, in an emotional public ceremony in Hanoi, Ho declared the independence of the Democratic Republic of Vietnam (DRV) (see document 8, appendix 1).

WHAT WAS THE SOURCE OF HO CHI MINH'S SUCCESS IN GAINING SUPPORT OF THE VIETNAMESE?

Journalist **David Halberstam** described Ho, whom Vietnamese often called Uncle Ho, as "part Gandhi, part Lenin, all Vietnamese." This succinct portrait captures well the assets Ho possessed when he stood before the cheering crowd that welcomed his declaration of Vietnamese independence. In the fashion of the great Indian leader Mohandas Gandhi, he appealed to his oppressed compatriots to seek the independence and social justice that colonial rule had denied them. Like Lenin, he was a theorist who developed a ruthless and disciplined plan for successful revolution inspired by Marx's concepts of class warfare. There is no question that he shrewdly donned simple clothes and sandals and muted the Marxist ideology behind his strategies in order to appeal to the masses of Vietnamese. His personal charisma and the attraction of his Viet-minh front, however, clearly derived from their tangible and deeply rooted Viet-namese identity.

Despite its bold claims of national leadership, the Vietminh had real limitations. Its core of Communist Party members numbered only about five thousand in a country of 24 million people. Most of its operatives were in Tonkin and Annam with only a small network in Cochinchina. Although most other political parties were weak, some, such as remnants of the VNQDD, had potential support from the Republic of China, whose troops came into Tonkin to accept the surrender of Japanese forces. British troops played a similar role in the south. In early 1946 the Vietminh used a combination of political bargains, staged elections, and carefully targeted assassinations to erect a tenuous government in Hanoi.

OUTBREAK OF THE FRANCO-VIETMINH WAR

While the Vietminh hurried to strengthen their position, France began to land troops in the south with the cooperation of British occupation forces. Well aware of strong sentiment in Paris to reclaim French Indochina, Ho Chi Minh negotiated a compromise agreement with French envoy **Jean Sainteny** that would have created a free Vietnam within an Indochina Federation of the French Union. It was never ratified, however, because in May 1946 the French high commissioner in Saigon declared the Republic of Cochinchina to be a separate state. Both sides then took part in a continuing series of violent encounters throughout Vietnam. Finally, major armed clashes in **Haiphong** and Hanoi, in November and December 1946, marked the beginning of what historians label the First Indochina War.

The war was divided along urban-rural lines, with French forces controlling the cities and the Vietminh fighters taking refuge in country villages and in the mountains. Major French military operations in 1947 that included aerial bombing with **napalm** failed to crush the enemy, but they inflicted heavy damage on civilians. The Europeans had difficulty in even finding the Vietminh, but their destructiveness helped increase the credibility of Ho's followers among the people. The Vietnamese communists, in fact, followed the example of people's war as developed by Mao Zedong in China. This strategy began with the establishment of remote base areas to avoid direct confrontation with the enemy's superior technology. It then relied on the development of clandestine political organizations among the people and the draining of French military strength through military tactics of feint and deception. The Vietminh goal was to develop gradually a power equilibrium that would make a general offensive possible.

WERE THERE VIABLE VIETNAMESE POLITICAL ALTERNATIVES
TO HO AND HIS VIETMINH?

To counter the Vietminh's claims to represent the Vietnamese nation, France tried to create an alternative through the 1949 Elysée Agreement with Bao Dai. Paris agreed to dissolve the Republic of Cochinchina and to recognize a single State of Vietnam with Bao Dai as its head. The former emperor sincerely wanted peace and unity for his country, but he was no match for either the French or Ho Chi Minh. Ho had immense prestige as a patriot. Many Vietnamese who were traditionalists, moderates, or outright French collaborators, however, feared the Vietminh and cast their lots with the State of Vietnam. Other Vietnamese tried to avoid association with either side. Often absent from his country and inclined to a playboy lifestyle, Bao Dai had no personal political base or effective way to recruit one. The French, however, bore primary responsibility for the weakness of the so-called Bao Dai solution because they never conceded to his regime the sine qua non for all Vietnamese, absolute independence.

In 1949 the Franco-Vietminh War was at a stalemate. The French Expeditionary Corps (FEC) had more fire power than the Vietminh but could not maneuver its elusive enemy into full battle. Ho's forces were surviving but were not able to drive the French out of the country. Politically, the Vietminh appealed to many Vietnamese but did not attract all groups in the factional and regional complexity of Vietnamese society. Immediately across Vietnam's northern border, however, a momentous historical change reached a climax, altering the Vietnamese equilibrium. The Chinese Communist People's Liberation Army pushed into southern China and forced the Chinese Nationalist regime to flee to Taiwan. Not only did China now have a communist government, but its leaders announced support for the Vietminh. Ho had a long association with the Chinese Communist Party, and, despite his instinctive Vietnamese distrust of China, he accepted military aid and advice from Beijing.

U.S. SUPPORT OF FRANCE IN INDOCHINA

The French war in Vietnam pitted Vietnamese against Vietnamese but was in its origins an international issue that attracted the attention of the United States from the outset. Before World War II the United States paid little official notice to French Indochina. Japan's occupation increased awareness of the strategic value of the area, but more important was the anticolonial momentum generated by Japanese actions. The prospect of the end of colonialism, including U.S. possession of the Philippines, brought the United States closer to its ideal of self-determination for oppressed peoples and also merged with the open-door concept of free trade. Franklin Roosevelt left no doubt that he opposed a French return to Indochina and vaguely suggested an international trusteeship for the region. No specific postwar plan emerged before Roosevelt's death, however, because of British resistance to the idea of dismantling colonial empires and a desire by policymakers in Washington to avoid alienating Paris, whose cooperation would be needed on European issues. After Japan's surrender, Harry Truman tried at first to continue his predecessor's example of neither condoning nor confronting French designs in Indochina.

WHY WAS THE OUTCOME OF THE FRANCO-VIETMINH WAR IMPORTANT TO THE UNITED STATES?

As tensions escalated into war between France and the Vietminh, the United States was unable to remain indifferent to the outcome and moved toward support of the French. American leaders never approved of the goal of recolonizing Indochina and repeatedly urged Paris to grant Vietnam its independence. Aware of this view, Ho had made a point of seeking contact with the United States during the war against Japan, and in his September 1945 declaration of independence, he quoted from the American Declaration of Independence as an example of the principles for which he and his followers struggled. Despite these appeals to American ideals, officials in Washington fastened on three reasons why French success over the Vietminh was in America's interest. Basically, Americans frowned upon colonialism but feared communism.

Washington's first reason for favoring France was that Europe not Southeast Asia was America's front line of defense in the emerging Cold War. U.S. strategists believed that the Soviet Union posed a political, economic, and military threat to Europe that required unity among the United States, Britain, and France. This presumption lay behind the Truman Doctrine and the policy of containment of Soviet power that became the foundation of U.S. foreign policy after World War II. The United States might criticize France for its behavior in Indochina, but it would not risk a rupture with Paris for the sake of the Vietnamese—especially not for a Vietnamese political movement headed by a man with a history of collaboration with Moscow and the Comintern. Indeed, by setting up the Bao Dai government, Paris tried not only to appeal to Vietnamese tradition but also to American officials by providing a noncommunist regime that would provide a rationalization for U.S. support of the French military in Indochina.

Asian geopolitics was a second reason to favor France. The victory of the Communist Party in China and the ideological and military closeness of the Vietminh with the new rulers in Beijing raised the specter of a "Red Menace" in Asia, similar to what Soviet communism represented in Europe. Just as the idea of containment in Europe symbolized a desire to avoid appeasement, such as had occurred at the Munich Conference, and meant the drawing of a line against aggression, so too did this idea apply to Asia. With the formation of the State of Vietnam, French officials frequently characterized their military effort as an anticommunist fight, not a colonial war.

The third reason why who won in Vietnam mattered to the United States was economics. Americans had no significant investment in Indochina, but they did have a large stake in the economic health of major U.S. allies. The open-door principle viewed a strong and open world economy as a vital American interest. The natural resources of Southeast Asia—such as rice, rubber, and tin—and the region's markets had long been vital to France and Britain. Japan had sought unsuccessfully to gain these benefits by force and still needed access to them for its recovery from the war. With China now considered hostile, American strategists began to think more about the welfare of their former Japanese enemy. If France, Britain, and Japan were to be effective political and economic allies of the United States, French interests in Southeast Asia were worth preserving as part of an American economic trading block.

For these reasons, in February 1950, the Truman administration extended diplomatic recognition to the State of Vietnam and in May committed $10 million in military assistance to the French-backed regime (see **Military Assistance Advisory Group**). At the time these actions seemed to be small and prudent steps, but they marked the beginning of what would be a twenty-five year involvement in Vietnam that would ultimately cost billions of dollars and thousands of American lives. In the short run, however, the intent was not to embark upon an American war in Vietnam but rather to encourage France to continue the burden of containment in Indochina and to cooperate with U.S. defense plans in Europe.

These American decisions on Indochina preceded the outbreak of war in Korea, in June 1950, and Truman's prompt deployment of U.S. troops to defend South Korea against attack from communist North Korea (see **Korean War**) The fighting in Korea confirmed the belief in Washington that Asian communist movements—Korean, Chinese, and Vietnamese—posed an aggressive military threat that must be countered by armed force. With U.S. soldiers fighting against North Korean and, after November 1950, Chinese troops and obligated to defend Europe through the North Atlantic Treaty Organization, it was imperative that France keep up the fight in Vietnam. To ensure that Paris not waver, especially after the FEC suffered heavy losses from 1950 to 1952, the Truman administration steadily increased the level of U.S. aid. By late 1952 U.S. funds were paying for more than a third of the French war costs.

DIENBIENPHU AND THE GENEVA CONFERENCE

The French War in Vietnam came to an end in 1954 with a major battle at **Dienbienphu** and a cease-fire agreement between France and the Vietminh negotiated at Geneva, Switzerland. The United States played a key role in both of these decisive developments largely by deciding not to play a key role. For three years the Truman administration had worked to sustain the French. Upon entering the White House in January 1953, **Dwight D. Eisenhower** and his advisers continued and, in fact, dramatically increased U.S. aid. When General Henri Navarre, the new commander of the FEC, presented a bold plan for offensive operations, the American subsidy jumped to 80 percent of the French costs. When the **Navarre Plan** produced a French disaster at Dienbienphu, however, the Eisenhower administration let events take their own course, which led to the Geneva agreements ending the war with Ho's Democratic Republic of Vietnam in control of North Vietnam.

WHY DID THE UNITED STATES NOT INTERVENE MILITARILY TO AID THE FRENCH AT DIENBIENPHU?

Navarre's aggressive tactics led him to construct a large French combat base in a remote valley in northeastern Vietnam near the village of Dienbienphu. His purpose was not entirely clear. He may have sought to block Vietminh access to nearby Laos or to position his forces for future operations. Whatever the case, he seriously underestimated the ability of his enemy and placed too much faith in his planes, tanks, and other technological resources. Vo Nguyen Giap, the Vietminh commander, occupied the high ground around Dienbienphu in March 1954 with a force twice the size of the French garrison. Giap's artillery rendered the French airstrip in the village useless. Some of France's best troops were isolated, besieged, and facing a humiliating defeat.

Dienbienphu presented the Eisenhower administration with a dilemma. A surrender there would not end France's ability to fight in Vietnam but could well end its will to fight. French opinion had turned against this "dirty war," and French leaders had already agreed to put the conflict on the agenda of an international conference to convene shortly in Geneva. On the other hand, the level of U.S. financial aid indicated that Washington placed a higher value on Vietnam than did Paris. On April 5, 1954, with Dienbienphu under siege, Eisenhower made his famous public remark about the domino principle, which became a U.S. description of the strategic importance of Vietnam for years to come (see **Domino Theory**). The president asserted that the loss of Indochina would set off a chain reaction imperiling Thailand, Malaya, Indonesia, Japan, Taiwan, the Philippines, and even Australia and New Zealand (see document 9, appendix 1).

Publicly Secretary of State **John Foster Dulles** called for "united action" by several countries to protect Southeast Asia from communist-led movements, and privately Eisenhower and his advisers weighed the possibility of a U.S. air strike to relieve the French fighters at Dienbienphu. On May 7, however, the Vietminh forced the surrender of the last French defenders without the United States having taken any meaningful military or diplomatic action. Some historians give

Eisenhower considerable credit for a statesman-like caution that seemed in sharp contrast to his successors' approval of American military intervention in Vietnam. There is ample evidence, however, that Eisenhower did not question the designation of Indochina as a vital strategic area worth defending. The disaster at Dienbienphu only confirmed that relying on France to carry the burden of that defense was not working. Some other approach would have to be found.

The talks at Geneva provided a way for France to extricate itself from the war. The governments of Great Britain and the Soviet Union convened the Geneva Conference that included representatives from France, the United States, the People's Republic of China, Laos, Cambodia, the State of Vietnam, and the Democratic Republic of Vietnam (that is, the Vietminh delegation). The U.S. envoys stayed out of the substantive talks. The French and Vietminh delegations negotiated and signed a cease-fire agreement in July 1954 that temporarily divided Vietnam at the seventeenth parallel. The DRV would control North Vietnam. The State of Vietnam would have administrative authority in South Vietnam, but, since French officials and not representatives of the State of Vietnam signed this document, the fate of the Bao Dai government was undefined. Separate agreements provided for Laotian and Cambodian governments in those countries. Finally, an unsigned declaration, released at the end of the conference, called for elections to be held throughout Vietnam in 1956 to decide the political future of the country. The diplomats at Geneva had found a formula for ending the Franco-Vietminh War but not a plan for the unification of Vietnam under one government (see document 10, appendix 1).

The U.S. delegation at Geneva issued a statement acknowledging the results of the conference but not endorsing them. Washington was not pleased that a Vietminh government in Hanoi, headed by Ho Chi Minh, now controlled North Vietnam. American leaders also recognized that they still had to deal with the State of Vietnam through French intermediaries. On the other hand, American planners were already at work on how to fashion their own solution for Vietnam that would keep the domino of North Vietnam from toppling South Vietnam, Laos, Cambodia, and other neighboring states.

Soon after the Geneva Conference, Secretary Dulles took the first steps in this direction by brokering a vaguely phrased defense pact composed of the United States, Britain, France, Australia, New Zealand, the Philippines, Thailand, and Pakistan. Designed to protect the status quo, this September 1954 treaty created the **Southeast Asia Treaty Organization** (SEATO), with a separate protocol listing Vietnam, Laos, and Cambodia not as members but as part of the SEATO security area. On paper, at least, Dulles had an arrangement for united action, such as he had proposed during the Dienbienphu crisis. In the years to come, including during the massive U.S. military deployment of the 1960s, American officials would often cite the SEATO pact as their basis for action in Indochina (see document 11, appendix 1).

Chapter 5

THE DIEM YEARS: EISENHOWER

Although intended to be temporary, the north-south division of Vietnam fashioned at the Geneva Conference endured for two decades until troops of the Democratic Republic of Vietnam occupied the southern capital of **Saigon** in 1975. For most of the first ten years of the separation, **Ngo Dinh Diem** headed the southern regime and appeared to the United States, at least for a time, as the best Vietnamese alternative to Ho Chi Minh and to a communist-led unification of Vietnam. The United States had made clear during and immediately after the Geneva Conference that it sought a way to counter the DRV, and the Eisenhower administration provided steadily increasing support to Diem for that purpose. The American hope for a successful government in South Vietnam did not by itself ensure that Diem's regime would survive, but it did cause Vietnamese to associate Washington and Saigon so closely that they often referred to the southern government as the "My-Diem" regime, which represented a combining of the Vietnamese word for "America" with Diem's name. Despite or because of U.S. assistance, the Saigon government found itself by the late 1950s facing danger not only from the North but from an armed insurrection in the South. When Eisenhower left office in 1961, there were serious questions as to whether the My-Diem government needed a greater commitment from the United States and whether American interests justified such a commitment.

THE DECISION TO BACK NGO DINH DIEM

Initial U.S. reaction to the prospect of a Vietnamese government headed by Ngo Dinh Diem was cautious because his political base was weak. Why Bao Dai named Diem prime minister of the State of Vietnam in June 1954 has never been entirely clear. From a mandarin family, Diem had served briefly in Bao Dai's powerless cabinet in the 1930s. The playboy emperor, who lived much of the time on the French Riviera, did not like Diem, who was intensely anti-French, was a devout and celibate Roman Catholic, and lived an ascetic and almost monkish life. With French power waning in Indochina, however, Diem had some genuine assets. He had a reputation for refusing to collaborate with either the French colonialists or the Vietminh. The latter was probably responsible for the murder of his oldest brother in 1945. Moreover, Diem had lived for a while in the United States and had met some prominent Americans. Although these contacts may not have been significant, it is likely that Bao Dai selected Diem in hopes of cultivating U.S. support for his government against the DRV.

WAS THE REPUBLIC OF VIETNAM (RVN) AN AMERICAN CREATION?

Although top policy makers, such as President Eisenhower and Secretary of State Dulles, knew little about Diem and took a wait-and-see attitude, they fairly quickly decided that he and his government deserved wholehearted American support. Diem himself was a very private person with none of the charisma of Ho, and he had no political organization to rival the Vietnamese Communist Party. He relied heavily on his four surviving brothers, especially **Ngo Dinh Nhu**, who was essentially his chief of staff. Because Vietnam is primarily a country of **Buddhists**, the Ngo family's religion also set them apart and led them to develop a network of Catholic minions, many of whom had fled from the North to the South after the Geneva-arranged cease-fire. French officials remaining in the South opposed Diem because they knew he was hostile to their aims to preserve what French influence they could in their former colony. Faced with lack of support or outright resistance from French officials, many Buddhists, admirers of Ho, and communist cadre, Diem needed U.S. help to have any chance of establishing a government.

Eisenhower sent General **J. Lawton Collins** to Saigon in November 1954 to evaluate Diem's potential and to try to get the French to cooperate with American efforts to strengthen South Vietnam. Collins concluded that a separate South Vietnamese state was possible, but he bluntly informed the White House that he did not believe Diem was qualified to lead it. At the same time, John Foster Dulles and his brother Allan, head of the **Central Intelligence Agency**

(CIA), sent Colonel **Edward G. Lansdale** to work secretly to advise Diem, and Lansdale recommended strong U.S. support for the South Vietnamese prime minister. These conflicting assessments came to a head in April 1955 when an odd alignment of religious sects and gangsters made a move to seize authority from Diem. The prime minister subdued the uprising with some help from Lansdale. Rather than risk further instability that might give Hanoi a political opening to exploit, Washington decided to give full support to Diem. Secretary Dulles informed Paris of U.S. determination to help Diem, and the French government responded by withdrawing its last military advisers in the South and leaving all future assistance to Saigon in American hands.

With the U.S. decision to try to build a nation in the South around Diem, the prime minister boldly announced a referendum to depose Bao Dai and convert the State of Vietnam into the Republic of Vietnam (RVN). U.S. officials were caught by surprise and thought the step was premature, but Diem and his brothers carried off a sham election in October 1955 that went overwhelmingly against the emperor (see **Elections in the Republic of Vietnam**). Some districts reported more votes for Diem to be head of state than there were voters. This "election" revealed the Ngos to be more clever than many had thought, but it also gave evidence of a problem that was to plague the RVN until its demise in 1975. The United States felt compelled to shore up an ally with questionable political support of its own. At the same time, the Saigon politicians, despite their dependence on American aid, would not hesitate to act as they pleased and assume that the United States had no choice but to go along.

THE NON-ELECTION OF 1956

The question of whether the United States was shaping or simply responding to events in Southeast Asia is apparent in the issue of an all-Vietnam election to decide on reunification. The diplomats at the Geneva Conference had called for a "free general election" in 1956 to determine the political will of the Vietnamese. The U.S. delegation at Geneva and the State of Vietnam's representatives never agreed to an election, and Washington was not inclined to help arrange a free ballot competition between the almost legendary Ho Chi Minh, who had forced the French colonialists to capitulate, and Ngo Dinh Diem, who was struggling just to keep politically afloat. Since no election occurred in 1956, the circumstantial evidence suggests that Washington blocked a peaceful resolution to Vietnam's internal political discord.

In truth, free elections throughout Vietnam had very little chance of being implemented. The Geneva conferees had provided no specific mechanism for elections. Neither of the conveners of the conference—Britain and the Soviet Union—nor any of the other major powers wanted to take responsibility for supervising an election. No officials in Hanoi or Saigon had any experience conducting free elections and likely would not have tolerated outside monitoring in areas under their control. Only the DRV kept up public calls for an election because it presumed its heroic defiance of France gave it the overwhelming popularity to carry it to a victory, whether the election was open or manipulated. Diem largely avoided any reference to an election. He eventually announced that he favored an election but said he would not agree to one as long as the North denied its citizens democratic liberty. Spokesmen in Washington endorsed this statement, but the election was already a dead issue.

When the summer of 1956 passed with no all-Vietnam election held or even being discussed, Washington grew more optimistic, with each month that the Diem government continued to function, that South Vietnam might actually hold the containment line against the North and thus against communist expansion in Asia. A nonpartisan advocacy group calling itself the **American Friends of Vietnam** was applauding Diem's accomplishments, and the Eisenhower administration issued self-congratulatory statements about how well U.S. assistance was working in Vietnam. In May 1957 Diem made a state visit to the United States during which he was repeatedly dubbed a "miracle man" for his regime's ability to take root despite the threat it faced from the North (see document 12, appendix 1).

THE ILLUSION OF NATION BUILDING

Despite the confident rhetoric out of Washington and Saigon, the Republic of Vietnam was not a self-sufficient nation and required life-sustaining support from the United States. The French had created under the State of Vietnam an army of 150,000 soldiers and a civil bureaucracy, but neither of these organizations had been given any independent authority. Both had been expected simply to carry out orders and hence had not developed their own leadership. Conspiratorial by nature, Diem and his brothers filled this leadership void by creating a government in the South resting largely on personal loyalty to them. From this narrow political base, Diem endeavored, with American help, to build a nation in the South to contest the DRV in the North.

WHICH WAS MORE URGENT FOR SOUTH VIETNAM IN THE 1950S, INTERNAL REFORM OR MILITARY SECURITY?

Diem's regime presented American officials with a debilitating dilemma. The Saigon government needed to build trust and loyalty among the South Vietnamese population but was well aware that it faced many internal enemies who could be ruthless in their opposition. With an instinct for survival, the Ngo family often resorted to dictatorial methods to intimidate or remove threats to its position. Diem's brothers Ngo Dinh Nhu and Ngo Dinh Can operated a largely secret party, the **Can Lao**, that ruled through bribery, arrests, imprisonment, and executions of alleged Vietminh suspects believed to be disloyal to the government. In one of its most fundamental moves, the regime abolished elected village councils and placed its own appointees (often Catholics who had fled from the North) in charge of local affairs. Such actions increased the isolation of the Ngos from the people and concerned American advisers, who hoped that the RVN would show greater respect for democratic principles.

Although urging Diem to reform his methods, Washington felt compelled to give him financial assistance or risk the collapse of his fragile nation. Americans reasoned that improved economic conditions among the peasants would help build support for the RVN, and they advanced plans for land reform, rent control, and agricultural development. U.S. officials also set up a system to subsidize commercial imports to boost the urban economy. These efforts translated into few actual changes in the agricultural and commercial economy of South Vietnam. Partly due to the regime's resistance to social innovation, this lack of economic change occurred primarily because 80 percent of U.S. aid went directly to the South Vietnamese armed forces.

Many American strategists envisioned a threat of an outright assault by North Vietnam on South Vietnam after the model of the North Korean attack on South Korea in 1950. Whether Diem shared this concern with external aggression or simply recognized the value of a strong military for defense against his internal foes, he often reiterated his need for military aid. The Eisenhower administration never had more than 740 uniformed U.S. soldiers in Vietnam for training and advising the **Army of the Republic of Vietnam** (ARVN), but 85 percent of the money for paying, equipping, and maintaining the southern military forces came from the United States. Some U.S. diplomats in Saigon questioned providing significant military assistance to such a politically unstable regime, but basic U.S. policy was that military security took precedence in Vietnam over economic and political reform.

NLF: RISE OF THE SOUTHERN INSURGENCY

In December 1960 Vietnamese Communists in South Vietnam created the **National Liberation Front** (NLF), an organization that also included noncommunists, with the goals of overthrowing the Diem government, seeking an end of U.S. military aid to the RVN, and forcing the creation of a coalition government that would seek reunification with the North. The appearance of the NLF followed months of increasingly violent incidents aimed at the ARVN, district chiefs, and other representatives of the RVN. American and Vietnamese officials in Washington and Saigon referred to these antigovernment rebels as **Vietcong** or Vietnamese Communists, whether they were communists or not.

WAS THE SOUTHERN INSURGENCY AND CREATION OF THE NLF
A PREDICTABLE RESPONSE TO DIEM'S OPPRESSIVE POLICIES
OR A NORTHERN CONSPIRACY TO SUBVERT THE RVN?

Although there was not an all-Vietnam election in 1956, the DRV Politburo continued to hold out for a political reunification of the country. Leaders in Hanoi were still struggling to consolidate their authority in the North and to convert agriculture and commerce to a socialist economy. They were not eager to launch any new military campaigns, especially if such attacks might provoke an American armed response. The DRV advised Communist Party cadre in the South to be patient.

The southern cadre informed Hanoi that it could not wait. With U.S. help, Diem's regime was managing to stay in power, and its policy of arrests, harsh punishments, and even executions of its opponents was decimating the party. Some party workers began to assassinate local RVN officials and to strike out in other ways. Finally, in 1959, the Politburo signaled approval of acts of self-defense, and an armed insurgency quickly emerged. A diverse coalition of communists, former Vietminh, some Catholics, Buddhist sects, and others threatened by Diem's suppression tactics began to coordinate resistance activities. They attacked ARVN outposts and government offices and claimed to have "liberated" scores of villages from government control. The momentum of the southern insurgency finally led Hanoi, in September 1960, to declare a two-part program of socialist revolution in the North and liberation of the South from the Americans and their Vietnamese henchmen. With that approval, the southern communists quickly formalized the organization of the dissatisfied southern elements into the NLF. Its strategy was to stage military actions in areas remote from government control, use political methods in the cities, and combine military and political means in other areas (see document 13, appendix 1).

As this new phase began in the struggle for control of South Vietnam, a crisis of international proportions was erupting in neighboring Laos. The Geneva Conference of 1954 had recognized an independent Royal Laotian Government. The United States gave considerable assistance to this government because of Laos's strategic proximity to North Vietnam and the existence of the communist **Pathet Lao**, who had worked with Hanoi against the royal government. In 1959 and 1960 a series of coups and other political maneuvers led to a very dangerous situation in which the United States and the Soviet Union were providing supplies to opposing factions in a tension-filled situation. Neither Washington nor Moscow desired a direct clash over Laos, but each superpower's connections to the contending parties in Vietnam had dragged it into this conflict. When **John F. Kennedy** met with Eisenhower in January 1961, on the eve of Kennedy's inauguration as president, the discussion of Southeast Asian issues concentrated on Laos, not Vietnam.

DID EISENHOWER LIMIT OR INCREASE U.S. COMMITMENT TO SOUTH VIETNAM?

Compared to the presidents who followed him, Eisenhower's commitment of U.S. resources to the survival of South Vietnam appeared limited. The number of U.S. forces in the country was only a few hundred engaged in training and advice, and no U.S. air or land forces had participated in combat in Vietnam. On the other hand, as Eisenhower's "domino" statement in 1954 had proclaimed and his concern for Laos in 1961 revealed, his administration had defined Southeast Asia and the containment of communist expansion there to be a global strategic interest of the United States. To protect that interest, Washington bankrolled and applauded the political survival of Ngo Dinh Diem in South Vietnam. With an armed insurrection rapidly expanding against the Saigon government, the level of American support was likely going to have to increase. The decision on whether to continue wholehearted support of Diem and how much more assistance to give South Vietnam was left, however, for Kennedy to make.

Chapter 6

THE DIEM YEARS: KENNEDY

Almost immediately upon entering the White House, John F. Kennedy received
a disturbing briefing from General Edward Lansdale, who had just returned
from an observation trip to Southeast Asia. The general reported that widespread guerrilla warfare and other subversive activities in South Vietnam would
soon bring down Ngo Dinh Diem's government if an effective **counterinsurgency** program did not begin at once. When campaigning for president,
Kennedy had criticized Eisenhower for being indecisive in foreign policy and
had further claimed that America's own survival required an assertive U.S. defense of "free" nations against communist aggression. It was especially important, the youthful Kennedy maintained, that the United States pay closer attention to the internal politics of developing nations that were vulnerable to
Soviet-sponsored **wars of national liberation**. For the new president, the
prospect of the defeat of the U.S.-backed Saigon regime carried global consequences dangerous to American interests. He moved quickly to increase U.S.
support of South Vietnam and continued thereafter to expand that assistance.
He eventually lost confidence in Ngo Dinh Diem and raised questions about
U.S. options in Vietnam, but at the time of his assassination in 1963, Kennedy
was still asserting the strategic value of South Vietnam to the United States.

COUNTERINSURGENCY WARFARE

DID KENNEDY MAKE ANY REASSESSMENT
OF EISENHOWER'S GOALS IN VIETNAM?

Despite his partisan criticisms of his predecessor's conduct of foreign policy, the new president agreed with the basic tenets of the containment strategy initiated by Truman and continued by Eisenhower. Kennedy considered the Soviet Union, with its hostile ideology and nuclear warfare capability, the principal threat to the United States. It followed logically that any country, such as the People's Republic of China or the Democratic Republic of Vietnam, allied with the USSR was the enemy of the United States.

Not only did Kennedy consider containment a prudent policy, he also believed that the United States had international commitments, whether formal as with NATO or implied as with SEATO, to oppose communist expansion, and that failure to uphold these commitments would have damaging consequences for the credibility of U.S. policy and the security of the world (see **Credibility Gap**). Despite his desire to demonstrate American determination, however, his initial months in office conveyed a different message. In April 1961 Cuban exiles suffered a disastrous failure when they attempted an invasion at the Bay of Pigs in an effort to unseat Fidel Castro's government. The thinly veiled U.S. hand in the assault on Cuba made the new administration appear reckless and inept. Unwilling to commit U.S. troops to the Cuban operation, Kennedy was even more wary of American forces going into the conflict in Laos. Consequently, and only days after the Bay of Pigs fiasco, he decided that the United States would participate in negotiations for a compromise political settlement in Laos (see **Geneva Conference [1961–1962]**). At a June summit meeting in Vienna, Soviet Premier **Nikita Khrushchev** sought to intimidate the inexperienced Kennedy, and soon afterward Moscow began construction of the Berlin Wall.

These apparent setbacks for U.S. foreign policy in Cuba, Laos, and Berlin led the Kennedy administration to put increasing attention on Vietnam. Washington felt that it could not afford another sign of weakness. It needed to stand firm somewhere. Kennedy had criticized Eisenhower for excessive reliance on nuclear deterrence as a diplomatic instrument. The new president advocated a strategy termed **flexible response**, that is, the notion that different types of aggression, such as guerrilla warfare in Vietnam, required different defenses, such as counterinsurgency warfare.

DID U.S. ADVICE ON COUNTERINSURGENCY WARFARE
HELP SAIGON DECREASE ITS POLITICAL VULNERABILITY?

Although Kennedy's initial efforts in 1961 to improve assistance to the Diem government contained psychological and economic elements, much of the help was in the form of military aid and advice. His administration increased U.S. funding to allow for a 200,000-man South Vietnamese armed force, and Washington deployed 400 U.S. **Special Forces** (Green Beret) advisers to provide training in antiguerrilla tactics. These moves did not deter the Vietcong, however, which actually increased its attacks, and infiltration of military reinforcements from North Vietnam doubled.

With Diem's government on more precarious footing than ever, two of Kennedy's top aides, **Walt Rostow** and **Maxwell Taylor**, traveled to Vietnam in October 1961 and returned with a recommendation that the United States send 8,000 troops to inject some confidence into the Saigon regime (see document 14, appendix 1). Other Kennedy aides suggested negotiations with the DRV to arrange a political compromise, such as had been done in Laos. Kennedy rejected both deployment of a U.S. combat force and negotiations, but during 1962 he significantly escalated the level of military aid. By the end of the year, there were 9,000 U.S. military advisers in South Vietnam, and a **Military Assistance Command, Vietnam** (MACV) had been created to direct the expanding American effort. The ARVN received modern military hardware, such as **helicopters**, tactical **aircraft**, and **armored personnel carriers**. To try to counter guerrilla attacks and Vietcong political organizing in rural areas, MACV helped the Diem government construct "**strategic hamlets**" or fortified villages. These activities gave the appearance that the RVN was becoming more secure. In January 1963, however, a Vietcong unit routed an ARVN force that was ten times larger and equipped with modern U.S. arms, including aircraft. The ARVN soldiers' lack of will to fight in this battle at **Ap Bac** symbolized a fundamental absence of allegiance to the Diem government that military equipment and training alone could not remedy.

THE BUDDHIST CRISIS

Low morale in ARVN units and disaffection among peasants in the strategic hamlets, into which many families had been forced after having to give up their ancestral homes, revealed widespread discontent with the Saigon leadership, but the most visible challenge to Diem came from some members of the Buddhist clergy. Although they usually avoided politics, monks began to criticize government oppression, especially prohibitions against public Buddhist observances when Catholic festivals were allowed. In June 1963 an elderly monk attracted worldwide attention to these complaints when he burned himself to death in a Saigon intersection with news reporters watching and taking photographs. Other acts of self-immolation followed. The particular target of these dramatic protests was Diem's brother Ngo Dinh Nhu, who headed the government's police and security forces. Nhu reacted callously to the priests' flaming sacrifices and in August even launched a massive military raid on major pagodas throughout the country. The Buddhist protests were a clear call for public resistance to the government, and the Ngos were not going to tolerate any opposition.

The Buddhist crisis brought to a head the long-running question about Diem's ability to govern South Vietnam. Since 80 percent of the population was Buddhist, his government's actions further alienated a population already feeling unserved and oppressed by Saigon. U.S. officials at all levels, from Saigon to Washington, were at the end of their patience with Diem. They tried to get him to remove or discipline his brother, but Ngo family cohesion was too strong. With Vietnamese and American sentiment against Diem readily apparent, members of South Vietnam's military began to plot against the government. Because U.S. policy since the mid-1950s had been to give Diem wholehearted support, disgruntled military and civil leaders in South Vietnam had been reluctant to threaten Diem. If these dissidents could be assured of American support for a new regime, however, they would be emboldened to act.

THE DIEM ASSASSINATION

WAS THE UNITED STATES RESPONSIBLE
FOR THE COUP AGAINST DIEM?

On November 2, 1963, South Vietnamese soldiers sent to arrest Diem and Nhu during a military coup murdered the two brothers. As with the Buddhist suicides, a violent act had once again punctuated events in South Vietnam. Although there is no evidence that U.S. officials desired or even anticipated that Diem would be killed, his death marked a major turning point in the history of South Vietnam and of the U.S. policy of noncommunist nation building there.

In August, after the raids on the pagodas, State Department officials in Washington had indicated to U.S. ambassador **Henry Cabot Lodge** in Saigon that he could pressure Diem for Nhu's removal, and, if Nhu remained, he could provide assurances to military leaders that the United States would not interfere in a coup. Despite this so-called green light, no move against Diem occurred in September, and the South Vietnamese president seemed as determined as ever to resist U.S. pressure for reform. After an inspection trip to Saigon, Secretary of Defense **Robert McNamara** and presidential aide Maxwell Taylor recommended that the United States cut back on the aid to the RVN and even on the number of military advisers as a further attempt to push Diem into less repressive policies. Although he expressed doubt about how to proceed, Kennedy approved the McNamara-Taylor report's finding in favor of increased pressure (see document 15, appendix 1). With U.S. displeasure with Diem more evident than ever, plotting within the military against Diem resumed. U.S. intelligence agents knew of this activity, but the American embassy in Saigon did not warn

Diem. On November 1 military forces took control of RVN government offices, and Diem and Nhu fled and took refuge in a Catholic church. The generals sent soldiers to retrieve them, and the assassinations occurred while the brothers were being transported to custody.

WHAT IF KENNEDY HAD LIVED?

Three weeks after the coup in Saigon, an assassin's bullet killed John F. Kennedy in Dallas, Texas. The president's death at this critical juncture in the Vietnam War has led to speculation about what might have occurred differently had Kennedy lived.

WOULD KENNEDY HAVE WITHDRAWN RATHER THAN ESCALATED THE U.S. MILITARY PRESENCE IN VIETNAM?

Many of Kennedy's associates and admirers have claimed that after his reelection in 1964 he would have removed U.S. forces from Vietnam. For evidence, among other things, they point to Kennedy's approval of the McNamara-Taylor recommendation to reduce the number of U.S. advisers in Vietnam. In the context of the report, however, that proposal was part of a plan to pressure Diem and not the product of a reassessment of the strategic value of South Vietnam. There is no question that Kennedy had doubts about U.S. military intervention in Indochina. In addition, after the world had stared into the face of nuclear war during the Cuban missile crisis in October 1962, he wanted to reduce international tensions. Kennedy's actual record in office from 1961 to 1963, however, documents his role in the growing militarization of the American role in Vietnam. He never challenged the proposition that the fate of South Vietnam was vital to U.S. security. In a television interview in mid-September 1963, he reaffirmed his belief in the domino theory and stated flatly that the United States should stay in Vietnam and influence the outcome of the struggle there in the most effective way it could (see document 16, appendix 1). By the time of his death, he had placed 16,000 American military advisers in Vietnam, and more than 100 of them had been killed in action. These figures were low compared to the staggering statistics generated later, but they represented a significant leap from those of the Eisenhower years.

Some historians note that it was Kennedy who injected excessive vigor, idealism, and overconfidence into U.S. policy in Vietnam. He had come into office in 1961, proclaiming in his inaugural address that the United States would "bear any burden" in the defense of liberty. By 1963 the burden that he had taken up for America in Vietnam was larger than when he began. With the removal of Diem, which Kennedy had countenanced, a morass of political instability emerged in South Vietnam that added to the challenge for Washington. History is not able to record if Kennedy would have responded with more or less U.S. activism in Vietnam in the face of worsening conditions for the Saigon government. Those conditions and the consequences of almost a decade of U.S. policy in Southeast Asia became the sudden and unwanted responsibility of **Lyndon B. Johnson**.

Chapter 7

THE AMERICAN WAR IN VIETNAM: ESCALATION

Between November 1963 and July 1965, President Lyndon B. Johnson made a series of decisions that ultimately led to a large-scale American war in Vietnam. After the death of Ngo Dinh Diem, the political viability of South Vietnam continued to decline. In part, this weakness was the result of tension within the South between those who sought a political settlement with Hanoi and others who wanted an invigorated military defense of South Vietnam. Aware that a major source of political support for the National Liberation Front had been the anti-Diem sentiment in South Vietnam, Hanoi decided to increase its infiltration of men and supplies into the South to bolster the NLF. Fearful that leaders in the South might agree with Hanoi to create a neutral Vietnam, strategists in Washington urged Saigon to strengthen its military defense and not to be lured into a compromise. In the weeks after Diem's murder, the tension within Vietnam began to reach crisis proportions, and the ten-year U.S. effort to build an independent nation in South Vietnam appeared to be at great risk.

WAS JOHNSON A WAR HAWK OR A RELUCTANT WARRIOR?

Because the Johnson administration was responsible for the American air war in Vietnam and the deployment of U.S. ground combat units to South Vietnam, many journalists, historians, and other observers have labeled the Vietnam War as "Johnson's War." While his leadership of the American combat escalation is undeniable, it is also apparent that he was engulfed in a political and strategic situation that he did not create and did not relish.

Johnson felt compelled to maintain U.S. defense of South Vietnam because of the tenets of the containment policy and the commitments that his predecessors had made to the Republic of Vietnam. As a leader in the U.S. Senate in the 1950s and as vice president, he had always endorsed the judgment of Eisenhower and Kennedy that Southeast Asia was an area of importance to U.S. security. Only four days after becoming president, he approved National Security Action Memorandum (NSAM) 273, which was originally drafted for Kennedy (see document 17, appendix 1). It affirmed that the United States would continue to aid South Vietnam against what it termed outside communist aggression (referring to North Vietnam). In signing this document, Johnson was not only pledging to continue Kennedy's policies, but he was renewing the promise of the Truman Doctrine of 1947 to assist any free people threatened by external pressure or internal subversion. In the months afterward, as Johnson made military decisions consistent with this pledge, he was in many respects implementing what could be termed Truman's War, Eisenhower's War, and Kennedy's War.

Johnson did not want a war in Vietnam and did not want to be a war president. His entire political career had been as a champion of domestic reform in the tradition of Franklin Roosevelt and the New Deal. At the time of his death, Kennedy had left an unfulfilled domestic program—the New Frontier, aimed at such problems as poverty, the environment, and racial discrimination. Johnson preferred to put his efforts into getting congressional action in these areas and not into grappling with the upheaval in Southeast Asia. The new president harbored even grander designs for a sweeping program of social benefits, which would later be labeled the **Great Society**. As a veteran of Capitol Hill, however, Johnson understood that the credibility he needed as a leader to achieve the bold Kennedy-Johnson domestic agenda required him to demonstrate that he could protect U.S. interests abroad. Also he did not want to give conservatives, who would likely oppose his reform program, a political weapon against him if he were to "lose" Vietnam. He recalled how the right-wing had attacked Truman for the "loss" of China. Hence, because of his belief that the survival of South Vietnam was a test of his ability to sustain America's global containment policy and in order to safeguard his domestic plans, he concluded that his administration could not tolerate defeat, or even compromise, in Vietnam.

Although unwilling to accept U.S. failure in Vietnam, Johnson did not want a large war that would divert resources and public attention from his domestic programs. Aware that the NLF continued to control many rural areas of the South and that the military government in Saigon had only a narrow base of political support, the president searched for solutions. Johnson sent General **William C. Westmoreland**, one of the most accomplished officers in the U.S. military, to head MACV, and he authorized an increase of U.S. military advisers in South Vietnam, from 16,000 to more than 23,000. Secretary of Defense Robert McNamara, Secretary of State **Dean Rusk**, and other top aides advised the president, however, that the real enemy of Saigon was Hanoi and not the southern guerrillas. They urged that he find a way to put greater pressure on the North.

THE GULF OF TONKIN INCIDENT

Although the Pentagon had developed contingency plans for air strikes against the DRV, such attacks on North Vietnamese territory without provocation were not possible. Other forms of harassment were tried. Through a secret program code-named OPLAN 34A, U.S. naval forces in the Gulf of Tonkin provided electronic intelligence to support South Vietnamese commando raids along North Vietnam's coast. On August 2, 1964, the U.S. Navy destroyer *Maddox* was engaged in one of these espionage patrols when it was approached by North Vietnamese torpedo boats. A brief exchange of hostile fire occurred. U.S. carrier-based aircraft joined in the fight, and one of the North Vietnamese boats was severely damaged. Washington ordered no further retaliation but declared its right to sail the open sea. It sent the destroyer *C. Turner Joy* to join the *Maddox* to continue the patrols.

On the night of August 4, in poor weather conditions, the two destroyers radioed that they were under attack. As soon as these first reports arrived in Washington, the instinctive response among the **Joint Chiefs of Staff** and other of Johnson's senior aides was to strike back with air attacks against North Vietnamese naval facilities. New messages quickly followed cautioning that the attack was not confirmed and that the initial radar and sonar reports may have been mistakes. The admiral in charge of U.S. Pacific forces cabled from Honolulu, however, that he was convinced there had been an attack. Relying on that judgment, Washington ordered retaliatory air raids (see **Gulf of Tonkin Incident**).

The best historical evidence available now suggests that there was no attack on U.S. ships on August 4, but it also shows that the Pentagon did not know with certainty what had occurred and did not willfully misrepresent the situation to the president. The decision makers in Washington wanted a pretext to send a forceful message to Hanoi not to defy the United States, and many of them believed they had the provocation they sought on August 4.

The president used this incident as an opportunity to obtain from Congress the **Gulf of Tonkin Resolution** that allowed him to use U.S. forces to repel aggression in Southeast Asia (see document 18, appendix 1). Johnson did not seek this authorization because he contemplated widening the war. He still wanted to limit the role of the U.S. military in Vietnam. He sought a show of support from Congress for his firm but restrained approach in Indochina that would help him in his impending election against Republican **Barry Goldwater,** who advocated greater use of U.S. forces in Vietnam. Johnson got the political result he desired and won the election, but the congressional resolution created future problems (see **Elections in the United States**). For one thing, Johnson misled congressional leaders by not divulging the secret patrols that had placed the destroyers in the gulf, and this deception created a basis for mistrust later. Also, having bombed the North and obtained congressional acquiescence, the president now faced less institutional restraint against future military escalation.

ROLLING THUNDER

Until he was elected in November, Johnson sought to preserve his image as a firm but restrained leader and authorized no additional attacks on North Vietnam, despite other incidents, including a guerrilla raid at **Bien Hoa** that killed Americans. Political instability in the Saigon leadership also prompted caution before the United States assumed any further risks. The continued lack of effective government in the RVN and unrelenting pressure of the NLF's armed insurgency supported by men and materiel from the North made South Vietnam's survival perilous. Most of Johnson's staff concluded that the United States would have no choice but to begin some type of air campaign against North Vietnam and the infiltration routes along the so-called **Ho Chi Minh Trail** through Laos. The notable exception among Johnson's inner circle was Undersecretary of State **George Ball**, who cautioned that bombing would be the start of a long and violent conflict, that it would not reverse Saigon's political decline, and that it risked confrontation with Hanoi's powerful Soviet and Chinese allies. Advocates of bombing responded that it would slow infiltration into the South, boost morale in Saigon, and send a message to Moscow and Beijing of the seriousness of U.S. intent in Southeast Asia and elsewhere in the world (see document 19, appendix 1).

On February 6, 1965, an NLF unit killed nine U.S. servicemen in an attack on an American barracks in **Pleiku**. The president ordered retaliatory air strikes on military installations in the North. Following another guerrilla assault on Americans at Qui Nhon on February 10, the administration began **Rolling Thunder**, a campaign of continuing and gradually mounting bombardment. Johnson shared many of Ball's misgivings about escalating the air war, but the president remained determined to avoid defeat in South Vietnam. Ball's warnings provided no action plan. The Joint Chiefs were not guaranteeing success, but doing something appeared better to Johnson than doing nothing.

JOHNSON DECIDES ON A LAND WAR IN ASIA

Having crossed the threshold of an **air war** against the North, the administration now faced the decision of inserting U.S. ground combat forces into the hostilities in Vietnam. No matter how terrifying or destructive, bombing alone could not control territory or provide population security. The ARVN was so beleaguered that it could not even protect the air bases from which the bombers flew their missions. At Westmoreland's request, Washington provided two battalions of U.S. Marines in March 1965 to help defend Danang air base. In the southern capital, political turmoil also hampered the launching of operations against the enemy. There had been five governments in Saigon since the death of Diem, and the current regime headed by a pair of military officers, **Nguyen Van Thieu** and **Nguyen Cao Ky**, inspired little confidence among Americans. Westmoreland and the JCS believed that the time had arrived for the United States to take over the ground war. They requested 150,000 troops in order to seek out and destroy enemy forces. Johnson knew this decision was momentous and weighed it for several days before deciding.

WHAT WAS JOHNSON'S RELATIONSHIP WITH HIS TOP ADVISERS?

This question is critical to historical assessments of how the United States took over conduct of the war from the South Vietnamese. The president's blustering and overbearing personality has been well documented. Both as Senate majority leader and later as president, he was known in Washington for the so-called Johnson treatment. He was a large man who could physically and verbally intimidate his subordinates. He was also a master of flattery and could charm and manipulate others. His advisers knew that he demanded personal loyalty and did not readily invite criticism. As is often the case with such strong personalities, he harbored a great deal of hidden insecurity about his ability. He was especially aware of his lack of experience and expertise in military and diplomatic affairs.

As Johnson pondered the decision on ground troops, he listened to McNamara, Rusk, Ball, **McGeorge Bundy** (his national security adviser), Maxwell Taylor (the U.S. ambassador in Saigon), and others. With the exception of Ball and **Clark Clifford** (a confidante whom Johnson often consulted), the aides either urged or accepted the deployment of U.S. forces. McNamara captured the prevailing view that the United States should act quickly or risk total collapse in Saigon. The introduction of U.S. troops would make later withdrawal difficult, he acknowledged, but the use of American combat units was the best hope for gaining an acceptable outcome in the conflict (see documents 20 and 21, appendix 1). It may appear that the staff was simply telling their formidable leader what he wanted to hear. On the other hand, these men were all experienced, established, and successful individuals in their own right, who understood the magnitude of the decision they all faced. They presumably believed what they were saying and shared a common outlook with the president on the strategic importance of South Vietnam.

The president himself remained fairly constant in his position throughout the evolution of Vietnam policy from the time he took office up to the July deliberations on ground troops. His thinking was driven by the containment notion that South Vietnam was an outpost on the front line of the global Cold War and by his political sense that this frustrating war was a real danger to his domestic agenda. By the spring of 1965 Johnson was in the midst of bringing his Great Society programs—such as, Medicare, civil rights protections, and the war on poverty—to passage in Congress. In a characteristically political move, he approved the sending of 50,000 troops with another 100,000 to follow, while he publicly downplayed the action as signaling no significant change in policy. In fact, a major decision had been made, but he did not want to derail his domestic momentum. As with the Gulf of Tonkin Resolution, Johnson sought to bolster Saigon while also protecting his domestic political position. In the longrun, however, it would become clear that he had Americanized the Vietnam War, greatly increased the human and financial costs to the United States, and not been honest with the American public in the process.

THEORIES OF CAUSATION

WHAT BEST EXPLAINS THE PATH THAT LED THE UNITED STATES TO TAKE OVER THE WAR?

Johnson has to bear responsibility for his escalation of the American commitment to Vietnam in 1965, but a long history defined the policy environment and options that he had inherited. What causes an event or determines the pattern of change over time is the fundamental challenge facing the historian and the essence of most historical debate. In the debate over the causes of the Vietnam War, there are several schools of thought. These interpretations take a number of different forms and are not always mutually exclusive. As with most major historical events, multiple causes are evident.

The most prevalent theory of the cause of the American war in Vietnam— what can be considered the orthodox interpretation—is the liberal-realist view. It is also referred to as the "flawed-containment theory" because historians who advance this thesis generally begin their explanations with what they see as the fixation on global communism in post–World War II U.S. foreign policy. These scholars note that the United States developed the containment policy to limit Soviet power in Europe for strategic and ideological reasons. Although American leaders were responding to the actual Soviet political and military presence in Eastern Europe, they characterized the danger of aggressive communism as global. Further, they cited such abstract ideals as the right of self-determination and the defense of freedom against tyranny as the reasons to oppose any communists anywhere who were connected in any way with Moscow. Both the Truman

Doctrine and Eisenhower's domino theory are examples of official expressions of containment that were applied to Southeast Asia. The realist critique of the liberal-realist school points out that a prudent concern for security may have justified caution about Soviet purposes in Europe, but there was no Soviet Red Army in Asia. U.S. officials failed to recognize that Vietnam had a low strategic value to the United States and that there could be high costs in trying to protect limited interests there. The liberal portion of the critique points out that many Asian revolutionaries who admired Lenin and were attracted to Marxism also had their own anticolonial desires for self-determination and social justice. In other words, the pattern of decisions that led to the Americanization of the Vietnam War was the product of a flawed interpretation of containment and a lack of understanding of the realistic conditions in Southeast Asia.

One of the most influential and persuasive scholars of the liberal-realist school is George Herring. In his book, *America's Longest War*, he cautions that precise lessons from the Vietnam War remain elusive. "That containment was misapplied in Vietnam, however, seems beyond debate," in his view. He concludes:

> The United States intervened to block the apparent march of a Soviet-dominated communism across Asia, enlarged its commitment to halt a presumably expansionist Communist China, and eventually made Vietnam a test of its determination to uphold world order. By wrongly attributing the conflict to external sources, the United States drastically misjudged its internal dynamics. By intervening in what was essentially a local struggle, it placed itself at the mercy of local forces, a weak client, and a determined adversary.

Herring adds that the war also demonstrated the limits of U.S. power. "Stopping wars requires settling the political questions over which they are fought," such as establishing borders and government structures, he says, and, "in Vietnam, such tasks ultimately proved beyond the ability of the United States."[1]

In *A Time for War*, Robert D. Schulzinger provides another concise example of the liberal-realist interpretation:

> The United States became involved in Vietnamese politics and eventually fought in Vietnam because of the Cold War. For more than forty years after 1947, Americans advanced containment of the Soviet Union as the central principle of U.S. foreign relations. Had American leaders not

---

1. George C. Herring, *America's Longest War: The United States and Vietnam, 1950–1975*, 3rd ed. (New York: McGraw-Hill, 1996), p. 314.

thought that all international events were connected to the Cold War there would have been no American war in Vietnam. American leaders persistently believed that their credibility was at stake there.[2]

Many other historians express similar liberal-realist conclusions. William Duiker declares: "As the decade of the 1950's dawned, Truman administration officials saw French Indochina, and specifically Vietnam, as the keystone of the U.S. policy of containment in Asia and an important link in the U.S. defensive perimeter throughout the region." Eisenhower and Kennedy agreed with this strategy assessment, he maintains, and Kennedy "defined Vietnam as a 'test case' of U.S. capacity to stem the advance of communism into vulnerable areas throughout the Third World."[3] Stanley Karnow writes that the United States was "playing for global stakes" in Indochina.[4] In the words of George Kahin, "Nearly all American officials . . . perceived Vietnamese communism as one of the fronts of contest with the Soviet Union and China—critically dependent on the two major communist powers rather than drawing most of its strength from a fundamentally autonomous national foundation. And in terms of American national interest, Vietnam remained a 'domino' whose fall would undermine and topple noncommunist regimes in neighboring states."[5] "By definition," Marilyn Young has asserted about U.S. policy, "Communists could not be genuine nationalists; by definition, America supported genuine nationalists. Therefore, those people the United States supported were nationalists, the rest were communist stooges."[6]

While these authors and most other scholars consider the massive U.S. intervention in Vietnam to have been a mistake, historians disagree over why reasonable people could not see the strategic errors they were making. Some characterize the decision-making process as a quagmire. They portray the United States as well intentioned and even cautious but claim that policy makers took a series of small steps to aid Saigon until Johnson found himself stuck in a commitment with no easy path forward or backward. As historian Arthur Schlesinger Jr. expressed it, the American war in Vietnam was "a tragedy with-

---

2. Robert D. Schulzinger, A Time for War: The United States and Vietnam, 1941–1975 (New York: Oxford University Press, 1997), p. 329.

3. William J. Duiker, U.S. Containment Policy and the Conflict in Indochina (Stanford, Calif.: Stanford University Press, 1994), p. 2.

4. Stanley Karnow, Vietnam: A History (New York: Viking, 1983), p. 169.

5. George McT. Kahin, Intervention: How America Became Involved in Vietnam (Garden City, N.Y.: Anchor Books, 1987), p. 126.

6. Marilyn B. Young, The Vietnam Wars, 1945–1990 (New York: HarperCollins, 1991), p. 24.

out villains."[7] Other analysts, however, have used a stalemate analogy to contend that leaders like Kennedy and Johnson and their aides well understood that there was no obvious U.S. solution to Vietnam's political division. "Virtually all important decisions were made without illusions about the odds of success," according to Leslie H. Gelb and Richard K. Betts.[8] Presidents kept doing just enough to avoid defeat, that is, to preserve a stalemate, however, so that they could not be blamed for failure in Vietnam. Both the quagmire and stalemate scenarios lead into a wide-ranging discussion by historians over the significance of presidential personalities and egos, bureaucratic inertia and careerism, determination to avoid Munich-like appeasement of aggressors, Western arrogance toward Asians, and Cold War political culture in the United States that made the risk of appearing soft on communism unacceptable.

As early as 1979, when they examined the literature then available on the war, Gelb and Betts discerned nine different but often overlapping causes of U.S. involvement. The first they labeled "the arrogance of power—idealistic imperialism." This American attitude arose from a long string of U.S. military successes that had created the illusion of invincibility and virtue. The second explanation was "the rapacity of power: economic imperialism," a radical interpretation that an industrial-financial elite seeking to control the world's economic resources shaped U.S. policy. "Bureaucratic politics" is third and highlights how factors such as departmental rivalries, career advancement, and institutional momentum can drive policy making. Fourth, "domestic politics" includes the pressure on elected officials to appear neither soft nor reckless toward communism or other threats. Gelb and Betts' fifth cause is the influence of "pragmatic security managers," nonideological technocrats who believe that they can fine tune the use of force in a precise way. "Ethnocentricity and misperception" is number six and relates to the quagmire notion of not understanding the history and culture of Vietnam. "The slippery slope," number seven, is another quagmire-like concept that describes American leaders, who did not truly understand the problems in Vietnam, as taking a series of small steps that added up into a most intractable and unforeseen commitment. Eight is "international power politics and containment"; and nine is "ideological anti-communism"—both of which incorporate the liberal-realist, or flawed-containment, critique that policy makers cast the issues in Vietnam as being of vital global and ideological significance to U.S. interests and values.[9]

---

7. Arthur M. Schlesinger, Jr., *The Bitter Heritage: Vietnam and American Democracy, 1941–1966* (Boston: Houghton Mifflin, 1967), p. 32.

8. Leslie H. Gelb and Richard K. Betts, *The Irony of Vietnam: The System Worked* (Washington, D.C.: Brookings Institution, 1979), p. 2.

9. Ibid., pp. 9–26.

More than a decade after Gelb and Betts made their thorough enumeration, one of the leading liberal-realist analysts, Gary Hess, offered an updated but similar list that revealed how well this catalog of causes remains instructive. For Hess, the factors that led the United States into Vietnam included:

> a global strategy that looked upon the confrontation with the Communist powers as a "zero-sum game" and cast Southeast Asian nations into potential "dominoes"; the "lessons of the past" that taught the importance of halting aggression and thus perceived Vietnam as another place where the Communist powers were "testing" Western resolve; the parallel growth of U.S. commitment and "credibility" that made disengagement tantamount to surrendering America's position of world leadership; and the historic conviction of American mission that encouraged leaders, as well as civilians and military personnel in the field, to see in Vietnam an opportunity to realize Western ideals.[10]

As Robert McMahon has perceptively commented, "Hess's liberal use of quotation marks . . . suggests that he sees American policy as rooted essentially in a series of illusions."[11] Terms such as "dominoes" or "credibility" misled policy makers, which is a basic contention of the liberal-realist interpretation.

The liberal realists represent the mainstream, but they have not been without their critics from the left and right. More radical interpretations take a systemic approach that downplays the judgments of individual policy makers and argues that the Western capitalist identity of the United States explains its conduct. These critiques vary considerably among themselves. A world systems analysis, such as that of Thomas McCormick, characterizes the United States as a hegemonic power in the mid-twentieth century, as Britain was in the nineteenth, that tried to use its tremendous economic and military advantages to defend its interests at the core of the world system at the expense of peripheral areas such as Southeast Asia. Gabriel Kolko and other writers place U.S. policies in Vietnam in the structural context of hegemonic capitalism and imperialism. Kolko explains: "The Vietnam War was for the United States the culmination of its frustrating postwar effort to merge its arms and politics to halt and reverse the emergence of states and social systems opposed to the international

---

10. Gary R. Hess, *Vietnam and the United States: Origins and Legacy of War* (Boston: Twayne, 1990), pp. 172–73.

11. Robert J. McMahon, "U.S.-Vietnamese Relations: A Historiographical Survey," in Warren I. Cohen, ed., *Pacific Passage: The Study of American-East Asian Relations on the Eve of the Twenty-First Century* (New York: Columbia University Press, 1996), p. 318.

order Washington sought to establish."[12] Less ideological but also giving important weight to the value of Southeast Asia to U.S. interests in an open global market are works by Andrew Rotter and Lloyd Gardner. Although he maintains that his interpretation is not strictly economic, Rotter concludes that U.S. policy makers were determined to prevent "Communist control of the Far East [that] would disrupt . . . commercial linkages, damage the West psychologically, enslave millions of Asians, and bring enormous economic and strategic benefits to the Soviets."[13] "From the beginning," according to Gardner, "Vietnam figured in the plans of policy makers to reconstruct the old prewar [colonial] order into a liberal capitalist system that would insure prosperity and peace."[14]

On the right, there are a number of writers who argue that the U.S. decision to fight a large war in Vietnam was not a mistake. They are sometimes termed revisionist because they challenge the standard view that the war was wrong. Their arguments are also labeled the "win thesis" because they generally assert that U.S. military victory was possible in Vietnam if Washington had authorized a greater use of force. Many of these authors, such as Harry Summers Jr. and Bruce Palmer Jr., are former military officers who served in Vietnam and who accept uncritically the official government position that the war was conventional aggression by the North against the South and not primarily a revolutionary or civil war. They maintain that Washington was morally and strategically justified in waging war against Hanoi and that the only problem was the decision by American political leaders to keep the war limited and to treat it as an unconventional or counterinsurgency war. In Summers's view, "the North Vietnamese had launched a strategic offensive to conquer South Vietnam." He does not contend that the U.S. forces should have countered with an invasion of the North, but rather they should have cordoned off the South from the northern threat. "We could have taken the tactical offensive to isolate the battlefield," he argues, "but instead of orientating on North Vietnam—the source of war—we turned our attention to the symptom—the guerrilla war in the south."[15] If the United States had used more air and ground force against the North, Summers and others reason, Hanoi could have been compelled to accept the independence of South Vietnam.

A number of military writers sharply disagree with the idea of treating the war as conventional aggression. Some, such as Andrew Krepinevich, find that the

---

12. Gabriel Kolko, *Anatomy of a War: Vietnam, the United States, and the Modern Historical Experience* (New York: Pantheon Books, 1985), p. 547.

13. Andrew J. Rotter, *The Path to Vietnam: Origins of the American Commitment to Southeast Asia* (Ithaca, N.Y.: Cornell University Press, 1987), p. 219.

14. Lloyd C. Gardner, *Approaching Vietnam: From World War II Through Dienbienphu* (New York: Norton, 1988), p. 15.

15. Harry G. Summers, Jr., *On Strategy: A Critical Analysis of the Vietnam War* (New York: Dell, 1984), pp. 126–27.

war was an insurgency, a conflict between the government and the guerrillas for control within the South. Rather than defending against attack from the North, the need was for pacification, that is, helping the Saigon regime protect itself and the population from the Vietcong and thereby building political support for the RVN. In his biography of U.S. military adviser and pacification advocate John Paul Vann, Neil Sheehan quotes Vann on the fundamental importance of counterinsurgency warfare: "Without security, nothing else we do will last."[16]

Although how the war came to be and what kind of war it was remains the subject of debate, by the summer of 1965 the United States had decided for its own purposes to take over the fighting from the South Vietnamese. Major ground operations against units of the Vietcong and the **People's Army of Vietnam** (PAVN), or **North Vietnamese Army** (NVA) as Americans usually termed it, were now conducted by American combat units with the ARVN providing security and supporting functions. A large-scale American air war was also in progress against targets in both North and South Vietnam and along the Ho Chi Minh Trail in Laos. He had not wanted the role, but Johnson was a war president.

---

16. Neil Sheehan, *A Bright Shining Lie: John Paul Vann and America in Vietnam* (New York: Random House, 1988), p. 67.

Chapter 8

THE AMERICAN WAR IN VIETNAM: STRATEGY

All wars have much in common, but, in many respects, the conflict in Vietnam was a different kind of war than Americans expected. National leaders, the general public, and men and women who went to Vietnam possessed images of war gained from the actual events of World War II and the Korean War and from the fictionalized versions of those conflicts in movies with such popular stars as John Wayne and Audie Murphy. World War II was the great example of American power and heroism coming to the rescue of oppressed peoples. The Korean War was a limited engagement that ended in stalemate and was more ambiguous, but it still had the noble image of Americans rushing to the aid of a nation threatened by communist aggression. Moreover, both World War II and the Korean War had been contests for territory with progress marked by lines on a map. The Vietnam War turned out to be unlike these other experiences. The geographical and political environment proved less responsive to American power. Determining who among the Vietnamese were friends and who were enemies was difficult in a guerrilla war with no fixed battles lines and a Vietcong enemy often wearing the same black peasant garb as the farmers American soldiers were supposedly defending. The Vietnam War became a tremendous military, political, and diplomatic frustration to the United States.

THE DRAFT

For the sake of his Great Society plans, Johnson wanted to keep the war at a low profile and to avoid full military mobilization. This political choice had a variety of consequences. His rejection of Robert McNamara's recommendation for a war tax to help finance the build-up, for example, contributed to more deficit spending and inflationary pressure. To maintain worldwide manpower levels during the Vietnam troop deployment, the Pentagon wanted to activate military reservists, but the president again said no because such action would involve Congress. To meet the need for additional personnel, the military had to rely on an increase in the **draft**.

HOW SOCIALLY EQUITABLE WAS THE BURDEN OF MILITARY SERVICE IN VIETNAM?

Even though U.S. troop levels in Vietnam leaped to almost 200,000 by the end of 1967, and that figure more than doubled in the following two years, not all young men in America were needed in the military. Throughout the Cold War era, the **Selective Service System** had functioned much as it was designed to do during the massive mobilization of World War II. Using a concept known as channeling, young men over age eighteen were either subject to military conscription or exempted from that obligation by a complex set of classifications intended to place people where the nation most needed them. Hence men who were in college or in certain professions or had certain medical conditions often could avoid service. After the Korean War and into the early 1960s, draft calls were low because of adequate voluntary enlistment and the reduced need for ground forces in an era of air power. With the escalation in Vietnam, draft calls went from 106,000 in 1965 to 339,000 in 1966. Over half of the draftees went to fill the ranks in Vietnam. Selective Service had always been a system designed to decide who would serve when all are not needed, but the fairness of the selection came under scrutiny as the risk of exposure to combat and death in Vietnam became very real (see document 22, appendix 1).

About two and a half million American men served in Vietnam, representing 10 percent of the males of the generation that reached age eighteen during the war. The draft exempted more men than it inducted into the service. Those who went to Vietnam were, as a group, poorer and less educated than the average of young Americans at the time. During the first year of the U.S. build-up, 20 percent of U.S. casualties were **African Americans**, although that group comprised only 13 percent of military personnel. The first units that went to Vietnam were comprised primarily of regular army troops, not draftees. Because the military represented a career opportunity for African Americans, the percentage of blacks was high in Vietnam at first. Eventually, the casualty rates for

African Americans dropped to more representative levels. Still, it appeared that because of class and race, some groups of Americans were more likely to serve in combat in Vietnam than others. A survey in 1964 indicated that 44 percent of Americans had white-collar jobs, but only 20 percent of U.S. soldiers came from white-collar families. Throughout most of the war, statistics for income, education, and parents' occupations show that about 80 percent of soldiers were from poor or working-class families.

ATTRITION STRATEGY AND BODY COUNT

HOW DID THE U.S. MILITARY COMMAND IN VIETNAM PLAN TO WIN THE WAR?

The Johnson administration chose a gradually increasing bombing campaign and an incremental deployment of U.S. troops to Indochina because the American objective in Vietnam was limited. The purpose was not to conquer North Vietnam or even to threaten its survival to a point that might risk a Chinese or Soviet military reaction. The intent was to sustain South Vietnam's political survival long enough and put enough pressure on North Vietnam to gain Hanoi's recognition of the RVN. Although the United States had tremendous power at its disposal, including nuclear weapons, the strategic assumption in Washington was that the full extent of U.S. force was not merited or needed in Vietnam.

Given these conditions, General Westmoreland devised an **attrition strategy**. This plan relied on America's advanced technology and vast material resources to limit U.S. casualties while inflicting so much damage on Vietcong and NVA forces in the South and military targets in the North that Hanoi would yield. The belief was that the air campaign, the ability to move U.S. troops easily by helicopter, modern weapons, and the other material advantages the United States had over the DRV in this technowar would ultimately exhaust the enemy's will and ability to fight (see document 23, appendix 1).

HOW WAS WINNING DEFINED?

Progress in the war of attrition could not be measured on a map since the possession of territory was not the objective. Instead, the Pentagon, under Secretary of Defense McNamara, devised a host of statistical measurements, such as the number of aircraft sorties flown and amounts of munitions expended. The most controversial yardstick was **body count**—the estimated number of enemy killed. If the primary objective was to wear down the opponent, a tally of his losses was logical, but this grim tabulation was an unreliable index. It was easily falsified, since unit commanders reported their own totals. Even worse, any dead Vietnamese might be counted, including noncombatants, which in effect encouraged indiscriminate targeting of people, especially villagers in rural areas. As the war progressed, U.S. air and ground warfare often resulted in the deaths of the very people U.S. policy claimed to be defending.

Of course, Westmoreland intended American military operations to search for and destroy enemy military units to weaken the enemy's ability to wage war. From the Battle of the **Ia Drang** Valley in 1965 through Operations Cedar Falls and Junction City in 1967, he mounted large unit sweeps of thousands of men to find and eliminate the Vietcong and NVA. Some areas were designated as "**free-fire zones**" in which U.S. arms, including B-52 bombers delivering tons of high explosives, could attack at will. These means did not go unchallenged in military circles. Some U.S. Marine commanders and civilian strategists concluded that **pacification** was a better approach. This alternate strategy called for smaller unit operations and more cooperation with villagers in order to build political capital for Saigon and weaken NLF influence among the people. Although some U.S. units engaged in pacification efforts, Westmoreland devoted most of his forces, which by the end of 1967 totaled 485,000, to **search and destroy** missions. Late in 1967, the general declared that a cross-over point had been reached in which U.S. forces were inflicting more losses on the Vietcong and NVA than the enemy could replace. The political viability of the Thieu-Ky government in Saigon, however, remained in doubt.

HUMPIN' IT: THE AMERICAN SOLDIER

Because of the heavy reliance on the draft and on voluntary enlistments induced by the draft, the average age of American enlisted men in the Vietnam War was nineteen or twenty, six or seven years younger than the World War II average and signifying what was probably the youngest foreign combat force in U.S. history. Without activation of reserves, there was also a shortage of junior officers and experienced noncommissioned officers to lead these young troops in an unconventional war in an Asian setting that was often unfathomable to Westerners. Added to these conditions were the vague political and military objectives of the struggle that usually got translated to the soldiers through the brutal shorthand of body count. As a result, many soldiers found themselves immersed in seemingly aimless violence in which their own survival and that of their buddies became the only discernible goal.

There is no one description that typifies the experience of American soldiers in Vietnam. Early in the war, morale was fairly high as soldiers accepted the validity of the Cold War purposes announced by their leaders. Later, as controversy and doubt about America's role in Vietnam grew, the morale declined. Where a soldier was in Vietnam also made a great difference. Marines in the mountains near the **demilitarized zone** between North and South Vietnam were at times in trench-like warfare reminiscent of World War I, while army troops in the marshes of the Mekong Delta far to the south often had to contend with elusive guerrillas. Since there were no actual battle lines, even the notion of forward and rear areas was imprecise.

WERE U.S. SOLDIERS PLACED IN BOTH PHYSICAL AND MORAL DANGER IN VIETNAM?

In all wars, combat places the warrior in some of the most extreme and stressful of situations, and the Vietnam War was no exception. Westmoreland's search-and-destroy strategy and the emphasis on body count, however, put American soldiers at tremendous physical and moral risk. While true that U.S. **artillery**, helicopter gunships, and tactical aircraft could devastate enemy forces, the difficulty was often in finding them. Consequently the "grunts," or foot-soldiers, went on long patrols through difficult terrain—they referred to these marches as "humpin' it"—in order to flush out the Vietcong and NVA. Many soldiers felt that they were bait for the high-tech trap. If an enemy force was found, then the great firepower at the unit commander's disposal could be unleashed via radio command. During these patrols, American soldiers experienced a significant number of deaths and maiming injuries from mines, **booby traps**, and hidden snipers. Over time, U.S. casualties mounted and so did the desire for revenge, or "pay back," against an often invisible foe. Fear, anger, and the incentive of promotion or commendation for a high body count could lead to an overapplication of U.S. weaponry bordering on or even constituting **atrocities**. Individual Vietnamese, and sometimes entire villages, could be "wasted" because they were suspected of being the enemy or simply got in the way. Reporting on an attack on one village, an American television crew recorded an officer's comment that it was necessary to destroy the village to save it. The tragic irony of that comment revealed much about the attrition strategy.

THE AIR WAR

Nowhere during the Vietnam War was American technological superiority over its enemy more apparent than in the air. The United States had helicopters for troop transportation, medical evacuation (see **Medical Support**), command and control, and close tactical fire support. It had fixed-wing propeller aircraft for troop and supply transportation, provisioning remote bases, fire support, and observing and marking targets for artillery and bombing. It had high-performance jet fighters and fighter-bombers for tactical and strategic bombing, and B-52 heavy bombers for delivering hundreds of tons of explosives on troop concentrations, supply lines, and other military targets. The United States spent more than $100 billion on these air operations. From 1962 to 1973 the total amount of explosives dropped on Indochina was about eight million tons: one million tons on North Vietnam, nearly a half million on Cambodia, about three million on the Ho Chi Minh Trail in Laos, and four million on South Vietnam. The level of bombing on the RVN in support of U.S. and ARVN ground operations made America's ally the most bombed country in history.

WHY DID THE MASSIVE U.S. BOMBING PRODUCE ONLY LIMITED OR NEGLIGIBLE RESULTS?

The air war did not force Hanoi to recognize the Saigon government or to stop infiltration of men and supplies along the Ho Chi Minh Trail. It did not make the Saigon regime more popular in South Vietnam. In fact, the bombing stiffened the DRV resistance and helped to solidify the perception in Vietnam of the RVN's dependence on the United States and lack of regard for the Vietnamese people. Air cover was often vital to the survival and success of American ground forces, but in a primarily agricultural country like Vietnam, there were few militarily valuable targets. Strategic bombing of North Vietnam and supply lines into South Vietnam was not effective in hastening an end to the fighting and was often counterproductive.

Washington persisted in bombing month after month and year after year for several reasons. Despite evidence from World War II, Korea, and Vietnam itself that strategic bombing did not force an enemy to capitulate, air power advocates continued to argue that bombing could produce victory. Civilian leaders liked air operations because they produced fewer American casualties than ground combat and thus generated less political opposition at home. In addition, the Johnson administration felt compelled to take some form of firm action to prevent the collapse of Saigon but had no clear-cut plan for victory. The air power option was available and possessed an enticing allure of a simple solution to a complex problem. The temptation to use it was irresistible.

DIPLOMACY

Johnson did not want a U.S. war in Southeast Asia and claimed that the United States was willing to negotiate with the DRV. In 1962 a diplomatic settlement had eased the risk of major power confrontations in Laos. Kennedy and later Johnson resisted applying the Laotian model of a coalition government to Vietnam because they judged that it would lead to a communist government there. Advocates of diplomacy, such as France's president **Charles de Gaulle** and United Nations Secretary General **U Thant**, argued on the other hand, that the problems in Southeast Asia were political, not military, and that to resort to arms only led to violence, not solutions. Sensitive to such criticisms, the Johnson administration proclaimed it was open to talks even as it turned to military escalation.

As the war grew in intensity from 1965 to 1967, both Hanoi and Washington remained more willing to endure the costs of hostilities than to make concessions. There were scores of private and public peace proposals offered from various sources. In April 1965, in a highly publicized speech at **Johns Hopkins University**, Johnson expressed an interest in "unconditional discussions" with Hanoi and offered a billion dollars in U.S. economic development funds for Southeast Asia as a sign of U.S. goodwill (see document 24, appendix 1). In fact, however, Washington was not prepared to yield at all on the demand that Hanoi recognize the legitimacy of the RVN. For its part, North Vietnam continued to resist talks and insisted that first U.S. forces withdraw from Vietnam and that Washington terminate its support of its puppet regime in Saigon. During 1966 and 1967 both sides made a few modest proposals about their troop deployments, and U.S. spokesmen offered some restrictions of the bombing campaign, but neither side would retreat from its basic position on the fate of South Vietnam. The United States and the DRV each continued to try to force its opponent to accept its terms.

THE RESILIENT ENEMY

Just as Washington had settled on an attrition strategy to try to wear down the Vietnamese communists, Hanoi had its own plan for victory in its doctrine of protracted war. Used successfully in the war against the French, this strategy sought to avoid large, fixed battles and to weaken the will of the enemy to fight through piecemeal attacks and guerrilla harassment (see document 25, appendix 1). This armed struggle was conducted by both regular PAVN units infiltrating from the North and Vietcong military formations of the **People's Liberation Armed Forces** (PLAF). The NLF and party cadre from the North also engaged in political struggle to recruit peasants and workers in South Vietnam for an anticipated general uprising against the ARVN. These plans constituted a reasonable way for the Vietnamese communists to use their patriotic and social appeal to the Vietnamese people to counter the technological superiority of the American forces and the U.S.-supplied ARVN. Still, Westmoreland's technowar against the North and South inflicted heavy losses on the Vietcong and NVA, and the longer the fighting continued the higher the costs became for the enemies of the RVN.

The communist commanders who led the struggle against the RVN and the United States were not infallible supermen. They argued among themselves and made mistakes, but they had certain advantages and did some things right. Hanoi's adherents were able to tap into the historical Vietnamese resistance to outside domination and to continue the nationalistic momentum gained by the Vietminh defeat of the French colonialists. Conversely, southern leaders such as Ngo Dinh Diem, Nguyen Van Thieu, and Nguyen Cao Ky suffered from the taint of collaboration with and dependence upon the Americans. The communists also had a more disciplined and effective political party organization than their Vietnamese opponents. The charismatic leadership of Ho Chi Minh, who remained the DRV president until his death in 1969, provided further legitimacy to his side. In their commitment to their goal of national liberation, the leaders of the NLF and DRV were also prepared to be ruthless with their opponents and to sacrifice the lives of large numbers of their own followers. In addition, assistance received from the PRC and the USSR helped North Vietnam recoup losses suffered from U.S. bomb attacks and to keep war materiels flowing into the South. At no time did U.S. strategists believe American interests in Indochina were worth the risk of war with China and the Soviet Union or the cost of an invasion of North Vietnam. The United States fought a limited war, and the DRV conducted what for it was a total war. After three years of heavy fighting, neither side was close to a military victory.

Chapter 9

THE AMERICAN WAR IN VIETNAM:
THE LIMITS OF POWER

At the end of January 1968, Vietcong assault forces began coordinated attacks on urban areas, provincial capitals, U.S. and ARVN military installations, and RVN government offices throughout all of South Vietnam. Dubbed the **Tet Offensive** because it coincided with the Vietnamese New Year's holiday of Tet, this event was a turning point in the war. It caused the Johnson administration, after three years of steady escalation of the U.S. commitment, to reevaluate the strategic importance of Vietnam against the known and potential costs to the United States. It set off a critical reaction to the war within the American **media** and gave greater credence to arguments against the war that a vocal protest movement had been voicing for some time. This public debate over the war became part of the presidential election campaign of 1968. In the year after Tet, the people of the United States and their leaders began looking for a way out of the Vietnam quagmire.

THE TET OFFENSIVE

IF THE TET OFFENSIVE WAS A TURNING POINT IN THE WAR, WHAT CHANGED?

Most historians of the war characterize the attack as a strategic success for Hanoi because of its psychological impact on the U.S. side. At a time when administration spokesmen were claiming that the U.S. military campaign was weakening the enemy, the Vietcong demonstrated surprising strength and morale in making this bold strike. Even though U.S. and ARVN troops withstood and repulsed the assaults, the official confidence and general public acceptance of U.S. purposes that had sustained the American intervention began to erode significantly. Why and how this change occurred has remained the subject of some debate.

Why the leaders in Hanoi decided to launch a broad offensive at this particular juncture is not entirely clear. They knew that the Saigon regime remained politically alienated from much of the South Vietnamese population, and they also had to be concerned about the heavy losses their forces were taking from the American ground and air operations. Vietnamese communist military doctrine since the French war had called for a protracted struggle until a point was reached at which a general offensive would set off a general uprising against the outside power and its Vietnamese puppets. In view of that doctrine and the battlefield stalemate at the end of 1967, the Tet Offensive can be seen as both an act of survival to initiate a general offensive before U.S. arms further weakened the PLAF and PAVN, and as an act of political faith that the people of the South would turn on the RVN and the United States.

Regardless of which line of reasoning carried the day in Hanoi, the general offensive did not lead to a popular uprising and also exposed the communist forces to enormous losses that they could not afford. At first their plan for the offensive went well. Between October 1967 and January 1968, the Vietcong and NVA attacked military targets in remote areas and laid siege to the U.S. Marine base at **Khe Sanh** near the Demilitarized Zone (DMZ). These feints drew U.S. forces away from the cities while the NLF moved men and supplies secretly into position to attack populated areas. Although U.S. intelligence detected some of these urban-directed movements, Westmoreland and his staff remained convinced that the fighting elsewhere, especially at Khe Sanh, was the principal enemy threat. When the offensive itself began in Saigon, Hue, three other cities, thirty-six provincial capitals, and sixty-four district capitals, the surprise was almost total. Within a few days, however, the mobility and firepower of U.S. forces and a surprising show of resilience by ARVN units reversed what gains the attackers had achieved. Thousands of Vietcong troops were killed or captured. In one notable exception, Hue became the scene of savage fighting that raged for three weeks for control of the old imperial capital. The American and ARVN troops prevailed, but much of the city was in ruins, thousands of civilians had died (some executed by the Vietcong), and 100,000 people were homeless.

In terms of both conventional and revolutionary warfare, the Tet Offensive was a tactical failure. The people of South Vietnam did not rise up behind the NLF's revolutionary banner, and the front's fighting forces were decimated. In other ways, however, Tet had significant positive implications for Hanoi. It revealed that the massive U.S. military presence had not been able to stop NVA infiltration into the South. That same flow of men and supplies could and did continue after Tet. U.S. deaths in the Tet fighting were significant, about 1,100 killed in action, which brought the total U.S. deaths in the war to about 17,000 at that time. The fighting in early 1968 also produced some 2,300 ARVN dead and enormous numbers of civilian casualties and refugees. This strain on the ARVN and the dislocation of the population severely handicapped pacification efforts. The Tet Offensive came as a shock and surprise to the American people and confronted them and their leaders with the prospect that much more time and money and many more lives would be required if the United States was to continue to defend South Vietnam.

THE ANTIWAR MOVEMENT AND THE MEDIA

Some Americans had always opposed U.S. military intervention in Vietnam, and that number had been growing even before Tet. In 1965, after the first U.S. combat troops went to Vietnam, organized protests began. In the spring of 1965 there were "**teach-ins**" on college campuses and a demonstration in Washington organized by the **Students for a Democratic Society** (SDS) (see document 26, appendix 1). Initially involving only a few thousand protesters, the **antiwar movement** grew significantly during 1966 and 1967 and involved a wide-range of activities: petitions, political campaigns, lobbying, street demonstrations, draft resistance, and even acts of violence. Although many protesters were students, peace activists also included ministers, mothers, traditional pacifists, conscientious objectors, and even some veterans embittered and disillusioned by the military experience in Vietnam (see **Vietnam Veterans Against the War**). Most members of Congress voted for the funds and authorizations needed to conduct the war, but some prominent legislative leaders, such as Senator **J. William Fulbright**, held hearings on the war or raised individual objections to the Americanization of the conflict. In the spring of 1967, an estimated 300,000 citizens gathered in New York City to protest the war, and in November some 30,000–50,000 demonstrators held an antiwar rally at the Pentagon (see document 27, appendix 1).

DID THE ANTIWAR MOVEMENT AND ITS ARGUMENTS AFFECT THE LENGTH OR OUTCOME OF THE WAR?

Lyndon Johnson and later Richard Nixon and their advisers were convinced that the existence of a large and public antiwar movement hurt the U.S. war effort by encouraging the enemy. Both administrations insisted that their own policies were not affected by protests, but their criticisms of the antiwar movement made plain that they believed it prolonged the conflict. Government authorities tried in various ways to harass and quiet the critics. Public opinion polls also showed that a growing number of Americans shared the same doubts about the war that the demonstrators expressed, even if the public disliked the image and methods of the generally young and often unkempt activists.

In a democracy like America, war, especially a limited war, has a significant domestic impact. In trying to disguise the magnitude of the U.S. military commitment in Vietnam, Johnson had not rallied the people in support of the war. As the size and costs of the conflict became apparent over the months, the vague official pronouncements on U.S. purposes in Vietnam generated demands for political accountability. In late 1967 Johnson compounded his earlier mistake with a public relations campaign to convey the idea that America was winning the war of attrition. The pressure that he felt indicated that the antiwar movement was having an impact.

Against the backdrop of official assurances of progress, the surprise and extent of the Tet fighting deepened public doubt. While true that U.S. and ARVN forces survived the attacks, that the enemy could move so forcefully at all damaged the credibility of official explanations of the course of the war. In one place in particular, American newspaper and **television** reporting of the Tet Offensive, this discrepancy between government pronouncements and actual events in the field was especially notable.

DID THE MEDIA TURN A MILITARY SUCCESS DURING THE WAR INTO A FAILURE?

There was a belief among some Americans, including General Westmoreland and some other military leaders, that American news reporting of the Tet Offensive was wrong, biased, and defeatist. Sometimes called the "stab-in-the-back" thesis, this view holds that the enemy took a desperate gamble, was soundly beaten back, and was extremely vulnerable to counterattack. Distortions in the media, this argument goes, caused civilian leaders in Washington to hesitate and to reassess Vietnam policy and thereby to miss the opportunity to strike a fatal blow to Vietcong and NVA military capability.

This interpretation greatly exaggerates the effect of the media. Until Tet, most of the major commercial media in the United States had accepted the official rationale for the war and the government reports of progress. A few intrepid reporters, such as David Halberstam and **Peter Arnett**, had been asking hard questions, but the government version had been getting out through the media. Hence, there was genuine dismay within news circles at the beginning of Tet. Television networks, newspapers, and magazines carried dramatic pictures of Vietcong soldiers in the U.S. Embassy compound in Saigon and on the streets of major cities. These real scenes left their own impression on the public. In the days that followed, respected journalists, such as the popular CBS News anchorman **Walter Cronkite**, declared that they could not see in all this fighting any quick end to the burden of this war (see document 28, appendix 1).

Basically, the professional media correspondents did their job and reported the dramatic twist of events as it was happening. Top-secret assessments of the fighting by the Joint Chiefs of Staff and others within the government that are now available to historians reveal the same questions and doubts about U.S. strategy and prospects in Vietnam that reporters such as Cronkite were voicing. For both the U.S. public and the Johnson administration, the heavy fighting in early 1968 brought with it a demand for reexamination of American policies.

JOHNSON'S DECISION TO STOP ESCALATION

Johnson was not a leader who would accept failure, and he did not interpret the enemy's Tet onslaught as a U.S. defeat. Always a reluctant warrior, however, the president had determined even before the surprise offensive that the size of the American military effort in Vietnam had about reached its reasonable limit. Consequently, when JCS Chairman General **Earle Wheeler** endorsed a proposal from Westmoreland for 206,000 more troops, Johnson ordered his new secretary of defense, Clark Clifford, to conduct a thorough policy review. Quickly leaked to the press, Westmoreland's request generated a burst of open opposition to the idea. Clearly, such public sentiments were a significant consideration, especially in a presidential election year, but additional influences were also at work within the administration.

Although Clifford had supported the war, he put detailed questions about future scenarios to the military brass, civilian strategists in the Pentagon, and a group of elder statesmen, the **Wise Men**, whom Johnson had consulted on other occasions. Wheeler painted a bleak picture of prospects without the additional troops, but he was purposefully vague on how the troops would be used. There was strong debate at the highest levels over whether to continue the attrition strategy or focus more on pacification and population security. Before he left the Pentagon, former secretary McNamara had come to believe that simply applying more force was not the answer, and his top aides remained in the department and continued to argue that point. Clifford found that members of America's business elite were concerned about the economic drag that the war was putting on the United States. Finally, a majority of the Wise Men, including former secretary of state **Dean Acheson**, who had helped to establish the global containment strategy, advised that America begin to disengage from the war.

After weighing these opinions, Johnson addressed the nation via television on March 31, 1968. The president had decided to reject Westmoreland's troop request and to authorize only an additional 13,500 U.S. forces. He announced that the United States would limit its bombing of North Vietnam to supply and staging areas just across the DMZ from the South and that he welcomed direct negotiations with Hanoi. Although the DRV quickly agreed to talks in Paris, there was no substantive diplomatic breakthrough (see **Paris Peace Talks**). Indeed, some of the heaviest fighting of the war occurred in the remaining months of 1968. In his March 31 speech, the president also shocked the nation when he withdrew himself as a candidate for reelection. The American war in Vietnam was far from over, but it was now going to be a different war under new U.S. leadership (see document 29, appendix 1).

THE PRESIDENTIAL ELECTION OF 1968

The Vietnam War was not the only national political issue in the United States in 1968. The civil rights revolution, urban violence, continuing debate over Johnson's social welfare agenda, an international trade deficit, and other issues also faced the nation's leaders. With over 500,000 American soldiers in Vietnam and 400 of them dying each week during the first half of 1968, however, the serious contenders for the presidency had to take and defend a clear position on the war. Especially once Johnson bowed out of the race, there seemed to be an opportunity for the voters to have a direct voice in foreign policy.

HOW DID THE U.S. POLITICAL PROCESS RESPOND TO THE WAR?

Despite the controversy surrounding U.S. policy in Vietnam, it was difficult at first to challenge Johnson politically. Potential candidates from his own Democratic Party and from the Republican opposition did not want to appear disloyal to the president during wartime or unwilling to support American soldiers exposed to the dangers of combat. One candidate who did come forward to contest the president on the war was Senator **Eugene McCarthy** (D-Minn.) (see document 30, appendix 1). He came close to upsetting the president in the New Hampshire primary on March 12. Senator **Robert Kennedy** of New York was a much stronger contender for the Democratic nomination and also opposed the president on the war. After the largely unknown McCarthy demonstrated Johnson's political vulnerability on the war, the younger brother of John Kennedy stepped forward as a candidate.

Without Johnson in the race, the charismatic Kennedy appeared to be the likely Democratic nominee. His stock rose higher on April 4 when he made a heartfelt plea for national harmony upon learning of the assassination of civil rights leader **Martin Luther King Jr.** In an unbelievably tragic sequence of events, however, Kennedy himself was murdered on June 6. McCarthy remained as an outspoken peace candidate, but the party organization turned its support to Johnson's vice president **Hubert H. Humphrey**. Because of his role in the administration, Humphrey had the image of being prowar, and his candidacy sparked little enthusiasm with many Democrats.

At the **Democratic National Convention** in Chicago in August, the war was the divisive issue inside and outside the meeting hall. On the convention floor, delegates loyal to McCarthy, Kennedy, and Senator **George McGovern** of South Dakota (another peace candidate) tried unsuccessfully to get the party platform to repudiate Johnson's conduct of the war. Humphrey then formally received the nomination, but dramatic events outside in the streets overshadowed the voting. Thousands of youths converged on the convention site condemning the war and taunting Chicago policemen massed to control them. On orders from Mayor Richard J. Daley, the officers brutally subdued and dispersed the crowd in full view of the national and international media assembled to cover the convention. It was a riveting and disturbing scene. In a much more orderly fashion, the Republican Party nominated **Richard M. Nixon**, who had served eight years as Eisenhower's vice president and had lost narrowly to John Kennedy in 1960. Nixon had supported the decisions of Eisenhower, Kennedy, and Johnson to back South Vietnam and had an image as an ardent anticommunist. As a presidential candidate, he suggested that he had a plan to end the war. His speeches contained no explicit proposals, and listeners were left to interpret for themselves how he meant to extricate the United States. Still, the public was becoming so sour on the war that many were prepared to accept his assurances that he had a solution.

As election day approached, the voters had three choices. Humphrey was tainted by his association with Johnson and the upheaval in Chicago, and Nixon had a reputation for political opportunism dating back throughout his political career. George Wallace, governor of Alabama, had broken with the Johnson administration over civil right legislation and ran as a third party candidate. On the war issue, Wallace's running mate, retired general Curtis LeMay, had made reckless and frightening statements about destroying North Vietnam with air power. The contest between Nixon and Humphrey was very close. Shortly before the voting, Humphrey came out unequivocally in favor of an end to U.S. bombing as a step toward negotiations, and many wavering Democrats who had long despised Nixon decided to back their party's choice.

Nixon won the election with a scant margin in the popular vote of only 510,000 and only 43.6 percent of the total vote. Nixon's vague platform and narrow victory would seem to have provided little indication of popular will. Yet, in the end, all the candidates had assailed Johnson's conduct of the war. The voters had spoken their desire to be rid of the burden of the war, and the responsibility for finding that exit had been entrusted to Richard Nixon.

Chapter 10

THE AMERICAN WAR IN VIETNAM: DE-ESCALATION

Despite all the frustration and agony that the United States had experienced in Vietnam, Richard Nixon entered the White House confident that he could end the American war with the credibility of U.S. power intact. Working closely with **Henry Kissinger**, his principal foreign policy adviser, the president rejected the notion of a unilateral American withdrawal as an admission of failure that would burden U.S. relations with friends and foes alike. Instead, Nixon and Kissinger believed that the United States could coerce Hanoi into a settlement while simultaneously satisfying the American public's desire to cut U.S. losses in the war. Just as Eisenhower, Kennedy, and Johnson had discovered, Nixon soon found that the challenge of Vietnam was not so readily managed. It took four more years of fighting, destruction, negotiating, and ultimately compromise before a formal agreement ended the American war in Vietnam in 1973. Two years later, Hanoi's quest, begun in 1945, to bring an independent and united Vietnam under its control reached its goal when North Vietnam's troops entered Saigon. On April 29 and 30, 1975, only hours before arrival of the enemy forces, U.S. Marine Corps helicopters evacuated the last remaining Americans and a few South Vietnamese from the U.S. Embassy compound in Saigon. Three decades of American policy in Vietnam had failed.

VIETNAMIZATION AND MORE BOMBING

During its first year, the Nixon administration pursued a two-part approach to the war. After the divisiveness of 1968, Nixon saw the need to try to maintain unity on the home front to gain the time he needed to deal with Hanoi. For the other part, he tried to bring new pressures and threats to bear on North Vietnam to force a diplomatic settlement that would allow the United States to leave South Vietnam with the Saigon government in place.

In June 1969 Nixon announced that the United States was withdrawing 25,000 combat troops from Vietnam. Fewer U.S. soldiers in Vietnam meant fewer American casualties and less need for the draft, both of which he knew would be popular at home. The move demonstrated his serious intention to end American involvement in the war. The president also proclaimed what became known as the Nixon Doctrine, which indicated that the United States would continue to back allies with aid and advice but expected them to make more use of their own troops in their own defense. In Indochina this policy was called **Vietnamization**, as U.S. troops would be slowly withdrawn to be replaced by a larger and better equipped ARVN. Although two nationally coordinated **Moratorium** demonstrations protested the slow pace of U.S. disengagement from Vietnam, Nixon countered these criticisms with a speech in which he asserted that a "**silent majority**" of Americans favored his firm and gradual strategy. Whether or not such a majority existed, Nixon promoted the possibility of an honorable settlement to the war at limited additional costs for Americans (see document 31, appendix 1).

ALTHOUGH IT COULD LAVISHLY EQUIP THE SOUTH VIETNAMESE MILITARY, COULD THE UNITED STATES GIVE THE ARVN THE WILL TO FIGHT FOR THE SAIGON GOVERNMENT?

Vietnamization was not a new concept. Eisenhower and Kennedy had tried to help Saigon help itself until the prospect of political collapse in the South had forced Johnson to insert U.S. ground troops and begin sustained bombing. After Tet Johnson had denied Westmoreland's request for more soldiers and then replaced Westmoreland with General **Creighton Abrams**, who began to shift more operational responsibility to the ARVN and to place greater emphasis on pacification. Vietnamization had already been in effect for a year when Nixon proclaimed it as a new plan, and, speaking from his initial experience with it, Abrams cautioned against moving too quickly in that direction. South Vietnamese leaders also protested that the plan was a cynical White House move to ease political pressure in America with the greater expenditure of ARVN lives. The program proceeded, however, and the South Vietnamese armed forces grew to over one million in number and were equipped with huge quantities of modern weapons, aircraft, and vehicles.

The infusion of these resources produced some improvement in the ARVN's efforts, and some units performed well. There were signs of less Vietcong and NVA activity in a number of places, although this lull may have been attributable to decisions by commanders of the revolutionary forces to avoid fighting and wait for U.S. troop strength to decline further. Much doubt remained about the ability of the RVN to protect itself. Desertions and corruption were endemic in the South Vietnam army. Worst of all, the Thieu government had failed to capture popular support and continued to remain almost completely dependent on U.S. financial support.

Aware that Americans were impatient to get the war over and that the Saigon regime was, as always, a fragile house of cards, Nixon and Kissinger tried to pressure Hanoi to yield. In addition to heavy bombing of the Ho Chi Minh Trail begun under Johnson, Nixon now added Operation Menu, air warfare against so-called enemy sanctuaries in Cambodia. This bombing of South Vietnam's neutral neighbor was not revealed publicly in the United States to avoid an antiwar outcry, but it was meant to send a message to Hanoi that Nixon was prepared to use more force. Indeed, according to H. R. Haldeman, Nixon's White House chief of staff, the president wanted to couple such action with his reputation as a fervent anticommunist to convince Hanoi that he was a madman capable of doing anything, even resorting to nuclear weapons. Despite Nixon's threat to increase the level of destruction against the North itself, the DRV's leaders, including Ho Chi Minh shortly before his death in September 1969, refused to make any concessions to the United States and persisted in their demand that Washington give up support of Thieu.

CAMBODIA AND KENT STATE

In 1970 Nixon still faced the twin challenges of containing antiwar sentiment at home and convincing North Vietnam of his determination to sustain South Vietnam. He revealed plans for gradual removal of another 150,000 American troops from Vietnam. While this step was meant to keep domestic critics at bay, it posed serious problems for Vietnamization. Abrams argued that the ARVN was far from ready to undertake the major burden of defense of the South. In March a sudden change in the leadership of Cambodia, however, presented Nixon with the opportunity to make a big play that could alter the military balance in Vietnam. Pro-American general **Lon Nol** overthrew Cambodia's neutralist leader Prince **Norodom Sihanouk**, opening the way for American ground forces to attack North Vietnamese bases inside Cambodia with approval of the government in **Phnom Penh**.

DID NIXON EXPAND THE WAR
OR REVERSE THE COURSE OF THE WAR?

On April 30, 1970, in a nationally televised address, the president explained his decision to send U.S. and ARVN troops into the "Fishhook" area across Cambodia's border, some fifty miles north of Saigon. The administration labeled this action a temporary "incursion," and critics called it an **"invasion" of Cambodia**. The purpose, according to the president, was to repel North Vietnamese aggression against Cambodia, to protect Vietnamization by neutralizing enemy sanctuaries along the border, and to destroy Hanoi's **Central Office for South Vietnam** (COSVN) that was reportedly located in the Fishhook area. Nixon ended his belligerent address with a claim that this bold stroke was an act of defense of free nations against totalitarianism and anarchy.

Nixon's expansion of the U.S. combat role into Cambodia set off a firestorm of protest. North Vietnam's violations of Cambodian territory were nothing new. There were doubts in official circles about the location of COSVN, and, in fact, it was not found by the invading Americans. The president might have been able to withstand these criticisms, but the controversy sparked by the invasion exploded into widespread outrage on May 4 when Ohio National Guardsmen, ordered onto the campus of **Kent State University** to quell antiwar protests, fired on a group of students, killing four and wounding at least nine. Student and faculty strikes and boycotts at hundreds of universities followed. Some campuses shut down completely, including the entire University of California system on orders from Governor **Ronald Reagan**.

Nixon had entered office promising to end the war. To many citizens, however, his continued use of air power, his actions in Cambodia, and his tough defense of his decisions suggested that he was not reversing course despite the troop reductions he had made. Although never conceding that protests swayed his policies, Nixon did remove all U.S. troops from Cambodia by the end of June, and he increased secret efforts by Henry Kissinger to reach a negotiated settlement with the DRV.

NEGOTIATIONS AND THE PARIS PEACE ACCORDS

On three occasions before the invasion of Cambodia, Kissinger had met secretly in Paris with **Le Duc Tho**, member of the Politburo of the DRV. These talks produced no agreement, but in September 1970 Kissinger resumed direct talks with North Vietnamese representatives. As a politician, Nixon well understood the need to find an exit from Vietnam before the 1972 presidential election. Public opinion polls, media commentaries, and congressional restiveness were pressing on the administration to act. In June 1971 the leak to the press of the **Pentagon Papers**, a secret summary and compilation of twenty years of documents, revealed the superficiality and lack of candor in the Vietnam policy process and strengthened the case for ending the American war. Shortly before the Pentagon Papers appeared, Kissinger had secretly presented a proposal in Paris that for the first time offered to accept the continued presence of North Vietnamese troops in the South after an American withdrawal, if Hanoi would pledge no further infiltration. The DRV indicated some interest but first wanted a U.S. pledge to end support of Thieu. The two sides remained at odds over the political questions involving the Saigon government, but there had finally at least been some discussion of the military issues of troop withdrawals and release of American prisoners of war (see **POW/MIA Issue**).

Early in 1972 Nixon and Kissinger made two dramatic diplomatic moves. Nixon went to Beijing in February. It was the first summit meeting with the PRC since the establishment of the Chinese communist government in 1949. Nixon's handshake with Mao Zedong began a process of reducing Cold War tensions in Asia, but his China visit did not result in making the DRV any more flexible in its demands. Nixon also traveled to Moscow in May and made progress in nuclear arms talks with Soviet leader Leonid Brezhnev. Again, however, improvements in U.S.-USSR relations did not translate into changes in the Washington-Hanoi stalemate. The United States still had to deal directly with the DRV.

DID NIXON GAIN A SETTLEMENT WITH HANOI THROUGH INTIMIDATION OR COMPROMISE?

As 1972 began, both sides were still trying to use military means to get better terms. In March the NVA began a massive conventional assault, including tank warfare, on the northern and central provinces of South Vietnam, followed by Vietcong attacks near Saigon and in the Mekong Delta. The United States responded with force to this **Easter Offensive**. Despite the risk of damage to Soviet ships on the eve of the Moscow summit, Washington ordered a naval blockade of North Vietnam and the mining of the North's major port at Haiphong. In an air operation code named **Linebacker**, U.S. planes conducted the largest bombing attacks up to that time against targets in North Vietnam and South Vietnam.

The intensity of Nixon's military reaction surprised Hanoi. DRV strategists had been waiting to strike as U.S. combat force levels fell, and those had dropped to less than 100,000 in early 1972 with only about 6,000 being combat soldiers. The North Vietnamese were also counting on White House political calculations in preparation for the approaching presidential election to restrain the United States. Instead, the heavy U.S. bombing helped reverse initial NVA and NLF gains against the ARVN and inflicted severe damage on North Vietnam and its forces in the South. Also, Nixon's decisive action helped raise his approval rating in public opinion polls, although he knew that the prevailing public sentiment still favored a peace settlement.

In late summer during the secret Paris talks, Le Duc Tho indicated for the first time that the DRV would accept the Thieu government in a coalition following a cease-fire. In October Hanoi dropped the coalition demand and offered a settlement based upon a cease-fire, U.S. troop withdrawal, exchange of POWs, and continued political discussions including the RVN, the **Provisional Revolutionary Government** (PRG) representing the NLF, and some neutral Vietnamese parties. Nixon and Kissinger were prepared to accept these terms, but Thieu vigorously objected to the provisions that left NVA troops in the South. Nixon won reelection in November over antiwar Democrat George McGovern, but the peace settlement remained elusive. Hanoi refused to consider Thieu's demands for an NVA withdrawal, and negotiations broke off in mid-December.

From December 18 to 29, 1972, in an operation formally designated Linebacker II and dubbed the **Christmas Bombing** by journalists, U.S. aircraft dropped 20,000 tons of bombs on North Vietnam. It was the heaviest bombing attack of the war and has been a source of controversy ever since. The Nixon administration was exasperated with both Hanoi and Saigon, and the bombing can be seen as a message to both. Washington wanted the DRV to sign the October agreement and wanted the RVN to cease being obstructionist. To both sides Nixon was saying that the United States remained strong and willing to use forceful action even as it was showing a readiness to compromise. Air power advocates have claimed that bombardments of this size should have been employed earlier and more often against the North because Hanoi quickly resumed talks and signed a cease-fire after the attack. Doubters of the necessity for and effectiveness of bombing note that the DRV had been prepared to sign even before the bombing and that it was Thieu who was the problem.

On January 27, 1973, the United States, DRV, RVN, and PRG signed an agreement in Paris to end the hostilities. The provisions were virtually identical to the October terms. There was to be a cease-fire in place, which left North Vietnamese troops in the South. The few remaining U.S. troops were to leave, and U.S. POWs would be released. Nixon privately assured Thieu that U.S. military aid to the RVN would continue, but, with the signing of the **Paris Peace Accords**, the American war in Vietnam was over (see document 32, appendix 1).

DRV VICTORY IN 1975

DID NIXON OBTAIN PEACE WITH HONOR OR SIMPLY A POLITICALLY ACCEPTABLE EXIT?

The president asserted that the United States military was departing Vietnam with American honor intact because Thieu's government still remained in of-

fice. In later years, Nixon wrote that the United States actually won the war because the final settlement was entirely reasonable and workable, if the DRV had
observed it. He contended, for example, that North Vietnam infiltrated 35,000
more troops into the South during 1973. Conversely, DRV historians of the war
charge that the ARVN never observed the cease-fire and immediately began to
attack the NLF and PAVN units.

The Paris settlement did not end the fighting in Vietnam and primarily provided a means for U.S. forces to depart and for American POWs to be repatri-
ated. Without U.S. air and land forces in the war, the ARVN with its vast supply
of American equipment was left alone to contest the PAVN and PLAF, who had
demonstrated throughout the war an effective fighting ability. Moreover, the
Thieu government in Saigon, which owed its political life to U.S. support, had
to compete with the revolutionary legacy that Ho Chi Minh's successors had inherited from him and his original Vietminh movement. For the Vietnamese,
the war did not end in 1973 but only entered a new phase.

Nixon had promised Thieu continued U.S. military aid after January 1973,
but the president underestimated the extent of the American public's desire to
leave the war behind. In 1973 Congress passed, over Nixon's veto, a **War Powers
Resolution** that prohibited any president from making an extended combat deployment of U.S. troops without congressional approval. Between 1973 and
1974, Congress cut the amount of money budgeted for military aid to the RVN
from over $2 billion to about $1 billion and reduced it further, down to $700
million, in 1975. At first Hanoi was cautious about escalating the fighting for fear
that the United States might reenter the war. It soon became clear, however,
that there was no base of support in Congress for such action. Also, in 1973 and
1974, the **Watergate** scandal began to unfold in Washington over criminal activities connected to Nixon's 1972 presidential campaign. Fighting for his political
life and finally resigning in August 1974, Nixon was in no position to pressure
Congress on further help for South Vietnam.

In the spring of 1975 the war in Vietnam ended much more rapidly than anyone had expected, even PAVN strategists. In March NVA and NLF forces
quickly took over the key towns of Ban Me Thout, Pleiku, and Kontum in the
Central Highlands. When Thieu ordered an ARVN retreat, mass confusion
and panic resulted with soldiers and civilians choking the narrow roads trying to
escape the fighting. The PAVN then attacked Danang and Hue, began moving
down the coast, and advanced on Saigon. Congress turned down a last-minute
request from President **Gerald Ford** for $300 million in emergency aid to the
RVN. Blaming the United States for abandoning him, Thieu resigned. The Republic of Vietnam had simply collapsed. The U.S. ambassador in Saigon, **Graham Martin**, refused to evacuate the American embassy until the last possible
moment. As enemy forces entered the city, the remaining Americans and what

few South Vietnamese associates they could hastily take with them made a chaotic escape. It was an inglorious end to U.S. nation building in Vietnam. On April 30, 1975, the flag of the Democratic Republic of Vietnam flew over Saigon, which the victors renamed **Ho Chi Minh City** (see document 33, appendix 1).

Chapter 11

THE WAR THAT WILL NOT GO AWAY

The Vietnam War was one of the major wars of the twentieth century. It lasted for thirty years in Vietnam, and for Americans it spanned twenty-five years, from the establishment of the U.S. Military Assistance Advisory Group in Vietnam in 1950 to the evacuation of the U.S. embassy in Saigon in 1975. The estimate of Vietnamese deaths, military and civilian, is about two million, and millions more Vietnamese were wounded, missing, or rendered homeless. Villages, forests, and farms throughout the country were destroyed by high explosives, napalm, and defoliants (see **Defoliation**). More than 58,000 Americans died, and 300,000 more were wounded. Direct U.S. government expenditures were about $140 billion, which added to the national debt, contributed to double-digit inflation by the 1970s, and took away resources needed for social services in the United States. Although the fighting in Vietnam ended in 1975, the high costs and long duration of the war had an enduring impact on the people and nations of Southeast Asia, on American **veterans** of the war, and on American politics, society, and culture. As with any major historical event, there was also the question of what lessons could be derived from all of this violence and sacrifice. Because the United States lost the war, coming to terms with its legacies and drawing conclusions from it have been difficult and divisive for Americans, and some issues remain highly contested (see document 34, appendix 1).

THE POSTWAR WARS IN SOUTHEAST ASIA

The Vietnam War was an internal conflict between rival Vietnamese groups, but it was always part of the broader regional and international political upheavals that followed World War II. As the fighting was ending in Vietnam, it was also ending in the other former French protectorates of Laos and Cambodia. Following the Paris Peace Accords for Vietnam, a similar document was signed by the rival parties in Laos. The communist Pathet Lao dominated the coalition created by this agreement and also had close ties with the Vietnamese Communist Party. With Hanoi's victory in 1975, the Pathet Lao took direct control of the government in Vientiane and began a concerted effort to kill all the **Hmong** minority who had fought together with the CIA against the Laotian and Vietnamese communists. Many Hmong died, but about 100,000 managed to escape to the United States.

In Cambodia the communist-led **Khmer Rouge** seized control in Phnom Penh from Lon Nol's government on April 17, 1975, even before the DRV captured Saigon. The rise to power of the Khmer Rouge ushered in one of the most horrific chapters in the violent chronicles of Southeast Asia. U.S. bombing of Cambodia beginning in 1969, the Lon Nol coup in 1970, and U.S. and ARVN cross-border operations had destabilized the fragile political balance that Norodom Sihanouk had maintained in Cambodia. In this turmoil the small Khmer Rouge rebel movement attracted followers and ultimately overwhelmed the weak government forces. Unlike the Pathet Lao, the Khmer Rouge had always resisted domination by the Vietnamese communists. In power they were determined not only to defy Hanoi, but also set out on a radical and ruthless program to empty the cities, exterminate all bourgeois Cambodians, and turn the country into an agrarian communist state. In the process, the Khmer Rouge, under the leadership of **Pol Pot**, murdered 1.5 million people in their country. The death total was so staggering that it can only be labeled a genocide conducted by a government against its own people in the name of revolution.

Despite the Cambodian holocaust, whose full reality was not immediately apparent to the outside world, the Khmer Rouge had an ally in the People's Republic of China. The Chinese communists and the Cambodian rulers claimed a common ideological goal of building rural socialism, but they also shared a historical concern with Vietnamese expansion at their expense. Beijing ended most of its military aid to Vietnam in 1975. Between 1975 and 1978, from the perspective of the Politburo in Hanoi, the PRC and Democratic Kampuchea, as the new regime had renamed Cambodia, appeared to be encircling Vietnam.

In 1976 the government of Vietnam renamed its country the Socialist Republic of Vietnam (SRV). Although it had won the war, the Hanoi regime confronted a host of domestic obstacles and needed international assistance. Ravaged by the war, Vietnam faced an enormous task of building an economic infrastructure and had hundreds of thousands of citizens needing help: orphans, amputees, homeless refugees, drug addicts, and other war victims. Many of these were concentrated in cities in the South. Hanoi created economic collectives and attempted other socialist reforms, most of which met resistance in the former South Vietnam. The communist authorities placed former South Vietnamese political and military officers in "**reeducation camps**" and executed some of them. The government then began to place restrictions on small entrepreneurs, most of whom were ethnic Chinese. Many of those threatened began to flee Vietnam by sea and became known to the world as "**boat people**."

Ironically, the SRV initially looked toward its former foe, the United States, for help in reconstruction. President **Jimmy Carter** had indicated that Washington would consider normalization of relations with the SRV if Hanoi provided a full accounting of all American POWs. In critical need of funds, Vietnam's leaders insisted that the United States pay $3.25 billion in war reparations. While the Paris Peace Accords and some statements by Nixon had referred to helping Vietnam rebuild from the war, no American political leader could agree to outright demands from the former enemy. Carter also sought to improve relations with China, which was not eager to see the SRV gain strength. Consequently, the Carter administration produced no U.S.-Vietnam reconciliation. Late in 1978 the proud leaders of the SRV turned reluctantly to Moscow for help and signed a treaty of friendship with the Soviet Union. Soon afterward, Carter announced that Washington was normalizing relations with Beijing.

On December 25, 1978, Vietnam invaded Cambodia and soon broke the grip of the tyrannical Pol Pot regime. Hanoi installed its own Cambodian allies in power backed by a large Vietnamese occupation force. China launched military attacks against the northern provinces of Vietnam to punish the SRV for expansionism. Beijing ended the campaign after about a month, having failed to deter Hanoi. Although the SRV had ended the murderous rule of the Khmer Rouge, the United States and Vietnam's Southeast Asian neighbors continued to isolate Vietnam from much needed economic markets and investments. The United States did not restore normal relations with Vietnam until 1995 (see **Clinton, Bill**).

DID THE REPRESSION AND HOSTILITIES THAT EMERGED IN VIETNAM AND CAMBODIA AFTER 1975 SUGGEST THAT U.S. INTERVENTION IN SOUTHEAST ASIA HAD BEEN JUSTIFIED?

The Vietnamese reeducation camps, flight of the boat people, and the Cambodian holocaust seemed to confirm that the Indochina communists were the evil dictators that American leaders had insisted they were. Furthermore, Hanoi's moves to control Laos and Cambodia also cast Vietnam as an aggressor. Conversely, the SRV's efforts to seek restored relations with the United States and to maintain its independence from China and the Soviet Union demonstrated that it valued its independence over ideology. Also, many of its actions were more awkward and desperate than calculated and reflected the heavy burden of thirty years of warfare. The politics of Southeast Asia became extremely complex after the Vietnam War because the international and ideological circumstances there had always been much more multidimensional than the simple communist and anticommunist labels the Cold War had imposed upon the region.

AMERICAN VIETNAM VETERANS

WHY HAVE VIETNAM VETERANS BEEN PLAGUED BY SO MANY POSTWAR ADJUSTMENT PROBLEMS?

All wars leave physical and emotional scars on the soldiers who fight them, and hence one should not assume that the Vietnam War was any more traumatic than other conflicts. With that caution in mind, the fact remains that military veterans of the Vietnam War often experienced social alienation. Part of America's self-image was a boast that the nation had never lost a war. In this war, however, U.S. forces failed to achieve the government's stated objective of preserving an independent South Vietnam. The controversial nature of the war and the ultimate lack of success caused many Americans to want to avoid discussing it at all and to forget about it as quickly as possible. The American warriors had no victory parades, and, in fact, they returned to a country that seemed pointedly disinterested in them and what they had experienced. Even worse, some citizens blamed them alone for what was, in truth, a shared national debacle.

The majority of veterans did not return from the war with severe physical and psychological problems, but all had to reintegrate into a society that largely ignored veterans as a group. Many veterans would not or could not discuss their experiences even with family and friends. Some had difficulty holding jobs or maintaining personal relationships. There was a lot of bitterness in the men and women (primarily military nurses) who had been through a difficult ordeal and now felt rejected and unappreciated by other Americans.

The plight of some veterans was extreme. Some had been exposed to the chemical defoliant **Agent Orange** during the war and were suffering serious health problems, such as rashes and cancers and birth defects in their children. Although laboratory research indicated a link between these conditions and the chemical dioxin in Agent Orange, the Veterans Administration health system resisted recognizing these ailments as war-related disabilities. There was an out-of-court settlement of a class action law suit with the chemical manufacturers in 1984, but the issue had caused much resentment.

More pervasive than dioxin poisoning was a psychiatric condition that in the 1980s came to be labeled "**post-traumatic stress disorder**" (PTSD). Medicine had long recognized that combat produces psychological trauma. Known by various terms, such as "shell shock" or "battle fatigue," this mental illness was not well understood, and, as with Agent Orange, official response to the problem after the Vietnam War was not always sympathetic. The symptoms of PTSD are severe personality changes that include agonizing grief, tormenting guilt, isolation, suicidal longings, violent outbursts, severe depression, and a sense of meaninglessness. Psychiatrists now view these patterns as normal reaction to abnormal stress, but during the first decade after the war many people, including health professionals, mistakenly assumed that such inability to readjust from the fear, rage, and guilt of war was caused by a dysfunctional personality prior to the war experience. Although diagnosis and treatment finally changed, much suffering had occurred.

Because Vietnam veterans often felt isolated and misunderstood, some found support in other veterans and sought ways for veterans to help each other help themselves. One of the most prominent outcomes of this process was the creation of the Vietnam Veterans Memorial in Washington, D.C. It is often referred to as "The Wall" because its design is a sloping black granite wall constructed in the side of a small rise in the Mall in the center of the nation's capital. On it are carved the names of the 58,000 Americans who died or remain missing in Vietnam and Indochina. A group of veterans conceived of the memorial idea, raised the funds to build it, and implemented its design and construction. It became the most visited site in Washington and had a remarkably positive impact on helping the veterans, the families of the dead, and the public confront the painful legacies of the war. With its dedication in 1982, the Wall helped lift the national amnesia about the war, and a healthy discussion and examination of the conflict has ensued since the mid-1980s.

One of the biggest obstacles to postwar readjustment for veterans, the public, and the government was the POW/MIA issue, which took on an almost religious devotion impervious to compromise or reason. In comparison to other American wars or to the Vietnamese experience, the 2,300 Americans still missing in action after the release of U.S. POWs in 1973 was a small number, and many of them were pilots killed in fiery crashes leaving few human remains. As U.S. public opinion had turned against the war after 1968, however, the Nixon administration had seized upon North Vietnam's accountability for all American prisoners of war and missing in action as a way to bolster American unity. Nixon helped turn the National League of Families of POWs and MIAs, who naturally wanted news of their loved ones, into a visible national lobby. Every president after Nixon felt politically compelled to reaffirm the demand that Hanoi satisfy all U.S. requests for POW/MIA information as a prerequisite for the establishment of economic and diplomatic ties. This stance delayed normalization of relations, which was in effect a way to punish Vietnam for winning the war, and it prolonged official sanction of the forlorn hope that some

Americans remained alive as prisoners in Indochina years after the war. For more than twenty years, numerous congressional and presidential investigations turned up no credible evidence to support this hope.

FILMS, FICTION, AND POETRY

Important indications of what the Vietnam War meant to Americans are found in movies, literature, and popular music. During the war, songs played a large role in cultural expression, especially in antiwar anthems, such as Country Joe McDonald's "I-Feel-Like-I'm-Fixin'-to-Die Rag" and John Lennon's "Give Peace a Chance." There were also prowar songs, for example, Merle Haggard's "Okie from Muskogee," and the popularity of the various types of songs with different groups underscored some of the domestic divisions that the war created. As the level of American involvement in the war increased, stories, poems, and novels about the war began to appear, many written by soldiers or journalists who experienced the conflict first hand, and the volume of these works grew after the war. Hollywood largely avoided the subject of Vietnam during the war, although a notable exception was John Wayne's 1968 prowar film, *The Green Berets*, based upon a 1965 novel by Robin Moore.

Movie portrayals of the war went through different phases and images. At first there were a series of films in the 1970s that portrayed psychologically damaged veterans as dangerous, often psychotic characters. This genre evolved into films, such as the Billy Jack movies, that made the veteran an action hero. In the late 1970s some serious movies, such as *The Deer Hunter, Coming Home*, and *Apocalypse Now*, began to explore what the war had done to the men who fought it. In the 1980s and concurrent with the Ronald Reagan conservative revolution in politics and its desire to restore American self-esteem, movies, such as the series with the character "Rambo," suggested that the military could have won the war if civilian leaders had allowed it. These films also exploited the POW/MIA obsession. Plots frequently dealt with rescue of captured Americans. Finally, in the late 1980s and early 1990s, a series of so-called reality films, such as *Platoon* and *Full Metal Jacket*, sought to combine an antiwar message with a grim depiction of the soldiers' horrific experiences. In the 1994 film *Forrest Gump*, the war was not portrayed in detail but was central to the story of the title character.

HOW CAN POETRY AND FICTION HELP CONFRONT THE HORROR, AMBIGUITY, AND MYSTERY OF THE U.S. EXPERIENCE IN VIETNAM?

Some of the most probing cultural examinations of the war have come from poems and novels written by Vietnam veterans. Many of these writers reflect on their own disillusionment with the war and how the war changed them and their country. They feel obligated to describe how old heroic myths and conventions about America died in the brutality and pointlessness of the United States application of its destructive might in a place largely unknown to most Americans and of only peripheral value to U.S. security interests. They wrote from a sense of loss and pain. In poetry and fiction, they find that they can convey the emotional stress and moral agony more clearly than in the sparse rhetoric of factual reporting. As the writer Tim O'Brien has noted, the novelist uses invention not to describe what happened in the world but what happened in the heart, the spirit, and the gut.

POSTMORTEMS

Since the end of the Vietnam War, there have been numerous autopsies to discover what caused the death of the notion of American invincibility. How could a great nation have gone so wrong? Should the United States have been involved at all in Vietnam? Was Washington trying to impose an American solution on what was always a Vietnamese struggle to discover and define its own independent identity? Was American security endangered by the instability and conflict in Indochina? If the survival of an independent South Vietnam was important to U.S. interests, did American leaders pursue the wrong kind of war to gain that objective? These are not idle questions. The United States failed to achieve its goals in Vietnam, but America was not a defeated nation. Its power and interests were still global in scope, and it remained certain that U.S. leaders would again face the decision of when, where, and how to intervene militarily in other conflicts in the world.

WERE THERE POLICY LESSONS FOR THE UNITED STATES IN THE VIETNAM WAR?

Policymakers looked to the Vietnam experience for guidance. Former president Richard Nixon complained that U.S. international behavior suffered from a "**Vietnam syndrome**," that is, a neo-isolationist desire to avoid all foreign involvement. When Ronald Reagan became president, he sought to reinstill a sense of confidence in U.S. foreign policy. He characterized the Vietnam War as a noble effort to try to defeat forces of tyranny, and he contended that lack of success in Indochina should not prevent America from seeking to help others elsewhere (see document 35, appendix 1). This perception of the Vietnam War led Reagan to approve American aid to the Contras, a force fighting an armed insurrection against the leftist Sandinista government in Nicaragua. A majority of members of Congress voted for legislation prohibiting the aid, however, because they drew a different lesson from Vietnam, namely, to avoid U.S. intervention in local political struggles. These policy differences eventually led to some members of the White House staff receiving criminal convictions for arranging aid to the Contras in violation of federal law.

In August 1990, when Iraq's army invaded and occupied neighboring Kuwait, President George H. W. Bush responded with a build-up of U.S. forces in the region that reached 540,000 military personnel. Unlike the conflicts in Vietnam and Nicaragua, Iraq's aggression was a clear violation of an international boundary in an oil-rich area of strategic importance. As a result, Bush was able to align a broad coalition of nations to support the U.S. use of force against Iraq. When the U.S. attack began in January 1991, Bush declared that the Persian Gulf War was not a repeat of the Vietnam War because the United States was prepared to strike decisively with overwhelming force rather than with the incremental pressure put on North Vietnam (see document 36, appendix 1). Despite the president's bold assertions, the shadow of Vietnam hung over his choices. Well aware that mounting U.S. casualties in Vietnam had eroded public support for that war, he ended the invasion of Iraq after only one hundred hours without a ground assault on Baghdad and before any significant number of U.S. losses could occur.

Presidential decisions, such as those on Nicaragua and Iraq, revealed that the Vietnam War had ended the Cold War consensus that had helped place U.S. troops in Vietnam. Before the Vietnam War, Congress and the American voters were usually willing to accept the judgment of the executive branch on foreign policy goals and strategies. After the Vietnam experience, there was no visible agreement among American leaders and the American public on what constituted interests or threats for which Americans were prepared to risk blood and treasure. When the Cold War itself ended with the collapse of the Soviet Union in 1991, the confusion over the meaning of Vietnam only increased. On a superficial level it appeared that the United States had suffered a major defeat in Vietnam, a Cold War battleground, but had won the Cold War itself. The idea of winning the Cold War was, of course, an extreme oversimplification of a multifaceted historic change that had more to do with the will of the people in Eastern Europe and with structural weaknesses in Russia than with specific American actions. The absence of a new American policy consensus on the use of U.S. military force was seen in the hesitancy of the Bush and Clinton administrations on how to respond to bloody civil conflicts in the Balkans in the 1990s.

Despite continuing disagreements over Vietnam, some lessons have emerged from the enormous outpouring of works on the war. Arguments about what might have been, for example, if Westmoreland had put more effort into pacification than attrition strategy, are difficult to prove because the evidence available addresses what was actually done. From the historical record it can be seen that global containment strategy, while not irrelevant to Southeast Asia, was misapplied. The local and historical conditions in Indochina were not the same as those in Greece, divided Germany, and other areas of Europe for which containment was initially conceived. The decision to apply U.S. power to Vietnam had more to do with maintaining U.S. credibility with America's friends and foes around the world and with the U.S. voters than it did with the political options in Saigon and Hanoi. It is also clear that, despite the vastness of American power and the strength of American principles, there were limits to that power and those ideals in the physical and cultural environment of Vietnam. Just as the terrain was not always suited for high-technology warfare, so too the people were not comprehensible to American soldiers and strategists. American wealth, weapons, and good will did not translate into political viability for the Saigon government. American students need to remind themselves continually that the Vietnamese—North and South, military and civilian—were principal actors in the war that engulfed their country. As questions about the causes, course, and consequences of the Vietnam War are investigated, these cannot be answered from an American perspective alone. In partial acknowledgement of that reality, President Bill Clinton formally extended U.S. diplomatic recognition to the Socialist Republic of Vietnam on July 11, 1995, fifty years after Ho Chi Minh had quoted the American Declaration of Independence as part of his declaration of Vietnamese independence (see document 37, appendix 1).

The asking and answering of questions about the war evoke competing visions of America. Writers and readers bring their own values and experiences to the study of historical subjects. Some come with a heroic image of the United States and others with a selfish image. Combined with these inherent biases, the elusive nature of historical facts also obscures truth. The details of history are always complex and often ambiguous or difficult to retrieve accurately. Those who seek to polemicize the Vietnam War and use its conflicted facts to argue their own narrow case will always be able to do so. Others who seek to exploit the controversy, horror, and valor of the war for their personal or partisan advantage will continue to do that. For those who truly seek an explanation for the origins and outcomes of the American war in Vietnam, however, there must be an appreciation for all of its complex reality.

PART II

The Vietnam War from A to Z

Abrams, Creighton (1914–1974)—General Creighton Abrams was commander of the U.S. Military Assistance Command, Vietnam (MACV), from 1968 to 1972 and U.S. Army chief of staff from 1972 to 1974. A celebrated tank commander in World War II, Abrams held many important positions and was the U.S. Army vice chief of staff from 1964 to 1967, the period of the huge American troop increase in Vietnam. In May 1967 he became deputy commander of MACV, and General William Westmoreland, the head of MACV, gave Abrams responsibility for improving the Army of the Republic of Vietnam (ARVN). The surprising effectiveness of the ARVN during the Tet Offensive in early 1968 was a credit to Abrams's efforts. In July 1968 he formally succeeded Westmoreland as MACV commander. He abandoned the attrition strategy of his predecessor and instead emphasized population security, pacification, and small-unit patrols. He continued to work on making the ARVN a more effective force, a process termed "Vietnamization" by the Nixon administration. Vietnamization also included a steady reduction in the number of U.S. troops in Vietnam, and Abrams thus led an ever smaller force. As chief of staff, beginning in June 1972, he began the process of rebuilding the pride and effectiveness of the army, which was beset by many problems of mission, organization, and training as a result of the war. He also started the transition to an all-volunteer force. He had command positions in Vietnam and at the Pentagon during some of the most difficult times for the

U.S. Army, and his fellow officers held him in the highest regard at the time of his death from cancer in 1974.

Acheson, Dean (1893–1971)—As secretary of state from 1949 to 1953, Dean Acheson was one of the principal creators of the containment policy. Although he disapproved of French colonialism, he considered Ho Chi Minh and the Vietminh to be agents of Chinese and Soviet communism. Thus he recommended that the United States support the French war against the Vietminh to prevent the spread of communism in Southeast Asia. He also viewed American aid to France in Indochina as helping cement U.S.-French cooperation in Europe against the Soviet Union. From 1965 to 1968 Acheson was also one of the Wise Men, an unofficial group of former officials who advised President Lyndon Johnson on Vietnam policy. Initially, he agreed with Johnson's use of American military power to defend South Vietnam, but early in 1968 Acheson joined the majority of the Wise Men who advised the president to begin de-escalation.

African Americans—African Americans appeared to pay a higher price in terms of combat deaths in Vietnam during the early phases of American escalation compared to other groups. In 1965 and 1966 black soldiers accounted for more than 20 percent of combat casualties at a time when 13.5 percent of men in America between ages 19 and 25 were African Americans. There were reports that 40 to 50 percent of the personnel in some ground combat units were black. The U.S. Army and Marine Corps responded to the inherent inequities in these numbers, and by 1967 the African American casualty rate had dropped to 13.4 percent and was below 10 percent thereafter.

In wars before Vietnam, most African Americans had been denied full participation, especially as combat soldiers, and black leaders had often demanded that members of the African American community be afforded the respect that military service conveys upon citizens. Harry Truman had ordered integration of the armed forces in 1948, but the process was slow and blacks participated in the Korean War largely in segregated support units, such as ambulance companies. The Vietnam War was America's first war in which African Americans were truly integrated into combat units. In fact, given the opportunity to enlist in the specialty of their choice, many young black men chose elite army units or the Marine Corps for the lure of adventure and the appeal of extra incentive pay for hazardous training and duty. Thus, when Johnson ordered the first combat brigades to Vietnam in 1965, many of them had a high percentage of African American personnel. There was also institutional racism in the draft because middle-class white students in college could get deferments while blue-collar black workers could not. Also, local draft boards were comprised of almost entirely white men, even in counties with large African American populations, which introduced further bias into the system. Eventually, reforms in the draft and the sheer number of men being drafted enabled military manpower planners to construct combat units with a racial make-up more reflective of American society.

Racial issues in American society also affected the military in other ways. The civil rights movement, urban violence in American cities, and the assassination of Martin Luther King Jr. in 1968 revealed racial upheaval to which the military was not immune. For example, African American prisoners in the Long Binh military stockade in South Vietnam rioted with resulting death and injury in 1968. Because most African Americans at the time did not have a high level of formal education, there were few black officers in Vietnam. Nevertheless, some were highly accomplished, and a few achieved the rank of general. Many African American soldiers were decorated for valor, including being awarded the prestigious Medal of Honor.

Agent Orange—see **Defoliation**.

Aircraft—The United States had available and employed a wide variety of aircraft in the Vietnam War. The fixed-wing aircraft ranged in size from the huge Boeing B-52 Stratofortress, a strategic bomber with eight jet engines and a payload capacity of up to 108 500-pound bombs, to the tiny Cessna O-1 Bird Dog, an unarmed single-engine plane used for forward air control to spot bombing and artillery targets. Out of bases in Thailand, the U.S. Air Force flew Republic F-105 Thunderchief and McDonnell Douglas F-4 Phantom fighter bombers. The U.S. Navy launched Phantoms and Douglas A-5 Skyhawk fighter bombers from aircraft carriers in the Gulf of Tonkin. Over North Vietnam these planes often encountered Mikoyan-Gurevich MiG-19 Farmer and MiG-21 Fishbed fighter interceptors flown by the DRV Air Force. The workhorse of the RVN Air Force was the Douglas A-1 Skyraider, a rugged Korean War–era, single-engine bomber used for close tactical air support. An aircraft model that dated back to the 1930s, the Douglas C-47 Skytrain, or "Gooneybird," was adapted for various uses in Vietnam, including as a gunship known as "Puff the Magic Dragon" that was equipped with rapid-fire 7.62 mm miniguns. For transporting men and supplies, the Douglas C-124 Globemaster II and the Lockheed C-130 Hercules carried much of the load. Eventually, jet-powered cargo planes, the Lockheed C-141 Starlifter and Lockheed C-5 Galaxy, were added.

Helicopters were some of the most widely used aircraft in the war. The U.S. ground war came to be designed around the capabilities of these versatile machines for troop and supply transportation, medical evacuation, and tactical air support. Serving all of these purposes and the helicopter most associated with the Vietnam War was the Bell UH-1H Iroquois, known as the "Huey." A larger and also widely used helicopter was the Boeing-Vertol CH-47 Chinook, which was capable of lifting heavy loads. The most effective and terrorizing fire support aircraft was the Bell AH-1 Huey Cobra. It came into use in 1967 and could be armed with a combination of miniguns, grenade launchers, cannons, and rocket launchers.

Air War—The air war was one of the most controversial features of the American war in Vietnam. The United States dropped more than twice as much bombing tonnage in Vietnam, Laos, and Cambodia during the Vietnam War than the total bombing tonnage dropped during World War II. About half of that tonnage was dropped on America's ally South Vietnam, making it the most bombed nation in history. And, after all of that destructive force, the United States failed to achieve its objective of preserving the survival of an independent South Vietnam. Some historians have argued that bombing was never an appropriate method for winning political support for the Saigon government and, in fact, turned people away from the regime. Some critics charged, during and since the war, that the use of air power was cruel and immoral. Conversely, other analysts have claimed that bombing could have achieved success for American aims if it had been greater in amount and better targeted, especially toward North Vietnam. Regardless of the merits of each of these views, it is evident that winning and losing in war is determined by a complex combination of factors and that destructive power alone does not assure victory.

Within South Vietnam, a wide variety of aircraft, from propeller-driven fighters to huge B-52 bombers flying what were called "Arc Light missions," provided tactical air support for ground operations or attacked enemy troop concentrations and supply areas. In addition to this bombing, both fixed-wing and helicopter gunships delivered massive devastation from the air. Another aspect of the air war in the South was defoliation with explosives or chemicals to expose enemy positions in forest and jungle areas. In Operation Ranch Hand the U.S. Air Force sprayed the chemical defoliant Agent Orange, which was later blamed for serious health problems in people exposed to it.

Several air operations targeted North Vietnam. From March 1965 to October 1968, Operation Rolling Thunder was a sustained bombardment of selected targets in North Vietnam. These bombing sorties were intended to weaken the will of the DRV to continue the war and to encourage the RVN to persevere in the conflict. The civilian population of Hanoi was not marked for attack. The principal targets were military facilities, roads, bridges, railroads, and power plants. Most analysts consider Rolling Thunder to have been ineffective, although some have claimed that this long campaign could have achieved its goals if it had been allowed to continue even longer.

Linebacker I and Linebacker II were heavy air attacks ordered against North Vietnam by the Nixon administration in 1972. Linebacker I was launched in May in response to North Vietnam's so-called Easter Offensive. This largely conventional assault by NVA troops against the South provided clear targets, such as supply lines and troop formations, that exposed themselves to air power. Consequently, this U.S. air operation was largely successful in halting the offensive. Linebacker II took place from December 18 to 29 and was consequently dubbed the Christmas Bombing by journalists. Air power advocates have credited this heavy attack, which included B-52 raids not far from the center of Hanoi itself, for bringing the DRV back to the conference table for the signing of the Paris Peace Agreement in January 1973. They also claim that more bombing of the North, if used earlier in the war, could have forced the DRV to accept a settlement years earlier. Skeptics of air power and of Nixon's motives for the bombing have noted that Hanoi had agreed to peace terms in October and that it was the Saigon, not Hanoi, regime that remained as the obstacle to settlement in December. These doubters have also observed that Washington had scaled back its objectives by 1972, compared to the goals at the outset of the war, and it was the American diplomatic concessions, not air power, that opened the way for settlement.

Throughout the war a number of aerial interdiction operations, such as Barrel Roll and Commando Hunt, were carried out along the Ho Chi Minh Trail. These campaigns eventually totaled about 3 million tons of high explosives dropped on the North's infiltration routes, but the resilient enemy managed to keep its troops and supplies moving into South Vietnam. The Nixon administration also conducted a secret bombing operation in Cambodia, code named Menu, which lasted from March 1969 to August 1973. Like the other campaigns of the air war, Menu sparked disagreement. Some observers have said that it denied the Vietcong access to sanctuaries in Cambodia and thus protected the gradual transfer of ground operations, from U.S. forces to Saigon's troops, in South Vietnam. Critics have claimed that the bombing placed intolerable strains on the fragile political structure of Cambodia and eased the way for the ruthless Khmer Rouge to take power.

American Friends of Vietnam (AFV)—A nonpartisan advocacy group, the American Friends of Vietnam formed in 1955 as a show of support for U.S. policy in Vietnam. Its original membership was a diverse group of prominent citizens, including liberals such as Senators John Kennedy and Hubert Humphrey and conservatives such as Senator William Knowland and publisher Henry Luce. Some of its organizers had close ties to Ngo Dinh Diem, and in the 1960s critics of the war characterized it as a "Vietnam Lobby" that had pushed the United States to intervene in Southeast Asia. Actually, U.S. leaders never required lobbying to support the Saigon government, and the AFV only represented a commonly held opinion that defense of South Vietnam was important to the United States. The AFV existed into the 1970s but had little significance after the death of Diem.

Annam — Under colonial rule, Annam was the name the French gave their protectorate in central Vietnam, from the southern edge of the Red River Delta southward through the Central Highlands. The Vietnamese historically called this region Trung Bo. The French often referred to all Vietnamese as Annamites, a term which patriotic Vietnamese abhorred.

Antiwar Movement — Historians disagree over the degree to which the antiwar movement affected U.S. government policies toward Vietnam, but public demonstrations and various forms of resistance to the war by individuals revealed that the war produced sharp divisions within American society. Long before the Vietnam War, there was a small peace movement in the United States, including Quakers and other religious groups and pacifist organizations, such as the Fellowship for Reconciliation and the War Resisters League. With the Cold War, the National Committee for a Sane Nuclear Policy (SANE) appeared, and its members, including the prominent pediatrician Dr. Benjamin Spock, protested the nuclear arms race. Also predating U.S. escalation in Vietnam was the Students for a Democratic Society (SDS). It formed in 1960 at the University of Michigan and spread to other campuses, and, in 1962, the SDS issued its Port Huron Statement, a manifesto of its self-labeled New Left beliefs. Basically, the SDS opposed the Establishment — that is, big business, big government, and big universities — which the students believed depersonalized and oppressed workers, minorities, students, and others. Similarly inspired was the Free Speech Movement begun at the University of California at Berkeley in 1964. Some of the earliest voices against American involvement in Vietnam came from these pacifist and New Left groups.

When U.S. bombing of North Vietnam and combat troop deployments to South Vietnam began in 1965, the anti–Vietnam War movement began. From then until American involvement in the war ended in 1973, the movement was an ad hoc, largely grassroots coalition of people from various backgrounds with diverse motivations and agendas. There was no centralized leadership, and, in fact, lack of coordination and agreement hampered antiwar efforts throughout the war. Some of the first signs of activism in the spring of 1965 were SDS protests at the Oakland, California, disembarkation point for troops going to Vietnam and a "teach-in" at the University of Michigan that was later replicated at other colleges. A teach-in was usually an all-night session in which faculty and students would gather to discuss the war in order to raise antiwar awareness. On April 17, 1965, a SDS rally against the war in Washington, D.C., attracted around 20,000 people. Also in 1965 an ecumenical group, Clergy and Laity Concerned About Vietnam (CALCAV), formed.

As the magnitude of U.S. intervention in Vietnam increased over the next two years, the level of antiwar activity also grew. There were rallies, marches, symposia, petitions, publications, draft protests (including burning of draft cards that young men were required to carry), and other expressions of dissent. In 1966 Senator J. William Fulbright became disillusioned with Johnson's policies and held televised hearings that challenged the president's policies. In 1967 there were several key protest developments. Martin Luther King Jr., already a Nobel Peace Prize winner for his civil rights leadership, publicly came out in opposition to the war on moral grounds and in the belief that the war was a drain on resources needed for domestic social improvements. A small group calling itself Vietnam Veterans Against the War (VVAW) appeared and, although never large, grew in subsequent years. Antiwar demonstrations became sizeable events, with 130,000 demonstrators in New York City and 70,000 in San Francisco in April. In October 100,000 people assembled in Washington, D.C., and about half of that group converged on the Pentagon.

In 1968 the antiwar movement took on some new dimensions. It entered the mainstream political process with the antiwar presidential candidacies of Eugene McCarthy and Robert Kennedy. After the Tet Offensive, a number of journalists, politicians, and other citizens who had given support to Johnson began to call for an end to American involvement in Vietnam. Among youthful or radical activists, the intensity of the protests escalated. Students occupied the administration building at Columbia University in April, protestors broke into draft offices and destroyed files, and, finally, the Democratic National Convention in Chicago became the scene of violent clashes between police and demonstrators.

During the Nixon administration, the antiwar movement played a mixed role in the eventual end of American military intervention. By gradually withdrawing U.S. combat troops and thus reducing American casualties, Nixon took some of the urgency out of the protests. He was also able to rally some popular backing for his Vietnam policies through skillful patriotic appeals. In October and November 1969 a record number of Americans participated in what were called "moratoriums" to voice opposition to the war. Nixon responded with a nationally televised speech in which he claimed a "silent majority" backed his "peace with honor" approach. He also focused national attention on making North Vietnam accountable for information about American prisoners of war and those who were missing in action (POWs and MIAs), which led many citizens to stand in support of the White House. Still, Nixon unleashed a firestorm of protest when he sent troops into Cambodia in April 1970. During a demonstration against this action, Ohio national guardsmen killed four students at Kent State University, which touched off major student strikes at hundreds of colleges. Indeed, the deaths of the these students and two others at a demonstration at Jackson State University, in Mississippi, revealed just how badly the war was straining American society. Expressions of antiwar sentiment continued. The public reacted to reports of American troops involved in atrocities like the My Lai massacre. The VVAW staged dramatic demonstrations. The theft and publication of the Pentagon Papers exposed poor decision making behind U.S. military intervention. Members of Congress also joined in the process with such symbolic actions as repealing the Gulf of Tonkin Resolution in 1970.

U.S. military intervention in Vietnam persisted for years despite significant levels of protest, and many citizens continued to support their government's policies contrary to the urging of the war's critics. It can be argued that the war did not end until leaders in Washington and Hanoi made their own military and political calculations of when and how to end the fighting. The antiwar movement brought pressure for an end to the war but cannot be singled out as having brought peace. On the other hand, the movement prepared the American public for withdrawal from Vietnam, and Americans welcomed the end of the war when it came, even if the United States had not achieved its originally stated aims.

Ap Bac—Located 40 miles (65 kilometers) southwest of Saigon, the village of Ap Bac was the site of a significant battle on January 2, 1963. An ARVN division that outnumbered its Vietcong opponents by ten to one and that was well equipped and advised by Americans failed miserably in an assault on its entrenched enemy. The ARVN officers' confusion and their troops' lack of will to fight revealed how far South Vietnam still had to go to be able to defend itself. Conversely, the Vietcong fighters, who downed five U.S. helicopters that day and inflicted heavy casualties on the ARVN, got a tremendous boost of confidence. Having suffered only minimal casualties themselves, they slipped away into the darkness after the battle. General Paul Harkins, the U.S. commander in Vietnam, declared Ap Bac a victory because the Vietcong left the area, but American journalists knew it had been a debacle and reported it as such. The battle of Ap Bac was a precursor of the difficulties the United States would face in Vietnam and of the credibility gap that developed between official U.S. reports and accounts carried in the press.

Armored Personnel Carriers (APCs)—Lightly armored, tracked vehicles, M-113 armored personnel carriers were widely used by U.S. and ARVN infantry. Their purpose was transportation over poor roads and flooded patty fields and not for use as a fighting platform. APCs had room for eleven men plus the driver and a gunner for the .50 caliber machine gun mounted on top. Enemy forces eventually learned how to use mines and rocket-propelled grenades against the APCs, but the vehicle remained useful for the mobility it provided. Also armored cavalry units modified the M-113 APC into the Armored Cavalry Assault Vehicle (ACAV) by adding more armor around the .50 caliber machine gun and adding two 7.62 mm M-60 machine guns.

Army of the Republic of Vietnam (ARVN)—With the assistance of U.S. advisers and monetary support, the Army of the Republic of Vietnam began in

1955 with a force of 150,000 and grew by 1975 to about one million troops, at least on paper. When at peak strength, the ARVN was divided into three levels: the regular army of thirteen combat divisions and various elite units, the Regional Forces (RF) assigned to four regional commanders, and less-trained Popular Forces (PF) that carried out security duties. U.S. soldiers called troops of these second two levels "Ruff-Puffs." As organized and trained by the Americans, the ARVN had considerable firepower but lacked effective command and control. Throughout its existence, the ARVN was plagued by low morale, desertion, and the corruption of its officer corps, which was more often chosen and promoted based on political loyalty to the president of the RVN than on military performance. Although U.S. forces conducted most of the large-unit combat operations, the ARVN did extensive fighting and had lost over 200,000 killed in action by the time of the Paris Peace Accords. It also held on for two years alone without the Americans before it fell before the North Vietnamese offensive in 1975. Some individual ARVN units were effective fighters, and on occasion the ARVN performed well, but overall it was not able to counter the more highly motivated Vietcong and PAVN during the course of the war.

Arnett, Peter (1934–)—A New Zealander, Peter Arnett reported on the Vietnam War for the Associated Press from 1962 to 1975. Not only did his long stay make him the senior war correspondent in Vietnam, but his colleagues also considered him among the most courageous and forthright of all reporters. His candid reporting gained him the enmity of U.S. and South Vietnamese officials, but he persisted nonetheless. He received a Pulitzer Prize for his work in 1966. He joined the Cable News Network in 1981, and in 1991 Arnett broadcast live reports from Baghdad as U.S. planes bombed the city during the Persian Gulf War.

Artillery—The U.S. Army and Marine Corps made extensive use of artillery in the war, firing millions of rounds. The U.S. Army deployed 68 artillery battalions to Vietnam, and the Marine Corps had 10 battalions. U.S. allies New Zealand, Australia, the Philippines, Thailand, and South Korea also supplied artillery units. The ARVN had 64 battalions by 1972. PAVN artillery was mostly arrayed along the DMZ, but the North Vietnamese used artillery in the South during their 1972 and 1975 offensives. Most northern artillery was from China and the Soviet Union, but some of it was U.S.-made weapons captured from the ARVN or even earlier from the French. The Vietcong forces did not usually have conventional artillery but used heavy infantry weapons, such as rocket launchers and mortars. The M101A1 towed 105-mm howitzer was the most commonly used artillery piece in the American arsenal. It could fire a 33-pound projectile a distance of eleven kilometers. Also available was a newer 105-mm towed howitzer (the M102), a self-propelled 105-mm howitzer, towed and self-propelled 155-mm howitzers, a self-propelled 175-mm gun, and an 8-inch self-propelled howitzer.

Much of the ordinance was high explosive projectiles, but there were also anti-tank, smoke, white phosphorus, illumination, and antipersonnel Beehive rounds and a so-called improved conventional munition (ICM) round that contained a cluster of explosive charges in one projectile.

Atrocities—Atrocities, such as the killing of noncombatant civilians or the torture of prisoners, occur in all wars but became a particular issue in the Vietnam War. It has been argued that the contending forces in this conflict made violence against civilians an intentional tactic or at least were indifferent to incidental destruction of noncombatants and their property. As guerrilla forces often do, the Vietcong utilized terrorism to intimidate people into cooperating with them and not cooperating with Saigon. Vietcong guerrillas assassinated or kidnapped thousands of local officials, priests, teachers, and others they classified as counterrevolutionaries. The RVN police arrested, imprisoned, and often executed alleged Vietcong suspects whose only offense might have been criticism of the regime. The PAVN and ARVN both abused prisoners in their custody. Most U.S. commanders were aware of the laws of ground warfare that had been established by various international agreements and maintained discipline of their troops, but atrocities were still committed by some American soldiers and officers. The military justice system convicted 278 soldiers and marines of murder, rape, and other violent crimes, but many incidents went unpunished or even unreported. On the level of U.S. policy, the heavy bombing in South Vietnam with high explosives and napalm by American forces to support ground operations in and around villages and the widespread use of artillery for the same purpose generated many accidental civilian casualties. In some cases, such as free-fire zones, the targeting of civilians as Vietcong supporters was intentional. Estimates of civilian death totals are difficult to make, but in the South it may have been 300,000 and in the North 65,000 from U.S. bombing.

Three specific atrocities were on a relatively large scale. The largest single American incident was the My Lai massacre on March 16, 1968. On that day a U.S. Army infantry company killed 504 unresisting women, children, and old men in the subhamlets of My Lai 4 and My Khe 4 of Son My village, Quang Ngai Province. The causes were complex and included psychological stress on the men, poor unit leadership, bad intelligence, and an overall American strategy that put more emphasis on killing—getting a high body count—than on protecting the people. The officers in charge covered up the incident for a year until Ron Ridenhour, a conscious-stricken soldier who had not participated but knew of the murders, managed to prompt an investigation. Only one officer, Lieutenant William L. Calley, received judicial punishment for the killings, and it was relatively light. On the Vietcong side, the Hue massacre was a major atrocity that occurred during the Tet Offensive in 1968. The NVA and Vietcong held the city of Hue for more than three weeks, and early in that occupation, Vietcong cadre searched house to house for civil servants, religious leaders, teachers, and others connected with the Americans. These people were arrested, executed, and buried in mass graves discovered on February 26 when U.S. and ARVN troops regained control of the city. There were 2,810 bodies found, and about 3,000 more residents were missing. Finally, an atrocity in a class by itself was the Khmer Rouge genocide of more than 1.5 million Cambodians from 1975 to 1978, as the revolutionary regime aimed to cleanse the country of all bourgeois and Western intellectual influence.

Attrition Strategy—Developed by General William Westmoreland, the attrition strategy aimed at destroying enemy forces at a higher rate than the PAVN and Vietcong could replace them. Since Washington wanted to avoid an invasion of North Vietnam, this strategy seemed a logical way to weaken the enemy's will and ability to continue the war. It had the appeal of aggressively carrying the war to the PAVN and Vietcong in the rural areas and not simply guarding urban enclaves. It also enabled U.S. commanders to use their helicopter mobility and massive firepower in "search and destroy" missions. The strategy had numerous weaknesses, however. It underestimated Hanoi's willingness to endure heavy losses and overestimated the patience of the American people with a long war in which U.S. casualties also mounted. It was also a largely conventional strategy in what was an unconventional political war, and the destructiveness of U.S. military sweeps and bombardment hurt pacification efforts to win the support of the people for the Saigon government. Finally, the strategy carried a moral cost because it measured progress in terms of killing rather than in territory or political allegiance.

The statistical indicator of success in the attrition strategy was body count, a tabulation of how many enemy soldiers were killed in an operation. Secretary of Defense Robert McNamara was obsessed with quantitative management, and the number of enemy dead or the ratio of enemy to friendly casualties put a number, or a score, on performance. Commanders and soldiers were aware that a high body count meant progress and would be rewarded. Hence numbers were often inflated, rendering them meaningless as indicators. An even worse problem was that Vietnamese civilians were sometimes killed, especially in remote areas, and counted as enemy losses. The troops called it the "gook rule": If it's dead and Vietnamese, it's Vietcong. The fabricating of body count and targeting of civilians had a devastating impact on many officers, men, and the military as a whole.

August Revolution (1945)—see **Vietminh**.

Ball, George W. (1909–1994)—A respected attorney and government official, George W. Ball served as undersecretary of state from 1961 to 1966. In both the Kennedy and Johnson administrations, he was referred to as the "Establishment

Dove." He was often the only high-ranking foreign policy aide to challenge decisions to expand U.S. involvement in South Vietnam. In 1961 he warned, accurately as it turned out, that sending 8,000 American advisers to Vietnam would lead to having 300,000 U.S. troops there in five years. He was equally prescient in his arguments against Johnson's decisions in 1965 to escalate U.S. bombing and troop deployments. In each case, his warnings went unheeded, and he finally resigned from the government.

Bao Dai (1913–1997) — The last emperor of Vietnam, Bao Dai succeed his father, Khai Dinh, to the Nguyen dynasty throne upon his father's death in 1925. He went to France to continue his education and returned to Hue to take up his imperial duties in 1932. Ernest and intelligent, Bao Dai appointed some energetic young mandarins to his royal cabinet, including Ngo Dinh Diem, but the French overlords would tolerate no reforms. Diem and others resigned their posts, and Bao Dai increasingly turned to a dissolute life of hunting, gambling, and womanizing. He spent much of his time on the French Riviera or at other resorts outside of Vietnam. In March 1945 Japanese occupation forces invited him to form a supposedly independent government in Vietnam, which he attempted to do. Bao Dai was no match for the politically skilled Ho Chi Minh, however, and during the August Revolution of 1945 the Vietminh secured Bao Dai's abdication of the throne. He soon left for the French Riviera.

During the war against the Vietminh, French officials began to look for a Vietnamese around whom to structure an alternative government to the DRV. In 1949 Bao Dai and the president of France signed the Elysée Agreements, also referred to as the Bao Dai Solution. These accords created the State of Vietnam with Bao Dai as head of state and Saigon as its capital. Despite promises about greater Vietnamese autonomy, the French never granted Bao Dai the independence of Vietnam that he, Ho, and most Vietnamese desired. In 1954 Bao Dai named Ngo Dinh Diem prime minister of the State of Vietnam, and in October 1955 Diem arranged a referendum in South Vietnam that deposed Bao Dai and supported creation of the Republic of Vietnam. Already in France, Bao Dai continued to live there until his death.

Bien Hoa — Located twenty miles (thirty-two kilometers) from Saigon, the city of Bien Hoa had a South Vietnamese air base where a Vietcong mortar attack killed five Americans and destroyed or damaged several U.S. planes on November 1, 1964. With the U.S. presidential election only days away, Lyndon Johnson chose not to retaliate. After the American build up of forces in South Vietnam, Bien Hoa became the site of a large U.S. air base and the headquarters for III Corps.

Boat People — Beginning in April 1975 with the fall of the Republic of Vietnam, many South Vietnamese began trying to escape life under the new regime by fleeing in boats, and eventually these refugees became known as "boat people." After the frantic exodus of about 60,000 Vietnamese during the departure of the last Americans on April 30, the flow of refugees almost ceased for awhile. In 1977 the number of people risking perilous sea voyages in overcrowded and often unseaworthy vessels spiked, and the number of boat people in 1979 reached 10,000 to 15,000 per month. Poor economic conditions and the release of inmates from reeducation camps contributed to this increase, but many of the boat people were ethnic Chinese who had two reasons for leaving. Many were business owners who had their businesses confiscated in socialist reforms, and all were discriminated against as an unwelcome minority. In fact, the government made possible the exit of those Chinese who paid a bribe and a "departure fee" of about $1,500. Ethnic Vietnamese trying to leave, however, faced severe punishment. Many of the boat people who managed to set sail for ports elsewhere in Southeast Asia drowned in the attempt or fell victim to pirates. The tens of thousands of boat people who survived added to the total of 1.5 to 2 million refugees estimated to have left from Laos, Cambodia, and the Socialist Republic of Vietnam in the decade after 1975. Almost a half million of the Vietnamese refugees eventually settled in the United States. Some of the displaced persons in Southeast Asia remained in refugee camps for years, and the last camp for boat people, located in Hong Kong, did not close until 2000, when the 1,000 remaining residents were given Hong Kong residency.

Body Count—see **Attrition Strategy**.

Booby Traps   More than 10 percent of the deaths and many of the maiming injuries suffered by U.S. forces in Vietnam were from booby traps, which were concealed explosives or other lethal devices. Some of them were quite simple, such as grenades attached to hidden trip wires. Punji sticks were bamboo stakes with needle sharp points, tipped with excrement to cause infection, and concealed in camouflaged pits. Some booby traps were more elaborate, such as the "Malay whip" log, which was a spiked log hung between trees and which would fly toward several men when triggered by a trip wire. These unseen weapons that were capable of inflicting pain and death without warning had a psychological effect on American soldiers, creating a mixture of fear and anger that led them to blame and even attack civilians for allegedly placing the booby traps. These terror devices were a way for the Vietcong and PAVN, who lacked the weapons and technology to confront the Americans directly and regularly, to inflict losses on their enemy and to disrupt U.S. operations.

Buddhists—About 80 percent of Vietnam's population during the twentieth century was at least nominally Buddhist. During the long Chinese rule of Vietnam and under the early Vietnamese emperors, Buddhism was the dominant religion. During the fifteenth century Confucian ideas began to shape political practice, and under French rule Catholicism was encouraged. Throughout Vietnam's history, however, Buddhism remained the popular religion of most of the people. Under the Catholic president Ngo Dinh Diem, Catholics controlled key government positions, and there was obvious favoritism for Catholics and discrimination against Buddhists. In general, the Buddhist clergy did not involve itself in politics, but monks began to challenge the increasing persecution of Buddhists. Diem's brother Ngo Dinh Nhu alleged that communist agitators were behind these protests, which only further angered the monks. On June 11, 1963, an elderly monk, Thich Quang Duc, burned himself to death on a Saigon street as an act of defiance. Government police cracked down harder with arrests and attacks on temples, which led to more self-immolations and to antigovernment riots. This Buddhist uprising contributed to the increasing consideration by U.S. officials and Buddhist officers in the ARVN of a change in government and helped set the stage for the coup that toppled the Diem government in November 1963. Another serious Buddhist protest, including self-immolations, erupted in 1966 against the policies of Premier Nguyen Cao Ky, but, with strong support from Washington, Ky survived the challenge. Organized Buddhist political action declined thereafter.

Bundy, McGeorge (1919–1996) — A former dean at Harvard University, McGeorge Bundy was special assistant to the president for national security affairs from 1961 to 1966 and one of the principal architects of U.S. policy in Vietnam under both Kennedy and Johnson. He believed strongly in American support of South Vietnam, and during the Kennedy years he fashioned the dramatic increase of the U.S. military advisory effort there as the best means to help Saigon. After Diem's death, Bundy gradually came to favor U.S. bombing of North Vietnam and the use of U.S. combat forces in the South to put pressure on Hanoi to agree to a negotiated settlement. Although he recommended U.S. military escalation in 1965, he eventually questioned the extent of U.S. military operations and the lack of attention to pacification efforts. He resigned in 1966 and became president of the Ford Foundation but continued to advise Johnson as part of a group of former officials known as the Wise Men. Because he had originally advocated escalation, his support for American de-escalation in Vietnam after the Tet Offensive had a profound influence on Johnson's 1968 decision to place a limit on the size of the U.S. military effort.

Bush, George H. W. (1924–) — As president of the United States (1989–1993), George H. W. Bush ordered a major U.S. military intervention into Kuwait to liberate that country from occupation by Iraq, and he was determined that this limited war would not be a repeat of the Vietnam War. His advisers persuaded him that America's lack of success in Vietnam occurred because insufficient power had been employed at the beginning of U.S. intervention. Thus he built up a force in the Persian Gulf region larger than the highest level of American troops ever in South Vietnam at any one time and supported it with a high-technology bombing campaign. Although Bush achieved a rapid and largely painless victory over the Iraqi army, the history of the conflict there and the nature of the enemy was very different from the Vietnam War. He declared that the success of U.S. arms had ended once and for all the Vietnam Syndrome, that is, the fear to use military intervention that had gripped American policy since the Vietnam War. Bush's own behavior contradicted his assertion, however, because he halted the U.S. attack after only one hundred hours rather than risk getting bogged down in a protracted and costly war in Iraq that might be similar to the war in Vietnam. With regard to Vietnam itself, Bush continued the trade embargo and withholding of diplomatic recognition that had been U.S. policy toward its former enemy since 1975. After his successor, Bill Clinton, established diplomatic ties with Hanoi, Bush made an unofficial visit to Vietnam in September 1995.

Cambodia, Invasion of (1970)—The invasion of Cambodia was a joint operation of U.S. and ARVN military forces into eastern Cambodia along the border with South Vietnam in May and June 1970. In March Prime Minister Lon Nol and others had ousted Cambodia's neutralist leader Norodom Sihanouk and had begun attacking communist Vietnamese forces in their country. The Nixon administration saw an opportunity to help the pro-American Lon Nol and at the same time attack National Liberation Front (NLF) and North Vietnamese Army (NVA) bases in Cambodia, which in the past had enjoyed the sanctuary of Sihanouk's neutrality. A bold military move across the border could also relieve pressure on the ARVN and gain time for Vietnamization, the transfer of responsibility for military operations in South Vietnam from U.S. to ARVN units. It could also be a forceful demonstration to Hanoi of American resolve that would aid U.S. negotiations with the DRV. Although some of Nixon's advisers, such as Secretary of Defense Melvin Laird, strongly opposed the idea, the president went ahead with an invasion of neutral Cambodia.

On April 30 Nixon made a tough-sounding television address announcing the operation and claiming it was a response to North Vietnamese aggression against Cambodia. He also declared that the objective was to destroy the Central Office for South Vietnam (COSVN), which he described as the "nerve center" of NVA operations in the South. A force of about 12,000 U.S. Army and 8,000 ARVN soldiers attacked along a 100-mile (160-kilometer) length of the border. The Americans struck an area called the "Fishhook" some fifty-five miles northwest of Saigon, and the ARVN concentrated on the "Parrot's Beak," which was thirty-three miles west of the RVN capital. These forces with tactical air support moved thirty miles into Cambodia. Although the attack resulted in approximately 2,000 enemy killed and a large number of weapons and supplies captured or destroyed, its military impact was slight. Combat activity decreased briefly within South Vietnam. If the U.S. forces had expected COSVN to be some type of jungle Pentagon, they were disappointed. A few abandoned huts were found but no major operations center. In fact, COSVN was little more than a mobile command post. It was a committee created in 1961 by the Communist Party (known then as Lao Dong or Workers' Party) Central Committee to coordinate NLF military activity, and it frequently moved about.

The Cambodian invasion had two serious negative consequences. First, the retreat of both Vietnamese and Cambodian communist forces deeper into the interior of Cambodia to escape the attack increased political instability throughout the country, and the escalation of the fighting and increase in bombing disrupted Cambodian society. This chaos provided political opportunities for the radical Khmer Rouge guerrillas. Second, the invasion generated a dramatic antiwar reaction in the United States. Protests occurred at hundreds of colleges. At Kent State University, in Ohio, the National Guard shot and killed four students on May 4, following a weekend of demonstrations, and on May 14 police killed two students at Jackson State University, in Mississippi. These violent incidents led to even more demonstrations. Nixon criticized the protests, but he had all U.S. forces out of Cambodia by June 30. In a largely symbolic act of defiance of the president, Congress repealed the Gulf of Tonkin Resolution in July.

Can Lao Party—The full name of the Can Lao Party was Can Lao Nhan Vi Cach Mang Dang, or Revolutionary Personalist Labor Party. Ngo Dinh Nhu controlled this largely secret organization and used it to spy on, bribe, and intimidate individuals to support his brother Ngo Dinh Diem. Created in 1954, the Can Lao provided a mechanism for the Ngo family to control civil and military leaders, who often were Can Lao members, and also contributed an official ideology to the RVN known as "personalism." Largely the work of Nhu, the family intellectual, personalism blended European and Asian concepts into a justification of absolute state power for the protection of the human person. After the deaths of Diem and Nhu, the party dissolved, and many of its members later supported Nguyen Van Thieu.

Carter, Jimmy (1924–)—During his one term as president of the United States (1977–1981), Jimmy Carter sought to address domestic and foreign policy issues created by the Vietnam War. James Earl Carter Jr. was a former naval officer, businessman, and Democratic governor of Georgia whose campaign pledge to always tell the truth and lack of Washington experience appealed to voters after the tensions created by the Vietnam War and Watergate scandal. To heal domestic wounds, he offered pardons to wartime draft resisters but would not grant amnesty, which would have given official sanction to violation of draft laws. He considered the establishment of normal diplomatic relations with the Socialist Republic of Vietnam, but ultimately his administration decided against it for several reasons: Hanoi's desire for reparations, the human tragedy of the "boat people" forced to risk death at sea in attempts to escape Vietnam, and Vietnam's invasion of Cambodia. In response to the crisis of the boat people, Carter doubled U.S. immigration quotas for Indochina refugees, an act of leadership that caused other countries also to agree to accept more refugees. His administration extended diplomatic recognition to the People's Republic of China in January 1979. He then tried to dissuade the PRC from attacking Vietnam after the SRV invaded Cambodia and cautioned the USSR against backing its ally Vietnam against China. Carter tried to find a post–Vietnam War role for the United States as international mediator. Burdened by the problems of high inflation at home and Iran's refusal to release American hostages, Carter lost the 1980 presidential election to Ronald Reagan.

Catholics—Roman Catholics comprised about 10 percent of the population of South Vietnam and were a key constituency of the government of Ngo Dinh Diem, who was himself a devout Catholic and whose brother, Father Ngo Dinh Thuc, became archbishop of Hue in 1961. Missionaries brought Catholicism to Vietnam in the fifteenth century, and by 1700 there were hundreds of thousands of Catholic Vietnamese. Under French colonial rule, the Church obtained land and built cathedrals, but the Vietnamese parishioners were divided between those who supported and those who resisted the Europeans. During the anticolonial war against France, the Vietminh treated all Catholics as collaborators, arrested priests, and confiscated Church property. Fearing persecution after the 1954 Geneva Agreements had left the Vietminh in control in the North, six hundred to eight hundred thousand Catholics fled to the South. Diem's government cultivated their support with political and economic favors, and this obvious pro-Catholic bias in the predominantly Buddhist RVN contributed to the dissension that ultimately led to the 1963 coup against Diem. Catholic influence in the RVN government waned but did not disappear after the coup, and Catholics remained targets of the Vietcong throughout the war. Many of the Vietnamese who fled from Vietnam during and after 1975 were Catholics.

Central Highlands—The Central Highlands of South Vietnam were the frequent site of heavy fighting because of their strategic location between the lower end of the Ho Chi Minh Trail and the heavily populated areas of the RVN. From a point about 50 miles north of Saigon, this heavily forested plateau and hill region covered an area about 200 miles long and 100 miles wide up to about 50 miles north of Kontum. Other important towns in the area were Dak To, Pleiku, and Ban Me Thuot, but in general the Central Highlands were sparsely populated by minority people referred to as Montagnards by the French and Americans. The PAVN's final offensive against the South in 1975 began with an attack on Ban Me Thuot in the Central Highlands.

Central Intelligence Agency (CIA)—The role and impact of the Central Intelligence Agency in Vietnam is difficult to know accurately because its work was highly secret. Created in 1947 to provide foreign intelligence information to the president, the CIA also acquired primary responsibility for espionage and covert operations. The CIA's World War II predecessor, the Office of Strategic Services (OSS), had worked with the Vietminh against the Japanese, and the chief of the OSS in Vietnam, Archimedes Patti, tried unsuccessfully to convince U.S. officials in Washington to cooperate with Ho Chi Minh in 1945. In 1954 Allan Dulles, the director of the CIA, sent Colonel Edward Lansdale to Saigon to bolster the new government of Ngo Dinh Diem, and Lansdale used bribes in South Vietnam and sabotage and propaganda in North Vietnam to aid Diem. Through intelligence gathering, CIA officers became well aware over time of Diem's limitations, and some of them were in direct contact with various plotters against Diem, including those ARVN officers who led the successful coup against Diem in 1963. CIA efforts to infiltrate South Vietnamese agents into the North were largely failures, but the agency had better success in its joint operation with U.S. Special Forces (Green Berets) in South Vietnam's Central Highlands to arm and train the Montagnard minority to defend the area. The CIA organized a secret war in Laos in which it armed Hmong tribesmen to fight the Pathet Lao and to attack the Ho Chi Minh Trail. Effective for a time, this tactic ended disastrously. Many Hmong died, although some managed to leave Laos.

The CIA often came into conflict with the military and the White House. The agency provided pessimistic assessments of progress in South Vietnam that Lyndon Johnson did not welcome. CIA leaders also argued for a pacification strategy in place of the large-unit military operations favored by General William Westmoreland. One specific pacification effort that was implemented, the Phoenix Program, became quite controversial when critics charged that this plan to capture Vietcong cadre became an indiscriminate assassination operation. Further complaints arose when the Nixon administration authorized Operation Chaos, the use of the CIA for domestic spying on antiwar activists. Because of controversy surrounding the CIA in relation to the war and in other areas of the world, Congress set additional limits on and oversight of the agency in the 1970s.

Central Office for South Vietnam (COSVN)—see **Cambodia, Invasion of**.

Champa—The Kingdom of Champa on the central coast of Vietnam was founded during the second century A.D. The Chams spoke a Malayo-Polynesian language, and most eventually became Muslims. After Vietnam gained its independence from China in the tenth century, Champa and Vietnam became rivals and fought several times over subsequent centuries. In the fifteenth century Champa became a dependency of Vietnam and was formally absorbed into Vietnam in the nineteenth century. The Chams remain an ethnic minority in central Vietnam and parts of Cambodia.

Christmas Bombing—see **Air War**.

Clifford, Clark M. (1906–1998)—An attorney and confidante of Democratic presidents beginning with Harry Truman, Clark Clifford served as secretary of defense from January 1968 to January 1969. Although he favored U.S. aid to South Vietnam, he advised Lyndon Johnson in 1965 to seek negotiations rather than begin a military escalation in Vietnam that could risk becoming an open-ended commitment. After Johnson decided to expand the war, however, Clifford advocated waging a determined military effort. He took this position as one of the Wise Men, an unofficial group Johnson consulted about the war. When Robert McNamara's growing doubts about Vietnam policy led him to step down as secretary of defense, Johnson appointed Clifford to the post in the belief that the new secretary would stand firm on continuing the war effort. The president felt betrayed when Clifford decided after the Tet Offensive that the time had come to reduce the American role. Clifford arranged a briefing for Johnson by the Wise Men, many of whom had come to share the same opinion as Clifford, and this meeting helped convince Johnson to begin limiting U.S. bombing and troop increases.

Clinton, Bill (1946–)—Bill Clinton served as president of the United States from 1993 to 2001, and during his administration the United States and the Socialist Republic of Vietnam (SRV) finally established normal diplomatic relations, twenty years after the end of the Vietnam War. William Jefferson Clinton was born after World War II and was part of the "Vietnam generation" that reached military age during the American war in Vietnam. After graduating from college in 1968, he avoided the draft through legal but questionable actions and participated in some antiwar demonstrations as a graduate student in England. When he ran for president in 1992, some journalists raised questions about his qualifications to be commander-in-chief based on his Vietnam-era activities. The issue had no significant impact on the election, but it did strain his working relationship with some senior military officers. As part of a broad program to increase U.S. foreign trade, Clinton lifted the long-standing U.S. embargo on trade with Vietnam on February 3, 1994. With no noticeably adverse public reaction to that step and after gaining assurances from Hanoi of continuing cooperation on locating the remains of American MIAs, Clinton announced diplomatic recognition of the SRV on July 11, 1995. He named Douglas "Pete" Peterson, a former Vietnam War POW, as the first U.S. ambassador to serve in Hanoi. In November 2000 Clinton made an official visit to Vietnam and encouraged the government there to open its economy to further trade with the West.

Cochinchina—When the French colonized Vietnam in the nineteenth century, they made Cochinchina a formal colony, whereas Tonkin and Annam in northern and central Vietnam were designated protectorates. Cochinchina was composed of six provinces in the Mekong Delta, an area known to the Vietnamese as Nam Bo.

Collins, Joseph Lawton (1896–1987)—From November 1954 to May 1955, General J. Lawton Collins served in Vietnam as President Dwight Eisenhower's special representative, or, in effect, U.S. ambassador to South Vietnam. Nicknamed "Lightning Joe" by his troops, Collins had been one of Eisenhower's most successful corps commanders in the D-Day invasion in 1944 and later became U.S. Army chief of staff. Eisenhower sent Collins to Saigon to assess the abilities of Ngo Dinh Diem and to assist the new prime minister in preparing to lead a new government. Collins endorsed U.S. support for South Vietnam but concluded that Diem was unsuited for leadership. Although many of Collins's perceptions of Diem's weaknesses later proved correct, at the time, the Eisenhower administration decided to continue its support of Diem as the best available leader in the South.

Containment Policy—During the Cold War, the containment policy became the basic U.S. strategy for responding to Soviet political and military power in Europe and by extension to any communist-led movement in the world. In February 1946 George F. Kennan, a leading State Department expert on the Soviet Union stationed in Moscow, sent a cogent explanation of the Kremlin's behavior that became known as the Long Telegram. His historical and ideological analysis so impressed officials in Washington that he was named head of the State Department's Policy Planning Staff. In July 1947 he published an essay under the pseudonym "Mr. X" that recommended "long-term, patient but firm, and vigilant containment of Russian expansive tendencies." From this basic concept came a long series of policy actions, including creation of the Marshall Plan and North Atlantic Treaty Organization in Europe and the offering of aid and the intervention of U.S. military forces in Korea and Indochina to combat perceived Soviet allies in Asia. Indeed the Kennedy and Johnson administrations believed that commitment of U.S. troops during the Korean War had contained communist aggression there, and this seeming lesson strongly influenced the decision to pursue military containment in Vietnam. Kennan himself became critical in the 1950s and 1960s of the militarization of containment, especially in Asia, because he maintained that his original arguments had applied only to a political threat in Europe.

Counterinsurgency—Counterinsurgency is the defense against armed or unarmed rebellion, that is, insurgency, aimed at overthrowing existing government authority. Counterinsurgency was a central issue in the Vietnam War because its importance and application depended on how the threat to the government of South Vietnam was defined. Official U.S. rationales for intervention in Vietnam declared that the DRV was an aggressor against the RVN or that, in other words, the enemy was external. While Hanoi wanted to reunite Vietnam under its control, the greatest pressure on the Saigon regime often came from political organizing and guerrilla warfare mounted by local Vietcong rebels in the South. Counterinsurgency meant providing security for the southern population against guerrilla attacks and creating government programs that would build popular support for the RVN. Through the dispatching of Special Forces teams to rural areas and the creation of fortified villages called "strategic hamlets," the Kennedy administration began a counterinsurgency plan. After Lyndon Johnson ordered bombing in North Vietnam and sent American combat divisions to South Vietnam, conventional tactics against northern aggression often overshadowed the counterinsurgency effort, which came to be called "pacification." Strategists then and historians later debated whether the United States gave counterinsurgency the level of effort needed to help Saigon and whether, as outsiders, Americans could devise any pacification program to remedy effectively the historical and political liabilities of the RVN leaders.

Credibility Gap—The term "credibility gap" referred specifically to a perceived disparity between U.S. government reasons for the American intervention in Vietnam and claims of progress in the war, on the one hand, and information available through the press and other sources about the physical and moral cost of the American war and the weakness of the RVN, on the other hand. The credibility of U.S. policies was also a frequently cited concern shared by the Kennedy, Johnson, and Nixon administrations. Throughout the war years, American officials wanted the nation's enemies and allies to believe that the United States stood behind its international commitments and would not forsake governments it had pledged to assist.

Cronkite, Walter (1916–)—A journalist since 1933, Walter Cronkite served as anchor and editor of the *CBS Evening News* from 1962 to 1981. His accuracy, impartiality, and understated style made him, in the view of many Americans, the nation's most respected and trusted news reporter. During the escalation of U.S. involvement in Vietnam, Cronkite largely accepted the government's rationales and reports of progress. After the Tet Offensive, he traveled to Vietnam and made his own special report for CBS News in February 1968. He shared with the public his conclusion that the war was a stalemate and that a negotiated settlement should be sought. Lyndon Johnson understood that Cronkite's view reflected and influenced the opinion of many other Americans.

Danang—Called Tourane under the French colonial regime, Danang was the second largest city in the Republic of Vietnam. Its protected harbor made it an excellent military base, port, and supply location on the northern coast of South Vietnam. The first U.S. ground combat units in Vietnam made an amphibious landing there in March 1965, and it eventually became the site of the headquarters of the ARVN I Corps, the U.S. III Marine Amphibious Force, the U.S. 1st and 3rd Marine Divisions, the XXIV Corps of the U.S. Army, and major U.S. air and naval bases. The city's China Beach was a rest area for U.S. troops. Danang's prewar population of slightly more than 140,000 mushroomed to more than 400,000 as refugees flowed into it during the war, and the city was a scene of chaos and high casualties during the NVA's final offensive in 1975.

Defoliation—From 1961 to 1972, the U.S. Air Force conducted a defoliation program under the code name Operation Ranch Hand. Thousands of gallons of chemical defoliants were sprayed throughout South Vietnam along roads and canals and around military bases to eliminate cover for enemy ambushes and attacks. This use had significant military utility. More difficult to assess was the effectiveness of defoliants to destroy forests and crops in order to deny those resources to the Vietcong in areas they controlled. One of the most commonly employed herbicides was known as Agent Orange for the color marking the containers. It contained a toxic impurity, dioxin, that could cause serious illness, including tumors and birth defects. As medical problems appeared among U.S. veterans and their offspring after the war, a legal battle began. It ended in 1984 with an out-of-court settlement between the veterans and some of the chemical manufacturers. The environmental impact of defoliation on Vietnam has been difficult to measure, but the ecosystem has recovered in some areas.

De Gaulle, Charles (1890–1970)—General Charles de Gaulle was provisional president of France's Fourth Republic from 1944 to 1946 and president of France's Fifth Republic from 1958 to 1969. He sent French troops to Indochina in 1945 because he strongly believed that, after its humiliation in World War II, France had to demonstrate its resolve by regaining control of its former colony. He resigned from the government in 1946 in a dispute with other political leaders over presidential powers. After France had experienced the hardships of trying to hold onto its claims to Indochina and Algeria, de Gaulle returned as president. He urged both Kennedy and Johnson to avoid military entanglement in Vietnam, and in 1964 he publicly proposed that the participants in the 1954

Geneva Conference reconvene to make an agreement on the neutrality of Southeast Asia in the Cold War. The Johnson administration rebuffed de Gaulle's suggestion and continued its military escalation in Vietnam.

Demilitarized Zone (DMZ)—Established as part of the 1954 Geneva cease-fire agreement, the demilitarized zone was a five-mile wide buffer area that followed the temporary demarcation line separating the Vietminh-controlled area to the north and the French-controlled area to the south. The line followed the Ben Hai River from the South China Sea to the village of Bo Ho Su and then west to the Laotian border at the 17th parallel. The DMZ became the de facto boundary between North Vietnam and South Vietnam. Although the DMZ was supposed to be a militarily neutral area, the DRV often moved troops and materiel in and out of it, and the United States bombed and shelled these troops in the DMZ. In both its 1972 and 1975 offensives against the RVN, the DRV sent troops directly across the DMZ.

Democratic National Convention (1968)—The 1968 Democratic National Convention was held in Chicago from August 26 to 29 and became the scene of some of the most dramatic antiwar protests of the Vietnam era. Vice President Hubert Humphrey arrived at the convention with enough delegates to ensure the nomination for president. Inside the Chicago Amphitheater the principal battle was over the party's platform plank on the Vietnam War. Humphrey himself wanted to include a proposal for stopping the bombing of North Vietnam, but Lyndon Johnson viewed this platform language as a repudiation of his administration. After a long and stormy debate, Johnson loyalists were able to gain passage of a plank endorsing Johnson's Vietnam policies. The delegates then nominated Humphrey with one ballot.

The tension inside the convention hall had been high, but outside on the streets a massive clash occurred between thousands of protestors and hundreds of Chicago policemen, state troopers, and national guardsmen. Mayor Richard J. Daley had pledged that the mostly young demonstrators who descended upon the city would not disrupt the convention. There were several violent incidents during the convention, some of which were provoked by the demonstrators, but on August 28 police discipline broke down, and hundreds of protestors were clubbed and dragged away under arrest in full view of the nation through the print and television media. The domestic divisions created by the war were clearly apparent.

Dienbienphu—The decisive battle of the French war in Indochina and one of the major military engagements of the twentieth century took place at the village of Dienbienphu in northwestern Vietnam from March 13 to May 7, 1954. In November 1953 French General Henri Navarre began building up a garrison at Dienbienphu to better control communication routes into Laos and to support ethnic minority groups in the area working with the French against the Vietminh. The general made a major miscalculation, one often repeated by American commanders later, when he greatly underestimated the ability of his Vietnamese adversaries to counter his move. The Vietminh realized the negotiating bonus a major victory would provide them at the international conference on Indochina slated to be held in Geneva in the spring. Over several weeks, General Vo Nguyen Giap assembled a force in the high ground overlooking Dienbienphu that outnumbered the French in their fortified but exposed outposts by about five-to-one. With supplies and advice from China's People's Liberation Army, the Vietminh even had more and better artillery and rockets than the French. On March 13 Giap began the siege with a heavy bombardment followed by infantry attacks. His artillery also rendered the Dienbienphu airstrip unusable for adequate resupply. Over the next seven weeks, the French fought back bravely, and both sides sustained high casualties. Near the end there was consideration of an American air strike to try to break the siege, but the Eisenhower administration declined. On May 7 the last of the small number of remaining French fighters surrendered.

The loss of a garrison that had numbered about 15,000, many of whom were elite paratroopers, had a devastating impact on the French public, which was already weary of the war. Although France still held Hanoi and had large forces in place elsewhere in Indochina, the end of the attempt to reestablish colonial rule had come. Paris's delegation at the Geneva Conference, which ironically began its Indochina deliberations on May 8, sought a negotiated exit from the war and achieved it. For the DRV and its army, the Battle of Dienbienphu was an enormous success that took on even more mythic symbolism over time. Although Giap had trucks available, much of the artillery, ammunition, and supplies were carried into the mountains above Dienbienphu by an army of laborers, including women. Some of his infantrymen, although not the majority, were irregulars. This glorious victory accomplished by what appeared to be a militia force became a central image in the official DRV portrayal of the selfless and heroic sacrifice of the people in the cause of national liberation.

Domino Theory—On April 7, 1954, President Dwight D. Eisenhower articulated the domino theory when he described how a French loss in Indochina would be like knocking over the first domino in a row, causing the others to go over quickly. Through this analogy he was saying that if Vietnam fell under communist control, then it would be difficult to prevent communist takeovers in Laos, Cambodia, Thailand, and possibly even India, Japan, the Philippines, and Indonesia. This chain-reaction concept was not new to U.S. containment policy. It was present in Harry Truman's rationale for aiding Greece and Turkey to prevent the spread of communist regimes in eastern Europe and the Middle East. The National Security Council applied the same idea in a report on Indochina in

1952. After Eisenhower made his 1954 comment, the domino theory became a simplified description of the broader strategic importance of South Vietnam to the United States. It was inherent in U.S. creation of the Southeast Asia Treaty Organization and American involvement in the Laotian civil war. When reporters asked John Kennedy about the domino theory in Southeast Asia, he responded emphatically that he believed it. Lyndon Johnson cited it as the reason the United States was in Vietnam. After Hanoi's final victory in 1975, however, the dominoes did not fall. Destabilized by war, Laos and Cambodia did see communist regimes emerge, but the remainder of Southeast Asia remained out of communist hands.

Draft—The draft, or conscription of young American men into the military during the Vietnam War, became one of the most controversial aspects of a controversial war. The Selective Service System was the U.S. government agency through which men were registered for, selected, and inducted into the U.S. Army, in most cases, but also into other services depending on manpower needs at the time. There was military conscription in the Civil War and World War I, but the draft legislation passed in 1940 on the eve of World War II provided the basic outlines of the system still in place when the Johnson administration decided to begin sending tens of thousands of U.S. soldiers to Vietnam in 1965. During World War II the draft had helped place millions of men in uniform and, although allowed to expire briefly after the war, resumed in 1948 to supplement voluntary enlistments and maintain U.S. military readiness during the Cold War, including the Korean War. Many men grumbled about the draft during those years and would have preferred to avoid it, but most accepted the possibility of conscription as a civic responsibility, much like paying taxes. Also, after the cease-fire in Korea in 1953 and until the escalation in Vietnam, monthly draft calls were fairly low, meaning that most men did not face a high likelihood of being tapped for induction.

Because Johnson sought at first to keep the war in Vietnam limited and to avoid a congressional debate on the war that might jeopardize his domestic plans, he rejected Pentagon recommendations to mobilize reserve forces. This decision left only the draft as the means for maintaining America's global force levels as the number of U.S. troops in Vietnam leaped past 100,000 in 1965 and climbed beyond 500,000 in 1968. More than two million men ultimately served in Vietnam, but that was less than 10 percent of the men who reached the minimal draft age of eighteen during the war. Thus, most young men did not serve in Vietnam, but almost all faced that possibility, and as the war grew more deadly and controversial, the issue of who should serve when not all were needed to serve became paramount.

There was a high potential for inequity in the selective service process. It was based on a concept known as "channeling," in which physical, mental, and occupational tests were used to place men where they could best serve the country. Hence many men received educational or job-related deferments on the theory that they had or were developing skills the nation needed. Also, local civilian draft boards, staffed largely by white, middle-aged men, had the authority to determine who received deferments. Combined, these various features of selective service produced an American military force in Vietnam that was young (the average draftee was nineteen) and that was drawn mostly from the working class. Minorities, such as African Americans and Hispanic Americans, also tended to be represented in higher percentages in Vietnam than in the U.S. population at large, in part due to draft inequities and in part due to the economic attraction of military service for underprivileged youth.

In 1967 a revision of the draft law eliminated student deferments for men in graduate and professional schools, which increased the number of middle-class college graduates among the draftees. Antiwar protestors also seized upon the draft as evidence of an oppressive government prosecuting an unpopular war, and this agitation prompted other changes. A national lottery to determine draft eligibility began in 1970, which produced greater fairness, but by that time draft calls were declining as Nixon lowered U.S. force levels in Vietnam. The draft ended completely in 1973 and was replaced by a system of all-volunteer service.

Dulles, John Foster (1888–1959)—As secretary of state (1953–1959), John Foster Dulles became a strong advocate of U.S. support of South Vietnam and especially of its president, Ngo Dinh Diem. Before joining the Eisenhower administration, he had acquired vast experience in world affairs as an international lawyer, churchman, and diplomat. Although he had served the Truman administration as negotiator of the U.S. peace treaty with Japan in 1951, he was the leading Republican foreign policy spokesman in Dwight Eisenhower's 1952 campaign for president. He condemned containment as passive and argued instead for liberation of communist-controlled areas. Although later as head of the State Department his policies did not depart noticeably from containment, his rhetoric remained strident and threatening. He was the administration's spokesman, for example, advocating a nuclear deterrent policy of "massive retaliation" against communist aggression. On Southeast Asia his recommendations were sometimes more aggressive than Eisenhower's, but basically the two worked well together. During the siege of Dienbienphu, he tried to organize "united action," that is, an international effort to aid France, but when that did not develop, he later created the Southeast Asia Treaty Organization to provide a mutual security arrangement covering South Vietnam. He initially had doubts about Diem's ability to lead the RVN, but he came to favor whole-hearted support of South Vietnam's president. Dulles died of cancer in 1959.

Easter Offensive (1972)—On March 30, 1972, the North Vietnamese Army (NVA) began a major infantry, artillery, and armor offensive against the northern provinces of South Vietnam. The attack marked the opening of the NVA's three-pronged Easter Offensive that continued into the middle of May. The DRV's General Vo Nguyen Giap massed his forces in conventional military operations in three places: (1) across the DMZ and out of Laos aimed toward Hue and Danang, (2) from Cambodia into the Central Highlands intended to cut the RVN in half by linking with NVA forces in coastal Binh Dinh Province, and (3) again out of Cambodia toward the town of An Loc, only 70 miles (110 kilometers) north of Saigon. With less than 100,000—mostly noncombat—U.S. forces remaining in the South, Hanoi's strategists reasoned that a conventional attack would result in either toppling the Nguyen Van Thieu government in Saigon or leaving the NVA in control of large areas of the RVN, thus forcing negotiations on DRV terms. An NVA success might also discredit Nixon's Vietnamization policy and make him vulnerable to defeat by a peace-minded Democrat in the approaching U.S. presidential election.

The offensive did extensive damage to South Vietnam and its forces and left the NVA in possession of some territory in the South along the Laotian and Cambodian borders, but the attack did not achieve its objectives. Although severely pressured, the ARVN forces held in each area largely because of some extremely accurate assessments of the NVA's intentions by U.S. military advisers and especially because of heavy American air attacks on Giap's conventional formations and lines of supply. Nixon also ordered extensive bombing of North Vietnam (Operation Linebacker) and the mining of Haiphong harbor, which prevented outside resupply of the NVA's huge operation. The northern forces suffered heavy losses in men and materiel that took about two years to recoup. The result was essentially a draw. The NVA lost the battle but would recover to fight again, and the ARVN survived the battle but only with decisive U.S. help, an ominous sign for Vietnamization and the future when U.S. advisers and bombers would not be available.

Eisenhower, Dwight D. (1890–1969)—Before he was president of the United States (1953–1961), Dwight D. Eisenhower had a distinguished career as a soldier-statesman. A West Point graduate, he was Allied Supreme Commander in Europe during World War II, and after the war he served as U.S. Army chief of staff, president of Columbia University, and commander of North Atlantic Treaty Organization forces. It is not surprising that, as president, he took an active interest in national security questions. He did not depart from Harry Truman's containment policy, but his administration added the New Look, a strategy of confronting the perceived threat of international communism with nuclear deterrence, regional defense alliances, and covert operations. In Indochina he authorized an increase in the level of U.S. aid to the French in 1953, and during the Battle of Dienbienphu in 1954 he offered the famous "domino theory" that blocking DRV success in gaining control of Vietnam would prevent the fall of neighboring states to communist control. He made the decision not to approve France's request for U.S. air support at Dienbienphu, but after the cease-fire arranged at the Geneva Conference, he authorized Secretary of State John Foster Dulles to pursue ways to assist South Vietnam. Dulles then led the creation of the Southeast Asia Treaty Organization in September 1954, which offered a limited pledge of U.S. security protection to the region. Although Eisenhower was personally less engaged in Vietnam policy development after 1954, his administration significantly expanded U.S. economic assistance to the RVN through the rest of the decade. Eisenhower bequeathed to John Kennedy a publicly-avowed American commitment to the survival of an independent South Vietnam.

Elections in the Republic of Vietnam (1955, 1967, 1971)—Elections in the Republic of Vietnam were held to attempt to legitimize government power, although that authority was not democratic. One of the most discussed elections in Vietnam was the one proposed for 1956 in the Final Declaration of the 1954 Geneva Conference but that was never held. It was to be a free election presumably to decide under whose leadership Vietnam would be united, but the delegates at Geneva provided no specific framework for the voting. No one in North or South Vietnam had any experience with free elections or really trusted them, and no outside government showed any desire to assume responsibility for conducting the vote. By the summer of 1955 it was clear there would be no national election. Diem then moved to arrange his own election in the South, and on October 23, 1955, he conducted a referendum to depose Bao Dai and to name himself chief of state. His brothers and other allies so thoroughly rigged the voting that over 98 percent of the ballots were cast in favor of the change.

In the fall of 1967 another election was held in the South in accordance with a new constitution that allowed for political parties and opposition to the government. Despite democratic appearances, the complicated voting procedures allowed the ruling junta of generals Nguyen Van Thieu and Nguyen Cao Ky to win election as president and vice president, respectively, while receiving only slightly more than one-third of the votes. In October 1971, in an obviously rigged election for president, Ky withdrew in protest from the contest, and Thieu won after receiving more than 90 percent of the votes cast. Both Diem in 1955 and Thieu in 1971 would likely have won handily in a fair election, but free and open elections were not the practice in Vietnam.

Elections in the United States (1964, 1968, 1972)—The presidential election contest of 1964 between incumbent Democrat Lyndon B. Johnson and Republican Barry M. Goldwater centered on their sharp ideological differences over domestic policy. The ultraconservative Goldwater opposed the social welfare programs that had grown since their inception in the New Deal of the 1930s. He even went so far as to suggest that Social Security be dismantled. Conversely,

Johnson's Great Society envisioned moving beyond the New Deal with initiatives such as national health insurance. On the mounting war in Vietnam, the militaristic Goldwater advocated U.S. bombing of North Vietnam, while Johnson presented himself as the peace candidate who wanted to limit the conflict. The president appeared appropriately firm but restrained in August when he ordered a single retaliatory air strike on North Vietnam during the Gulf of Tonkin Incident. Johnson easily defeated Goldwater with 61.1 percent of the popular vote and a margin of 486 to 52 in the electoral vote.

The 1968 election came at the height of the Vietnam War and in the wake of major upheavals in the struggle for civil rights. Senator Eugene McCarthy of Minnesota and Senator Robert F. Kennedy of New York challenged President Johnson for the Democratic nomination. As part of his review of Vietnam policy after the Tet Offensive, Johnson withdrew as a candidate for reelection on March 31, leaving Kennedy as the front runner. Kennedy, however, was assassinated in June, and the nomination ultimately went to Johnson's vice president, Hubert Humphrey of Minnesota. Before his nomination was official, the Democratic Party went through a tumultuous convention in Chicago marred by violent clashes between the police and youthful protestors opposed to the war. Meanwhile, the Republicans chose former vice president Richard Nixon as their candidate. There was also a third-party candidate, Governor George Wallace of Alabama, a segregationist, who ran as the American Independent Party nominee. In the campaign, Nixon led voters to believe that he had a secret plan for ending the war in Vietnam. Humphrey too wanted the war to end but for most of the campaign defended Johnson's policies and did not come out clearly for a negotiated settlement until shortly before the election. The contest was very close with Nixon winning 43.4 percent of the popular vote, Humphrey 42.7 percent, and Wallace 13.5 percent. Nixon got 301 electoral votes, Humphrey had 191, and Wallace had 46.

The Vietnam War remained a principal issue during the 1972 election, although voters were also concerned about inflation and unemployment. Nixon easily won renomination, and opinion polls showed that he had slightly more than a 50 percent approval rating for his performance in office. Many in the public appreciated his policy of gradually reducing the number of American troops in Vietnam, but he also had many critics for other controversial actions, such as the invasion of Cambodia. On the Democratic side there were several contenders for the nomination, including Wallace, who did well in some Democratic primaries until he was seriously injured by an assassination attempt and forced to end campaigning. Senator George McGovern of South Dakota won the nomination largely through reforms in the delegate selection process that made the voting at the party convention more open. McGovern took a strong moral position in opposition to American involvement in Vietnam and proposed immediate withdrawal of all U.S. forces from South Vietnam. His extreme position on the war did not resonate well with many voters who did not want out of Vietnam in a manner that appeared to be surrender or abandonment of an ally. McGovern was also unable to get voters interested in the arrest of five men inside the Democratic National Headquarters in the Watergate office complex in Washington in June. Finally, Nixon's aide Henry Kissinger announced in late October that "peace is at hand," although his secret negotiations still faced tough obstacles. The final outcome of the election was a landslide victory for Nixon with 60.7 percent of the popular vote and 520 electoral votes to McGovern's 37.5 percent and 17 electoral votes.

Flexible Response — Proposed in a 1959 book by General Maxwell Taylor, flexible response was a strategic doctrine in which the United States would prepare to use different levels of force depending on the level of threat posed by an adversary. Taylor contended that Eisenhower's massive retaliation doctrine presented an impossible choice of annihilation or capitulation not applicable to every situation. With the United States and the Soviet Union at a nuclear standoff by the late 1950s, their conflicting global interests increasingly involved them in hostilities in the so-called Third World. These were often wars of national liberation, that is, revolutionary wars or insurrections aimed at overthrowing existing governments. The internal conflict in Vietnam was typical of these wars because the insurrectionary force, the Vietcong, coupled its political goal with a radical program of economic and social change. In a 1961 speech Soviet premier Nikita Khrushchev declared that his government would sponsor wars of national liberation. The Kennedy administration adopted the flexible response concept to counter Khrushchev's challenge, and the president made Taylor his military adviser. Thus the creation of a counterinsurgency strategy and the expansion of U.S. aid to South Vietnam under Kennedy flowed directly from the flexible response idea.

Ford, Gerald R. (1913–) — During Gerald R. Ford's brief term as president of the United States (1974–1977), he presided over the final acts of the American war in Vietnam. A long-time member of Congress, Ford agreed to become Richard Nixon's vice president after Spiro Agnew resigned that post in 1973, and Ford then became president when Nixon resigned in August 1974 in the aftermath of the Watergate scandal. Congressman Ford had supported U.S. involvement in Vietnam and had criticized Lyndon Johnson for not using enough American military force, especially air power. By the time he entered the White House, Ford understood that the American people were ready to cast off the burden of the war. He created a Presidential Clemency Board to review cases of draft evaders. As the Khmer Rouge prepared to seize Phnom Penh in April 1975, he ordered the evacuation of the U.S. embassy there. Later in April North Vietnamese forces made their final assault on Saigon. Ford asked Congress to provide some additional funds to help the RVN, but he did not order into action or request from Congress permission to use U.S. forces to help the collapsing southern regime. On April 28 he ordered the evacuation of the U.S. embassy in Saigon. In May 1975 Cambodian soldiers seized a U.S. merchant ship, the *Mayaquez*, and Ford ordered a military rescue of the crew. Although forty-one U.S. Marines died in the rescue attempt while the crew was being released elsewhere, polls indicated that the public approved his decisive action. Ford gained the Republican nomination for president in 1976 but lost the general election to Democrat Jimmy Carter.

Free Fire Zones—Termed "specified strike zones" after 1965, free fire zones were areas of South Vietnam determined by Vietnamese provincial chiefs to be controlled by the National Liberation Front and thus enemy territory. U.S. forces could then use aerial bombing and artillery fire against any target in such a designated zone. Although warnings were sent to civilians to leave such areas for protected villages, many refused to leave or never received the warnings. It was also impossible to draw lines on maps indicating areas that were populated entirely by Vietcong supporters, but under the rules of engagement for U.S. commanders, anyone remaining in a free fire zone could be assumed to be the enemy. Civilian casualty numbers in free fire zones were often high. Antiwar protestors in the United States frequently cited free fire zones as examples of the oppressive and criminal way the war was conducted.

Fulbright, J. William (1905–1995)—Senator J. William Fulbright was chairman of the Senate Foreign Relations Committee (1959–1974). A Democrat from Arkansas, he served in the Senate from 1945 to 1974. A friend and political ally of Lyndon Johnson, he helped persuade his fellow senators to give the Gulf of Tonkin Resolution of August 1964 overwhelming support. He soon learned that Johnson had misrepresented the issues behind the resolution, and Fulbright also shifted his opinion on the war. He decided that intervention in Vietnam was not in America's interest and, in fact, threatened to weaken U.S. society. He convened hearings in 1966 to give war critics a platform for their views. In 1967 he published *The Arrogance of Power*, a book that offered a cogent liberal intellectual warning of the threat the war posed to American democracy and the nation's position in the world.

Geneva Conference (1954)—On May 8, 1954, this international conference in Geneva, Switzerland, began discussions aimed at ending the war between France and the Vietminh. The meeting produced two agreements of great significance in the history of the wars in Indochina. On July 20 France, the Democratic Republic of Vietnam, and Cambodia signed a cease-fire agreement ending hostilities in Vietnam, Cambodia, and Laos. On July 21 an unsigned Final

Declaration on Indochina was announced at the concluding plenary session. The conference had convened on April 26 and had first attempted unsuccessfully to arrive at a political settlement in Korea. The diplomats then took up the subject of Indochina, ironically, the day after the fall of the French garrison at Dienbienphu to Vietminh forces.

Great Britain and the Soviet Union, represented respectively by their foreign ministers, Anthony Eden and Vyacheslav M. Molotov, served as co-chairs of the Geneva Conference. The talks also included delegations from France, the United States, the People's Republic of China, Laos, Cambodia, the DRV (for the Vietminh), and the State of Vietnam (the government of Emperor Bao Dai). Secretary of State John Foster Dulles headed the U.S. contingent for the beginning of the Korean talks, but he left the conference on May 3. Undersecretary of State Walter Bedell Smith or Ambassador U. Alexis Johnson led the American delegation thereafter and had instructions to avoid direct participation in substantive negotiations. With the conference in progress, Pierre Mendèz-France became premier and foreign minister of France on June 17 and pledged to achieve a settlement by July 20 or resign.

The cease-fire arranged between France and the DRV provided for the temporary partition of Vietnam at the seventeenth parallel with French forces to regroup south of that line and Vietminh forces to the north. The terms allowed free movement of populations between the zones for three hundred days, prohibited either zone from receiving military reinforcement or from joining a military alliance, and created a commission with members from India, Poland, and Canada to monitor compliance. The unsigned declaration of July 21 also called for a "free general election" to be held throughout Vietnam in July 1956 to decide on reunification of the country. The partition and election formula allowed the fighting to end but left the political future of Vietnam undecided. Although present at the conference, the United States and the State of Vietnam were not formal parties to any of the agreements, but the American delegation issued a statement on July 21 taking note of the agreements and "refraining from the threat or use of force to disturb them." The 1956 election called for in the Final Declaration was never held.

Geneva Conference (1961–1962) — The Geneva Conference of 1961–1962 arranged a compromise settlement to the civil war in Laos, which had escalated due to U.S. and Soviet military aid to competing factions. Convened by Britain and the Soviet Union, this fourteen-nation conference began negotiations in May 1961. On July 23, 1962, an agreement was signed making Laos a neutral nation governed by a three-party coalition. Neutralist Prince Souvanna Phouma headed the government, which also included a pro-Western and a communist faction. The neutrality was immediately violated as the communist Pathet Lao, who controlled the eastern provinces and was a long-time ally of the Democratic Republic of Vietnam, allowed thousands of PAVN troops into the area. This border region became the site of the Ho Chi Minh Trail from North Vietnam into South Vietnam. At the same time, the Kennedy administration authorized the CIA to begin organizing military operations in Laos against the Pathet Lao and PAVN. The failure of the neutralization scheme in Laos also prompted Kennedy, and later Johnson, to be skeptical of proposals for a diplomatic settlement in the Vietnam conflict.

Goldwater, Barry M. (1909–1998)—An outspoken Cold War conservative, Senator Barry M. Goldwater of Arizona was the unsuccessful Republican nominee for president in 1964. He criticized Lyndon Johnson's Great Society platform as an expensive and excessive expansion of government power, and he challenged the restrained, advisory approach of U.S. policy in Vietnam. He advocated seeking "total victory" by carrying the war directly and massively to North Vietnam. Although he never actually advised using nuclear weapons against the North, the Johnson campaign was able to convey the impression that he had. His doctrinaire domestic views and saber-rattling international rhetoric hurt him with voters, and he received only 39 percent to Johnson's 61 percent in the 1964 balloting. He returned to the Senate in 1969. He remained a hawk on the Vietnam War and a major conservative force within the Republican Party.

Gook—A derogatory slang expression referring to anyone of Asian origin, the term "gook" was used by American troops in Vietnam with regard to any Vietnamese, whether enemy or ally. The origin of the word is unclear, but it was also used by U.S. soldiers during the Philippine War, the Pacific war against Japan, and the Korean War.

Great Society—The Great Society was Lyndon Johnson's term for the sweeping social reform legislation that he sought and gained from Congress primarily in 1964 and 1965 as he was also escalating American involvement in Vietnam. Many of these programs have changed the landscape of American public policy: Medicare, federal aid to education, federal protection of civil rights, and public television. The Great Society also created the multi-billion dollar War on Poverty program aimed at eliminating hunger and deprivation in America. These initiatives were always more important to Johnson than the war in Vietnam, and his initial decisions to expand U.S. help to Saigon while also keeping the size of that commitment concealed were an effort to manage foreign policy to protect his domestic policy. In 1970 he revealed to a biographer that the Great Society was "the woman I really loved" and that, from the beginning, he feared involvement "with that bitch of a war" that would cost him his dream of providing food, housing, education, and healthcare to those most in need. Although Medicare and some other reforms survived, much of his ambitious plan fell short of funds as the war effort grew and left a legacy of unfulfilled expectations criticized by both liberals and conservatives from their differing perspectives.

Gulf of Tonkin Incident—The Gulf of Tonkin Incident marked an important turning point in the American involvement in Vietnam. It began on August 2, 1964, when three North Vietnamese torpedo boats attempted to attack the U.S. destroyer *Maddox* in the Gulf of Tonkin off the coast of the DRV. The American vessel was on a highly secret DeSoto patrol to collect information about the North's defenses in support of small-scale South Vietnamese raids against DRV targets, a program known as OPLAN 34A. The *Maddox* and U.S. carrier-based fighters drove off the torpedo boats. Although the Johnson White House had already concluded that ways needed to be found to increase military pressure on North Vietnam to reverse the sagging fortunes of the Saigon government, it ordered no further retaliation but resumed the patrols on August 3 with the U.S.S. *C. Turner Joy* joining the *Maddox*.

On the night of August 4 the crews of the two destroyers reported that they were under attack again. Weather conditions were poor with extremely limited visibility. The indications of hostile activity came from radar and sonar interpretations and interceptions of enemy communications. The captain of the *Maddox* sent a follow-up radio message urging caution about the accuracy of the initial reports. Although aware of the confusion on the scene, officials in Washington prepared to retaliate, and on August 5 Johnson ordered single air raids against naval facilities in the DRV. Historical studies of the Gulf of Tonkin Incident have generally concluded that there was no attack on the American ships on August 4, but they also show that Johnson believed that there had been an attack when he ordered retaliation. It is also clear that many of Johnson's aides were eager to strike a blow against North Vietnam and were quick to conclude that the presumed second attack provided a welcome provocation. Having used armed force directly against the DRV once would now make it easier to do so in the future, and Johnson followed up this incident with a request for a congressional resolution giving him that authority.

Gulf of Tonkin Resolution—On August 7, 1964, the Gulf of Tonkin Resolution received unanimous approval in the U.S. House of Representatives and passed with only two dissenting votes in the Senate. Approved hastily in the wake of what legislators believed to be two unprovoked North Vietnamese attacks on U.S. Navy ships in the Gulf of Tonkin, the resolution authorized the president "to take all necessary measures to repel any armed attack against the forces of the United States and to prevent further aggression" and to use the armed forces "to assist any member or protocol state of the Southeast Collective Defense Treaty [SEATO] requesting assistance in defense of its freedom." Except for annual military spending approvals, this document was the single congressional authorization for what became the massive American war in Vietnam.

When the war later grew in size and controversy, many members of Congress regretted their vote for the resolution and, in fact, learned that the White House had concealed from them many of the facts of the Gulf of Tonkin Incident. Discovery of the secret DeSoto patrols behind the first attack raised doubts that it was unprovoked, and information about the confusion surrounding the second attack presented the possibility that Johnson had actually lied about it. Such doubts became major elements of the loss of credibility Johnson suffered as the war progressed. Finally in 1970, after Richard Nixon ordered U.S. forces into Cambodia, Congress repealed the Gulf of Tonkin Resolution in an expression of defiance to presidential war power.

Haiphong—The second largest city in North Vietnam, Haiphong is located 70 miles (112 kilometers) from Hanoi, and the Hanoi-Haiphong corridor was the economic center of the DRV. Haiphong was the North's principal seaport through which Soviet military aid and other foreign commerce entered the country. There were also railyards, shipyards, heavy industry, and electrical power plants in and around Haiphong that were targets for U.S. bombing. In 1972 the United States placed mines in the harbor that were removed after the 1973 cease-fire.

Halberstam, David (1934–)—A correspondent in South Vietnam for the *New York Times* in 1963 and 1964, David Halberstam became well known as one of several young journalists who began reporting on the weakness of the Diem government. His hard-hitting dispatches encouraged other reporters to question the optimistic assessments in official U.S. government reports on the progress of the RVN in combating the Vietcong insurgency. Halberstam shared a Pulitzer Prize in 1964 for the honesty of his reporting and also gained the unique distinction of having President John Kennedy ask the *New York Times* to transfer him from Vietnam. The *Times* refused. Halberstam wrote several books on or related to the war, including his best-selling, critical portrait of America's war leaders, *The Best and the Brightest*, which won the National Book Award in 1973.

Hanoi—The administrative capital of French Indochina from the 1880s until the Franco-Vietminh War, Hanoi became the capital of the Democratic Republic of Vietnam in 1954 and remains the capital of the Socialist Republic of Vietnam. Located in the heart of the Red River Delta, Hanoi is one of the oldest cities in Vietnam and has essentially been the country's capital since the eleventh century. Ho Chi Minh declared Vietnamese independence there in September 1945. His government was driven out of the city by the French in

1946 but made a triumphal return in 1954 after the Geneva Conference. North Vietnam's largest city and second in population only to Ho Chi Minh City (Saigon) in all of Vietnam, Hanoi experienced periodic bombardment during the war with the United States. These air strikes targeted military and industrial sites in the metropolitan area and usually not the center of the city. The population generally managed to withstand these air raids and the economic dislocation they caused, and most of the buildings in the city survived the war.

Helicopters—see **Aircraft**.

Hmong—The Hmong people of Laos were closely allied to the U.S. military effort in Indochina and provided an army of guerrilla soldiers for a CIA-directed secret war in Laos. Living in the mountains around the Plain of Jars in northern Laos, the Hmong used slash-and-burn agriculture to grow rice, corn, vegetables, and opium. They were often called "Meo" by the French and Americans, although that term had derogatory Chinese origins. During the French Indochina War, most of the Hmong supported the French against the Vietminh. In the early 1960s, the CIA worked with Hmong leader Vang Pao to recruit and supply guerrillas to attack communist Pathet Lao and North Vietnamese forces in the Plain of Jars and to protect U.S. radar facilities in the Laotian mountains critical to the air war against the DRV. During the American war, the Hmong lost much of their small population in the fighting. After the war Vang Pao and some Hmong came to the United States. Others fled from the communist regime in Laos to refugee camps in Thailand.

Ho Chi Minh (1890–1969)—Often called the father of the Vietnamese revolution, Ho Chi Minh organized the Indochina Communist Party and served as the founding president of the Democratic Republic of Vietnam from 1945 until his death. Ho was born in Nghe An Province in northern Annam, and his name at birth was Nguyen Sinh Cung. Educated in Hue at one of the leading schools in Vietnam, Ho first became a teacher like his father. In 1911 he left Vietnam working aboard a ship as a kitchen helper and began an odyssey that would not return him to Vietnam for thirty years. After stops and brief stays in Europe, Africa, and the United States, Ho went to France at the beginning of World War I. There he began using the pseudonym Nguyen Ai Quoc (Nguyen the Patriot). Much impressed by the anticolonial writings of Vladimir Lenin, he joined the French Socialist Party and helped organize Vietnamese in France who opposed French rule of their country. After failing to gain the attention of the Versailles Peace Conference to his country's plight, he helped found the French Communist Party. For colonial peoples, he believed, the class struggle and the struggle for national independence were the same.

During the 1920s and 1930s, Ho worked in the Soviet Union and China for the Communist International (Comintern). In 1925, in South China, he organized the Vietnamese Revolutionary Youth League, which trained communist activists, and in 1930, in Hong Kong, he helped form the Indochina Communist Party (ICP). Comintern leaders were not pleased, however, with his fuzzy blend of nationalism with communist doctrines and his tendency to act independently of Moscow. He was back in the Soviet Union during the mid-1930s but kept a low profile. In 1938, after the outbreak of the Sino-Japanese War, the Comintern allowed him to return to South China as a party organizer. He soon established contact with ICP members, such as Pham Van Dong and Vo Nguyen Giap, inside Vietnam. In the spring of 1941, after French colonial officials began collaborating with the Japanese on the possession of military bases in Indochina, Ho and the ICP created the League for the Independence of Vietnam, the Vietminh. Using the appeal of national independence and land reform, the Vietminh recruited Vietnamese into a united front to resist both the French and Japanese presence. Later in 1941 Ho secretly moved into an area in the mountains of northern Vietnam known as the Viet Bac. It was apparently his first return to Vietnam since 1911, and it was about this time that Nguyen Ai Quoc began using the name Ho Chi Minh (He Who Enlightens).

As resistance leaders, Ho and the Vietminh gained a following among Vietnamese, and at the time of Japan's defeat by the United States, in August 1945, they moved to assume leadership of an independent Vietnam. Quoting from the American Declaration of Independence and the French Declaration of the Rights of Man, Ho publicly proclaimed in Hanoi the founding of the Democratic Republic of Vietnam. He attempted unsuccessfully during 1946 to negotiate a peaceful transition from French colony to independent state. During the Franco-Vietminh War, 1946–1954, Giap was the chief military strategist, but, from his camp in the Viet Bac, Ho was the political head of the DRV. Ho was the diplomat who secured Soviet and Chinese assistance for the DRV forces, and he was the leader from whom the revolution gained its patriotic inspiration.

Following the French war, Ho was the best-known and most-respected, even revered, political figure in Vietnam. Despite his fame, he was always an enigma. He presented conflicting images as a Vietnamese nationalist and an international communist, as the people's beloved "Uncle Ho" and a ruthless political operative. Within the DRV government in Hanoi, he played an active role in the leadership and was determined to achieve reunification of his country. Although others increasingly made policy decisions, especially as Ho's health declined in the 1960s, he was influential in deciding on DRV support for the armed rebellion in the South and on responding to the American escalation with a strategy of protracted struggle. He died of a heart attack before his life's quest for an independent and united Vietnam was realized.

Ho Chi Minh City—see **Saigon**.

Ho Chi Minh Trail—The Ho Chi Minh Trail was the network of roads, trails, bridges, and camps that made up the main infiltration route for transporting men and supplies from the DRV into the RVN. It passed through Laos and Cambodia and entered into South Vietnam at various points from the Demilitarized Zone down through the Central Highlands. Originally a system of old, well-hidden jungle paths suitable only for foot and bicycle traffic, the trail eventually included hundreds of miles of all-weather, concealed roads built and maintained by the North Vietnamese Army with the assistance of Russian and Chinese engineers. Moving at night and hiding in camouflaged camps during the day, trucks traversed the trail carrying hundreds of reinforcements and hundreds of tons of modern weapons, medical supplies, and other war materiel each week. American military planners were well aware that this incredible logistical system made it possible for the NVA and Vietcong forces in the South to withstand the enormous fire power of U.S. forces and to replace battlefield losses. Many U.S. military operations, especially bombing campaigns, specifically targeted the trail, but none were any more than temporarily effective. Beginning in 1965, the air campaign known as Rolling Thunder included the trail as one of its targets. In 1968 Operation Commando Hunt began, and it concentrated solely on the supply route in Laos. Over a five year period it unleashed 3 million tons of bombs, the longest aerial interdiction campaign ever, but the soldiers and supplies continued to flow. The NVA's ability to obscure targets, provide antiaircraft protection, and quickly repair damage countered this massive assault. Arguably, the labor and sacrifice that the DRV put into building and keeping open the Ho Chi Minh Trail was the key to its ultimate success in the war against the RVN and the United States.

Hue—The city of Hue was South Vietnam's third largest city with an official population during the war of about 140,000 and an unofficial refugee population of many more. Located on the Perfume River 50 miles (80 kilometers) south of the Demilitarized Zone, it was the capital of the Nguyen dynasty from 1802 to 1945 and an educational and cultural center. Its impressive imperial palace, surrounded by a high-walled citadel, remained as a symbol of the traditional Vietnamese state. During the 1968 Tet Offensive, Hue, and especially the citadel, became the scene of intense and brutal fighting that required almost a month for U.S. and ARVN forces to dislodge the well-positioned Vietcong and NVA troops. In addition to the enormous military and civilian casualties caused by this battle, hundreds of civilian bodies in mass graves were found after the fighting, apparently victims of systematic executions when the Vietcong first took control of the city. Also, an estimated 50 percent of the once beautiful city was in ruins, and thousands of people were homeless.

Humphrey, Hubert H. (1911–1978) — Hubert H. Humphrey from Minnesota was first elected to the U.S. Senate in 1948 and became one of the leaders of the liberal Democrats in Congress. He worked hard for passage of John Kennedy's and Lyndon Johnson's reform programs, and Johnson chose him to be his vice-presidential running mate in 1964. Although he always backed the president in public, he disagreed privately with Johnson on the decision to begin bombing North Vietnam in 1965, and Johnson then excluded him from later discussions on troop deployments. After a visit to South Vietnam in 1966, however, Humphrey shifted to support military intervention, causing dismay among liberals. In 1968, after Johnson decided not to run for reelection and an assassin's bullet ended the life of Robert F. Kennedy, Humphrey emerged as the Democratic Party's nominee for president. His formal selection came at the party's national convention in Chicago that was marred by massive antiwar protests and clashes between police and young demonstrators. He began the campaign constrained by loyalty to the president and obligated by the party's platform to defend Johnson's handling of the war. He believed, however, that the time had come to end the bombing and seek a negotiated settlement, and in late September, despite Johnson's disapproval, Humphrey publicly endorsed that policy. At the end of October and only a week before the balloting, Johnson finally agreed to a bombing halt. Humphrey began rapidly closing the lead that his Republican opponent Richard Nixon had held and narrowly lost the election by less than 1 percent of the popular vote. Many observers believed he could have won if a few more days had remained to campaign. He was reelected to the Senate in 1970 and unsuccessfully contested George McGovern for the presidential nomination in 1972.

Ia Drang — The battle of Ia Drang Valley was the first major engagement between regular U.S. and North Vietnamese troops. Located below Chu Pong Mountain, the valley was a PAVN infiltration route from Cambodia into South Vietnam's Central Highlands. From November 14 to 17, 1965, heavy fighting occurred between units of the U.S. Army's First Cavalry Division and three PAVN regiments. The American commanders made good use of helicopter air mobility and air bombardment. Although U.S. losses totaled 305 killed, the estimate of enemy dead was ten times greater. Westmoreland considered the battle a success, and it led him to design further operations around air mobility with the goal of bringing unbearable losses on Hanoi's forces, the so-called attrition strategy. The PAVN commanders also learned lessons from Ia Drang about avoiding head-on clashes with large U.S. forces and moving in close — "clinging to the belt" of the Americans — to make it more difficult for U.S. officers to use air and artillery support.

Indochinese Communist Party — Created in 1930 at a conference in Hong Kong chaired by Ho Chi Minh, the Indochinese Communist Party (ICP) provided the primary political organization for the revolution against French colonialism. Although the party was dominated by Vietnamese throughout its existence, the Comintern had insisted on the name Indochinese to mute Ho's nationalist proclivities and in the belief that Vietnam alone could not break the French grip on Indochina. The Central Committee of the ICP created and led the Vietminh united front against the Japanese from 1941 to 1945. In 1945 Ho announced the dissolution of the party in the name of political harmony, but in fact it continued in secret. In 1951 the party took the name Vietnamese Workers Party, or Lao Dong, and created separate parties in Laos and Cambodia. The Lao Dong concluded the French war, undertook the implementation of socialism in North Vietnam, and conducted the war against the United States. In 1976 the party renamed itself once again. It returned to Ho's original choice of a name, the Vietnamese Communist Party, and was the only political party of the Socialist Republic of Vietnam.

Johns Hopkins University Speech — On April 7, 1965, Lyndon Johnson delivered a carefully prepared speech at Johns Hopkins University, in Baltimore, Maryland, in which he declared that he was ready for "unconditional discussions" in pursuit of peace in Vietnam. He further offered a billion-dollar economic development program for the Mekong River, modeled on the Tennessee Valley Authority in the United States, as a sign of good faith. As it was intended, the speech helped quiet mounting criticism that Johnson was not interested in negotiations, but read carefully the president's remarks offered no modification of the U.S. goal of preserving an independent, non-communist South Vietnam. The speech produced no diplomatic breakthrough, and the administration continued on its path of military escalation.

Johnson, Lyndon Baines (1908–1973) — As president of the United States (1963–1969), Lyndon B. Johnson made the decisions that eventually placed more than 500,000 U.S. military forces in Vietnam and launched an air war against targets in North and South Vietnam that surpassed World War II in the total tonnage of bombs dropped. These momentous decisions, coupled with his overbearing and devious personal style, led many observers to label the American war in Vietnam as Johnson's War.

As a powerful leader of the U.S. Senate, he supported the containment policies of Truman and Eisenhower, and as Kennedy's vice president he had traveled to South Vietnam to demonstrate American backing of Ngo Dinh Diem. When Johnson became president in November 1963, following Kennedy's assassination, he was determined to maintain the long-established U.S. commitment to the defense of South Vietnam. He shared the common belief in Washington that, if Hanoi gained control of all of Vietnam, success would fuel the ambitions of the Soviet Union and China and would pose the risk of a global nuclear war.

His political calculations also convinced him that a communist victory in Southeast Asia would expose his liberal Democratic administration to a fatal attack by Republicans and conservative Democrats. Although determined not to lose South Vietnam, he campaigned in 1964 by assuring voters that he was less likely to involve the United States in war in Asia than his opponent Barry Goldwater, who advocated bombing North Vietnam. In August of that election year, however, he managed to appear statesman-like when he ordered a limited bombing of the North in retaliation for an attack on U.S. ships in the Gulf of Tonkin and gained a near unanimous resolution from Congress authorizing the use of military power to defend U.S. forces. These firm but restrained moves helped him defeat Goldwater, but he failed to be candid with Congress and the public about the ambiguous circumstances surrounding the events in the gulf.

As political conditions deteriorated in South Vietnam in February 1965, Johnson approved regular bombing attacks against the North to bolster the South. In March he sent Marines to guard the Danang air base and then in July approved sending 40,000 U.S. combat troops to South Vietnam. Publicly he downplayed each of these steps. He did not want to provoke China or the USSR into direct intervention, but more significantly he did not want to invite a debate in the United States over a declaration of war against North Vietnam. Johnson's dramatic Great Society program for domestic reform was about to be voted on in Congress, and he wanted no conservative demand for a foreign war to defeat his agenda at home. His Great Society passed and Saigon was strengthened, but Johnson had embarked on a tragic course.

For most of the remainder of his term as president, Johnson tried to have "guns and butter." This expression meant that he fought a war that grew to huge proportions while simultaneously trying to advance the public welfare of Americans. Domestic programs were under funded, inflation increased, and the war stalemated. As the costs of the war became apparent, a credibility gap appeared between the president's public reassurances and the harsh realities of the conflict. Antiwar criticism grew, and Johnson increasingly resorted to efforts to quiet the protestors and to claim progress in the war. Finally in 1968, during the Tet Offensive, the contradictions within Johnson's conduct of the war brought his leadership to a crisis. He came to realize the escalation of the American war had gone far enough. On March 31, 1968, in a national television address, he announced that he was limiting U.S. bombing, was offering negotiations, and would not seek reelection as president. Johnson's political fear of losing in Vietnam had ended up destroying his political career, dividing Americans, frustrating his domestic reforms, and increasing the level of violence in Vietnam to the point that thousands of Americans and Vietnamese had died in the war.

Joint Chiefs of Staff (JCS) — In the National Security Act of 1947, Congress formalized the Joint Chiefs of Staff as advisers to the president on national defense strategy, logistics, and personnel. The JCS is composed of the chiefs of the Army, Navy, Air Force, and Marine Corps and a fifth member who is chairman. During the French war in Indochina, members of the JCS often expressed reservations about U.S. military involvement in Southeast Asia. Later, when the Eisenhower, Kennedy, and Johnson administrations had decided that the survival of South Vietnam was in America's interest, the JCS often favored a higher use of force than the White House desired. In fact, under Kennedy and Johnson, the JCS frequently felt frustrated and ignored as civilian officials, such as the secretary of defense and the president's national security adviser, decided force levels and strategies. The chiefs were also handicapped by interservice rivalries, a reluctance to appear disloyal to the commander in chief, and their natural tendency to recommend military solutions for what was largely a political conflict. Richard Nixon claimed that he was willing to remove political constraints from the JCS options, but, like his predecessors, he often found their suggestions unimaginative.

Kennedy, John Fitzgerald (1917–1963) — During his brief term as president of the United States (1961–1963), John F. Kennedy dramatically increased the number of U.S. military advisers in and the level of economic aid to South Vietnam. As a congressman and senator, Kennedy had supported Truman's containment policy and Eisenhower's decision to build a nation in South Vietnam around Ngo Dinh Diem. In the White House, Kennedy agreed to a compromise settlement of the Laotian civil war that gave the communist Pathet Lao a role in the government, and he endured seeming setbacks to the containment policy in Europe with construction of the Berlin Wall and in Cuba in dealing with Fidel Castro. Against this background, he became determined to uphold the U.S. commitment to support the RVN. He sent several key aides and Vice President Lyndon Johnson on trips to Saigon to show support of Diem and also to evaluate progress there. He became increasingly doubtful of Diem's ability but did not waver from belief in the vital importance of an independent South Vietnam to U.S. interests. When the Buddhist crisis of 1963 revealed the high level of domestic opposition to Diem in the RVN, Kennedy accepted a shift away from U.S. support of Diem himself but reaffirmed his agreement with the domino theory. With this knowledge, ARVN officers staged a coup against Diem on November 1, 1963, confident that American support of the RVN would continue. Kennedy was assassinated in Dallas, Texas, on November 22, and thus it is impossible to know how he might have responded to the ever greater threats to the survival of America's client state in South Vietnam that President Johnson eventually faced.

Kennedy, Robert F. (1925–1968) — A younger brother of John F. Kennedy, Robert F. Kennedy served as attorney general from 1961 to 1964 and as senator from New York, 1966–1968. He supported his brother's decisions to increase U.S. assistance to South Vietnam, and in 1965 he backed Johnson's escalation of American military involvement in Vietnam. Through 1966 and 1967 he became concerned about the growing magnitude of the conflict and the weakness of the Saigon government. He eventually came to favor a negotiated settlement of the war, but, being careful not to appear as a political opportunist, he was cautious not to challenge Johnson directly. The decline in the president's public approval ratings after the Tet Offensive and the strong political showing against Johnson in the New Hampshire primary of the less well-known Senator Eugene McCarthy as an antiwar candidate prompted Kennedy to declare his candidacy for president in 1968. Johnson withdrew from the race, and Kennedy appeared headed toward gaining the nomination when he won the California Democratic primary on June 4. That evening, however, he was assassinated by a lone gunman. With memories of the murders of his brother John in 1963 and of Martin Luther King Jr. only a month earlier still plaguing the public, the violent death of the charismatic Robert Kennedy profoundly shocked the nation.

Kent State University—On May 4, 1970, Ohio National Guardsmen shot and killed four students and wounded at least nine others following a weekend of antiwar protests on the campus of Kent State University. It was one of the worst moments in the history of domestic conflict over the Vietnam War. Following President Nixon's April 30 announcement of the invasion of Cambodia by U.S. forces, demonstrations occurred on campuses across the nation. On May 2 a group burned the Reserve Officers' Training Corps (ROTC) building at Kent State, and the governor ordered national guardsmen to the campus. On May 4 the soldiers used tear gas to disperse a noon rally protesting both the war and the guard's presence on campus. As the crowd retreated, some guardsmen inexplicably fired their weapons and killed Allison Krause, Jeffrey Miller, Sandra Scheuer, and William Schroeder and injured several others. Some of the victims were simply onlookers or students walking to class. News of the killings ignited more demonstrations and student strikes at hundreds of universities. On May 14 police fired on a dormitory at Jackson State University in Mississippi, killing two and injuring twelve. No criminal charges were made against the guardsmen or police, but in Ohio the state made a civil settlement with the victims' families. Public reaction to the Kent State incident ranged from outrage against the guardsmen's excessive use of force to approval of suppression of violent protests, such as burning buildings. The extent to which the war had divided American society was obvious.

Khe Sanh—In January 1968 the U.S. Marine base at Khe Sanh became the focus of U.S. attention in Vietnam, and the battle there with parts of three divisions of PAVN infantry remains one of the most discussed engagements of the war. The base was 14 miles (23 kilometers) south of the DMZ and 6 miles (10 kilometers) from the Laotian border. It was located on Route 9, the principal road from northern South Vietnam into Laos. General William Westmoreland declared Khe Sanh to be an important strategic location and built up the Marine garrison there to about 6,000 men, including about 300 ARVN rangers. He may also have been trying to lure the NVA into battle by providing a tempting target. On January 21 Hanoi's forces began ground assaults and artillery barrages that continued for weeks. U.S. resupply of the base was by parachute drops, and B-52 bombers and tactical aircraft dropped tons of high explosives on the attackers in what Westmoreland dubbed Operation Niagara.

The White House and the press followed the battle closely out of concern that Khe Sanh might become another Dienbienphu, with the DRV forces overrunning the garrison and achieving a dramatic victory. Westmoreland expressed assurance that U.S. air power prevented that from happening. When Hanoi launched its Tet Offensive late in January, however, Khe Sanh took on a different appearance. If it was a diversion planned by the DRV's General Vo Nguyen Giap, it had worked well to preoccupy the Americans and tie up valuable men and resources far from the cities. On the other hand, Giap's ploy cost his army dearly. Although the marines actually counted only 1,600 dead NVA soldiers during the weeks of fighting, a reasonable estimate of the casualties caused by the heavy bombing of the surrounding hills was ten to fifteen thousand.

Westmoreland later expressed pride in his decision to defend Khe Sanh and viewed it as a victory that prevented the enemy from gaining the valuable northwest corner of South Vietnam and that inflicted heavy losses on the PAVN. The general's critics said he fell victim to Giap's diversion. Operation Niagara ended on March 31, and by April 15 a joint Army-Marine-ARVN ground advance, Operation Pegasus, had relieved the base. On July 5 General Creighton Abrams, Westmoreland's successor as MACV commander, closed the Khe Sanh base.

Khmer Rouge—Meaning Red Khmer in French, the term "Khmer Rouge" referred originally to any Cambodian communist, but in the early 1970s it came to denote specifically an extremely radical faction of the Communist Party of Kampuchea (CPK) under the leadership of Pol Pot. This group seized control of the CPK by murdering hundreds of Khmer communists it considered too moderate or too closely connected with the Vietnamese communists. After overthrowing the inept government of Lon Nol in 1975, the Khmer Rouge embarked on a brutal effort to turn Cambodia, which they called Kampuchea, into a rural collective society. They forced the population out of the cities and turned the country into a forced labor camp. Worst of all, they exterminated more than 1.5 million people in the name of purifying the masses. Some of the victims were ethnic minorities but most were Khmers whom they characterized as contaminated with bourgeois, Western, and Vietnamese ideas. In 1979 the

Socialist Republic of Vietnam invaded Cambodia, installed a Cambodian communist government in place of the Khmer Rouge, and kept an occupation army in the country until 1989. The Khmer Rouge continued to survive in rural base areas, however, and remained a factor in Cambodian politics through the 1990s. Efforts to bring Khmer Rouge members to trial for the murders of the 1970s were frustrated because some members of later Cambodian governments were former Khmer Rouge members themselves.

Khrushchev, Nikita Sergeyevich (1894–1971)—Premier of the Soviet Union (1958–1964), Nikita S. Khrushchev tested the mettle of the youthful John Kennedy with assertive Soviet moves toward Berlin and with a declaration of support for wars of national liberation. Kennedy's determination to be firm in Vietnam was due in part to Khrushchev's challenges. The Soviet leader initially aided the DRV in the belief that a U.S. failure to sustain South Vietnam would hurt American influence in Asia and that Soviet assistance to Hanoi would improve his country's appeal to developing nations over that of its communist rival China. After the Cuban missile crisis of 1962, however, Khrushchev sought to lower tensions with the United States and began to reduce aid to the DRV. Leonid I. Brezhnev replaced Khrushchev as Soviet leader in 1964 and immediately increased help to Hanoi.

King, Martin Luther, Jr. (1929–1968)—Civil rights leader Martin Luther King Jr. received the Nobel Peace Prize in 1964 in recognition of his nonviolent methods in pursuit of human rights. He worked closely with Lyndon Johnson to help secure passage of the landmark Civil Rights Act of 1964 and Voting Rights Act of 1965, but he disagreed with Johnson's escalation of U.S. military force in Vietnam. To preserve the political alliance between the civil rights movement and the White House on domestic issues, King avoided criticizing Johnson's Vietnam policy directly through 1965 and most of 1966. Late in 1966 he became a co-chair of Clergy and Laity Concerned About Vietnam (CALCAV), and on April 4, 1967, he delivered a major address, "A Time to Break Silence," at a CALCAV meeting held at the Riverside Church in New York City. King specifically condemned America's use of violence in Vietnam, criticized the diversion of billions of dollars to the war that could be helping the disadvantaged through Johnson's Great Society programs, and voiced concern about the disproportionate percentage of African Americans in the combat forces and casualty figures in Vietnam. Some in the civil rights movement criticized him for mixing their cause with the antiwar movement. King's outspokenness angered Johnson, and administration officials characterized him as a radical. Actually, King's recommendation for a change in policy was moderate, namely, to end the bombing and begin negotiations. He continued to speak out against the war abroad and injustice at home until he was assassinated on April 4, 1968, in Memphis, Tennessee.

Kissinger, Henry A. (1923–) — A former professor of international relations at Harvard University, Henry A. Kissinger was the top foreign policy adviser of Presidents Richard Nixon and Gerald Ford and the principal U.S. negotiator of the Paris Peace Accords that ended the American military intervention in Vietnam. Nixon appointed Kissinger to be his national security adviser in 1969 and gave him the concurrent position of secretary of state in 1973. In 1975 Brent Scowcroft took over the office of national security adviser under Ford, but Kissinger remained secretary of state until 1977.

For Nixon and Ford, Kissinger was a major architect of détente with the Soviet Union and rapprochement with China, and he took an active diplomatic role in the Middle East. His first official connection with Vietnam policy actually came during the Johnson administration in 1967, when he served as a facilitator of eventually fruitless talks in Paris between U.S. and DRV representatives. In the Nixon White House he worked closely and privately with the president on developing aggressive approaches to the DRV. He encouraged secret bombing in Cambodia, the 1970 invasion of Cambodia, the 1971 ARVN thrust into Laos, and the heavy bombing of North Vietnam in Linebacker I and Linebacker II in 1972. He also conducted so-called back-channel negotiations with DRV diplomats Xuan Thuy and Le Duc Tho in Paris separate from the publicly known Paris Peace Talks. Through this military pressure and these secret contacts, Kissinger reached an agreement with Le Duc Tho, in October 1972, for a cease-fire, withdrawal of U.S. forces, release of U.S. prisoners, authorization of PAVN troops in South Vietnam, and continuation of the existing Saigon government while political realignments took place in the South. Kissinger announced to the press that "peace is at hand," which gave a further boost to Nixon's successful presidential race against George McGovern. President Nguyen Van Thieu of the RVN, however, rejected the proposed terms, and fighting continued. After Linebacker II (the "Christmas bombing" of North Vietnam in December) and Nixon's lavish but secret promises to Thieu of continued U.S. aid to the South, Kissinger and Tho signed the Paris Peace Accords on January 27, 1973, basically replicating the October agreement.

The Nobel Peace Prize for 1973 went to both Kissinger and Tho, but Tho declined to accept his portion because peace had not come to Vietnam. Fighting between North and South forces continued, and Washington became preoccupied with the Watergate investigation. A major Arab-Israeli war in October 1973, followed by the Organization of Petroleum Exporting Countries' (OPEC) drastic increase of oil prices, consumed Kissinger's energy and attention. As the RVN began to collapse in 1975, Kissinger advised President Ford that the United States must respond with military and economic assistance to Saigon to preserve America's international credibility as a great power. Ford understood, however, that there was no longer a military option for America in Vietnam, and Congress clearly was in no mood to authorize more American money or military might in

Indochina. Saigon fell, and Kissinger's diplomatic accomplishment in the Paris Peace Accords came to be viewed as having only created a "decent interval" between the departure of U.S. troops and the end of the RVN.

Korean War (1950–1953)—The Korean War paralleled the Vietnam War in several ways, and it influenced later U.S. decisions on Vietnam. North Korea had a communist government, which received support from the Soviet Union and China and was not recognized by the United States. In June 1950 its army invaded the Republic of Korea (ROK) in the South and almost overran the Korean peninsula. With authorization from the United Nations, the United States rushed troops to Korea and helped reverse the North Korean advance. By late 1950 U.S. troops were approaching Korea's border with China, and units of the Chinese army attacked south, pushing U.S. and ROK forces back to about the thirty-eighth parallel, which had originally divided the two Koreas. Heavy fighting ensued for more than two years until a cease-fire was arranged in 1953.

As it did later in Vietnam, Washington considered the war in Korea to be evidence of global communist aggression and thus believed that the containment policy required a military response to this threat. Harry Truman deployed thousands of U.S. troops to Korea without a congressional declaration of war, setting a precedent later followed by Lyndon Johnson in Vietnam. Truman also kept the war limited to Korea and did not want to engage China elsewhere, another similarity to later decisions in Vietnam. During the Korean War, the president removed General Douglas MacArthur from command of U.S. forces for publicly criticizing the limited war strategy, and this example may have made top American officers hesitate about challenging presidential choices in Vietnam. There were also significant historical and geographical differences between the two wars, especially the contrast between conventional invasion in Korea and armed insurrection in Vietnam. Regardless, the example of successfully defending South Korea against a communist military assault contributed to the U.S. decision to offer military defense to South Vietnam. During the Vietnam War, the ROK provided some 50,000 soldiers to supplement U.S. and ARVN troops.

Lansdale, Edward Geary (1908–1987)—A U.S. Air Force officer who often worked secretly with the Central Intelligence Agency, Edward G. Lansdale became legendary in Southeast Asia as a counterinsurgency expert. After having helped Ramon Magsaysay establish a political base in the Philippines, Lansdale went to Saigon in 1954 on orders from CIA chief Allen Dulles to do the same for Ngo Dinh Diem. He befriended Diem and helped him with advice on how to win popular support. He arranged for bribes to some of Diem's political rivals to gain their cooperation, and he organized sabotage and propaganda operations aimed at North Vietnam. He did not have the level of success with Diem, however, that he had achieved with Magsaysay in broadening his political base.

Lansdale and his activities served as a model for the character "Alden Pyle" in Graham Greene's novel *The Quiet American* (1955). In 1956 Lansdale went to the Pentagon as a specialist on covert operations, and in 1961 he advised the Kennedy administration on creating a counterinsurgency plan for Vietnam. Lansdale worked on Operation Mongoose, a secret effort to weaken or remove Cuban leader Fidel Castro, and in 1963 he retired from active military duty as a major general. In 1965 he went back to Vietnam as a civilian pacification aide to the U.S. ambassador, but he was largely frustrated in his effort to give some political legitimization to the Saigon government.

Le Duc Tho (1910–1990)—Le Duc Tho was the principal negotiator for the Democratic Republic of Vietnam (DRV) in the Paris Peace Talks and personally conducted most of the secret negotiations with Henry Kissinger beginning in 1969. Tho (whose real name was Phan Dinh Khai) was a founding member of the Indochinese Communist Party in the 1930s and spent six years in a French prison. During the Vietminh war against France, he headed the resistance movement in southern Vietnam. Elected to the Politburo in 1955, Tho continued as a principal party leader in South Vietnam during the war against the Americans. He was a determined and disciplined diplomat who held firm in the Paris talks to Hanoi's insistence on combining political and military issues. He worked out the compromises with Kissinger that led to the tentative agreement of October 1972. The two men signed the final Paris Peace Accords on January 27, 1973. He declined the 1973 Nobel Peace Prize (to be shared with Kissinger) because, he said, the war in Vietnam continued. Returning to South Vietnam, he helped direct the final DRV assault on Saigon in 1975. He also supervised Vietnam's invasion of Cambodia in 1978–1979. He resigned his leadership positions and retired in 1986.

Linebacker I and Linebacker II—see **Air War**.

Lodge, Henry Cabot (1902–1985)—A former senator, ambassador to the United Nations, and Republican nominee for vice president, Henry Cabot Lodge filled key diplomatic roles during the Vietnam War. As U.S. ambassador in Saigon, August 1963 to June 1964, he implemented Washington's decision to allow the coup against Ngo Dinh Diem to proceed, but he denied claims in some accounts that he encouraged the coup. During a second tour as ambassador in Saigon, July 1965 to April 1967, he participated in unsuccessful talks with Polish diplomats to start peace negotiations with Hanoi. In 1968 Lodge was one of the Wise Men, a group of former officials, who advised Lyndon Johnson against further escalation of the war, and in 1969 he went as a U.S. delegate to the Paris talks with representatives of the DRV.

Lon Nol (1913–1985)—From March 1970 to April 1975, Lon Nol headed the government of Cambodia. For many years he was a trusted official, often in military positions, in the government of Prince Norodom Sihanouk. Although Sihanouk tried to maintain Cambodia's neutrality during the Vietnam War, Lon Nol was strongly anticommunist and often urged the prince to deny North Vietnam and the Vietcong use of Cambodian territory. In March 1970, while Sihanouk was away from Cambodia, the National Assembly voted to oust Sihanouk and to give full power to Prime Minister Lon Nol and Deputy Prime Minister Prince Sisowath Sirik Matak. Opinions among historians differ over responsibility for this coup. Some accounts portray Lon Nol as ambitious, but others find evidence that he was a reluctant leader. U.S. officials welcomed Lon Nol's hostility toward the Vietnamese communists, but direct American involvement in the change of government was not apparent. Lon Nol remained prime minister until 1972, when he became president of a newly designated Khmer Republic. He was unable to force the PAVN and Vietcong out of their Cambodian sanctuaries and could not counter the rise of the internal Cambodian communist movement, the Khmer Rouge. He proved to be an inept leader, and Cambodia fell into violence and social chaos. In 1975 he fled to the United States as the Khmer Rouge seized power in Cambodia.

Mao Zedong (Mao Tse-tung) (1893–1976)—The leader of the Chinese Communist Party from 1935 until his death, Mao Zedong had a great influence on Ho Chi Minh and other Vietnamese communists, both as a revolutionary theorist and as a direct supporter. Mao was a founding member of the Chinese Communist Party in 1921 and led it to victory over the Nationalist Party in the Chinese Civil War. He became the first president of the People's Republic of China (PRC) in 1949 and remained the supreme Chinese leader throughout the rest of his life. As a theorist of Marxism-Leninism, he adapted that ideology, inspired by industrial Europe, to agrarian rebellions in Asia. From his experience, Mao also developed the strategy of "people's war," a form of protracted guerrilla warfare in which a disciplined and politically conscious force can withstand and defeat a materially stronger but less motivated adversary. The Vietnamese communists followed his people's war model, although they modified it to include external assistance and conventional tactics. After creation of the PRC, Mao took an active role in advising and aiding the Vietnamese revolutionary war against the French and the Americans. He met with Ho on several occasions and arranged substantial assistance in materiel and technology. Mao used support for the Vietnamese as part of his campaign, known as the Cultural Revolution, to maintain revolutionary fervor in China. As tensions grew in the 1960s between the PRC and USSR, however, Mao began to contemplate a rapprochement with the United States. Mao and Richard Nixon had a dramatic meeting in Beijing in

1972 that greatly eased tensions between China and America, lowered the strategic importance of Vietnam to the United States, and helped set the international stage for the negotiated exit of all U.S. combat troops from Vietnam in 1973.

Martin, Graham A. (1912–1990)—Serving as the last U.S. ambassador to South Vietnam from 1973 to 1975, Graham A. Martin tried to assure President Nguyen Van Thieu of continued U.S. support, while he also lobbied Congress for support of the RVN. His encouragement of Thieu and his optimistic reports to Washington about the situation in Saigon delayed U.S. embassy preparations for the final North Vietnamese offensive against the South's capital city. When he belatedly began the evacuation of the embassy on April 29–30, 1975, it turned into a harrowing helicopter lift of people from rooftops. The hasty departure also left behind many South Vietnamese who were closely associated with the Americans and who fell victim to the North Vietnamese. Martin himself was one of the last Americans to leave Saigon.

Mayaquez Incident (1975)—see **Ford, Gerald R.**

McCarthy, Eugene J. (1916–)—In November 1967 Senator Eugene McCarthy declared himself to be an antiwar candidate for president of the United States to challenge the policies of President Johnson. A Democrat from Minnesota who entered the Senate in 1959, McCarthy had voted for the Gulf of Tonkin Resolution but, like some other liberal senators, became a critic of the massive use of U.S. force in a conflict he came to view as essentially a civil war. As a senator and as a candidate for the Democratic nomination for president, he challenged Johnson's policies on moral and constitutional grounds and advocated a negotiated American withdrawal from the war. Although a long-shot candidate against the politically powerful Johnson, McCarthy attracted many liberal, intellectual, and college-student supporters. After the Tet Offensive, he won 42 percent of the vote in the New Hampshire primary to Johnson's 48 percent. His surprisingly strong showing encouraged Senator Robert F. Kennedy of New York to also enter the race with an antiwar platform. After Johnson withdrew as a candidate, Kennedy pulled ahead of McCarthy for the nomination until Kennedy was assassinated in June. The Democratic nomination ultimately went to Vice President Hubert Humphrey, but McCarthy's bold challenge to Johnson had injected the antiwar position into the mainstream political process. An idealist, McCarthy was disappointed by the political process and chose not to run for reelection to the Senate in 1970. He later wrote extensively on politics and took on the role of a political gadfly.

McGovern, George S. (1922–)—Senator George S. McGovern was one of the leading congressional critics of the Vietnam War and ran unsuccessfully against Richard Nixon in the 1972 presidential election. After serving as a bomber pilot in World War II and receiving a Ph.D. degree in history at Northwestern University, he entered Democratic Party politics in South Dakota and won election to the U.S. Senate in 1962. Domestically, he took extremely liberal positions on medical care, aid to education, labor, and agriculture, and in foreign policy he argued for restraint in military spending and criticized Washington's preoccupation with Fidel Castro and assistance to corrupt dictatorships in the name of anticommunism. Although he voted for the Gulf of Tonkin Resolution, he was an early opponent of U.S. military escalation in Vietnam. He eventually called for withdrawal of U.S. forces and cosponsored a Senate resolution with Republican Senator Mark Hatfield of Oregon urging that course in 1970. With some good political strategy, he received the Democratic nomination for president in 1972 and boldly pledged an immediate end to the war if voted into office. Although, like McGovern, much of the American electorate wanted peace in Vietnam, the Nixon campaign was able to portray the Democrat as a dangerous radical who was far from mainstream America. Also, McGovern could not interest voters in the suspicious role of the White House in the burglary of the Democratic National Headquarters at the Watergate building in Washington, D.C. Nixon won a landslide victory. In 1974 McGovern successfully held on to his Senate seat, but he lost it in 1980 during the conservative political surge led nationally by Ronald Reagan.

McNamara, Robert S. (1916–) — As secretary of defense (1961–1968), Robert S. McNamara was one of the architects of U.S. military intervention in Vietnam, but he later came to doubt and then regret his policy decisions. A successful president of Ford Motor Company, he brought his style of business management based upon quantitative measurements to his leadership position in the Pentagon. Arrogant about his own ability and the power of the American military, McNamara shared the Cold War beliefs of his generation of national leaders that the United States should and could defeat communist aggressors anywhere, including Vietnam. He favored the concept of "flexible response" to bring just the right level of force to bear on a situation. Consequently, he urged Lyndon Johnson in 1964 and 1965 to bomb North Vietnam and send U.S. combat troops to South Vietnam in gradually increasing numbers in order to shore up the faltering Saigon government. Before the end of 1965, however, he privately began expressing doubts to Johnson about achieving a military solution in Indochina. Through 1966 and 1967 he maintained a confident outward image of satisfaction with U.S. progress in aiding South Vietnam, while his private doubts grew to virtual despair as the killing and destruction increased with no sign of victory. Johnson came to question McNamara's judgement and allowed the secretary to resign to take a position as head of the World Bank. McNamara remained publicly silent about the war until 1995, when he published his memoir, *In Retrospect*, in which he acknowledged that he and others were wrong to favor military intervention. Although it was a remarkable confession by a powerful official, the book renewed old criticisms of his role in what many Americans had called "McNamara's War."

Media—Media coverage of the war, specifically newspaper, magazine, and television reporting, became a point of controversy among Americans. Some American political and military leaders came to believe that negative and distorted coverage by antiwar journalists eroded public support for the American war effort and contributed to U.S. defeat. The reporters themselves, and other Americans critical of the war, often responded that the media simply reported the flaws in U.S. policies and performance and did not create them. In fact, media coverage of the war was neither as biased as its critics claimed nor as objective as its defenders maintained.

Historical studies of journalism during the war reveal that major print and electronic news outlets generally reflected the views of national leaders and that public opinion often followed its own course independent of the press. Early in the war up to the Tet Offensive, the principal newspapers, magazines, and television networks overwhelmingly supported U.S. intervention. Their reporters relied heavily on official sources of information—news releases, official press briefings, and interviews with officials—and thus their stories basically followed government explanations and accounts. There were some intrepid young correspondents, such as David Halberstam and Neil Sheehan, who wrote about discrepancies between what they observed and what they were told, but even they seldom questioned basic U.S. policies. When the Tet Offensive erupted, some journalists reported that the U.S. command had been caught unprepared and had suffered a serious setback. Others, such as senior CBS News correspondent Walter Cronkite, were more cautious in their assessments, but they expressed doubts about Johnson's previous claims of progress and called for a negotiated withdrawal from Vietnam. Westmoreland later alleged that such reports were defeatist, but, in fact, they were remarkably similar to reevaluations of policy then secretly occurring within the White House. As for public opinion, polls indicated that support for the war had started declining long before Tet. There was an actual increase in public approval of the military's performance throughout the heavy Tet fighting, but Johnson's personal approval rating dropped sharply. As the war continued through 1968 and beyond, polls showed the American people increasingly turning against U.S. involvement because of the ever-growing number of American casualties, a fact the press reported but did not create. As a significant portion of the public and members of Congress criticized Nixon's continuation of the fighting, and especially his sending of troops into Cambodia in 1970, the media joined this chorus. In his political career, Nixon often had a stormy relationship with the press, and he became convinced that the media was his enemy and tried to retaliate against journalists in various ways.

One media critic labeled the Vietnam War "the living-room war" because of film footage from Vietnam broadcast into people's homes daily on popular television news programs. This technology had not been available in previous wars, and it could at times project dramatic images, such as the execution of a Vietcong suspect on a Saigon street in 1968 or the chaotic helicopter evacuation of the U.S. embassy in 1975. In general, however, television camera crews seldom caught scenes of actual fighting nor took close-ups of wounded Americans. Instead, the televised images consisted of generic shots, such as helicopters landing or soldiers wading in flooded rice patties. The narration of these two-to-three minute reports was seldom very analytical. Television also broadcast pictures of antiwar protests in the United States to the delight of the demonstrators and discomfort of the government. Because the cameras frequently focused on picturesque and unkempt members of the crowd, many viewers got a distorted impression that all protestors were bums or so-called hippies. Television and the other media reported on the war in less than perfect ways, but it is historically inaccurate to conclude that journalism determined the outcome of the war.

Medical Support—U.S. military medical support in Vietnam provided for higher survival rates for injured soldiers than in previous wars. An official U.S. Army study indicates that 19 percent of U.S. casualties died from their wounds in the Vietnam War, compared with 26 percent in the Korean War and 29 percent in World War II. Several factors accounted for this change. More effective medicines and therapies were available, and, because the PAVN and Vietcong often used low-technology weapons, such as booby traps, more wounds were treatable injuries to the extremities than in other wars where wounds might be from high-explosive artillery or bombs. Another factor was the absence of shifting geographical fronts in Vietnam, which meant that dozens of basically permanent hospitals were constructed, equipped, and staffed throughout South Vietnam to provide quality medical care. There were also general hospitals in Okinawa and Japan for more severe cases. The single greatest innovation in medical support, however, was the extensive use of medical evacuation with specially outfitted "medevac," or "dustoff," UH-1 helicopters. These air ambulances could sometimes have a wounded soldier out of combat and in a hospital within twenty minutes of his injury. The average time from injury to hospitalization was 2.8 hours, compared to 6.3 hours in Korea and 10.5 hours in World War II. In addition to wounds received in action or injuries from accidents, tropical diseases and fevers also placed troops in hospitals. One of the most common ailments was falciparum malaria, which was resistant to treatment. It could be controlled if soldiers took a preventative medicine called chloroquine, but many did not and became infected with malaria.

Mekong River and Delta—Originating in Tibet, the Mekong River travels 2,700 miles (4,184 kilometers) to where it empties into the South China Sea south of Ho Chi Minh City (Saigon) from a huge 26,000 square-mile delta. The river forms much of the border between Thailand and Laos, goes through Cambodia, and then into Vietnam. Despite its rich soil, the delta was sparsely populated until the seventeenth century. French planters built canals and dikes and converted the delta into a highly productive rice-growing region largely populated by tenant farmers working for absentee landlords. The harshness of the labor system and the thick jungle terrain, which provided cover for bases, made the delta a center of guerrilla resistance against the French and later the Republic of Vietnam. Despite the RVN's strategic hamlet program and U.S. and ARVN operations in the region, much of it remained a base area for the Vietcong and NVA. The delta was the scene of heavy fighting on many occasions, especially during the Tet Offensive. Well-supplied NVA units attacked Saigon from the delta during the final Northern offensive of 1975.

Military Assistance Advisory Group (MAAG)—Created by the Truman administration in 1950, the Military Assistance Advisory Group, Indochina (MAAG-I) initially monitored U.S. aid to French forces. After withdrawal of the last French troops from Indochina in 1955, Washington redesignated MAAG-I as Military Assistance Advisory Group, Vietnam (MAAG-V) with a separate MAAG created for Cambodia. MAAG-V supervised the training and organization of the Army of the Republic of Vietnam (ARVN). The number of these U.S. military advisers in Vietnam was never more than 740 during the 1950s. By 1960 they had fashioned a South Vietnamese army of 150,000 men, but it was better prepared for defense against conventional invasion than for defeating an armed insurgency. As part of its moves to improve the ARVN's counterinsurgency effort, the Kennedy administration increased the size of the U.S. advisory force, created the Military Assistance Command, Vietnam (MACV) in 1962, and phased out MAAG-V.

Military Assistance Command, Vietnam (MACV)—Established in February 1962, the Military Assistance Command, Vietnam, was a joint service headquarters that directed all U.S. forces in the Republic of Vietnam. Its chain of command and geographical responsibilities were complex, which hampered its effectiveness from its beginning until it was dissolved in March 1973. Through most of its existence, MACV's commander in chief was General William C. Westmoreland (June 1964–July 1968) or General Creighton W. Abrams (July 1968–June 1972). They were not independent theater commanders but reported to the commander in chief, Pacific (CINCPAC), in Honolulu. They did have direct communication access, however, to the Pentagon and the U.S. ambassador in Saigon. MACV controlled all U.S. military assets—army, navy, air force, and marines—in the RVN, but CINCPAC directed the air war against North Vietnam, naval operations at sea, and operations in Laos. The MACV commander and senior staff officers also had advisory responsibility for the ARVN but not command and control of the South Vietnamese units. While this arrangement made organizational and political sense, the MACV headquarters paid less attention to ARVN problems and development as it got more involved in larger U.S. operations. This same preoccupation with large unit sweeps also led to MACV neglect of pacification programs.

Moratorium (1969)—The Moratorium demonstrations in the fall of 1969 marked the largest organized nationwide protests against the Vietnam War. Several veteran organizers of antiwar activities worked together during 1969 to try to find a way to overcome the anarchic image of the peace movement conveyed by televised reports of violence at the Democratic National Convention in August 1968. They also wanted to enlist more moderate and mainstream opposition to the war. As a result of their efforts, millions of citizens in dozens of cities across America expressed opposition to the war on October 15, 1969. The activities varied: 100,000 people gathered on Boston Common to hear George McGovern speak; 250,000 marched in Washington, D.C.; the mayor of New York City decreed a day of mourning and ordered flags lowered to half-staff; special church services were held; candlelight vigils remembered those killed in the war; some people honked their car horns in protest; a few soldiers in uniform wore black arm bands. Overall, the actions were moderate and orderly and demonstrated widespread opposition to the war. In a televised address on November 3, President Nixon tried to diminish the impact of the Moratorium by calling upon the "silent majority" of patriotic Americans to back his Vietnamization policy and bring about an honorable peace in Vietnam. On November 15 a second Moratorium day brought out 750,000 to rally in the nation's capital, 250,000 in San Francisco, and other large demonstrations elsewhere. The organizers were unable to continue such large events on a regular basis, but millions of Americans had made opposition to the war respectable and undeniable.

Munich Analogy—Among the presumed lessons of World War II, the Munich analogy was one of the strongest in the minds of postwar U.S. leaders. At the 1938 Munich Conference, British prime minister Neville Chamberlain agreed to German possession of part of Czechoslovakia in an effort to appease Adolph Hitler's demands for territorial expansion. Six months later Nazi forces took all of Czechoslovakia, and Hitler then demanded territory in Poland. This experience convinced American strategists that aggressive dictators could only be deterred by prompt and forceful action. Believing that the Soviet Union, People's Republic of China, North Korea, and North Vietnam posed a similar threat, U.S. presidents approved American military intervention in Korea and

Vietnam to stop communist expansionism before it could spread. The containment policy and the domino theory were other expressions of the same idea.

My Lai Massacre—see **Atrocities**.

Napalm—A jellied gasoline mixture, napalm is an incendiary weapon developed during World War II, used by the French against the Vietminh, and widely employed by the U.S. Air Force for close tactical air support in South Vietnam. It is an effective and terrifying weapon that produces an intense heat that kills by burning or asphyxiation. When used in or near villages, it often caused civilian casualties and became a particular concern of the antiwar movement. The manufacturer of napalm, Dow Chemical Company, often had its offices, plants, and campus job recruiters targeted by protestors. A nationally circulated newspaper photograph in 1972 of a naked Vietnamese girl injured by and running from a napalm attack became one of the most powerful images of the cruelty of the war.

National Liberation Front (NLF)—Organized in December 1960, the National Front for the Liberation of South Vietnam, or the National Liberation Front as it was commonly known, became the Communist Party's vehicle for armed insurgency against the Ngo Dinh Diem government. Like its predecessor, the Vietminh, the NLF was a classic model of communist united-front strategy. The Diem regime's oppression in South Vietnam had created genuine hatred for and fear of the Saigon government, and many of the people who joined the NLF were not communist but were simply angry. Communist Party (then known as Lao Dong or Workers Party) leaders in Hanoi authorized their members in the South to organize this resentment but to avoid the name Communist and to emphasize Diem's repression and the goal of national reunification, not radical ideology. Although the NLF was not entirely communist and never called itself communist, South Vietnamese and American officials labeled it the Vietcong, meaning Vietnamese Communist. The term "Vietcong" was also widely used for the soldiers of the NLF, whether they were regulars or guerrillas, of what the NLF called its People's Liberation Armed Forces (PLAF).

Because the NLF was able to mount a serious military and political challenge to the RVN, the United States steadily increased its military role in South Vietnam until Lyndon Johnson finally ordered a massive U.S. intervention. During the war there was an almost continuous debate among Americans between the official U.S. position that the NLF represented DRV aggression against the South and the view of many critics of U.S. policy that the NLF was a movement in the South, and hence its insurrection amounted to civil war. There was an element of truth in both arguments. Many of the NLF's best fighters led the Tet Offensive in 1968 and were lost in the heavy fighting that followed. After Tet, North Vietnamese forces increasingly took a greater role in the war in the South. When the PAVN took control of South Vietnam in 1975, only a few NLF officials ended up being included in the new national government.

Navarre Plan—Designed by the commander of French forces in Indochina, General Henri Navarre, and his staff, the Navarre Plan of 1953 was portrayed as a strategy for French victory after seven years of war. Actually, French leaders understood that it was, at best, a plan that would help secure continued U.S. support and make possible an honorable French withdrawal from the Indochina conflict. The new Eisenhower administration welcomed the appointment of Navarre in 1953 to head the French forces. He was a competent and aggressive officer. The general's plan provided a larger and better trained Vietnamese National Army, the Vietnamese soldiers who served Bao Dai's State of Vietnam. It pledged greater independence for Vietnam, Laos, and Cambodia within the French Union. It also envisioned more offensive operations and less static defense. The United States responded to the plan positively with increased aid, but it was never really implemented because the course of events at Dienbienphu increasingly occupied Navarre and his staff.

Ngo Dinh Diem (1901–1963)—As prime minister of the State of Vietnam (1954–1955) and president of the Republic of Vietnam (1955–1963), Ngo Dinh Diem left an ambiguous legacy in South Vietnam as both a nationalist alternative to Ho Chi Minh and as the source of his own regime's failure. Diem's father was an official of the emperor's court but resigned when the French stripped the emperor of all political power. The Ngo family was Roman Catholic, and Diem considered entering the priesthood. He was the third of six sons in a family of nine children, and his next elder brother, Ngo Dinh Thuc, became a priest and eventually an archbishop. Diem graduated from the University of Hanoi's law school, however, and began a promising career as a public administrator. He was a provincial governor at age twenty-five and at age thirty-two joined the cabinet of the youthful emperor Bao Dai. He soon resigned when it was clear that French authorities would continue to disallow power to the court, and he dropped out of politics for more than a decade. In 1945, after the August Revolution, he rejected an offer from Ho Chi Minh of a position in the DRV government. Diem believed the Vietminh were responsible for the murder of his eldest brother, Ngo Dinh Khoi, and Diem left Vietnam in 1950 after an assassination attempt on him.

With his reputation as being an anti-French and anticommunist nationalist growing, Diem was in Europe and the United States from 1950 to 1954. He lived in a Maryknoll seminary in New Jersey for two years and met several prominent American Catholics, including Cardinal Francis Spellman and Senators John

Kennedy and Mike Mansfield. Through his youngest brother, Ngo Dinh Luyen, Diem also kept in contact with Bao Dai. As the French negotiated their exit from Indochina at the Geneva Conference, Bao Dai named Diem prime minister in June 1954. It is likely that Bao Dai believed Diem would be able to attract U.S. support and protection against the DRV.

In 1955, with the help of his large family, especially his younger brother Ngo Dinh Nhu, Diem staged a referendum that deposed Bao Dai and made Diem president of the RVN. Most of the key positions in his government went to his family or to Catholics, who comprised only 10 percent of the population. Diem himself was personally honest and patriotic, but his regime was characterized by nepotism and favoritism, and the government's secret police, directed by Nhu, sought to repress all political opposition. Discontent in the South grew into an armed insurgency, which Hanoi helped organize as the National Liberation Front (NLF).

U.S. officials harbored doubts about Diem's leadership from the time he became prime minister in 1954. He was reclusive, eccentric, and clannish—qualities not well suited to building political support. For a time, Washington overlooked these liabilities and trumpeted him as a miracle man who was creating an independent Republic of Vietnam despite the legacies of colonialism and the threat of communist attack. As he became more oppressive, including forbidding Buddhist observances in a country that was 80 percent Buddhist, he faced growing challenges from Buddhist monks, students, peasants, NLF guerrillas, and even members of his own armed forces. A group of generals plotted a coup against Diem, which U.S. officials knew about and chose not to stop. The coup began on November 1, 1963, and the next day Diem and Nhu were murdered by soldiers supporting the coup. President Kennedy was shocked. He had wanted Diem removed but not killed.

Ngo Dinh Nhu (1910–1963)—Younger brother of Ngo Dinh Diem, Ngo Dinh Nhu was the ruthless gray eminence of Diem's government. Educated in France as an archivist, he worked on colonial archives in Indochina and also became an organizer of Catholic labor unions. Indeed, his talent was organization, and his principal work was promoting and protecting his brother's career. His official position in the RVN government was minister of the interior, but his real source of power was as head of a secret, Mafia-like party, the Can Lao. Membership in the Can Lao was required to obtain important government and military positions in South Vietnam, and it was used to spy on people and to operate lucrative criminal activities. More openly, Nhu headed the government police, created a fascist-style uniformed youth force, and promoted an obscure philosophy called "personalism." His wife, Tran Le Xuan, but usually referred to as Madame Nhu, was a forceful and controversial woman who participated fully in these and related groups and who served as somewhat of a First Lady for the RVN, since Diem was never married. Nhu's manipulation and intimidation even came to include suppression of religious observances by the Buddhist majority, and he became a genuine political liability for Diem. U.S. officials urged the RVN president to remove him, but Diem refused. Nhu had some secret talks with the DRV in 1963, but whether they were peace overtures or a bluff to counter American pressure on him is not clear. Nhu was widely despised in South Vietnam, and when the coup against Diem occurred on November 1, 1963, he was brutally murdered along with Diem.

Nguyen Cao Ky (1930–)—A colorful pilot and air force officer, Nguyen Cao Ky was premier of the Republic of Vietnam from 1965 to 1967 and vice president from 1967 to 1971. Born in Son Tay province near Hanoi, Ky took pilot training in France and returned to Vietnam in 1954 at the end of the French-Vietminh War. He rose rapidly in rank in the RVN Air Force and participated in the anti-Diem coup in 1963. The Saigon regime made him a major general and air vice marshal, in effect the head of the air force. As the principal leader of the rebellious Young Turks in the military, Ky became premier when this group took political power in 1965. Although his fellow general Nguyen Van Thieu had the title of head of state, Ky directed the daily operations of the government and played the principal role in meetings with Lyndon Johnson in Hawaii in 1966. In preparation for elections in 1967, however, the Armed Forces Council put Thieu at the head of its ticket and gave Ky the vice-presidential slot primarily because Ky was junior to Thieu. Ky then steadily lost political influence. He attempted to challenge Thieu in the 1971 elections only to be disqualified from running. Although the RVN Supreme Court later permitted his name on the ballot, he chose to withdraw as a candidate. He publicly criticized Thieu's leadership in the last days of the RVN and proclaimed that he would never leave Vietnam. On April 29, 1975, however, he flew a helicopter out of Vietnam to a U.S. aircraft carrier and later settled in America.

Nguyen Dynasty (1802–1945)—Established by Emperor Gia Long in 1802, the Nguyen dynasty occupied the throne of Vietnam until the abdication of Emperor Bao Dai in 1945. In the seventeenth century the Nguyen family was one of several strong families competing for power. Despite losing control of their home area in central Vietnam at the hands of the Tay Son Rebellion in the eighteenth century, the family returned to prominence under Nguyen Anh. With the help of arms and mercenaries provided by a French priest, Pigneau de Béhaine, Nguyen Anh gained power over all of Vietnam, took the name Gia Long, and installed his court at the family center in what is now the city of Hue. Although Gia Long's descendants continued to maintain the appearances of an imperial court in Hue, they progressively lost actual power to the French. During the reign of Emperor Tu Duc (1847–1883), formal French colonial control began. A youthful Bao Dai assumed the throne in 1925 but relinquished the title of emperor in 1945, at the time that Ho Chi Minh declared the establishment of the Democratic Republic of Vietnam.

Nguyen Van Thieu (1923–2001)—General Nguyen Van Thieu was president of the Republic of Vietnam from 1967 to 1975. Born near Phan Rang, he served as a combat officer with French forces during the French-Vietminh War. He received military command and staff training in the United States in the 1950s, converted from Buddhism to Catholicism, and joined the Can Lao Party to gain advancement in the ARVN. As a colonel, he led an ARVN division against the presidential palace during the coup against Diem and gained promotion to general from the new government. Along with Air Vice Marshal Nguyen Cao Ky, Thieu became a leader of a military faction known as the Young Turks, who gained control of the government in June 1965. With Thieu as head of state and Ky as premier, the two men shared power for awhile. They met with Lyndon Johnson in 1966 and pledged to strengthen the South's armed forces and to prepare a constitution. Rivalry developed between the two officer-politicians, and Thieu was able to secure the presidency of the RVN in a manipulated election in 1967 that made the younger and brasher Ky vice president. In 1971 Thieu gained reelection as president in another rigged process from which Ky ultimately withdrew, leaving the South basically with one-man rule.

As president, Thieu made some attempts at allowing elected village governments, initiating land reform and rent controls, and removing corrupt officials, but he also repressed dissent, eventually suspended local elections, and amassed a personal fortune. He consistently resisted a negotiated settlement with Hanoi, and on several occasions—most notably in November 1968 and November-December 1972 during U.S. elections—he refused to cooperate with major American diplomatic efforts. With secret promises of generous financial support from Richard Nixon, Thieu took the offensive in attacking North Vietnamese Army forces in the South in 1973. The NVA began effective counterattacks in 1974, and in the spring of 1975 the North launched its final successful offensive against the South. Military, political, and economic conditions in the RVN were poor, and Thieu's government had little popular support. Nixon had resigned, and the American Congress was not willing to provide Thieu more aid. He resigned as president nine days before the NVA occupied Saigon. Thieu bitterly denounced the United States for abandoning his government and then fled to Taiwan before the fall of the southern capital. He later settled in the United States.

Nixon, Richard Milhouse (1913–1994)—As president of the United States (1969–1974), Richard M. Nixon ended U.S. military intervention in Vietnam but became the only American president forced to resign from office. He began his political career after World War II in the House of Representatives and the

Senate, advocating a tough line against communists abroad and at home. From 1953 to 1961 he was vice president, and, during the siege of Dienbienphu in 1954, he publicly endorsed the idea of U.S. military intervention in Indochina to back the French. President Eisenhower did not send American forces at that time, but after the French war, the Eisenhower administration chose to defend and support South Vietnam, a policy that Nixon fully embraced. Nixon attempted to convert his experience as vice president into election to the presidency, but he lost a very close race with John Kennedy in 1960. During the campaign, both candidates had pledged to continue the containment policy.

After a humiliating failure to become governor of California in 1962, Nixon was out of public office during the period that Kennedy and Lyndon Johnson led the United States into the huge military commitment in Vietnam. The Republican developed a public critique of the Democratic presidents that they had not exerted enough American force, especially against North Vietnam. As the war reached a stalemate in 1967 and 1968, Nixon also argued that Johnson was too focused on Vietnam and not concentrating enough policy effort toward America's principal adversaries, the Soviet Union and the People's Republic of China. As debate over the war created internal divisions within the Democratic Party, Nixon went about methodically gaining the Republican nomination for president in 1968. He allowed the press to believe and report that he had a "secret plan" to end the war, although later he acknowledged that no such plan existed. In the 1968 voting, he won an extremely narrow victory over Vice President Hubert Humphrey.

Once in the White House, Nixon was determined not to let the war overwhelm him as it had done Johnson, and he set out to end it as quickly as possible. Always an insecure politician, he became very secretive in his approach to policy making and relied almost entirely on one person, his national security adviser Henry Kissinger, for planning war strategy. Nixon tried to intimidate Hanoi into accepting a cease-fire and recognizing South Vietnam by what Nixon's White House chief of staff, H. R. Haldeman, called the "mad man" approach, namely, that the zealously anticommunist Nixon might unleash horrendous destruction on North Vietnam. To emphasize the threat, the administration began Operation Menu, the secret bombing of communist base areas and supply lines in neutral Cambodia. The DRV leaders made no concessions, however, and the new president experienced the same frustration that Johnson had faced. Nixon and Kissinger then settled into a policy labeled Vietnamization, which meant reducing the number of U.S. ground forces in Vietnam, increasing the level of materiel aid to the ARVN, and greatly expanding American bombing of enemy targets. Nixon also authorized Kissinger to pursue secret talks with DRV representatives in Paris.

While trying to pressure Hanoi and move forward the negotiations, Nixon also tried to manage dissent at home. In November 1969 he responded to the large Moratorium protests with his "silent majority" speech, in which he asserted that most Americans backed his efforts at gradual disengagement. To protect Vietnamization, Nixon allowed U.S. and ARVN troops to cross into Cambodia in April 1970. This move gained little military benefit but set off a storm of antiwar protests, including one at Kent State University that ended with four students being killed by the Ohio National Guard. In 1971 a stolen copy of a secret Department of Defense history of the war, the Pentagon Papers, was leaked to the press, and Nixon fought back with the "plumbers," White House agents assigned to spy on officials in order to stop leaks.

In 1972, with the presidential election approaching, Nixon increased military and diplomatic activity. He traveled to Beijing in February and to Moscow in May for dramatic face-to-face meetings with Chinese and Soviet leaders aimed at reducing global tensions. When the PAVN began a spring offensive against South Vietnam, the president ordered massive air raids against the North, including Hanoi and Haiphong. Nixon also allowed Kissinger to relax some of the American demands in the secret Paris negotiations. In response to these moves, the DRV responded with some concessions of its own with regard to the Saigon government, and in October a tentative agreement emerged, which Kissinger prematurely mentioned to the press. Nixon was already leading antiwar Democrat George McGovern in the polls, and with peace seemingly imminent, he buried McGovern in the November election. During twelve days in December, Nixon unleashed Operation Linebacker II, the most concentrated bombing of North Vietnam of the entire war. In January the Paris talks resumed, and on January 27, 1973, Kissinger and the DRV's Le Duc Tho signed the Paris Peace Accords, ending the U.S. military role in the war.

Nixon declared that he had obtained "peace with honor" in Vietnam. In fact the fighting continued, but the United States was out of it. Having finally extracted all U.S. forces from Vietnam and having achieved a landslide election victory, Nixon should have been politically secure for his second term. During 1973 and 1974, however, a journalistic, judicial, and finally congressional investigation of illegal White House activities during Nixon's 1972 reelection campaign—known by the single term "Watergate"—forced Nixon from office on August 9, 1974. In his memoir and other writings, Nixon claimed that the Watergate controversy prevented him and his successor Gerald Ford from providing the support to South Vietnam that it needed to survive past 1975. He blamed Congress for failing to vote more aid to the RVN and, thus, for losing the peace, but, in fact, his own misconduct, the American public's war weariness, and political realities within Vietnam shaped the final outcome of the war.

North Vietnamese Army (NVA)—see **People's Army of Vietnam (PAVN)**.

Pacification—Sometimes called "the other war" or the "war for hearts and minds," pacification was the collection of programs by which the United States attempted to assist the Saigon government to gain control over and build popular support throughout the RVN. The first requirement of pacification was to provide people with security to go about their daily affairs, and, beyond security, pacification programs included health care, education, food and shelter for refugees, agricultural assistance, and other services. Basic reforms, such as land redistribution or elections, were also included in pacification.

Under the Eisenhower and Kennedy administrations, pacification took the form of nation building, as Washington sought to assist the Diem government with military and civilian advisers and various aid packages to make South Vietnam a viable government. Diem's communist-led enemies had their own political agenda for gaining the allegiance of the people, and as the Saigon government actually began to function with U.S. help and to suppress its opponents, armed insurrection mounted in the South. One of the RVN's responses was the largely unsuccessful Strategic Hamlet program, which was a pacification plan to create fortified villages protected from Vietcong intimidation.

When Johnson introduced large numbers of U.S. combat forces into South Vietnam in 1965, pacification took on secondary importance. Indeed, the need for greater force to combat the insurrection was evidence that pacification was failing. General Westmoreland put most of his command's resources into the attrition strategy and the waging of a conventional war and left village security largely to the ARVN. Still, American leaders could not deny that the war was basically political, a struggle for the allegiance of the Vietnamese people, and that pacification remained important. Johnson himself pressured RVN leaders Nguyen Van Thieu and Nguyen Cao Ky to devote more effort to the "other war," which Saigon labeled "Revolutionary Development." Johnson sent White House aide Robert Komer to South Vietnam to be Westmoreland's deputy for pacification, and Komer created an office of Civilian Operations and Revolutionary Development Support (CORDS) to manage all military and civilian pacification programs. One part of CORDS was the Phoenix Program, which was intended to coordinate intelligence gathering on Vietcong cadre, find them, and arrest them in order to disrupt the Vietcong Infrastructure (VCI). Critics alleged it was an assassination operation, and abuse and killing of Vietcong suspects did occur. Although it weakened the VCI, the Phoenix Program more often suffered from its own organizational problems.

After the Tet Offensive, the United States instituted the Accelerated Pacification Campaign to try to take advantage of Vietcong losses during the Tet fighting. The new U.S. commander in Vietnam, General Creighton Abrams, gave pacification more support than had Westmoreland, and late in 1968 William Colby succeeded Komer as head of CORDS. By 1972 rural security and economic development were improving, and a debate about pacification has persisted ever since then. Its advocates maintain that, if pacification had been given more emphasis and resources earlier, the Saigon government could have survived. Doubters note that the RVN had enormous political handicaps compared to the DRV and that the regime in the South never had the organizational strength and discipline of the communist movement. Regardless of the merits of pacification, after Tet the American public grew increasingly weary of the burden of Vietnam, and it became unwilling to continue paying a price in blood and treasure while South Vietnam, especially under a corrupt Thieu regime, failed to get its house in order.

Paris Peace Accords (1973) — The full title of the Paris Peace Accords, signed January 27, 1973, was the "Agreement on Ending the War and Restoring the Peace in Vietnam." Primarily the work of Henry Kissinger for the United States and Le Duc Tho for the Democratic Republic of Vietnam (DRV), the document was signed by its authors and by representatives of the Republic of Vietnam (RVN) and the Provisional Revolutionary Government (PRG) of South Vietnam. Similar to the terms reached in the Paris Peace Talks between Kissinger and Tho in October 1972, the accords provided for a cease-fire with Vietnamese forces remaining in place (although the location of those forces was not specified). All U.S. and other foreign troops were to be out of Vietnam in sixty days, and all U.S. prisoners of war were to be released over the same period. "The two South Vietnamese parties" — the RVN and PRG — were to "end hatred and enmity" and to create a National Council of National Reconciliation and Concord to implement the agreements and decide upon elections. There were also provisions alluding to the reunification of North and South Vietnam "step by step through peaceful means." Except for the withdrawal of the 23,000 U.S. troops remaining in the South and Hanoi's release of 591 U.S. prisoners, the parties to the agreement observed none of these provisions. There was no cease-fire; the fighting never stopped. There was no recognition of who possessed what specific territory. There was no reconciliation council, no elections, and no steps toward peaceful reunification. President Nixon hailed it as a "peace with honor" because the United States was able to leave Vietnam with the government of the RVN still in place in Saigon. Critics alleged, however, that the accords only provided for a "decent interval" between the American departure and the end of an independent South Vietnam.

Paris Peace Talks — On May 13, 1968, W. Averell Harriman for the United States and Xuan Thuy for the Democratic Republic of Vietnam formally opened the Paris Peace Talks. For more than four and a half years and with the fighting continuing, this diplomatic effort failed to produce an agreement to end the war. The talks began when they did because of the results of the DRV's Tet Offensive of January and February 1968. The psychological shock of the offensive in the United States put the Johnson administration under intense political pressure to take steps to disengage its forces from Indochina, which led the president to offer to open negotiations with Hanoi. Reeling from its own losses in the Tet fighting, the DRV surprised Washington by agreeing to talks in Paris. When the two sides met, however, neither was prepared to make substantive concessions for peace.

At first, Hanoi's delegation refused to talk as long as U.S. bombing continued north of the DMZ. Johnson finally halted the air attacks at the end of October, in large part to attempt to give a last minute boost to Hubert Humphrey in his presidential contest with Richard Nixon. The diplomatic proceedings had also been held up by the issue of participation by the Republic of Vietnam and National Liberation Front. Since neither of these parties would deal with the other, Harriman devised a formula of referring to "our side" and "your side" that skirted this issue. The participants also wrangled over the shape of the conference table (two sides, four sides, or round). These procedural obstacles basically prevented any substantive exchanges before Nixon took office in January 1969. The new president selected Henry Cabot Lodge as chief U.S. negotiator, and Lodge was succeeded after a year by David K. E. Bruce. In June 1969 the NLF declared the creation of the Provisional Revolutionary Government, which joined the talks on behalf of the NLF. In August 1969 Nixon's national security adviser, Henry Kissinger, began secret conversations in Paris with Hanoi's representatives, usually led by Le Duc Tho, a high ranking member of the Politburo.

For many months during both the Johnson and Nixon administrations, the official talks and the later secret talks were stalemated. The basic U.S. proposal was that both Hanoi and Washington withdraw their troops from the South and then negotiate for a political settlement. The DRV insisted that U.S. forces withdraw and that the Thieu regime be replaced by a coalition government before Hanoi would agree to a truce. In order to gain concessions, Nixon attempted to convince Hanoi that he would increase military pressure on the North, but the DRV leaders would not yield. Finally, in the summer of 1972, both sides began to move toward compromise. Nixon wanted to try to reach a settlement before the November presidential election, and Kissinger indicated in the secret talks that the United States might accept a cease-fire in place, which would leave North Vietnamese troops in the South. With the DRV's forces having taken heavy losses during their May offensive, Le Duc Tho responded that Hanoi would not insist on the removal of Thieu as a precondition to a truce. With both sides yielding on key points, an agreement along these lines was reached in October. Thieu objected strongly, however, to allowing the PAVN to remain in the RVN and to the arrangements for further political negotiations. The talks collapsed in November as Hanoi made new demands in view of Thieu's recalcitrance. In December Nixon unleashed Linebacker II, an intense bombing of North Vietnam as a demonstration of American strength to both Hanoi and Saigon. In January the parties returned to Paris, and on January 23, 1973, Kissinger and Tho initialed the Paris Peace Accords, which provided for an end of hostilities along the lines of the October agreement.

Pathet Lao—Meaning "Land of the Lao," Pathet Lao was a communist-led nationalist front created in Laos in 1950 to fight with the Vietminh against the French effort to restore its colonial control in Indochina. The Pathet Lao remained closely linked politically and militarily with the DRV thereafter. During the Laotian Civil War (1960–1962), the United States backed forces opposed to the Pathet Lao, but the Geneva Agreements of 1962 created a coalition government in Laos in which the front had a small role. During the Vietnam War, Pathet Lao soldiers helped keep open the Ho Chi Minh Trail through Laos. The United States secretly bombed Pathet Lao bases, and the CIA organized a war against the Pathet Lao using the Meo and Hmong people of Laos. The Pathet Lao survived, however, and gradually came to dominate the coalition government. After the DRV victory in Vietnam in 1975, the leader of the Pathet Lao became president of the Lao People's Democratic Republic.

Pentagon Papers—The official title of the Pentagon Papers was *United States-Vietnam Relations, 1945–1967*. It was a secret history of U.S. decision making prepared by the Department of Defense at the request of Secretary of Defense Robert McNamara. The report contained a narrative, written by staffers such as Leslie Gelb and Daniel Ellsberg, and supporting documents, primarily from Defense Department and State Department files. It came to 7,000 pages bound in forty-seven volumes. With the exception of some sections dealing with diplomacy, the documents did not contain particularly sensitive secrets, but, as McNamara himself had come to think, they showed an often simplistic and not well-considered decision-making process.

Ellsberg was a top-level defense analyst who had decided that the war was wrong, and he believed that the information in the Pentagon Papers should be more widely available. He secretly photocopied the report and tried unsuccessfully to interest some antiwar senators in it. In March 1971 he gave his purloined copy to Neil Sheehan of the *New York Times*. A team of writers from the paper prepared reports based upon the Pentagon Papers, and on June 13, 1971, the *Times* began publishing what was to be a series of these articles. The Nixon administration, whose decisions were not part of the study, immediately went to court to seek an order preventing publication on the grounds of protecting national security. The *Washington Post* and the *Boston Globe* also began printing material from the Pentagon Papers, and Senator Mike Gravel of Alaska read portions into the record of a Senate subcommittee hearing. On June 30, in a six-to-three vote, the Supreme Court ruled that the *New York Times* had the right under the First Amendment's protection of freedom of the press to publish the papers. The majority of the justices found that the government had not shown that printing the Pentagon Papers posed a threat to national security. Soon after this ruling, two editions of the Pentagon Papers appeared in print—the items released by Senator Gravel and a version released by the Department of Defense. The more sensitive diplomatic documents were not published until 1983.

The Nixon administration obtained a criminal indictment against Ellsberg and an alleged accomplice, Anthony Russo, for conspiracy, espionage, and stealing government property. A federal judge dismissed the charges in May 1973, however, because of government misconduct. Most notably, a secret White House team known as the "plumbers" had burglarized the office of Ellsberg's psychiatrist in a search for information to discredit Ellsberg. This same "plumbers" operation was involved in the bungled break-in at the Watergate offices in 1972 that began the scandal leading to Nixon's resignation in 1974.

People's Army of Vietnam (PAVN) — Known to Americans during the war as the North Vietnamese Army (NVA), the People's Army of Vietnam was the army of the Democratic Republic of Vietnam. Its organization included some air and naval units, but it was primarily composed of infantry units and their related support units, including artillery, armor, and logistics. It was also divided into a hierarchy of regular, regional, and self-defense forces with varying levels of equipment and training. The PAVN provided leaders, supplies, and reinforcements to the People's Liberation Armed Forces (PLAF) or Vietcong, but the two armies often operated separately and had separate identities.

The PAVN, as a military organization, was largely the creation of Vo Nguyen Giap. He was its original commanding officer, and, although other generals challenged and even eclipsed his leadership during the American war, he remained an influential and heroic figure. Giap created an armed propaganda brigade in 1944 as part of the Vietminh resistance to the Japanese. From this modest beginning, he and others built a force of mostly peasant irregulars to fight the French after 1945, and this organization became known as the People's Army of Vietnam in 1950. PAVN leaders adopted the Chinese Communist model of protecting base areas, harassing their enemy, and avoiding set battles with the better-equipped French, but they also had organized six combat divisions by 1952. PAVN strategy against the French and later the Americans was a variant of what the Chinese called "People's War," but it adapted more flexibility between regular and irregular tactics than in Mao Zedong's theories. When the PAVN scored its decisive victory over the French garrison at Dienbienphu in 1954, its assault was largely a conventional operation by regular troops.

Between the French and American wars, Hanoi modernized its army and built it up to a size of about 160,000 by 1960. Aided by Chinese and Soviet advisers, the PAVN introduced standardized practices for unit organization, uniforms, ranks, recruitment, and training. It remained three-fourths infantry, but added engineering, air defense, air transport, communication, and other technological elements. The DRV also had compulsory military service, which created a large reserve pool of trained personnel. The PAVN had a good supply of soldiers but was often lacking in sufficient materiel. Consequently, it gave its troops heavy political indoctrination in the glory of patriotic sacrifice and prepared them to use guerrilla, as well as conventional, tactics as needed.

After the Politburo decided in late 1959 to aid the armed insurrection in the South, the PAVN began logistic and advisory support of the PLAF and the infiltration into the South of southern-born fighters living in the North. In 1964 units of northern-born troops were also sent into the RVN, and regular PAVN brigades eventually clashed with ARVN and U.S. forces, primarily in the Central Highlands. High PLAF losses during and after the Tet holiday fighting in 1968 required an increase in the number of PAVN troops in the South and their use in low-land areas that they previously had avoided. As the Nixon administration began lowering the number of American combat forces in South Vietnam in 1969, Hanoi felt less risk in sending more combat divisions, as well as tanks and artillery, into the RVN. The PAVN felt emboldened to launch its so-called Easter Offensive against the northern provinces of South Vietnam and isolated targets in the Mekong Delta and Central Highlands in May 1972, but it was repulsed by ARVN forces with heavy U.S. air support. In 1975, however, with U.S. air power unavailable and with the PAVN expanded to 685,000 main force troops, the DRV's army swept through disintegrating ARVN defenses with troops, tanks, and heavy artillery and had complete control of the South by April 30.

After 1975 the PAVN continued to grow until its forces surpassed one million, making it one of the four largest standing armies in the world. In 1978 it occupied Cambodia and successfully withstood a brief clash with China's army in 1979. The PAVN withdrew from Cambodia in 1989, and economic problems and loss of Soviet aid led to sharp cut backs in its size in the 1990s.

People's Liberation Armed Forces (PLAF) — see **National Liberation Front**.

Pham Van Dong (1906–2000) — Often considered to be Ho Chi Minh's closest political ally, Pham Van Dong was premier of the DRV from 1955 to 1975 and of the Socialist Republic of Vietnam from 1975 to 1986. Son of a gentry family from central Vietnam's Quang Ngai Province, he attended school in Hue with Vo Nguyen Giap and Ngo Dinh Diem. In 1926 he joined Ho's Revolutionary Youth League, and from 1931 to 1937 he was in France's infamous Poulo Condore prison. With Ho and Giap he founded the Vietminh. He was named finance minister of the DRV in 1946 and, as foreign minister, represented the DRV at the Geneva Conference of 1954. As prime minister, he strongly opposed a negotiated settlement with the United States, and upon Ho's death in 1969 he became the most visible international leader of the DRV. He played a key role in approving Hanoi's tactical concessions in the 1973 cease-fire agreement and then the subsequent decisions to continue the fighting. Within Vietnam he received considerable blame for the economic collapse that occurred after 1976, and the Politburo replaced him as prime minister in 1986. He retained respect, however, as one of the heroes of the revolution.

Phan Boi Chau (1876–1940)—Born in Nghe Anh Province, Phan Boi Chau became one of the leading anticolonial activists of the early twentieth century. Although he had passed the examinations to be a gentry official, he embarked on a revolutionary course in the model of the Chinese and Japanese self-strengthening movements of the late nineteenth century. In 1904 he formed the Modernization Society, which advocated that Vietnam should follow a model like that of Meiji Japan and adopt Western technology, political practices, and economic institutions if it was to be a free nation. Inspired by Sun Yat-sen's Revolutionary Alliance and later Nationalist Party in China, however, Phan Boi Chau changed his Modernization Society, which basically advocated constitutional monarchy, into the Vietnamese Restoration Society, which called for the creation of a democratic republic. His activities generated resistance to French control, and French police captured him in Shanghai in 1925. He was convicted of treason and sentenced to life in prison. Although he failed to ignite a successful revolution, he is remembered as one of Vietnam's first nationalists, who tried to rally a broad spectrum of the population to defy foreign rule.

Phnom Penh—The capital of Cambodia, Phnom Penh was once a beautiful city, but it was emptied of its population after the anti-urban Khmer Rouge took power in 1975. Forced into rural areas, many of the city's inhabitants died of starvation or illness, and the Khmer Rouge killed others because they were intellectuals or professionals or had been Westernized. In 1979 the Vietnamese army took control of the city, and during the Vietnamese occupation some of the population returned. After the departure of the Vietnamese in 1989, the city began to be restored and rebuilt with the aid of foreign investment.

Pleiku—A provincial capital and market town in South Vietnam's Central Highlands, Pleiku became the location of a major U.S. command center and combat base. On February 7, 1965, a Vietcong attack on the U.S. advisers' base at Pleiku killed eight Americans. Along with a concurrent attack on Americans at Qui Nhon, it provided the Johnson administration the provocation it desired to launch air attacks that became the on-going Operation Rolling Thunder. In 1975 a poorly executed South Vietnamese army retreat from Pleiku set off a military and civilian panic that began the final rout of Saigon's forces.

Pol Pot (1928–1998)—The leader of the Khmer Rouge when they seized power in 1975, Pol Pot more than any other individual was responsible for the

Cambodian holocaust that brought death to over 1.5 million people. His real name was Saloth Sar. He was always very secretive, and many details about his life are vague. He lived in France in the 1940s and early 1950s and became a member of the French Communist Party. Back in Cambodia after 1953, he was active in the secret Communist Party of Kampuchea and became its secretary general in 1963. Many within the party knew him only as Brother Number One. Despite his own experience in Europe and the influence of the French Revolution, Maoism, and Stalinism on his thinking, he claimed that Cambodia had nothing to learn from outside and that eventually Cambodia would be restored to the former glory of the old Angkor kingdom. He ruthlessly imposed his ideas about Cambodian purity on his party, which came to be known as Khmer Rouge, or Red Khmer. When Khmer Rouge forces defeated the ineffective Lon Nol government in 1975, Pol Pot declared the "Year Zero" and set out to remake Cambodia as a rural collectivist society. He emptied the city of Phnom Penh, ordered millions into forced labor in which many died of starvation and overwork, and had thousands of others executed to create his classless Cambodian utopia. A Vietnamese invasion broke his grip on power in 1979, but he continued to be a dangerous guerrilla leader with secret bases in Thailand and Cambodia. The Khmer Rouge divided into factions, and, as was often the case in his life, his role was unseen and unknown. In 1997 Khmer Rouge leaders conducted a trial and convicted him of murdering other Khmer Rouge. He died while being held prisoner, supposedly of natural causes.

Post-Traumatic Stress Disorder (PTSD)—see **Veterans**.

POW/MIA Issue—One of the most enduring Vietnam War controversies was over the fate of Americans who were either a prisoner of war (POW) or missing in action (MIA). By terms of the Paris Peace Accords, the DRV released 591 U.S. prisoners in February and March 1973. Many of them had endured terrible hardships—torture, neglect, malnutrition, and lack of health care—and were greeted as heroes upon their return. Controversy immediately developed and lasted for years, however, over whether or not living American prisoners still remained in Vietnam and also in Laos. Dozens of men were known to have died in captivity, but a precise number was impossible to ascertain because prisoners had been captured and held in many different places. There were more than 2,300 personnel officially listed as missing in action. Most of these were known or presumed to have died in fiery plane crashes or as captives of local guerrillas, but the location of their remains or their precise fates were unknown. Separate congressional and Department of Defense investigations in the 1970s concluded that there were no American prisoners remaining anywhere in Indochina.

Although the number of missing Americans after the Vietnam War was small compared to other U.S. conflicts, the issue of accounting for all American

POWs and MIAs took on a political, diplomatic, and mythical life. Richard Nixon first drew attention to the return of all prisoners as a way of maintaining public support for his policies. The National League of Families of American Prisoners and Missing in Southeast Asia became a powerful political lobby. Reports of "live sightings" of POWs required the government to keep MIA searches going, although none of these reports were ever confirmed and most were shown to be hoaxes. Presidents from Ford through Clinton felt compelled for political reasons to keep open the possibility of live captives, and U.S. insistence upon full accountability for missing Americans was a major obstacle to normalization of U.S.-Vietnam relations for years. When Washington and Hanoi established diplomatic ties in 1995, the two sides indicated they would work together to try to resolve remaining MIA cases.

Provisional Revolutionary Government (PRG)—Created in 1969 in the South Vietnam-Cambodia border area, the Provisional Revolutionary Government was a combining of National Liberation Front and other rebel leaders to form a political alternative to the RVN. At Hanoi's insistence, PRG representatives, most notably Madame Nguyen Thi Binh, participated in the Paris Peace Talks. Several communist governments recognized the PRG as the legitimate government of South Vietnam. In January 1973 Madame Binh signed the Paris Peace Accords on behalf of the PRG, and the PRG was a party to the National Council of National Reconciliation and Concord created by the accords to address with the RVN the political future of the South. After the DRV's final offensive in 1975 eliminated the RVN government, the Hanoi regime quickly absorbed the PRG as well.

Reagan, Ronald (1911–)—A conservative Republican and staunch anticommunist, Ronald Reagan strongly supported U.S. intervention in Vietnam while he was governor of California (1967–1975). Later as president of the United States (1981–1989), he continued to maintain that the American war in Vietnam was morally and strategically justified. As governor, he used the national guard and state police to quell student antiwar demonstrations and declared that there would be "no appeasement" of protestors. As a candidate for president in 1980 and then as president, he continued to assert that the American effort in Vietnam had been a "noble cause" in opposition to the evil of international communism. Through such rhetoric he sought to restore the confidence of Americans in their nation's power, something that he believed was lost during the war, but he also was reluctant to make long-term U.S. military commitments abroad in volatile areas like the Middle East. An exception was in Central America and the Caribbean where he advocated support of "freedom fighters" opposing leftist governments in circumstances his critics said were similar to the Cold War rationales that had involved the United States in Vietnam.

Red River and Delta—Originating in South China, the Red River flows 700 miles (1,120 kilometers) southward to the Red River Delta, which empties into the Gulf of Tonkin. About 316 miles (554 kilometers) of the river lies within Vietnam. The Red River Delta is an agriculturally productive area around which the Vietnamese first appeared as a distinct people and state. Today's capital of Vietnam, Hanoi, and the major Vietnamese seaport on the Gulf of Tonkin, Haiphong, are located in the delta. Ordinarily shallow, the river rises to dangerous levels during heavy rains, and an extensive system of high dikes along the river and its tributaries controls flooding. U.S. strategists considered bombing these dikes during the war but did so only once in an attack on Nam Dinh in 1972.

Reeducation Camps—Following a model found in the early Soviet Union and in the People's Republic of China and used in North Vietnam after the French war, the victorious Hanoi regime set up reeducation camps for its southern enemies in 1975. Whole categories of people, such as ARVN officers, RVN officials and bureaucrats, teachers, and clergy, went into these centers to be indoctrinated into the new system. Others who came to be perceived as dissidents, including even some former Vietcong, and some common criminals were incarcerated in the camps as well. The length of stay ranged from a few weeks to many years. The conditions of the camps also varied widely. All required hard labor and meted out severe punishments, including executions, for even minor infractions of rules. There were "courses" that often consisted of forced confessions of crimes against the people. The number of people incarcerated can only be estimated, but the Socialist Republic of Vietnam acknowledged that a million people spent some time in the camps. Other sources indicate that about half of these were detained for two to five years, and some 50,000 were held longer. The principal effect was punishment more than reeducation. Many of those released left the country, and the influence of capitalist culture endured in southern Vietnam. The communist governments in Laos and Cambodia also sent domestic enemies to reeducation camps that were much harsher than those in Vietnam and in which thousands died.

Rolling Thunder—see **Air War**.

Roosevelt, Franklin D. (1882–1945)—Similar to other U.S. officials, Franklin D. Roosevelt (president of the United States, 1933–1945) did not give much thought to French Indochina before Japanese expansion began to threaten the colony in 1940. During the American war against Japan in Asia and the Pacific (1941–1945), Roosevelt on occasion mentioned an ambiguous concept of postwar trusteeship for colonial areas. In a January 1944 memorandum, the president specifically criticized French rule in Indochina and suggested that all colonies should be aided in a transition to independence. He publicly endorsed the idea of a trusteeship for French Indochina in a February 1945 press conference. He raised the issue because of humanitarian sympathy for the subject peoples and a desire to see the closed economic spheres of European colonial powers ended. Before his death in April 1945, however, Roosevelt never articulated a specific trusteeship plan for Indochina or elsewhere. Britain and France clearly wanted no tampering with their colonies, and growing tensions with the Soviet Union had caused Roosevelt to avoid raising issues that would produce strains in Washington's relations with London and Paris.

Rostow, Walt Whitman (1916–)—An early advocate of the use of American air power and ground forces in Vietnam, Walt W. Rostow never deviated from his hawkish advice as long as he served as a top presidential aide. A professor of economics at the Massachusetts Institute of Technology, Rostow joined John Kennedy's White House staff in 1961, headed the State Department's policy planning staff from 1961 to 1966, and was Lyndon Johnson's national security adviser from 1966 to 1969. Based in part on his advice, Kennedy greatly increased U.S. support of South Vietnam in 1961. Rostow believed that pressure on the DRV was the key to defense of the South, and he consistently recommended bombing of the North, blockading its harbors, and deploying U.S. forces in the South. After Johnson began bombing and sent troops to Vietnam in 1965, Rostow favored further escalation. His views were not moderated by the growing public criticism of the war in 1967, and he opposed the idea of using a halt to bombing to prompt negotiations. He was one of the president's few top aides to argue for further escalation after the shock of the Tet Offensive. Johnson had always admired Rostow's optimism and bold recommendations, but this time the president did not follow his advice. When Johnson left office, Rostow joined the faculty of the University of Texas. He continued to maintain even after the DRV victory that U.S. intervention in Vietnam had been correct and that it had provided time for other Southeast Asian nations to gain the strength they needed to withstand the threat of communist takeover.

Rusk, Dean (1909–1994)—As secretary of state in the Kennedy and Johnson administrations (1961–1969), Dean Rusk was one of the principal U.S. policy makers during the Vietnam War, and he never wavered in his conviction that American military intervention in Vietnam had been justified. As assistant secretary of state for Far Eastern affairs in the Truman administration, he strongly supported the containment policy, and he considered U.S. support for France in Indochina to be an extension of that policy. As Kennedy pondered U.S. options in Southeast Asia, Secretary of State Rusk argued that the United States must prevent North Vietnam from taking over South Vietnam by force. Rusk believed that the credibility of U.S. global power and its commitments to allies were at stake and that a victory by Hanoi would be a strategic gain for Moscow and Beijing. In the Kennedy White House, he tended to defer to Secretary of Defense Robert McNamara and the military on Vietnam policy. When Johnson became president, Rusk developed a closer personal relationship with the chief executive than he had ever had with Kennedy. Cautious by nature, Rusk preferred a negotiated settlement of the war, but he concluded that the high stakes in Southeast Asia required the United States to fight rather than to make political concessions with regard to the independence of South Vietnam. As McNamara, Clark Clifford, and others wavered on using American force, Johnson came to highly value Rusk's personal loyalty to him and his uncompromising, even stubborn, conviction that the United States was countering aggression and defending freedom in Vietnam. Many people in the antiwar movement detested Rusk for his unapologetic attitude, but he saw himself as a Wilsonian internationalist committed to world peace.

Saigon—Renamed Ho Chi Minh City by the victorious DRV in 1975, Saigon was the largest city in French Indochina and the capital of the French-created State of Vietnam (1949–1955) and the Republic of Vietnam (1955–1975). As a commercial and administrative center during the colonial period, it was home to a relatively affluent population, and, consequently, it had elegant homes, restaurants, and a beautiful park-like appearance that caused it to be known as the "Paris of the Orient." Its location in the long-time French colony of Cochinchina made the Vietminh presence less evident there than other areas during the French Indochina War. As South Vietnam's capital under Ngo Dinh Diem and his successors, Saigon became the center of much military and political activity and of the massive U.S. presence in the country. The flow of Americans and their money into Saigon turned it into a city of corruption, vice, and hustlers. Refugees also poured in and ballooned the population to more than three million by the war's end. The once picturesque city had become infested with squatter's shacks and other pervasive signs of poverty. Even with huge U.S. bases on the outskirts—Long Binh, Bien Hoa, and Ton Son Nhut—Vietcong terrorism could strike the city, and during the Tet Offensive of 1968, some of the heaviest fighting was in and around Saigon. The arrival of the North Vietnamese Army in Saigon on April 29, 1975, preceded only hours before by the chaotic final evacuation of Americans from the U.S. embassy, marked the end of the Vietnam War.

Sainteny, Jean (1907–1978)—A French diplomat who was personally close to Ho Chi Minh, Jean Sainteny signed an agreement with Ho in March 1946 that provided a formula for French recognition of the DRV but that was never implemented because of actions by other French officials. Over the next three decades, Sainteny continued to provide both official and unofficial French and

American contact with the DRV, and he even helped arrange Henry Kissinger's secret meetings with Hanoi's representatives in Paris in 1972.

Search and Destroy—Search and destroy was the most common tactic used to implement the U.S. attrition strategy from 1965 to 1968. Developed by General William Westmoreland and his deputy General William DePuy, search and destroy often involved sending U.S. troops on long patrols—what the soldiers called "humpin' the boonies"—or inserting them in suspected enemy areas by helicopter in order to find the elusive Vietcong and North Vietnamese forces. Once the enemy was found, air and artillery support could then be called upon to destroy the adversary. Many military experts criticized this aggressive tactic as ineffective and argued that U.S. forces could have been better utilized in pacification operations to protect the South Vietnamese population.

Selective Service System—see **Draft**.

Sihanouk, Norodom (1923–)—Prince Norodom Sihanouk had many titles over the years—prince, king, prime minister, head of state—but from 1941 to 1997 he was often the actual, or symbolic, leader of Cambodia. A charismatic and committed Cambodian nationalist, Sihanouk had a base of support among rural Cambodians but often struggled with other political leaders within his country. A descendent of Cambodia's ancient royal dynasty, he became king by choice of French colonial officials in 1941. When Cambodia gained its independence at the Geneva Conference of 1954, Sihanouk headed the government—a constitutional monarchy—but took the title of prince. During the Vietnam War, he skillfully attempted to maintain Cambodia's neutrality. Although his government had received aid from the United States during the 1950s and early 1960s, he broke diplomatic relations with the United States in 1965 and leaned toward better relations with China. In 1969 he reestablished relations with Washington and even allowed American bombing of targets in Cambodia because of his growing concern with Vietnamese communist use of eastern Cambodia for bases and supply routes. Impatient with Sihanouk's continuing desire for neutrality, however, the National Assembly in Phnom Penh voted to depose him in March 1970 while Sihanouk was away in Europe. The prince blamed the United States for this action, moved to Beijing, and lent his credibility with the peasants to the Khmer Rouge, although these communist insurgents had killed some members of his family. When the Khmer Rouge gained power in 1975, Sihanouk returned to Cambodia but fled to China in 1978 when Vietnamese troops ousted the Khmer Rouge. He came back to the royal palace in Phnom Penh after Vietnamese forces withdrew in 1989. Sihanouk's son, Prince Norodom Ranariddh, became first prime minister in an internal power-sharing arrangement with second prime minister Hun Sen, but

Sihanouk again left Cambodia in 1997 after Hun Sen forced Ranariddh out of the country.

Silent Majority—On November 3, 1969, President Richard Nixon made a nationally televised address in which he asserted that there was a "great silent majority" of Americans to whom he was appealing for support of his policies in Vietnam. On October 15 so-called Moratorium demonstrations had brought out millions of mainstream Americans in protest against the war. Another such Moratorium was scheduled for November 15. Nixon sought to turn Americans away from protest. He declared that "North Vietnam cannot defeat or humiliate the United States. Only Americans can do that." Nixon criticized the war's critics for calling for an immediate U.S. withdrawal from Vietnam. He defended, instead, his preference for continued negotiations and gradual withdrawal of American forces while strengthening South Vietnam through Vietnamization. Nixon claimed that the White House received thousands of positive responses to the speech, although the November 15 Moratorium protest went on as scheduled with millions again participating.

Southeast Asia Treaty Organization (SEATO)—Created by the Manila Pact of September 8, 1954, the Southeast Asia Treaty Organization included Britain, France, the United States, Australia, New Zealand, the Philippines, Thailand, and Pakistan. The idea for SEATO occurred in March 1954 when French officials inquired about possible U.S. military intervention at Dienbienphu. There was no framework at that time for what Secretary of State John Foster Dulles termed "united action" to counter security threats in the area. After the Geneva Conference adjourned in July, the United States took the lead in arranging SEATO to fill that gap. It was a very loose alliance, not at all like NATO in Europe. The members were not required to act in cases of aggression, but only to confer. The Geneva Agreements did not allow the states in Indochina to join alliances, but a separate protocol to the treaty declared Laos, Cambodia, and South Vietnam to be within the treaty area. Dulles later described SEATO as a "no trespassing sign" directed at China and the Soviet Union. In the 1960s Secretary of State Dean Rusk inaccurately cited the SEATO treaty as obligating the United States to aid South Vietnam. Of the SEATO nations other than the United States, only Australia, New Zealand, and Thailand sent troops to participate in the Vietnam War.

Special Forces—The U.S. Army Special Forces, also known as Green Berets, were specially trained for counterinsurgency, antiguerrilla warfare. President John Kennedy took a particular interest in these elite soldiers and ordered 400 to South Vietnam in 1961 to begin training Saigon's forces to combat Vietcong guerrilla tactics. At their peak strength in Vietnam, the Special Forces numbered 3,500, most of whom were assigned to the 5th Special Forces Group, but they typically operated in small teams in remote areas of the country. They trained the South Vietnamese Special Forces, and some Green Berets participated in highly secret intelligence missions with MACV's Studies and Observation Group. Most of them were in the Central Highlands where they trained thousands of Montagnards and organized them into Civilian Irregular Defense Groups (CIDG). With the CIDG they garrisoned forts to guard border areas against PAVN infiltration, and they helped the CIDG defend villages. The ARVN did not like the idea of the CIDG, which it feared could become a separate army of the Montagnard minority, and Saigon merged it with the regular army in 1968. The U.S. Special Forces did a lot of pacification work in villages, such as providing medical care, digging wells, and constructing schools. They also conducted long-range reconnaissance patrols (LRRPs), often with the South Vietnamese Special Forces, and they trained other U.S. Army personnel in LRRP operations. Many Green Berets received the nation's highest citations for bravery, but their counterinsurgency mission was often at odds with MACV large-unit search-and-destroy tactics.

Strategic Hamlets—From 1961 to 1964, strategic hamlets were a visible and controversial pacification program to counter Vietcong political and military influence in rural areas. In 1959 the Republic of Vietnam began construction of what it called "agrovilles"—newly built, fortified villages into which the rural population could be moved to strengthen government control of strategic areas. Less than twenty were attempted, and all failed because the peasant population resisted movement from their ancestral homes and complained that promised government services were never provided. British counterinsurgency expert Sir Robert Thompson had implemented an effective system of armed hamlets in Malaya for rural security against rebel forces, and several officials in the Kennedy administration believed Thompson's plan should be tried in Vietnam. In 1962 Ngo Dinh Diem's government began construction of these strategic hamlets following Thompson's model and with U.S. aid.

These strategic hamlets were supposed to require less relocation of population, to be smaller, and to provide better living conditions than the agrovilles, and they were to be located in more secure areas. In operation, however, the program fell victim to the weaknesses of the Diem government. Saigon valued them more for political control than for providing services to the people and thus tended to build them in contested areas, to force people into them, and to treat villagers oppressively. Corruption often rendered the strategic hamlets militarily and economically weak and easy prey for the Vietcong. They ceased to function in 1963 and 1964, and their demise strengthened the arguments of strategists like General William Westmoreland, who favored offensive military operations against enemy forces over pacification or static population control.

Students for a Democratic Society (SDS)—see **Antiwar Movement**.

Taylor, Maxwell Davenport (1901–1987)—One of America's most accomplished military officers, General Maxwell D. Taylor served as John Kennedy's special military representative (1961–1962), chairman of the Joint Chiefs of Staff (1962–1964), ambassador to South Vietnam (1964–1965), and presidential consultant on Vietnam (1965–1968). His 1959 book, *The Uncertain Trumpet*, advocated a "flexible response" strategy that shaped the Kennedy administration's counterinsurgency plan in Vietnam. He coauthored a 1961 report with Walt Rostow that expressed confidence about the effectiveness of U.S. aid to the RVN and led to a dramatic increase of U.S. money and advisers in Vietnam. Taylor and Secretary of Defense Robert McNamara prepared an influential but ambiguous report in 1963 that affirmed optimism about progress against the Vietcong but cast doubts on the leadership of Ngo Dinh Diem, and shortly afterward a coup toppled Diem's government. As ambassador in Saigon, Taylor grew impatient with the political maneuvering of Diem's successors. He also argued unsuccessfully against General William Westmoreland's plan to use large numbers of U.S. troops for aggressive patrolling. Taylor favored a limited use of American ground forces in an "enclave strategy" of guarding cities and military installations while using U.S. air power against North Vietnam. Despite his criticisms of Saigon's leaders and American strategy, he remained convinced, even after the 1968 Tet Offensive, that U.S. power could prevail in Vietnam, but he also acknowledged that the United States should avoid "this dirty kind of business" in the future.

Tay Son Rebellion (1771–1789)—Taking its name from the home village of the three brothers who led this uprising, the Tay Son Rebellion is remembered in Vietnam as a major peasant challenge to corrupt leaders and for a victory over an intervening Chinese army in the Battle of Dong Da in 1789. The movement defeated the Nguyen family in the south in 1785 and the Trinh lords in the north in 1788. The three brothers briefly ruled the nation and attempted a redistribution of land to aid the peasants. After they died, an heir to the Nguyen court gained control of all of Vietnam in 1802, established the Nguyen dynasty, and ruled under the name Gia Long.

Teach-ins—see **Antiwar Movement**.

Television—see **Media**.

Tet Offensive—The Tet Offensive of 1968 was the turning point of the American war in Vietnam. The lunar new year celebration, Tet was the most important holiday on the Vietnamese calendar and in the past had been a time for a brief, unofficial truce. In the early morning hours of January 30, 1968, however, as Vietnamese were beginning their family observances of Tet, Vietcong forces attacked thirteen cities in central South Vietnam. Twenty-four hours later, these premature moves were followed by coordinated attacks throughout the RVN on cities, towns, government facilities, and U.S. and ARVN military bases. A Vietcong platoon managed to get inside the courtyard of the U.S. embassy in Saigon for a few hours in what was one of the boldest attacks. U.S. troops destroyed the platoon but not before photos and reports of this challenge to American power gained wide circulation. In heavy fighting over the next few days, all of the attacks throughout the South were countered by U.S. and ARVN forces with high losses to the Vietcong. Only in Hue and in the Cholon suburb of Saigon did brutal house-to-house fighting continue for about a month. A related PAVN siege of the U.S. Marine base at Khe Sanh, near the DMZ ,was broken in April.

Militarily, the Tet Offensive failed to achieve the objectives conceived by General Vo Nguyen Giap, the PAVN commander. Giap had thought that his plan would break the bloody stalemate between his troops and the large American expeditionary force. By launching a general offensive of simultaneous attacks throughout the South, he thought the ARVN would collapse and the people of the RVN would join the Vietcong in a general uprising against the Saigon regime. With its puppet overthrown, he reasoned, the United States would have no will to continue the war. Initially his scheme went well. In several well-conceived diversions by his troops, including the siege of the Khe Sanh marine base, he lured many U.S. units to outlying areas. Meanwhile, he secretly supplied Vietcong units and moved them in position for attacks on the cities and towns. When the offensive began, however, the ARVN fought surprisingly well, no uprising occurred, and the PAVN and Vietcong suffered 45,000 casualties. The National Liberation Front's units were so decimated that troops from the North had to take over most of the combat operations for the remainder of the war.

The fighting turned into a strategic success for the DRV, however, because the magnitude of the surprise attack led Washington to begin a searching reassessment of U.S. costs and objectives in the war. Spokespersons for the Johnson administration, including General Westmoreland, had been claiming before Tet that the end of the war was in sight, but the offensive led many to challenge that claim. Johnson's credibility declined, and his leadership was discredited. Westmoreland requested 206,000 additional troops after the attacks began. He saw an opportunity to mount a decisive counteroffensive, but, when news of his request appeared in the *New York Times*, many Americans interpreted it as an act of desperation and demanded an end to escalation. Several close advisers whom Johnson trusted and who had supported the U.S. military buildup in the past, such as Secretary of Defense Clark Clifford, now urged the president to scale back in Vietnam. Johnson yielded to these pressures and announced on March 31 that he was limiting the bombing of North Vietnam, was calling for negotiations, and, moreover, would not be a candidate for reelection. The Tet Offensive did not end the American war, but it began what was still a slow process of extricating the United States from the mire of Vietnam.

Thant, U (1909–1974)—From Burma, U Thant was secretary general of the United Nations from 1962 to 1972. Although the United States resisted UN involvement in peace efforts in Vietnam, Thant spent several months in personal and private initiatives in 1964 and 1965 trying unsuccessfully to arrange for talks between the United States and North Vietnam. Hanoi agreed to discussions, but Washington gave Thant no reply. When Thant finally voiced public criticism of the Johnson administration for not cooperating in efforts to start negotiations, the White House denied there had been any authorized communications with him, although U.S. ambassador to the UN Adlai Stevenson had been talking with Thant for more than a year.

Tonkin—Also spelled "Tonking" in English, Tonkin is the name of the French protectorate established in 1883 in northern Vietnam. It was comprised of the area of the Red River Delta northward to the Chinese border. Derived from the Chinese name for Hanoi and meaning Eastern Capital in Chinese, Tonkin was known by the Vietnamese as Bac Bo.

Truman, Harry S. (1884–1972)—As president of the United States (1945–1953), Harry S. Truman made several key decisions with lasting impact on U.S. policy in Southeast Asia. Although designed for Europe not Asia, his Truman Doctrine speech of March 1947 pledged the United States to aid any free people in the world threatened by totalitarian regimes. This idea led to the globalization of his administration's containment policy, which included economic and military assistance in areas like Korea and Indochina where communist-led movements sought to extend their political control. With the advice of Secretary of State Dean Acheson in 1950, Truman extended U.S. aid to French forces fighting the Vietminh and increased that assistance after he ordered American forces to fight in the Korean War. His administration also formally recognized the French-backed State of Vietnam headed by Bao Dai and thereby initiated an American search for an alternative Vietnamese government to that of Ho Chi Minh.

U Thant—see **Thant, U.**

Veterans—Although readjustment problems for returning soldiers have occurred in all wars and most Vietnam veterans made the transition to civilian life in the United States successfully, many men and women who had served in Vietnam experienced difficulties particular to this conflict. In World War II more than half of the males of military age participated in the war, and many of them went off to combat as a member of the unit with which they had trained. The Korean War differed from World War II and was more like the Vietnam War in that only a minority of the available men were called to serve. World War II was a great victory for American arms, and veterans could feel pride in their accomplishment. In Korea the fighting ended with an uneasy truce, but the American soldier had not been defeated. In Vietnam, however, more than 2.5 million men and some 6,400 women (mostly nurses) participated in a war in which the purposes were not always clear to them, they were a minority of their own age group, they were aware of the divisions over the war among Americans, they often went off to the war and returned back again alone and not with a unit, and there were no victory parades or public recognition of service when they came home. In fact, Vietnam veterans were often treated with indifference or even scorn by people who were either opposed to the war or ambivalent about it. Because the United States lost the war, some citizens blamed the veterans for the nation's failure or ignored the veterans out of a desire to forget the war. Even government services for veterans through the Veterans Administration were often inadequate because of a lack of political will to provide support for the veterans.

Veterans themselves could not forget the war. Feeling alienated from the rest of society, many bonded together into a special brotherhood of those who had been there. Slowly they began to help rehabilitate themselves. The Vietnam Veterans Memorial in Washington began as a project by veterans and finally provided a way for society to begin to connect with those who had served. Movies, which at first had often portrayed Vietnam veterans as drug-addicted killers, began in the 1980s to present more positive, sympathetic, and even heroic images. Another belated but positive development was the American Psychiatric Association's confirmation in 1980 of a clinical diagnosis of a condition known as post-traumatic stress disorder (PTSD). Many soldiers who had been in heavy combat and many nurses who had faced, almost daily, the physical toll of warfare had come home with severe personality changes, similar to what in previous wars had been termed "shell shock" or "battle fatigue." What had happened to them was at first misunderstood and often misdiagnosed. Their symptoms included agonizing grief, tormenting guilt, suicidal longings, violent outbursts, severe depression, and feelings of isolation. The recognition that their illness, PTSD, was a normal human reaction to abnormal traumatic experiences greatly helped in the treatment of thousands of veterans.

Vietcong— see **National Liberation Front**.

Vietminh—Created by the Indochinese Communist Party in May 1941, the Vietminh represented a classic tactic in pursuit of long-term revolutionary objectives through a patriotic front organization in a war of national liberation. Vietminh was the common name for Vietnam Doc Lap Dong Minh Hoi, or

League for the Independence of Vietnam. Ho Chi Minh and other leaders of the Vietminh de-emphasized the principle of class conflict and welcomed Vietnamese of whatever class to join the struggle for national independence against the French colonialists and the Japanese occupiers. In March 1945 the Japanese command dispersed the forces of their French collaborators, and in August 1945 the Japanese troops themselves surrendered their claims of authority. This temporary political void was the moment for which Ho had been waiting. The Vietminh leaders ordered their network of branch committees and patriotic associations and their armed brigade under Vo Nguyen Giap to seize control throughout the country. This August Revolution is one of the key events in modern Vietnamese history. Although actual Vietminh control was tenuous or nonexistent in most areas, Ho Chi Minh read aloud in Hanoi his Declaration of Vietnamese Independence on September 2, 1945, and inaugurated the Democratic Republic of Vietnam.

During the ensuing war with France over authority in Indochina, the Vietminh and the Indochinese Communist Party went through various name changes and public postures. Regardless of these propaganda maneuvers, Vietminh remained the name used within and outside Vietnam to designate the movement and army that defeated the French and placed the DRV government in power in North Vietnam in 1954. In 1960 some former Vietminh cadres who remained in the South played major roles in organizing the National Liberation Front.

Vietnamization—Vietnamization was the name the Nixon administration gave to the American policy of helping South Vietnam defend and develop itself. The approach actually marked a return to what had been U.S. policy in Vietnam before Lyndon Johnson's massive military escalation had Americanized the war. Also prior to Nixon's presidency, General Creighton Abrams had begun what he termed "Vietnamizing" when he succeeded General William Westmoreland as MACV commander in 1968. The basic idea of Vietnamizing, or Vietnamization, was for the U.S. military to turn over more of the ground combat effort against the Vietcong and PAVN to the ARVN. In the process, the United States provided more war materiel and advanced technology to its South Vietnamese allies and increased U.S. air support. The program also included more attention on pacification, that is, on population security, political reform, and economic development.

Although the Republic of Vietnam needed to become less dependent on the United States if it was to survive, Vietnamization was more an American political move than a change in strategy. It allowed Nixon to begin reducing the number of American troops in South Vietnam while giving the appearance of progress in the war. Nixon even proclaimed it as part of a global policy—a so-called Nixon Doctrine—that the United States would help its allies but could not itself undertake the defense of all nations. Vietnamization paid some political dividends for the president and left a better equipped ARVN, but it did not improve the long-term military and political effectiveness of the RVN. Only extensive U.S. bombing averted disaster for the ARVN in its attempted offensive into Laos in 1971 and in its defense against the DRV's Easter Offensive of 1972. Without American air support after 1973, the failure of Vietnamization was evident in the RVN's inability to survive on its own.

Vietnam Quoc Dan Dang (Vietnam Nationalist Party)—Organized as a clandestine, radical party in 1927, the aim of the Vietnam Quoc Dan Dang (VNQDD) was to ignite a violent overthrow of French rule and create a democratic republic. Its members were moderate socialists but not communists, and it modeled itself after the Chinese Nationalist Party. In February 1930 VNQDD units of 50 to 300 fighters each suddenly attacked several French military bases in Tonkin and inflicted the heaviest losses at Yen Bay, where they killed a dozen French soldiers. A French counterattack crushed the poorly armed rebels, and the French executed or imprisoned hundreds of VNQDD members in the following weeks. Others fled to China. After the August Revolution of 1945, hundreds returned to Vietnam only to be killed by the Vietminh, who saw them as rivals. The remaining members were fervent anticommunist, and many gathered in South Vietnam after 1954 and formed a minority party in the RVN. Although poorly led, the VNQDD represented a significant expression of anticommunist nationalism in Vietnam.

Vietnam Syndrome—The term "Vietnam syndrome" came into use in the 1980s to denote the palpable reluctance in American public opinion to support U.S. military intervention abroad. Prowar politicians in the '80s, such as former president Richard Nixon and Presidents Ronald Reagan and George H. W. Bush, worried that this feeling—often expressed in the phrase "no more Vietnams"—would prevent American leaders from being able to defend legitimate national interests or to stand up to communist aggressors. These concerned conservatives had their own interpretation of "no more Vietnams." To them the phrase did not mean no interventions whatsoever, but it meant to intervene only when there was clear political backing and a willingness to use America's full resources. As President Bush prepared to send U.S. forces to the Persian Gulf region to counter the Iraqi invasion of Kuwait in 1990–1991, he first built up a massive force, sought international and domestic approval, and then launched the attack. After the U.S. attack had liberated Kuwait, the president exclaimed: "By God, we've kicked the Vietnam syndrome once and for all." The American public and their leaders did not forget the Vietnam experience so completely, however, and U.S. strategists continued to be cautious about employing American troops in hostilities abroad.

Vietnam Veterans Against the War (VVAW) — Founded by a half dozen veterans in New York City in 1967, the Vietnam Veterans Against the War eventually claimed several thousand members, although the group remained a tiny minority of men who served in Vietnam. Questions exist as to whether all the members were Vietnam veterans or even veterans at all, but many indeed were authentic. The image of the returned warrior protesting his own war was a powerful antiwar statement. They participated in antiwar demonstrations, and the New York City chapter formed "rap groups" in which veterans could obtain group therapy for psychological problems related to their war experiences. These rap groups became models for counseling centers later developed by the Veterans Administration. Two of the VVAW's most well-known activities came in 1971. In February the VVAW conducted what it called the "Winter Soldier Investigation" in Detroit to present evidence of alleged war crimes in which the speakers said they had participated or which they had witnessed. In April VVAW members and others went to Washington for an operation they called Dewey Canyon III, which received much media attention. They camped out for a week, held memorial services, presented antiwar skits, and testified before Congress. The most dramatic gesture of the week came when some participants threw military medals and decorations for Vietnam service onto the steps of the Capitol.

Vietnam Veterans Memorial — Dedicated in 1982, the Vietnam Veterans Memorial on the Mall in Washington, D.C., contains the names of more than 58,000 U.S. military personnel who were killed in the war or who remain missing. The names are carved in chronological order of date of loss on a polished, black granite wall that forms a "V" with each arm 246 feet long. "The Wall," as it is called, is placed on a hillside so that it slopes downward toward the center where the panels containing the names rise ten feet. The idea of the monument came from three Vietnam veterans, Jan Scruggs, Bob Doubek, and John Wheeler. In 1979 they and others set up the nonprofit Vietnam Veterans Memorial Fund that raised some $9 million, most of it in small contributions from veterans, to build the monument. The design by Maya Lin was initially criticized by some as too modern or negative in connotation, but time has shown the memorial to be a powerful attraction for veterans, families and friends of those killed, and other Americans. It has become the most visited monument in the nation's capital. Often those who stand before its reflective panels and focus on the individual names are deeply moved by the experience. Many make rubbings of the names and leave small mementos, which are carefully saved by the National Park Service. In 1984 a flagpole and a bronze statue by Frederick Hart depicting three soldiers were added. In 1993 the Vietnam Women's Memorial Project dedicated a statue by Glenna Goodacre. It represents three nurses assisting a soldier. The Wall, the statues, and the flagpole have played a significant role in public remembrance of a controversial conflict.

Vo Nguyen Giap (1911–)—As senior general in the People's Army of Vietnam (1946–1972) and minister of national defense (1946–1982), Vo Nguyen Giap was one of the acknowledged architects of the Vietminh and DRV military successes against France and the United States. As one of the founders of the Vietminh, with Ho Chi Minh and Pham Van Dong, and a member of the Politburo from 1951 to 1982, he was also a key political leader. In fact, his military genius came from a combination of historical study of warfare and the ability to combine politics and military strategy. Born in Quang Binh Province in central Annam, he attended the National Academy in Hue but was expelled as a trouble maker. He joined the Indochinese Communist Party in 1930 and graduated from the University of Hanoi in the mid-1930s with a degree in law. He briefly taught history in Hanoi before the party sent him to southern China in 1940. He left his wife behind, and she later died a painful death in a French prison. He joined Ho in creating the Vietminh and organized an Armed Propaganda Brigade of thirty-four men who represented what would become the PAVN. His troops underwent political indoctrination as well as military training to instill high motivation. His strategic doctrine followed Mao Zedong's model of People's War that mixed political and military activity leading to a final offensive and political revolution.

Giap gained his fame for the dramatic PAVN siege and capture of the French fortress at Dienbienphu in 1954. During the DRV's war against the Americans, Giap retained his leadership offices but often encountered intense debates with other commanders over strategy. He generally cautioned patience, while others wanted to be more aggressive against the U.S. forces. He designed the Tet Offensive of 1968 that produced high casualties for his own troops and no popular uprising in the South. It had enough initial success, however, to produce an unexpected psychological victory for Hanoi. Controversy continued to surround his military leadership, and before the end of the war he no longer commanded the PAVN. His political power declined as well, and after the war he was dropped from the Politburo. In his retirement the government designated him as a "national treasure."

War Powers Resolution (1973)—Also known as the War Powers Act, the War Powers Resolution was a joint resolution with the power of law passed by Congress over Richard Nixon's veto on November 7, 1973. Its intent was to attempt to limit the power of the president to commit U.S. forces to extended combat or risk of combat without congressional approval, either through a declaration of war as the Constitution provides or at least by specific enabling legislation. The resolution clearly was a response to displeasure in Congress with presidential conduct of the Vietnam War, but the practice of chief executives using their constitutional authority as commander in chief to conduct a war went back to Truman and the Korean conflict. Specifically, the War Powers Resolution required the president to notify Congress within forty-eight hours of any commitment of U.S.

troops to actual or possible foreign conflict and to terminate that deployment within sixty days unless Congress acted to authorize the action. The period could be extended thirty more days, if necessary, for safe evacuation of U.S. troops. Congress could also order a withdrawal of U.S. forces. Since 1973 the sixty-day limit on the president's action has only been activated twice. President Ford notified Congress of troop deployment during the 1975 *Mayaguez* incident with Cambodia, but the incident ended almost immediately. In 1983 Congress, not President Reagan, started the sixty-day limit on sending Marines to Lebanon, but it actually ended up authorizing an eighteen-month limit. In most cases, presidents have claimed that the War Powers Resolution was not applicable, although they have often followed its spirit. For example, President George H. W. Bush sought authorization from Congress on the eve of the Gulf War in 1991 to send American troops into combat, but he insisted that he was not required to do so.

Wars of National Liberation—see **Flexible Response**.

Watergate—The term "Watergate" denotes the major scandal that enveloped the presidency of Richard Nixon and led to his unprecedented resignation on August 9, 1974. It takes its name from the attempted burglary of the Democratic National Committee offices in the Watergate office-hotel complex in Washington, D.C., on June 23, 1972, by a team of men working for the Committee to Re-elect the President (CREEP). Although the White House was able initially to cover up any direct connection of these men to the president, the continued prodding by the judge in the trial of the burglars and an investigation by reporters for the *Washington Post* newspaper found a wide conspiracy reaching to Nixon's closest personal advisers.

The Vietnam War figured directly in the origins of this conspiracy and other illegal White House activity. From the beginning of his administration, Nixon and his aides had used the FBI, CIA, and the military to spy on antiwar groups and had used the Internal Revenue Service and other government agencies to intimidate people on their political "enemies list." After Daniel Ellsberg leaked the Pentagon Papers to the press in 1971, the White House created the "plumbers," a secret group of operatives to stop political leaks and get damaging information on Ellsberg and others. The June 1972 burglary was a plumbers operation. After Senate and House investigations found widespread wrongdoing, the House Judiciary Committee voted to impeach Nixon for "abuse of power." Tapes of White House conversations established that the president himself had authorized the cover-up of illegal activities, and such obstruction of justice was a felony offense. Facing virtually certain removal from office, Nixon resigned.

Nixon's behavior in office contributed to passage of the War Powers Resolution in 1973 in the midst of the Watergate revelations. Nixon and later President Ford faced increased congressional oversight on the use of American troops abroad. Nixon and his aide Henry Kissinger later claimed that Watergate made it impossible for the United States to provide effective assistance to South Vietnam after 1973. This contention is debatable, however, because Congress and the public had rejected continuing U.S. defense of the RVN long before the Watergate scandal ended with Nixon's resignation.

Westmoreland, William C. (1914–) — General William C. Westmoreland commanded the U.S. Military Assistance Command, Vietnam, from June 1964 to June 1968, and, as the officer in charge of most of the American military assets in Vietnam during that period, he became the principal strategist for the U.S. war effort. Born in South Carolina, he graduated in 1936 from West Point, where he had been commander of the Corps of Cadets. He had an outstanding combat record in World War II and the Korean War, held many important command and staff positions, and was superintendent of West Point when President Kennedy selected him to head MACV. He was an energetic and dedicated but conventional military leader. Despite his communist adversaries' known skills for irregular warfare and political tactics, he designed an attrition strategy of large unit sweeps and aerial bombardment aimed at regular North Vietnamese and Vietcong units and intended to inflict more losses on his enemies than they could sustain. He requested and received ever-higher numbers of U.S. ground forces until the total exceeded 500,000. He employed these in "search and destroy" operations utilizing helicopter mobility and high-technology weaponry. He paid much less attention to pacification efforts.

Although Westmoreland's approach inflicted heavy losses on the enemy and he made public claims of progress (often at Washington's prompting), by the end of 1967 he had, in fact, achieved only a military stalemate, which became apparent in the Tet Offensive in early 1968. His forces in South Vietnam repulsed the surprise enemy attacks, but it was clear that the war was far from over, and its burden on Americans and Vietnamese would only continue. Some military historians have claimed that Westmoreland never received the freedom or resources from Washington he needed for success, but it was also evident that his troops were often just flailing about without any clear plan for victory. Consequently, Johnson turned down his request for 206,000 more troops after Tet and reassigned him as U.S. Army chief of staff. He was succeeded at MACV by his deputy commander, General Creighton Abrams. Westmoreland retired from the army in 1972 and published his memoir in 1976. A 1982 CBS News investigation claimed that he had knowingly misrepresented enemy troop strength to Washington prior to the Tet Offensive. He sued the network for libel, and the case was settled out of court in 1985 with both sides claiming victory.

Wheeler, Earle G. (1908–1975) — General Earle G. Wheeler was U.S. Army chief of staff from 1962 to 1964 and chairman of the Joint Chiefs of Staff (JCS) from 1964 to 1970. Like other senior U.S. officials, Wheeler underestimated the political strength of the Vietnamese communists and remained convinced that American military power was the key to success in Vietnam. He and the other service chiefs disagreed with Secretary of Defense Robert McNamara's preference for gradual escalation of force and favored massing U.S. ground and air power from the beginning. Such a move would also have required activating the military reserves to maintain global readiness. He never gained presidential approval on the reserves, and his constant requests for more troops and bombing were only partially met. It was at Wheeler's urging that, after the start of the Tet Offensive, Westmoreland asked for 206,000 more troops, which the White House denied. Some military writers have criticized Wheeler and the JCS under him for not making clear to the president their estimation that the piecemeal strategy would fail, but Wheeler chose to remain the loyal military subordinate to the civilian commander in chief.

Wise Men — Beginning in July 1965, as he faced the decision to send U.S. combat troops to Vietnam, Lyndon Johnson began meeting occasionally with an unofficial group of senior advisers that became known as the Wise Men. Most of them were former high-ranking civil and military officials, and the composition of the group varied over time. The Wise Men were Dean Acheson, George W. Ball, Omar Bradley, McGeorge Bundy, Arthur Dean, Douglas Dillon, Abe Fortas, Arthur Goldberg, Henry Cabot Lodge Jr., John J. McCloy, Robert Murphy, Matthew Ridgway, Maxwell Taylor, and Cyrus Vance. Through 1967 most of them endorsed Johnson's policies at every stage, and thus the president was shaken when the majority of them concluded after the Tet Offensive that an American military solution in Vietnam was no longer attainable. On March 26, 1968, the Wise Men met for the last time with the president and advised him "to take steps to disengage" the United States from Vietnam. On March 31 Johnson announced that the United States would reduce bombing of the North and enter into negotiations, and that he would not seek reelection.

PART III

Chronology

207 B.C.	Kingdom of Nam Viet founded.
111 B.C.	China's Han dynasty conquers Nam Viet.
39 A.D.	Revolt led by Truong Sisters against Chinese rule fails, but sisters eventually become legendary heroes.
938	Vietnamese defeat Chinese at Battle of Bach Dang River and end a thousand years of Chinese rule.
1009	Ly dynasty founded.
1288	Vietnamese defeat invading Mongols at second Battle of Bach Dang River.
1407	China's Ming dynasty conquers Vietnamese state called Dai Viet.
1428	Le Loi, having defeated Ming army, establishes Le dynasty.
1471	Vietnamese establish protectorate over Champa and begin 300-year March to the South.
1627	French priest Alexander of Rhodes uses Latin alphabet to create Vietnamese written language.
1630s	Nguyen family in the South and Trinh family in the North divide control of Vietnam at approximately the seventeenth parallel.

1771–1789	Tay Son Rebellion ends the balance of power between the Nguyen and Trinh families.
1802	Nguyen Anh unites Vietnam under his rule as Emperor Gia Long and begins Nguyen dynasty with its capital at Hue.
1858	French naval force occupies Tourane (Danang).
1859	French take control of village of Saigon.
1862	Emperor Tu Duc cedes Cochinchina to France as a colony; France makes Cambodia a protectorate.
1883	France creates protectorates in Annam and Tonkin.
1893	France establishes protectorate in Laos.
1897	France formalizes its colonial government of Indochina Union.
1899	U.S. Secretary of State John Hay asks nations to preserve an "open door" in China.
1904	Phan Boi Chau forms Modernization Society.
1912	Phan Boi Chau founds Vietnamese Restoration Society.
1917, January 18	President Woodrow Wilson includes in his Fourteen Points an appeal for all nations to be free to determine their own institutions.
1919	Nguyen Ai Quoc (Ho Chi Minh) unsuccessfully petitions Versailles Peace Conference for Vietnamese independence.
1925	Phan Boi Chau arrested; Ho Chi Minh founds Vietnamese Revolutionary Youth League.
1927	Vietnam Quoc Dan Dang (VNQDD), or Vietnam Nationalist Party, founded.
1930	VNQDD rebellion crushed by French authorities; Ho Chi Minh founds Indochinese Communist Party.
1932	French authorities prevent young emperor Bao Dai from carrying out his modest efforts to shape a political role for the royal court.
1940	Japanese forces occupy military bases in Tonkin.
1941	Vietminh created by Indochinese Communist Party; President Franklin Roosevelt declares in the Atlantic Charter that nations have a right to self-government.
1944	Vietminh forms Armed Propaganda Brigade.
1944, February	President Roosevelt endorses the idea of a trusteeship for French Indochina but offers no specific plan.
1945, March	Japanese troops remove French officials in Indochina and recognize royal government of Emperor Bao Dai.

1945, August	Japan surrenders to Allied powers; Vietminh begins August Revolution; Bao Dai abdicates his throne.
1945, September 2	Ho Chi Minh declares the independence of the Democratic Republic of Vietnam.
1946, March 6	Ho-Sainteny agreement makes preliminary provision for a "free" Vietnam.
1946, May 30	French officials in Saigon declare Republic of Cochinchina a separate state.
1946, December 19	French-Vietminh War begins with Vietminh attack on French forces in Tonkin.
1947, March 12	President Harry Truman in his Truman Doctrine speech pledges U.S. assistance to free people seeking to work out their own destinies.
1947, July	George Kennan publishes an article in the journal *Foreign Affairs*, providing the rationale for what becomes the U.S. policy of containment of the USSR and its allies.
1949, March 8	Elysée Agreement between French government and Bao Dai creates State of Vietnam with Bao Dai as head of state.
1950, January	People's Republic of China and Soviet Union recognize Democratic Republic of Vietnam.
1950, February	United States and Great Britain recognize State of Vietnam.
1950, May	United States begins economic and military aid to French in Indochina.
1950, June 25	Korean War begins.
1953, July 27	Korean War armistice is signed.
1953, September 30	Eisenhower administration grants $385 million to France to finance its Navarre Plan, which Paris claims will end the war; with this new aid, the United States funds 80 percent of French war costs in Indochina.
1954, March 13	Vietminh siege of French garrison at Dienbienphu begins.
1954, April 7	Eisenhower employs the "domino theory" to explain strategic importance of Vietnam.
1954, May 7	French forces at Dienbienphu surrender to Vietminh.
1954, June 19	Bao Dai appoints Ngo Dinh Diem prime minister of the State of Vietnam.
1954, July 20–21	Geneva Agreements provide for an armistice in the French-Vietminh War, the temporary partitioning of Vietnam between North and South, further talks to

	plan all-Vietnam elections for 1956, and recognition of independence of Laos and Cambodia.
1954, August	Hundreds of thousands of refugees, mostly Catholics, begin moving from North Vietnam to South Vietnam under terms of Geneva Agreements.
1954, September 8	Southeast Asia Treaty Organization established.
1954, November 8	General J. Lawton Collins arrives in Saigon as President Eisenhower's special representative and a few months later recommends that the United States should back some South Vietnamese leader other than Ngo Dinh Diem.
1955, April 27–30	Ngo Dinh Diem survives armed challenge to his authority from religious sects and Binh Xuyen gangsters.
1955, October 23	Ngo Dinh Diem stages a referendum that deposes Bao Dai and allows Diem to create Republic of Vietnam with Diem as president and its capital in Saigon.
1956, July 20	Second anniversary of Geneva Agreements passes with no all-Vietnam elections held.
1957, May	Ngo Dinh Diem makes state visit to United States and is hailed for his success.
1959, May	North Vietnam forms a military group to provide men and supplies to support armed struggle in South Vietnam; this operation marks beginning of Ho Chi Minh Trail through Laos.
1959, July 8	Guerrilla attack at Bien Hoa kills two U.S. soldiers, who are later declared the first American casualties of the Vietnam War.
1960, August	Laotian civil war begins.
1960, December 20	National Liberation Front, also called Vietcong, established in South Vietnam by the Lao Dong, or Communist Party, of North Vietnam.
1961, January 19	President Eisenhower tells President-elect Kennedy that Laos is the most serious problem the United States faces in Southeast Asia.
1961, May 12	Vice President Lyndon Johnson visits South Vietnam.
1961, May 16	Geneva Conference begins that produces international agreement on July 23, 1962, on a coalition government in Laos.
1961, October 18–24	Kennedy aides Maxwell Taylor and Walt Rostow visit South Vietnam and recommend increased U.S.

	economic aid and deployment of 8,000 American combat troops.
1961, November 3	President Kennedy receives the Taylor-Rostow report and soon after approves additional aid but not combat troops.
1962, February 6	U.S. Military Assistance Command, Vietnam (MACV) is created with General Paul Harkins as its first commander.
1962, June	Students for a Democratic Society (SDS) issues its Port Huron Statement.
1963, January 2	Battle of Ap Bac is defeat for U.S.-aided Army of the Republic of Vietnam (ARVN) forces.
1963, May 8	South Vietnamese police fire on and kill Buddhist demonstrators in Hue.
1963, June 11	Buddhist monk Thich Quang Duc burns himself to death on Saigon street corner to protest Republic of Vietnam suppression of Buddhists.
1963, August	South Vietnamese soldiers attack Buddhist pagodas and arrest hundreds of Buddhists; Henry Cabot Lodge becomes U.S. ambassador to South Vietnam.
1963, October	American officials signal South Vietnamese military that United States will not interfere in coup against Diem; Kennedy approves report by Robert McNamara and Maxwell Taylor recommending greater pressure on Diem to reform.
1963, November 1	Military coup overthrows Diem government.
1963, November 2	Ngo Dinh Diem and his brother Ngo Dinh Nhu are assassinated.
1963, November 22	President Kennedy is assassinated in Dallas, Texas; Vice President Lyndon Johnson becomes president.
1964, January 30	General Nguyen Khanh seizes control of Saigon government.
1964, June 20	General William C. Westmoreland becomes commander of Military Assistance Command, Vietnam (MACV).
1964, July 30–31	South Vietnamese Navy conducts commando raids along North Vietnamese coast.
1964, August 2	North Vietnamese torpedo boats attack U.S. destroyer *Maddox* in Gulf of Tonkin.
1964, August 4	U.S. destroyers *Maddox* and *C. Turner Joy* report being attacked (although doubts about the attack soon arise);

	President Johnson orders retaliatory air raids against military facilities in North Vietnam.
1964, August 7	Congress passes by overwhelming vote the Gulf of Tonkin Resolution authorizing the president to use armed force in Southeast Asia to protect American personnel and to counter aggression.
1964, November 3	President Lyndon Johnson defeats Barry Goldwater by wide margin.
1965, February 7	Vietcong attacks U.S. base at Pleiku, and United States responds with air attacks on North Vietnam.
1965, February 20	Armed Forces Council makes civilian Phan Huy Quat prime minister of the Republic of Vietnam.
1965, March 2	Operation Rolling Thunder begins regular bombing of North Vietnam.
1965, March 8	U.S. Marine brigade lands at Danang.
1965, March 24–25	First teach-in held at University of Michigan.
1965, April 7	President Johnson makes Johns Hopkins University speech offering "unconditional discussions" with Hanoi and massive economic development aid for Southeast Asia.
1965, April 17	Students for a Democratic Society (SDS) organizes an antiwar protest of about 20,000 in Washington, D.C..
1965, June	Military government headed by Air Marshal Nguyen Cao Ky as prime minister and General Nguyen Van Thieu as president takes over in Saigon.
1965, July 28	Lyndon Johnson approves Westmoreland's request for 100,000 additional troops, basically Americanizing the war.
1965, November 14–17	Battle of Ia Drang Valley is first major clash between regular U.S. and North Vietnamese troops.
1965, December 24	President Johnson suspends bombing of North Vietnam to encourage negotiations.
1966, January 31	President Johnson resumes bombing of North Vietnam.
1966, February 4	Senate Foreign Relations Committee begins televised hearings on U.S. military intervention in Vietnam.
1966, February 7	President Johnson meets with Nguyen Cao Ky and Nguyen Van Thieu in Honolulu.
1966, March	Buddhist-led antigovernment demonstrations begin in Hue, Danang, and Saigon and last until June.
1966, April 11	First use of U.S. B-52 bombers against targets in North Vietnam.

1966, September 11	Republic of Vietnam elects a constituent assembly; Buddhist leaders complain of voting fraud.
1966, December 9	Diplomatic initiative through Polish intermediaries to start negotiations collapses after U.S. bombing raid strikes targets near Hanoi.
1967, January	Large U.S. and Army of the Republic of Vietnam (ARVN) offensive sweep, Operation Cedar Falls, targets People's Army of Vietnam (PAVN) and Vietcong bases in area near Saigon known as the Iron Triangle.
1967, February	Operation Junction City is major U.S. and ARVN attack on enemy base areas near South Vietnam-Cambodia border.
1967, March 10	Republic of Vietnam Council of Ministers approves new constitution.
1967, March 20	President Johnson meets with Nguyen Cao Ky and Nguyen Van Thieu in Guam.
1967, April 4	Martin Luther King Jr. delivers his speech, "A Time to Break Silence," in New York City.
1967, April 15	Large antiwar demonstrations occur across the United States, including an estimated 300,000 protestors at a peace rally in New York City.
1967, May 10	Johnson administration establishes Civilian Operations and Revolutionary Development Support (CORDS) organization to coordinate pacification programs in South Vietnam.
1967, September 3	Nguyen Van Thieu elected president and Nguyen Cao Ky elected vice president of Republic of Vietnam.
1967, September 29	In speech at San Antonio, Texas, President Johnson offers to stop bombing in return for serious negotiations from North Vietnam.
1967, October	People's Army of Vietnam (PAVN) begins attacks near U.S. Marine base at Khe Sanh.
1967, October 21–23	Antiwar protestors, numbering about 50,000, march on Pentagon.
1967, November 21	General William Westmoreland makes speech at the National Press Club in Washington, D.C., reporting military progress in Vietnam and that the end of the war is coming into view.
1967, December	North Vietnam reiterates its position that the United States must stop bombing before serious negotiations can begin.

1968, January 21	People's Army of Vietnam (PAVN) siege of U.S. base at Khe Sanh begins and lasts until April 6.
1968, January 30	First attacks of Vietcong and PAVN Tet Offensive begin in central South Vietnam.
1968, January 31	Tet Offensive begins throughout South Vietnam.
1968, February 25	U.S. and South Vietnamese troops retake control of Hue.
1968, February 26	More than 2,500 bodies found in mass graves in Hue are evidence of Vietcong massacre of Republic of Vietnam supporters in the city.
1968, February 27	CBS News airs a television documentary in which respected reporter Walter Cronkite concludes that the time has come for the United States to seek a negotiated end to the war.
1968, February 28	General Earle Wheeler supports General Westmoreland's requests for 206,000 additional troops.
1968, March 12	Senator Eugene McCarthy makes strong showing as antiwar candidate against Lyndon Johnson in the New Hampshire Democratic presidential primary.
1968, March 16	My Lai massacre occurs in which members of an American infantry company kill 504 unresisting Vietnamese civilians in the My Lai and My Khe subhamlets of Son My village in Quang Ngai Province, but incident is not publicly revealed at the time.
1968, March 22	President Johnson announces that General Westmoreland will become U.S. Army chief of staff and General Creighton Abrams will become commander of Military Assistance Command, Vietnam (MACV).
1968, March 26	Wise Men advise Johnson against further military escalation in Vietnam.
1968, March 31	President Johnson makes televised speech revealing bombing restrictions, offer to negotiate with North Vietnam, increase of only 13,500 U.S. troops in South Vietnam, and his decision not to run for reelection.
1968, April 4	Martin Luther King Jr. assassinated in Memphis.
1968, April 23–30	Student protestors occupy several buildings at Columbia University until forcibly removed by police.
1968, May	So-called Mini-Tet Offensive includes Communist attacks throughout South Vietnam that are quelled by

	U.S. and Army of the Republic of Vietnam (ARVN) forces.
1968, May 13	Paris Peace Talks begin between U.S. and Democratic Republic of Vietnam representatives.
1968, June 4	Robert F. Kennedy wins the Democratic presidential primary in California and is assassinated in Los Angeles the same evening.
1968, August 28	Democratic National Convention is scene of violent clash between Chicago police and radical antiwar demonstrators.
1968, October 31	President Johnson announces the end of Rolling Thunder, that is, of all U.S. bombardment of North Vietnam.
1968, November 5	Richard Nixon narrowly defeats Hubert Humphrey in U.S. presidential election.
1969, January 25	Paris Peace Talks expand to include representatives of the Republic of Vietnam and the National Liberation Front.
1969, March 18	United States begins Operation Menu, the secret bombing of Cambodia.
1969, March 19	Nixon administration announces its Vietnamization policy.
1969, April 5–6	Antiwar demonstrations in several U.S. cities.
1969, April 30	U.S. troop strength in Vietnam reaches its highest level of the war at 543,400.
1969, June 8	Richard Nixon announces withdrawal of 25,000 U.S. troops as beginning of gradual reduction of American forces in South Vietnam.
1969, June 10	National Liberation Front and other opponents of Saigon regime form the Provisional Revolutionary Government of South Vietnam.
1969, July 25	President Nixon declares in the Nixon Doctrine that the United States will aid allies, but that they must be responsible for their own defense.
1969, August 4	Henry Kissinger begins secret talks in Paris with Democratic Republic of Vietnam representative Xuan Thuy.
1969, September 2	Ho Chi Minh dies.
1969, October 15	Moratorium demonstrations against the war occur across the United States.
1969, November 3	President Nixon asserts in televised speech that "silent majority" favors his Vietnamization plan of gradual American withdrawal from Vietnam.

1969, November 15	Moratorium demonstrations draw larger participation than in October.
1969, November 16	Military officials reveal investigation of My Lai massacre.
1969, December 1	U.S. Selective Service begins draft lottery.
1970, February 21	Henry Kissinger begins secret talks with Le Duc Tho in Paris.
1970, March 18	Cambodia's National Assembly ousts Prince Norodom Sihanouk and makes Lon Nol head of state.
1970, April 20	President Nixon reveals plan to reduce U.S. forces in Vietnam by 150,000 over next year.
1970, April 30	President Nixon announces that U.S. troops are attacking Communist sanctuaries in Cambodia; widespread campus protests follow in the United States.
1970, May 3	U.S. military spokesman acknowledges resumed bombing of North Vietnam.
1970, May 4	Ohio National Guardsmen shoot and kill four Kent State University students and wound at least nine others.
1970, May	Widespread campus demonstrations and strikes, and other large public demonstrations, protest the events at Kent State and Nixon's policies in Southeast Asia.
1970, May 14	Police kill two students and wound twelve others during student protests at Jackson State College in Mississippi.
1970, June 24	U.S. Senate repeals the Gulf of Tonkin Resolution.
1970, June 30	U.S. troops complete their withdrawal from Cambodia.
1970, September 1	Senators George McGovern and Mark Hatfield make unsuccessful attempt to obtain a Senate resolution setting a deadline for all U.S. troops to be out of Vietnam.
1971, February 8	Army of the Republic of Vietnam (ARVN) offensive into Laos, code-named Lam Son 719, begins with U.S. air support and continues to March 24.
1971, March 29	Military court convicts Lieutenant William L. Calley Jr. of murder for his role in 1968 My Lai massacre; he is originally sentenced to life in prison but is paroled in 1974.
1971, April 7	President Nixon declares Vietnamization a success and announces a reduction of 100,000 more U.S. troops from South Vietnam.

1971, April 19–23	Vietnam Veterans Against the War stages dramatic protests in Washington, D.C., that it calls Operation Dewey Canyon III.
1971, April 24	Antiwar demonstration in Washington, D.C., draws 200,000 participants, and rally in San Francisco gathers 156,000 protestors.
1971, June 13	*New York Times* publishes the first article based on the Pentagon Papers, the secret history of government decision making leaked to the press by Daniel Ellsberg.
1971, October 3	Nguyen Van Thieu wins reelection as president of the Republic of Vietnam after opposing candidates withdraw from race charging that the election is rigged for the incumbent.
1972, February 21	President Nixon meets in Beijing with Mao Zedong, the leader of the People's Republic of China.
1972, March 30	North Vietnam launches Easter Offensive intended to topple Thieu government.
1972, April	United States bombs People's Army of Vietnam (PAVN) forces in North Vietnam and South Vietnam; demonstrations in the United States protest the bombing.
1972, May 8	President Nixon orders Operation Linebacker, which includes heavy bombing of North Vietnam's military supply network and the mining of Haiphong harbor.
1972, May 20	President Nixon meets with Soviet President Leonid Brezhnev in Moscow.
1972, June	General Creighton Abrams becomes U.S. Army chief of staff and General Frederick Weyand becomes commander of Military Assistance Command, Vietnam (MACV).
1972, September 15	Army of the Republic of Vietnam (ARVN) retakes Quang Tri City, which is virtually destroyed by intense fighting since North Vietnamese Army occupied it in May.
1972, October 26	Henry Kissinger announces "peace is at hand," after he and Le Duc Tho reach a tentative agreement that provides for withdrawal of remaining U.S. troops, allows North Vietnamese Army units to remain in the South, and leaves the Republic of Vietnam government in place to deal directly with the Provisional Revolutionary Government on political issues.

1972, November 1	President Thieu makes public his opposition to the tentative Kissinger-Tho agreement.
1972, November 7	President Nixon defeats George McGovern in a landslide vote.
1972, December 14	United States and Democratic Republic of Vietnam break off peace talks.
1972, December 18–29	United States carries out Operation Linebacker II, also called the Christmas Bombing, which is the most intense air attack on Hanoi and Haiphong of the entire war.
1973, January 5	Nixon provides Thieu private assurance that United States will respond with "full force" if Hanoi violates diplomatic settlement.
1973, January 8	Kissinger and Tho resume negotiations in Paris.
1973, January 23	Kissinger and Tho initial a peace agreement very similar in terms to their October 1972 agreement.
1973, January 27	Paris Peace Accords are signed by representatives of United States, Democratic Republic of Vietnam, Repubic of Vietnam, and Provisional Revolutionary Government; Nixon calls it "peace with honor," but fighting continues in Vietnam; military draft in United States formally ends.
1973, February 21	United States ends bombing in Laos.
1973, March 29	Last U.S. POWs leave Hanoi and last U.S. troops leave South Vietnam, with only U.S. Marine embassy guards and a Defense Attaché's Office remaining in Saigon.
1973, August 14	U.S. bombing of Cambodia ends in accordance with deadline set by Congress.
1973, October 16	Henry Kissinger and Le Duc Tho awarded Nobel Peace Prize; Tho declines to accept.
1973, November 7	Congress overrides Richard Nixon's veto and passes War Powers Resolution, which limits presidential authority to send troops into combat abroad.
1974, February	Army of the Republic of Vietnam (ARVN) begins major offensive against areas controlled by the Provisional Revolutionary Government in central South Vietnam and west of Saigon; intense fighting follows.
1974, August 6	U.S. Congress makes deep cuts in military aid to the Republic of Vietnam.

1974, August 9	Richard Nixon resigns as president because of revelations of criminal acts connected to the Watergate scandal; Vice President Gerald R. Ford becomes president.
1975, January 1	Khmer Rouge begins offensive against Cambodia's capital Phnom Penh.
1975, January 8	North Vietnamese take control of South Vietnam's Phuoc Long Province on the Cambodian border; there is no U.S. military response.
1975, March 10	People's Army of Vietnam (PAVN) Spring Offensive begins with capture of Ban Me Thuot in Central Highlands.
1975, March 15	Army of the Republic of Vietnam (ARVN) begins chaotic retreat from Central Highlands.
1975, March 26	Hue falls to the People's Army of Vietnam (PAVN) advance, which Hanoi has named the Ho Chi Minh Campaign.
1975, March 30	Danang falls to North Vietnamese offensive.
1975, April 9–11	Army of the Republic of Vietnam (ARVN) makes strong but futile defensive stand at Xuan Loc.
1975, April 10	Congress rejects President Ford's request for $722 million in military aid for Army of the Republic of Vietnam (ARVN).
1975, April 12	U.S. personnel evacuate Phnom Penh.
1975, April 17	Khmer Rouge captures Phnom Penh.
1975, April 21	Nguyen Van Thieu resigns as president of the Republic of Vietnam.
1975, April 29	Americans remaining in Saigon begin making desperate, last-minute escapes by helicopters from building rooftops as North Vietnamese and Vietcong troops enter the city; many South Vietnamese closely associated with the United States are left behind.
1975, April 30	North Vietnamese forces capture Saigon and rename it Ho Chi Minh City, thereby bringing an end to the Vietnam War.
1975, May 12–14	President Ford orders military rescue attempt of crew of U.S. merchant ship *Mayaguez* after the vessel is seized by Khmer Rouge near the Cambodian coast.
1975, December	Pathet Lao gains control of Laos.
1976, July 2	Newly created National Assembly names reunited Vietnam the Socialist Republic of Vietnam.

1976, November 2	Jimmy Carter defeats Gerald Ford in U.S. presidential election.
1977, January 21	President Carter pardons most Vietnam-era draft law violators.
1977, September 20	Socialist Republic of Vietnam is admitted to the United Nations.
1978, May	Refugees flee Vietnam (many who escape by boat are termed "boat people"); China cuts economic aid to Vietnam in response to Hanoi's mistreatment of the many refugees who are ethnic Chinese.
1978, June 29	Socialist Republic of Vietnam becomes member of the Soviet-sponsored economic group COMECON.
1978, November 3	Socialist Republic of Vietnam signs Treaty of Friendship with the USSR.
1978, December 25	Vietnamese Army invades Cambodia.
1979, January 1	United States and People's Republic of China establish normal diplomatic relations.
1979, January 7	Vietnamese remove Khmer Rouge regime and replace it with communist government in Phnom Penh headed by Heng Samrin; Vietnamese troops remain as occupying force.
1979, February 17	Chinese forces attack northern Vietnam but withdraw on March 15.
1980, November 4	Ronald Reagan defeats Jimmy Carter in U.S. presidential election.
1982, November 13	Vietnam Veterans Memorial dedicated in Washington, D.C.
1984, May	Chemical manufacturers of Agent Orange agree to out-of-court settlement with Vietnam veterans.
1986, December 15–19	Vietnamese Communist Party elects Nguyen Van Linh as general secretary, and war-time leaders, such as Truong Chinh and Pham Van Dong, resign from the Politburo.
1989, September 15	Vietnam withdraws its troops from Cambodia.
1990, August	Cambodian political parties agree to UN-supervised elections.
1991, January 16	President George H. W. Bush begins Persian Gulf War against Iraq and pledges to American people that it "will not be another Vietnam."

1993, November 13	Vietnam Women's Memorial dedicated at Vietnam Veteran's Memorial in Washington, D.C.
1994, February 3	President Bill Clinton ends embargo on trade with Vietnam.
1995, July 11	President Bill Clinton extends U.S. diplomatic recognition to the Socialist Republic of Vietnam.

PART IV

Resource Guide

1

GENERAL WORKS

BIBLIOGRAPHIES
AND HISTORIOGRAPHICAL ESSAYS

Brune, Lester H., and Richard Dean Burns. *America and the Indochina Wars, 1945–1990: A Bibliographic Guide.* Claremont, Calif.: Regina Books, 1992. Containing more than 3,000 citations, this bibliography offers an excellent list of items published through the 1980s.

Burns, Richard Dean, and Milton Leitenberg. *The Wars of Vietnam, Cambodia, and Laos, 1945–1982: A Bibliographic Guide.* Santa Barbara, Calif.: ABC-Clio, 1984. Although listing somewhat older works, this volume identifies nearly 5,000 useful items.

Divine, Robert A. "Vietnam Reconsidered." *Diplomatic History* 12 (Winter 1988): 79–93. The author notes that the first histories of the war criticized U.S. policy and that so-called revisionist works later aimed to justify U.S. actions.

Edmonds, Anthony O., ed. *Sources for Teaching the Vietnam War: An Annotated Guide.* Pittsburgh, Penn.: Center for Social Studies Education, 1992. This list of books, magazines, and films available through 1991 is helpful for courses on the war.

Herring, George C. "America and Vietnam: The Debate Continues." *American Historical Review* 92 (April 1987): 350–62. This review essay notes the importance of placing the U.S. war in Vietnam in international perspective.

Hess, Gary R. "The Unending Debate: Historians and the Vietnam War." *Diplomatic History* 18 (Spring 1994): 239–64. This essay considers many of the significant works and arguments on the war and urges more studies that combine American, Vietnamese, and international perspectives.

Gilbert, Marc Jason, ed. *The Vietnam War: Teaching Approaches and Resources.* Westport, Conn.: Greenwood Press, 1991. This anthology of essays provides discussion of sources and approaches for teaching about the war drawn from the experiences of college teachers.

Kimball, Jeffrey. "The Stab-in-the-Back Legend and the Vietnam War." *Armed Forces and Society* 14 (Spring 1988): 433–58. The author finds unconvincing the argument by some writers that the U.S. military could have won the war if civilian politicians had allowed it to win.

————., ed. *To Reason Why: The Debate About the Causes of U.S. Involvement in the Vietnam War.* New York: McGraw-Hill, 1990. This collection is a balanced presentation of the variety of reasons scholars, policy makers, and others have advanced on the causes of the American war in Vietnam.

McMahon, Robert J. "U.S.-Vietnamese Relations: A Historiographical Survey." In *Pacific Passage: The Study of American-East Asian Relations on the Eve of the Twenty-First Century*, edited by Warren I. Cohen, 313–36. New York: Columbia University Press, 1996. McMahon identifies the major historical interpretations of the war and connects these positions to other themes in U.S. history.

Olson, James S., ed. *The Vietnam War: Handbook of Literature and Research.* Westport, Conn.: Greenwood, 1993. Twenty-three specialized essays (with bibliographies) in this book pose numerous research questions.

Paterson, Thomas G. "Historical Memory and Illusive Victories: Vietnam and Central America." *Diplomatic History* 12 (Winter 1988): 1–18. Paterson argues that flawed histories of how the United States could have won in Vietnam led to U.S. interventionism in Latin America in the 1980s.

Peake, Louis A. *The United States in the Vietnam War, 1954–1975: An Annotated Bibliography.* New York: Garland Publishing, 1985. The items contained in this book are standard, older works.

Sugnet, Christopher L., and John T. Hulsey, eds. *Vietnam War Bibliography.* Lexington, Mass.: Lexington Books, 1983. This research guide catalogs the extensive primary and secondary sources in the Echols Collection at Cornell University.

Wittman, Sandra M. *Writing About Vietnam: A Bibliography of the Literature of the Vietnam Conflict.* Boston: G. K. Hall, 1989. This specialized bibliography concentrates on Vietnam War fiction, poetry, and drama.

DICTIONARIES, ENCYCLOPEDIAS, AND ATLASES

Bowman, John S., ed. *The Vietnam War: An Almanac.* Foreword by Fox Butterfield. New York: Pharos Books, 1985. Organized chronologically, this reference work covers military, diplomatic, and domestic events and has separate sections with biographical sketches and essays on land, air, naval, and irregular forces.

Duiker, William J. *Historical Dictionary of Vietnam.* 2d ed. Metuchen, N.J.: Scarecrow Press, 1997. Events and individuals from Vietnam's history are arranged alphabetically.

Edmonds, Anthony O. *The War in Vietnam.* Westport, Conn.: Greenwood Press, 1998. Intended as a guide for students, this book provides a brief narrative, biographies, glossary, some documents, and a bibliography.

Hillstrom, Kevin, and Laurie Collins Hillstrom. *The Vietnam Experience: A Concise Encyclopedia of American Literature, Songs, and Films.* Westport, Conn.: Greenwood Press, 1998. The authors describe forty-four novels, songs, and movies about the war.

Kutler, Stanley, ed. *Encyclopedia of the Vietnam War.* New York: Macmillan Library Reference USA, 1996. In addition to brief alphabetic entries on all aspects of the war, this book contains a chronology, table of acronyms, bibliography, list of Medal of Honor winners, ten interpretive essays on broad topics, and two documents (Gulf of Tonkin Resolution and Paris Peace Accords).

Olson, James S., ed. *Dictionary of the Vietnam War.* Westport, Conn.: Greenwood Press, 1988. This dictionary is especially good on military topics and Vietnam-era terminology.

Reinberg, Linda. *In the Field: The Language of the Vietnam War.* New York: Facts on File, 1991. This extensive list defines technical terms, slang, and Vietnamese phrases.

Stanton, Shelby. *Vietnam Order of Battle: A Complete Illustrated Reference to the U.S. Army Ground Forces in Vietnam, 1961–1973.* New York: Galahad Books, 1981. An extremely useful reference, it is filled with military facts of all kinds.

Summers, Harry G., Jr. *Historical Atlas of the Vietnam War.* Boston: Houghton Mifflin, 1995. In this atlas, there are more than 400 color maps accompanied by brief historical explanations.

———. *Vietnam War Almanac.* New York: Facts on File, 1985. Focusing on military subjects, the entries in this work convey a view that a successful U.S. military strategy was possible in Vietnam.

Thayer, Thomas C. *War Without Fronts: The American Experience in Vietnam.* Boulder, Col.: Westview, 1986. This book provides a mass of statistical data on the war and suggests that political pacification would have been possible in South Vietnam but was not given a chance.

Tucker, Spencer C., ed. *Encyclopedia of the Vietnam War: A Political, Social, and Military History.* 3 vols. Santa Barbara, Calif.: ABC-CLIO, 1998. These three volumes are the most detailed reference work available and include more than 200 documents.

SURVEYS AND SYNTHESES

Anderson, David L., ed. *Shadow on the White House: Presidents and the Vietnam War, 1945–1975.* Lawrence: University Press of Kansas, 1993. Written by experts on their subjects, the essays in this book examine the Vietnam decisions of each president from Truman through Ford.

Boettcher, Thomas D. *Vietnam: The Valor and the Sorrow.* Boston: Little, Brown, 1985. This good general history is illustrated by more than 500 photographs.

Buzzanco, Robert. *Vietnam and the Transformation of American Life.* Malden, Mass.: Blackwell Publishers, 1999. The author examines how the American war in Vietnam and concurrent social-cultural upheaval in America together produced significant changes in the United States.

Cooper, Chester L. *The Lost Crusade: America in Vietnam.* New York: Dodd, Mead, 1970. An official who was involved in policy making, Cooper reflects on U.S. policy mistakes in Vietnam from the end of World War II through the Johnson administration.

Davidson, Philip B. *Vietnam at War: The History, 1946–1975.* Novato, Calif.: Presidio Press, 1988. A general who served in a key position in Vietnam, Davidson describes U.S. Army operations in detail and contends that the U.S. military did not understand revolutionary war and how to conduct it.

DeGroot, Gerard J. *A Noble Cause? America and the Vietnam War.* Harlow, England: Longman, 2000. DeGroot sees the war as providing some painful but useful lessons for the United States about the limits of its power. The book's introduction provides a good summary of various historical interpretations of the war.

Duiker, William J. *U.S. Containment Policy and the Conflict in Indochina.* Stanford, Calif.: Stanford University Press, 1994. This careful examination of how U.S. containment strategy influenced U.S. decisions in Vietnam up to 1965 places heavy responsibility on the Kennedy administration for exaggerating the strategic importance of Indochina to the United States.

Ellsberg, Daniel. *Papers on the War.* New York: Simon and Schuster, 1972. Ellsberg helped write and then leaked the Pentagon Papers to the press and maintains that U.S. policy makers knew all along that there were no good U.S. policy options in Vietnam.

Errington, Elizabeth Jane, and B. J. C. McKercher, eds. *The Vietnam War as History.* New York: Praeger, 1990. These essays by some major historians of the war provide thoughtful reflections on key topics.

Fall, Bernard B. *Last Reflections on a War.* Garden City, N.Y.: Doubleday, 1967. Fall's expert knowledge of Vietnamese history helps place the American war in historical context.

——. *The Two Vietnams: A Political and Military Analysis.* 2d ed. New York: Praeger, 1967. Fall is critical of both communist and American actions in Vietnam from 1945 to 1965.

Fitzgerald, Frances. *Fire in the Lake: The Vietnamese and the Americans in Vietnam.* Boston: Little, Brown, 1972. The author is quite critical of America's lack of understanding of the Vietnamese revolution, which she analyzes in detail.

Gibbons, William Conrad. *The U.S. Government and the Vietnam War: Executive and Legislative Roles and Relationships.* 4 vols. Princeton: Princeton University Press, 1986–1995. Although primarily concerned with congressional actions, these volumes are a good survey of U.S. policy from 1945 to 1968.

Hearden, Patrick J. *The Tragedy of Vietnam.* New York: HarperCollins, 1991. The theme of this book is the connection between U.S. policy in Vietnam and American interest in an open international economic system.

Herring, George C. *America's Longest War: The United States and Vietnam, 1950–1975.* 4th ed. New York: McGraw-Hill, 2002. This concise yet comprehensive account is one of the standard and most consulted works on the U.S. war.

Hess, Gary R. *Vietnam and the United States: Origins and Legacy of War*. Rev. ed. Boston: Twayne Publishers, 1998. This survey is good on placing U.S. policies in the context of Vietnamese, Laotian, and Cambodian history.

Hunt, Michael H. *Lyndon Johnson's War: America's Cold War Crusade in Vietnam, 1945–1965*. New York: Hill and Wang, 1996. This book contends that American cultural disregard for Asia and U.S. global strategies led to the U.S. war in Vietnam.

Joes, Anthony James. *The War for South Viet Nam, 1954–1975*. Rev. ed. Westport, Conn.: Praeger, 2001. Joes argues that the United States could have won the war militarily.

Kahin, George McT. *Intervention: How America Became Involved in Vietnam*. New York: Knopf, 1986. This significant book traces how U.S. actions from the end of World War II to 1966 left America in support of a weak Saigon government against a politically stronger Hanoi regime.

Kahin, George M., and John W. Lewis. *The United States in Vietnam*. Rev. ed. New York: Delta, 1969. This older but valuable work argues that U.S. policy makers failed to recognize the nationalism that motivated their enemies in Vietnam.

Karnow, Stanley. *Vietnam: A History*. Rev. ed. New York: Viking Press, 1992. Written to accompany the Public Broadcast System's *Vietnam: A Television History*, this book is an excellent narrative history by a veteran journalist.

Kattenburg, Paul M. *The Vietnam Trauma in American Foreign Policy, 1945–75*. New Brunswick, N.J.: Rutgers University Press, 1980. A wartime policy maker, the author places decisions on Vietnam in the overall context of U.S. foreign policy.

Kolko, Gabriel. *Anatomy of a War: Vietnam, the United States, and the Modern Historical Experience*. New York: Pantheon Books, 1985. This sweeping analysis of the social revolution in Vietnam argues that U.S. policy there was part of a global American opposition to radical nationalist movements.

Langguth, A. J. *Our Vietnam: The War, 1954–1975*. New York: Simon and Schuster, 2000. Focusing on individual participants, this veteran journalist, who was a correspondent in Vietnam, portrays the war as a futile U.S. military adventure.

Lowe, Peter, ed. *The Vietnam War*. London: Macmillan, 1998. Written by prominent scholars, the essays in this volume examine the international aspects of the war.

Maclear, Michael. *The Ten Thousand Day War: Vietnam, 1945–1975*. New York: St. Martin's, 1981. A companion volume to a television documentary series, the book contains many interviews with participants in the war.

Mann, Robert. *A Grand Delusion: America's Descent Into Vietnam*. New York: Basic Books, 2001. Mann organizes this general political account of the war around U.S. presidents and key senatorial leaders.

McMahon, Robert J. *The Limits of Empire: The United States and Southeast Asia Since World War II*. New York: Columbia University Press, 1999. McMahon portrays U.S. policy as empire building and an over-extension of U.S. power.

Moss, George Donelson. *Vietnam: An American Ordeal*. 4th ed. Upper Saddle River, N.J.: Prentice Hall, 2002. This book is a reliable military, diplomatic, and political survey.

Olson, James S., and Randy Roberts. *Where the Domino Fell: America and Vietnam, 1945 to 1995*. 3d ed. St. James, N.Y.: Brandywine Press, 1999. This concise survey offers basic and accurate coverage of the war.

Post, Ken. *Revolution, Socialism, and Nationalism in Viet Nam.* 5 vols. Aldershot, England: Darmouth, 1989–1994. A Marxist analysis, this work highlights successes and failures by the Vietnamese communists.

Schlesinger, Arthur M., Jr. *The Bitter Heritage: Vietnam and American Democracy, 1941–1966.* Boston: Houghton Mifflin, 1966. The author advances the quagmire thesis that ignorance undermined U.S. good intentions in Vietnam.

Schulzinger, Robert D. *A Time for War: The United States and Vietnam, 1941–1975.* New York: Oxford University Press, 1997. This synthesis of secondary literature and primary sources provides a useful survey of many issues both in Vietnam and the United States.

Steinberg, Blema. *Shame and Humiliation: Presidential Decision Making on Vietnam.* Toronto: McGill-Queens University Press, 1996. This book is a psychological study of how the personalities of Eisenhower, Johnson, and Nixon affected each president's Vietnam decisions.

Tucker, Spencer C. *Vietnam.* Lexington: University Press of Kentucky, 1999. This volume is primarily a military history of Vietnam since 1945.

Turley, William S. *The Second Indochina War: A Short Political and Military History, 1954–1975.* Boulder, Col.: Westview Press, 1986. This work argues that the containment policy developed for Europe could not be applied in the same way in Vietnam.

Young, Marilyn B. *The Vietnam Wars: 1945–1990.* New York: HarperCollins, 1991. Young provides a dual analysis of the civil war within Vietnam and the tensions that the Vietnam War produced within the United States.

DOCUMENT COLLECTIONS

Barrett, David M., ed. *Lyndon Johnson's Vietnam Papers: A Documentary Collection.* College Station: Texas A&M University Press, 1997. These carefully selected documents illustrate Johnson's significant decisions on the war from 1963 through 1968.

Gettleman, Marvin E., Jane Franklin, Marilyn B. Young, and H. Bruce Franklin, eds. *Vietnam and America: A Documented History.* Rev. and enlarged 2d ed. New York: Grove Press, 1995. This interesting collection groups U.S. government documents with related Vietnamese and antiwar views.

Herring, George C., Jr., ed. *The Secret Diplomacy of the Vietnam War: The Negotiating Volumes of the Pentagon Papers.* Austin: University of Texas Press, 1983. These documents relate to various possibilities of a negotiated peace during the Johnson administration.

Porter, Gareth, ed. *Vietnam: The Definitive Documentation of Human Decisions.* 2 vols. Stanfordville, N.Y.: Coleman, 1979. There are a number of significant documents translated from Vietnamese in this collection.

Pratt, John Clarke, ed. *Vietnam Voices: Perspectives on the War Years, 1941–1982.* New York: Viking Penguin, 1984. This documentary history utilizes fiction, poetry, memoirs, and official documents.

Sheehan, Neil, et al. *The Pentagon Papers as Published by the New York Times.* Chicago: Quadrangle, 1971. This single volume contains the newspaper's summary of the multivolume Pentagon study and some of the major documents from that study.

U.S. Department of Defense. *The Pentagon Papers: The Defense Department History of United States Decision Making on Vietnam: The Senator Gravel Edition.* 5 vols. Boston: Beacon, 1971–1972. This edition is the most complete and easily used version of the secret Defense Department history of Vietnam policy decisions.

U.S. Department of Defense. *United States-Vietnam Relations, 1945–1967: Study.* 12 vols. Washington, D.C.: U.S. Government Printing Office, 1971. This government printing of the Pentagon Papers is valuable but not as easily used as the edition published by Beacon Press.

Williams, William Appleman, Thomas McCormick, Lloyd Gardner, and Walter LaFeber, eds. *America in Vietnam: A Documentary History.* New York: Norton, 1985. The editors' introductions and the documents they have selected pose important questions about the U.S. war.

BIOGRAPHIES

Ambrose, Stephen E. *Eisenhower.* Vol 2., *The President.* New York: Simon and Schuster, 1984. Ambrose characterizes Eisenhower as wary of U.S. military involvement in Vietnam.

———. *Nixon.* Vol. 2., *The Triumph of a Politician, 1962–1972.* New York: Simon and Schuster, 1989. The author provides a rather straightforward narrative of Nixon's Vietnam policies and his decision to employ U.S. military forces in Cambodia.

———. *Nixon.* Vol. 3., *Ruin and Recovery, 1973–1990.* New York: Simon and Schuster, 1991. Although Nixon negotiated a settlement with Hanoi, Ambrose notes, he could not make peace with his domestic opponents.

Anderson, David L., ed. *The Human Tradition in the Vietnam Era.* Wilmington, Del.: Scholarly Resources, 2000. Twelve biographical essays in this collection recount the personal Vietnam-era experiences of some well-known and unknown Americans.

Ashby, LeRoy, and Rod Gramer. *Fighting the Odds: The Life of Senator Frank Church.* Pullman: Washington State University Press, 1994. A large part of this biography deals with Church's opposition in the U.S. Senate to the Vietnam War.

Bill, James A. *George Ball: Behind the Scenes in U.S. Foreign Policy.* New Haven: Yale University Press, 1997. This book studies the career of the man who, virtually alone among Johnson's advisers, argued against U.S. military escalation in Vietnam.

Bird, Kai. *The Color of Truth: McGeorge and William Bundy: Brothers in Arms: A Biography.* New York: Simon and Schuster, 1998. Key advisers to Kennedy and Johnson, these brothers were major architects of U.S. policies in Vietnam.

Cohen, Warren I. *Dean Rusk.* Edited by Samuel F. Bemis and Robert H. Ferrell. Vol. 19, *American Secretaries of State and Their Diplomacy.* Totowa, N.J.: Cooper Square, 1980. This critical biography ascribes Rusk's advocacy of U.S. defense of South Vietnam to his desire to contain the aggressiveness of the People's Republic of China.

Currey, Cecil B. *Edward Lansdale: The Unquiet American.* Boston: Houghton Mifflin, 1989. This account is a favorable assessment of the most secretive and legendary U.S. intelligence agent to serve in Vietnam.

———. *Victory at Any Cost: The Genius of Viet Nam's Gen. Vo Nguyen Giap.* Washington: Brassey's, 1997. With sources that include interviews with Giap, Currey notes the strengths and shortcomings of North Vietnam's famous military leader.

Dallek, Robert. *Flawed Giant: Lyndon Johnson and His Times, 1961–1973.* New York: Oxford University Press, 1998. This major biography examines Johnson's decisions on Vietnam and how the war, in turn, affected his life and career.

Duiker, William J. *Ho Chi Minh.* New York: Hyperion, 2000. Based upon archival research in five languages and written by one of the leading authorities on Vietnamese communism, this biography is the most detailed and revealing account available of Ho Chi Minh's life and his role in the Vietnamese revolution.

Fisher, James T. *Dr. America: The Lives of Thomas A. Dooley, 1927–1961.* Amherst: University of Massachusetts Press, 1998. Dr. Tom Dooley's humanitarianism and anticommunism were emblematic of U.S. purposes in Vietnam, and his story reveals much about appearance versus reality in U.S. policies.

Giglio, James N. *The Presidency of John F. Kennedy.* Lawrence: University Press of Kansas, 1992. Giglio argues that Kennedy, at the time of his death, had U.S. policy committed to involvement in Vietnam.

Greene, John Robert. *The Presidency of Gerald R. Ford.* Lawrence: University Press of Kansas, 1995. This biography provides a short discussion of the end of the war and the *Mayaguez* incident with Cambodia.

Halberstam, David. *Ho.* New York: McGraw-Hill, 1993. This slim volume seeks to explain Ho Chi Minh's appeal to the Vietnamese.

Hendrickson, Paul. *The Living and the Dead: Robert McNamara and Five Lives of a Lost War.* New York: Knopf, 1996. This study of McNamara is set against sketches of how the war he helped conduct affected him and five other Americans.

Isaacson, Walter. *Kissinger: A Biography.* New York: Simon and Schuster, 1992. This book is an especially good description of Kissinger's negotiations to end the U.S. military role in Vietnam.

Kinnard, Douglas. *The Certain Trumpet: Maxwell Taylor and the American Experience in Vietnam.* Washington: Brassey's, 1991. The author is very critical of General Taylor's failure to give candid advice to Kennedy and Johnson about their Vietnam policies.

Lacouture, Jean. *Ho Chi Minh: A Political Biography.* New York: Knopf, 1968. A French journalist, Lacouture emphasizes Ho's nationalism over his communism.

Powers, Thomas. *The Man Who Kept the Secrets: Richard Helms and the CIA.* New York: Knopf, 1979. This book examines Helms's role in key calculations of U.S. troop levels and enemy strength estimates.

Schoenbaum, Thomas J. *Waging Peace and War: Dean Rusk in the Truman, Kennedy, and Johnson Years.* New York: Simon and Schuster, 1988. Secretary of State Rusk was personally modest, according to Schoenbaum, but was overconfident about U.S. power and good intentions in Vietnam.

Schulzinger, Robert D. *Henry Kissinger: Doctor of Diplomacy.* New York: Columbia University Press, 1989. Schulzinger analyzes Kissinger's impact on Nixon's and Ford's policies in Vietnam and Cambodia.

Shapley, Deborah. *Promise and Power: The Life and Times of Robert McNamara.* Boston: Little, Brown, 1992. This study notes McNamara's arrogance, excessive loyalty to superiors, and eventual torment over U.S. policy in Vietnam.

Sheehan, Neil. *A Bright Shining Lie: John Paul Vann and America in Vietnam.* New York: Random House, 1988. A gifted journalist who reported on the war, Sheehan uses the medium of a biography of this American military adviser to illustrate the weaknesses in U.S. nation-building efforts in South Vietnam.

Small, Melvin. *The Presidency of Richard Nixon.* Lawrence: University Press of Kansas, 1999. Small debunks Nixon's assertions that his policies won a peace with honor in Vietnam.

Sorley, Lewis. *Thunderbolt: General Creighton Abrams and the Army of His Times.* New York: Simon and Schuster, 1992. Sorley writes approvingly of the life of the general who replaced William Westmoreland as the top U.S. commander in Vietnam and of how Abrams ended the controversial attrition strategy of his predecessor.

Warner, Denis. *The Last Confucian.* New York: Macmillan, 1963. This biography of President Ngo Dinh Diem of South Vietnam is dated but still useful.

Woods, Randall Bennett. *J. William Fulbright, Vietnam, and the Search for a Cold War Foreign Policy.* New York: Cambridge University Press, 1998. This powerful senator moved from support to opposition of White House policies toward Vietnam.

Zaffiri, Samuel. *Westmoreland: A Biography of General William C. Westmoreland.* New York: Morrow, 1994. This conventional biography is only mildly critical of Westmoreland's leadership in Vietnam.

Zeiler, Thomas W. *Dean Rusk: Defending the American Mission Abroad.* Wilmington, Del.: Scholarly Resources, 2000. Zeiler portrays Rusk as a Wilsonian internationalist who never swayed from his conviction that North Vietnam was an aggressor nation.

MEMOIRS

Adams, Sam. *War of Numbers: An Intelligence Memoir.* Introduction by David Hackworth. South Royalton, Vermont: Steerforth Press, 1994. A CIA analyst in Vietnam, Adams has written a memoir critical of how intelligence was used. He was a source of information for CBS News in the libel case *Westmoreland v. CBS.*

Balaban, John. *Remembering Heaven's Face: A Moral Witness in Vietnam.* New York: Simon and Schuster, 1991. This powerful personal account is by a conscientious objector who went to Vietnam as a civilian medical worker.

Ball, George W. *The Past Has Another Pattern: Memoirs.* New York: Norton, 1982. Part of Johnson's inner circle of advisers, Ball describes his dissenting role on the war and provides insights into the decision-making process.

Broyles, William, Jr. *Brothers in Arms: A Journey from War to Peace.* New York: Knopf, 1986. A journalist and former Marine, Broyles reflects on his return to postwar Vietnam and his sense of camaraderie with former enemies.

Bui Diem, with David Chanoff. *In the Jaws of History*. Boston: Houghton Mifflin, 1987. Saigon's ambassador to Washington describes how the South Vietnamese viewed their alliance with the Americans.

Caputo, Philip. *A Rumor of War*. New York: Holt, Rinehart, and Winston, 1977. Caputo's memoir graphically describes the Marine lieutenant's disillusionment with the war.

Clifford, Clark M., with Richard Holbrooke. *Counsel to the President: A Memoir*. New York: Random House, 1991. This account is an excellent source on policy discussions throughout the Johnson administration and especially in reaction to the Tet Offensive.

Donovan, David. *Once a Warrior King: Memories of an Officer in Vietnam*. New York: McGraw Hill, 1985. The U.S. military advisory effort is well described in this memoir.

Harris, David. *Our War: What We Did in Vietnam and What It Did to Us*. New York: Random House, 1996. This book is a thorough condemnation of the American war in Vietnam by one of the nation's most well-known draft resisters.

Hayslip, Le Ly, with Jay Wurts. *When Heaven and Earth Changed Places*. New York: Doubleday, 1989. Hayslip describes her life as a child and young woman in Vietnam during the war and her return to Vietnam from America a decade after the war.

Herr, Michael. *Dispatches*. New York: Knopf, 1977. A young war correspondent, Herr captures much of the personal experience of the war and provides good details on the battle at Khe Sanh.

Johnson, Lyndon B. *The Vantage Point: Perspectives of the Presidency, 1963–1969*. New York: Holt, Rinehart, and Winston, 1971. Although more bland than the man himself, Johnson's memoir is a good source on how he sought to explain his decisions on Vietnam.

Kovic, Ron. *Born on the Fourth of July*. New York: McGraw-Hill, 1976. Paralyzed by a war injury, Kovic became a bitter critic of the war and the Veterans Administration.

Mason, Robert. *Chickenhawk*. New York: Viking Press, 1983. Mason vividly recalls his experiences flying more than 1,000 missions as a combat helicopter pilot.

McNamara, Robert S. *In Retrospect: The Tragedy and Lessons of Vietnam*. New York: Times Books, 1995. Controversy greeted the publication of this book by Kennedy and Johnson's secretary of defense. Despite his remarkable admission of error in advising U.S. military intervention in Vietnam, his confession seems to lack contrition.

Nguyen Cao Ky. *Twenty Years and Twenty Days*. New York: Stein and Day, 1976. One of the principal leaders of South Vietnam, Ky describes the inner workings of the Washington-Saigon connection and points blame at U.S. officials and his South Vietnamese colleagues.

Nixon, Richard M. *RN: The Memoirs of Richard Nixon*. New York: Grosset and Dunlap, 1978. Although self-serving, Nixon's memoir reveals much about his war decisions and peace negotiations.

Nolting, Frederick. *From Trust to Tragedy: The Political Memoirs of Frederick Nolting, Kennedy's Ambassador to Diem's Vietnam*. Foreword by William Colby. New York:

Praeger, 1988. Nolting views the coup against Ngo Dinh Diem as the mistake that led to war for the United States.

O'Brien, Tim. *If I Die in a Combat Zone: Box Me Up and Ship Me Home*. New York: Dell, 1987. An award-winning writer of Vietnam fiction, O'Brien narrates his personal story as a combat infantryman.

Rusk, Dean, as told to Richard Rusk. *As I Saw It*. Edited by Daniel S. Papp. New York: Norton, 1990. The secretary of state for Kennedy and Johnson makes no apologies for his support of the war and professes respect for Lyndon Johnson.

Safire, William. *Before the Fall: An Inside View of the Pre-Watergate White House*. New York: Doubleday, 1975. A senior Nixon aide, Safire supplies details and insights on important Vietnam decisions.

Schlesinger, Arthur M., Jr. *A Thousand Days: John F. Kennedy and the White House*. Boston: Houghton Mifflin, 1965. This inside account of the Kennedy administration includes White House discussions about Vietnam.

Sharp, U.S. Grant. *Strategy for Defeat*. San Rafael, Calif.: Presidio Press, 1978. This admiral who commanded U.S. Pacific forces asserts that U.S. air power could have won the war if Washington had allowed it.

Tran Van Don. *Our Endless War: Inside Vietnam*. San Rafael, Calif.: Presidio Press, 1978. This South Vietnamese military commander describes the factionalism in the Saigon regime.

Van Devanter, Linda, and Christopher Morgan. *Home Before Morning: The Story of an Army Nurse in Vietnam*. New York: Warner Books, 1983. Van Devanter's memoir describes the challenges of being a surgical nurse in Vietnam and the trouble she faced resuming life back in the United States.

Vo Nguyen Giap. *Unforgettable Days*. 3d ed. Hanoi: Gioi, 1994. Giap's central military leadership role in the Democratic Republic of Vietnam makes this a significant work.

Westmoreland, William C. *A Soldier Reports*. Garden City, N.Y.: Doubleday, 1976. The senior U.S. commander in Vietnam at the height of the war blames civilians for not supporting the war effort. His memoir is valuable on U.S. military strategy.

ORAL HISTORIES

Baker, Mark. *Nam: The Vietnam War in the Words of the Men and Women Who Fought There*. New York: Morrow, 1981. This oral history provides a diverse cross-section of views of more than 150 interviewees.

Beesley, Stanley W. *Vietnam: The Heartland Remembers*. Norman: University of Oklahoma Press, 1988. These interviews with veterans from Oklahoma are valuable for the ethnic diversity of the contributors.

Lehrack, Otto J. *No Shining Armor: The Marines at War in Vietnam*. Lawrence: University Press of Kansas, 1992. These interviews focus on the men of one particular Marine unit.

Marshall, Kathryn, ed. *In the Combat Zone: An Oral History of American Women in Vietnam*. Boston: Little, Brown, 1987. This collection contains the personal stories of twenty women who served in Vietnam as nurses and in other jobs.

Santoli, Al. *Everything We Had: An Oral History of the Vietnam War as Told by Thirty-three American Soldiers Who Fought It*. New York: Random House, 1981. These interviews, including two with women, relate military experiences.

——. *Leading the Way: How Vietnam Veterans Rebuilt the U.S. Military, an Oral History*. New York: Ballantine Books, 1993. Fifty-six career officers describe how the military regained its sense of purpose after the Vietnam War and was able to succeed in the Gulf War.

——. *To Bear Any Burden: The Vietnam War and Its Aftermath in the Words of Americans and Southeast Asians*. Bloomington: Indiana University Press, 1999. Santoli interviewed a varied but mostly nonmilitary group connected in various ways to the U.S. side of the war.

Terry, Wallace. *Bloods: An Oral History of the Vietnam War by Black Americans*. New York: Random House, 1984. Terry's interviews with African Americans who served in Vietnam reveal a full spectrum of opinions on the war.

Tollefson, James W. *The Strength Not to Fight: An Oral History of Conscientious Objectors of the Vietnam War*. Boston: Little, Brown, 1993. Conscientious objectors recall the difficulties they encountered.

Trujillo, Charley, ed. *Soldados: Chicanos in Viet Nam*. San Jose, Calif.: Chusma House, 1990. This book provides the rare opportunity to hear Hispanic veterans describe what their war experiences meant to them.

HISTORY OF SOUTHEAST ASIA
AND U.S. FOREIGN RELATIONS

GENERAL HISTORY OF VIETNAM

Bradley, Mark Philip. *Imagining Vietnam and America: The Making of Postcolonial Vietnam, 1919–1950.* Forward by John Lewis Gaddis. Chapel Hill: University of North Carolina Press, 2000. The author contends that the colonial history of Vietnam as much as the global Cold War determined the U.S. approach to the country.

Buttinger, Joseph. *Vietnam: A Dragon Embattled.* 2 vols. New York: Praeger, 1967. This history of the Vietnamese people ends with the death of President Ngo Dinh Diem.

Hess, Gary R. "Franklin D. Roosevelt and Indochina." *Journal of American History* 59 (September 1972): 353–68. Hess argues that Roosevelt's trusteeship plan to end French colonialism could have avoided war in Southeast Asia but was not given enough consideration by Roosevelt and others.

LaFeber, Walter. "Roosevelt, Churchill, and Indochina, 1942–1945." *American Historical Review* 80 (December 1975): 1277–95. LaFeber maintains that Roosevelt's trusteeship plan for colonial Indochina was part of a U.S. attempt to supplant Britain's position in East Asia.

Long, Ngô Vinh. *Before the Revolution: The Vietnamese Peasants Under the French.* 2d ed. New York: Columbia University Press, 1991. Through translations of Vietnamese accounts, this book graphically reveals the burdens of French colonialism on Vietnamese peasants.

Marr, David G. *Vietnamese Tradition on Trial, 1920–1945.* Berkeley: University of California Press, 1981. This book provides a good analysis of Vietnamese nationalism and the origins of Vietnamese communism.

McAlister, John T., Jr. *Vietnam: The Origins of Revolution*. Garden City, N.Y.: Doubleday, 1971. This excellent study examines the social and historical origins of the Franco-Vietminh war.

SarDesai, D. R. *Vietnam: The Struggle for National Identity*. 2d ed. Boulder, Col.: Westview, 1992. This book surveys Vietnamese history from its beginning through the American war.

HISTORY OF U.S. FOREIGN RELATIONS

Chambers, John Whiteclay, II, ed. *The Oxford Companion to American Military History*. New York: Oxford University Press, 1999. The entries in this volume are written by specialists and provide both details and discussion of key military and diplomatic issues.

DeConde, Alexander, Richard Dean Burns, and Fredrik Logevall, eds. *Encyclopedia of American Foreign Policy: Studies of the Principal Movements and Ideas*. 2d ed. 3 vols. New York: Scribner's, 2002. The topical essays in this reference work offer expert analysis on a broad range of important themes.

Graebner, Norman A. *Ideas and Diplomacy*. New York: Oxford University Press, 1964. Including numerous excerpts from key documents, Graebner's book presents a realist critique of U.S. foreign policy since the founding of the republic

Hogan, Michael J., ed. *America in the World: The Historiography of American Foreign Relations Since 1941*. New York: Cambridge University Press, 1995. The essays in this volume thoroughly discuss the debate among historians over issues in U.S. foreign policy beginning with World War II.

———., ed. *Paths to Power: The Historiography of American Foreign Relations to 1941*. New York: Cambridge University Press, 2000. There are eight chapters in this anthology that examine the historical debate over U.S. diplomacy from the early republic to Pearl Harbor.

Hogan, Michael J., and Thomas G. Paterson, eds. *Explaining the History of American Foreign Relations*. New York: Cambridge University Press, 1991. The articles in this book address conceptual categories, such as bureaucratic politics, dependency theory, corporatist models, national security approaches, culture, gender, and ideology.

Kennan, George F. *American Diplomacy, 1900–1950*. Chicago: University of Chicago Press, 1951. Kennan is a leading exponent of a realist analysis of foreign policy.

LaFeber, Walter. *The American Age: United States Foreign Policy at Home and Abroad Since 1750*. 2d ed. New York: Norton, 1994. This text weaves together diplomatic, economic, political, and military themes in U.S. history.

McCormick, Thomas J. *America's Half-Century: United States Foreign Policy in the Cold War*. 2d ed. Baltimore: Johns Hopkins University Press, 1995. McCormick stresses the dominance but impermanence of U.S. economic power in the capitalist world system by the middle of the twentieth century.

Schulzinger, Robert D. *U.S. Diplomacy Since 1900*. 5th ed. New York: Oxford University Press, 2002. The author examines the competing ideas and interests that shaped U.S. foreign policy since the Spanish-American War.

Williams, William Appleman. *The Tragedy of American Diplomacy*. New ed. New York: Norton, 1972. Williams advances the so-called open-door interpretation of U.S. foreign policy that a perceived need for markets compelled U.S. leaders to contradict American ideals of nonintervention and self-determination.

THE FRENCH INDOCHINA WAR

Billings-Yun, Melanie. *Decision Against War: Eisenhower and Dien Bien Phu, 1954*. New York: Columbia University Press, 1988. The author gives a favorable assessment of Eisenhower's decision against U.S. military intervention at Dienbienphu.

Blum, Robert M. *Drawing the Line: The Origins of the American Containment Policy in East Asia*. New York: Norton, 1982. The emphasis in this account is the domestic politics of Truman's decisions on Southeast Asia.

Cable, James. *The Geneva Conference of 1954 on Indochina*. New York: St. Martin's Press, 1986. This useful monograph was written by a British diplomat who attended the conference.

Chen Jian. "China and the First Indo-China War, 1950–54." *China Quarterly* (March 1993): 85–110. The author says that Chinese evidence indicates the importance of Chinese advice to the Vietminh.

Dunn, Peter M. *The First Vietnam War*. New York: St. Martin's, 1985. This study focuses on British policy in 1945 and 1946.

Fall, Bernard B. *Hell in a Very Small Place*. Philadelphia: Lippincott, 1967. Fall has written the standard military analysis of the Battle of Dienbienphu.

——. *Street Without Joy*. Rev. ed. New York: Schocken, 1972. This military history of the French war also comments on U.S. policy.

Fifield, Russell H. *Americans in Southeast Asia: The Roots of Commitment*. New York: Crowell, 1973. This older work remains useful on the period before 1954.

Gardner, Lloyd C. *Approaching Vietnam: From World War II Through Dienbienphu*. New York: Norton, 1988. Gardner's primary themes are U.S. anticolonialism and containment in Vietnam and the policies of John Foster Dulles in 1953 54.

Gurtov, Melvin. *The First Vietnam Crisis: Chinese Communist Strategy and United States Involvement*. New York: Columbia University Press, 1967. Gurtov argues that the Eisenhower administration misperceived China's position in 1954.

Hammer, Ellen J. *The Struggle for Indochina, 1940–1955: Viet Nam and the French Experience*. Rev. ed. Stanford, Calif.: Stanford University Press, 1966. This book is one of the best on the French war in Indochina and criticizes French and American actions.

Herring, George C. "The Truman Administration and the Restoration of French Sovereignty in Indochina." *Diplomatic History* 1 (Spring 1977): 97–117. Herring notes how U.S. support of France in Vietnam served U.S. interests in Europe.

Herring, George C., and Richard H. Immerman. "Eisenhower, Dulles, and Dienbienphu: 'The Day We Didn't Go to War' Revisited." *Journal of American History* 71 (September 1984): 343–63. The authors contend that Eisenhower was more inclined to intervene militarily at Dienbienphu than he later admitted.

Hess, Gary R. "The First American Commitment in Indochina: The Acceptance of the Bao Dai Solution." *Diplomatic History* 2 (Fall 1978): 331–50. Concerns about Ho Chi Minh's communism outweighed American doubts about Bao Dai's political viability.

———. *The United States' Emergence as a Southeast Asian Power, 1940–1950.* New York: Columbia University Press, 1986. Hess portrays U.S. policies in Southeast Asia as driven by considerations of American policy elsewhere in the world.

Immerman, Richard H. "The United States and the Geneva Conference of 1954: A New Look." *Diplomatic History* 14 (Winter 1990): 43–66. The author suggests that the United States missed a chance in 1954 to deal separately with China and the Soviet Union in Indochina.

Joyaux, François. *La Chine et le règlement du premier conflit d'Indochine (Genève 1954).* Paris: Publications de la Sorbonne, 1979. Joyaux presents a good explanation of Chinese actions at Geneva.

Kaplan, Lawrence S., Denise Artaud, and Mark R. Rubin, eds. *Dien Bien Phu and the Crisis of Franco-American Relations, 1954–1955.* Wilmington, Del.: Scholarly Resources, 1990. Essays in this volume by prominent U.S. and French scholars address several aspects of the end of the French war.

Marr, David G. *Vietnam, 1945: The Quest for Power.* Berkeley: University of California Press, 1995. Marr takes a detailed look at French, Vietnamese, and U.S. actions in 1945.

Nordell, John R., Jr. *The Undetected Enemy: French and American Miscalculations at Dien Bien Phu, 1953.* College Station: Texas A&M University Press, 1995. Nordell's military analysis deals primarily with French blunders before the siege of Dienbienphu.

Patti, Archimedes L. A. *Why Viet Nam? Prelude to America's Albatross.* Berkeley: University of California Press, 1980. An American intelligence officer who met Ho Chi Minh, Patti contends that the United States could have worked with Ho.

Prados, John. *The Sky Would Fall: Operation Vulture, the Secret U.S. Bombing Mission to Vietnam, 1954.* New York: Dial Press, 1983. Prados finds evidence that the Eisenhower administration had made preparations for U.S. air strikes at Dienbienphu.

Randle, Robert F. *Geneva 1954: The Settlement of the Indochinese War.* Princeton: Princeton University Press, 1969. This detailed account makes clear the flaws in the Geneva Agreements.

Rotter, Andrew J. *The Path to Vietnam: Origins of the American Commitment to Southeast Asia.* Ithaca, N.Y.: Cornell University Press, 1987. Rotter contends that U.S. officials considered Southeast Asia important to U.S. interests in rebuilding the global economy after World War II.

Shaplen, Robert. *The Lost Revolution: The U.S. in Vietnam, 1946–1966.* Rev. ed. New York: Harper and Row, 1966. This book provides a good journalistic account of the First Indochina War.

Short, Anthony. *The Origins of the Vietnam War.* London: Longman, 1989. This account of the French war is very good on the Geneva Conference.

Tønnesson, Stein. *The Vietnamese Revolution of 1945: Roosevelt, Ho Chi Minh, and de Gaulle in a World at War*. Oslo: International Peace Research Institute, 1991. The author describes how Ho Chi Minh was able to gain power and legitimacy at the end of World War II.

Zhai Qiang. "Transplanting the Chinese Model: Chinese Military Advisors and the First Vietnam War, 1950–1954." *Journal of Military History* 57 (October 1993): 689–715. This article details the significant assistance that the Vietminh received from China.

LAOS AND CAMBODIA

Becker, Elizabeth. *When the War Is Over: The Voices of Cambodia's Revolution and Its People*. New York: Simon and Schuster, 1986. The author has collected gripping stories of life and death under the Khmer Rouge, 1975–78.

Castle, Timothy. *At War in the Shadow of Vietnam: United States Military Aid to the Royal Lao Government, 1955–1975*. New York: Columbia University Press, 1993. Castle assembles a wealth of information on the highly secret U.S. role in Laos.

Chandler, David P. *Brother Number One: A Political Biography of Pol Pot*. Rev. ed. Boulder, Col.: Westview, 1999. The author indicts Pol Pot personally for the slaughter in Cambodia.

——. *The Tragedy of Cambodian History: Politics, War, and Revolution Since 1945*. New Haven: Yale University Press, 1991. Chandler provides a good overview of Cambodian history after World War II.

Clymer, Kenton J. "Cambodia: The View from the United States, 1945–1954." *Journal of American-East Asian Relations* 6 (Summer-Fall 1997): 91–124. This article is one of the few analyses of U.S. strategic considerations about Cambodia during the French war in Indochina.

——. "The Perils of Neutrality: The Break in Cambodian-American Relations, 1965." *Diplomatic History* 23 (Fall 1999): 609–31. Clymer is critical of America's negative response to Norodom Sihanouk's neutral posture.

Deac, Wilfred P. *Road to the Killing Fields: The Cambodian War of 1970–1975*. Foreword by Col. Harry G. Summers Jr. College Station: Texas A&M University Press, 1997. This book is primarily a military history of Cambodia from 1970 to 1975.

Dommen, Arthur. *Conflict in Laos: The Politics of Neutralization*. Rev. ed. New York: Praeger, 1971. This account is a useful study by an experienced journalist.

Fall, Bernard B. *Anatomy of a Crisis: The Laotian Crisis of 1960–1961*. Rev. ed. Garden City, N.Y.: Doubleday, 1969. Although agreeing with U.S. concern about communism in Laos, Fall argues that Washington's actions helped strengthen the Laotian communists.

Guilmartin, John F., Jr. *A Very Short War: The Mayaguez and the Battle of Koh Tang*. College Station: Texas A&M University Press, 1995. This military analysis deals with only part of the *Mayaguez* incident.

Hamilton-Merritt, Jane. *Tragic Mountains: The Hmong, the Americans, and the Secret Wars for Laos, 1942–1992*. Bloomington: Indiana University Press, 1993. The author is sharply critical of what she describes as American betrayal of the Hmong, who allied with the Americans in Laos.

Hannah, Norman B. *The Key to Failure: Laos and the Vietnam War.* Lanham, Md.: Madison Books, 1987. Hannah views the 1963 neutraliation agreement in Laos as a first step in the ultimate U.S. failure in Vietnam.

Kiernan, Ben. *How Pol Pot Came to Power: A History of Communism in Kampuchea, 1930–1975.* London: Verso, 1985. Kiernan traces the historical origins and development of the Khmer Rouge.

Pelz, Stephen E. "'When Do I Have Time to Think?' John F. Kennedy, Roger Hilsman, and the Laotian Crisis of 1962." *Diplomatic History* 3 (Spring 1979): 215–29. Pelz finds that the Kennedy administration lacked an orderly approach to Laotian policy.

Rowan, Roy. *The Four Days of Mayaguez.* New York: Norton, 1975. This journalistic account is a reliable narrative, but it is not particularly analytical.

Schanberg, Sydney H. *The Death and Life of Dith Pran.* New York: Viking Penguin, 1985. Schanberg tells the dramatic story of the survival of his *New York Times* colleague under the Khmer Rouge terror. This account inspired the movie *The Killing Fields.*

Shawcross, William. *Sideshow: Kissinger, Nixon, and the Destruction of Cambodia.* New York: Simon and Schuster, 1979. Shawcross blames Nixon and Kissinger for ill-considered policies that spread the Vietnam War into Cambodia and thereby opened the way for the rise of the vicious Khmer Rouge.

Smith, R. B. "The International Setting of the Cambodia Crisis, 1969–1970." *International History Review* 18 (May 1996): 303–35. Smith reviews the Cambodian, Laotian, and Vietnamese factors behind Nixon's order sending U.S. armed forces into Cambodia.

Stevenson, Charles A. *The End of Nowhere: American Policy Toward Laos Since 1954.* Boston: Beacon, 1972. This thorough analysis finds an excess of ideology in U.S. policy making.

Warner, Roger. *Back Fire: The CIA's Secret War in Laos and Its Link to the War in Vietnam.* New York: Simon and Schuster, 1995. This book has considerable information on CIA support of the Hmong but less on policy links to Vietnam.

3

THE DIEM YEARS

Anderson, David L. *Trapped by Success: The Eisenhower Administration and Vietnam, 1953–1961*. New York: Columbia University Press, 1991. According to this monograph, the Eisenhower administration created much of the U.S. commitment to the survival of South Vietnam that limited the policy choices of Kennedy and Johnson.

Bassett, Lawrence J, and Stephen E. Pelz. "The Failed Search for Victory: Vietnam and the Politics of War." In *Kennedy's Quest for Victory: American Foreign Policy, 1961–1963*, edited by Thomas G. Paterson, 223–52. New York: Oxford University Press, 1989. These authors contend that Kennedy dramatically increased U.S. involvement in Vietnam with little positive results.

Chomsky, Noam. *Rethinking Camelot: JFK, the Vietnam War, and U.S. Political Culture*. Boston: South End Press, 1993. Contrary to assertions by Kennedy admirers, Chomsky finds no evidence that the president planned to disengage the United States from Vietnam without a victory.

Combs, Arthur. "The Path Not Taken: The British Alternative to U.S. Policy in Vietnam, 1954–1956." *Diplomatic History* 19 (Winter 1995): 33–57. Combs finds that London tried for a time to urge adherence to the political reunification provisions of the Geneva accords.

Ernst, John. *Forging a Fateful Alliance: Michigan State University and the Vietnam War*. East Lansing: Michigan State University Press, 1998. This monograph details Michigan State's advisory efforts to help Ngo Dinh Diem establish a civil bureaucracy and police force.

Greene, Daniel P. O'C. "John Foster Dulles and the End of the Franco-American Entente in Indochina." *Diplomatic History* 16 (Fall 1992): 551–71. Greene examines the decisive meetings in 1955 when the United States and France agreed to separate their policies toward Saigon.

Greenstein, Fred I., and Richard H. Immerman. "What Did Eisenhower Tell Kennedy About Indochina? The Politics of Misperception." *Journal of American History* 79 (September 1992): 568–87. The authors engage in informed speculation about what Eisenhower advised Kennedy on Indochina.

Halberstam, David. *The Making of a Quagmire.* New York: Random House, 1964. This journalist's account remains one of the most significant descriptions of the Kennedy administration's actions in Vietnam.

Hammer, Ellen J. *A Death in November: America in Vietnam, 1963.* New York: Dutton, 1987. Hammer points out Diem's weaknesses and strengths and criticizes U.S. involvement in his death.

Hatcher, Patrick Lloyd. *The Suicide of an Elite: American Internationalists and Vietnam.* Stanford, Calif.: Stanford University Press, 1990. The author gives a favorable assessment of Ngo Dinh Diem and a negative evaluation of U.S. intervention in South Vietnamese politics.

Hilsman, Roger. *To Move a Nation: The Politics of Foreign Policy in the Administration of John F. Kennedy.* Garden City, N.Y.: Doubleday, 1967. A key Kennedy aide, Hilsman gives an inside account of Kennedy's Vietnam policies.

Lansdale, Edward G. *In the Midst of Wars.* New York: Harper and Row, 1972. This U.S. Air Force officer and CIA operative gives only guarded details on his activities but offers a dramatic description of Saigon in the early Diem years.

Morgan, Joseph G. *The Vietnam Lobby: The American Friends of Vietnam, 1955–1975.* Chapel Hill: University of North Carolina Press, 1997. Morgan's judicious study concludes that organized lobbying on behalf of the Diem government did not have as significant an impact on U.S. policy as some opponents of the war alleged.

Newman, John M. *JFK and Vietnam: Deception, Intrigue, and the Struggle for Power.* New York: Warner Books, 1992. Newman speculates that Kennedy's assassination was related to an alleged secret plan the president had for decreasing U.S. involvement in Vietnam. The scenario in the Hollywood movie *JFK* parallels this account in some ways.

Rust, William J. *Kennedy in Vietnam.* New York: Scribners, 1985. Rust notes that Kennedy had great expectations for counterinsurgency measures in Vietnam but would not have committed U.S. forces to the extent that Johnson eventually did.

Scigliano, Robert. *South Vietnam: Nation Under Stress.* Boston: Houghton Mifflin, 1964. This book provides details on Diem's Vietnam not readily available elsewhere.

4

NORTH VIETNAM AND THE VIETCONG

Andrews, William R. *The Village War: Vietnamese Communist Revolutionary Activities in Dinh Tuong Province, 1960–1964.* Columbia: University of Missouri Press, 1973. This older work remains useful on the social and political struggle in rural South Vietnam.

Brigham, Robert K. *Guerrilla Diplomacy: The NLF's Foreign Relations and the Viet Nam War.* Ithaca, N.Y.: Cornell University Press, 1999. From Vietnamese sources, Brigham details the often strained relations between the National Liberation Front and the Hanoi government.

Duiker, William J. *The Communist Road to Power in Vietnam.* 2d ed. Boulder, Col.: Westview Press, 1996. This general history is a standard work on the Communist Party's revolutionary strategy against the French and the Americans.

——. *Sacred War: Nationalism and Revolution in a Divided Vietnam.* New York: McGraw-Hill, 1995. Duiker's brief survey explains how the Vietnamese communists developed a successful strategy against the powerfully armed Americans.

Harrison, James P. *The Endless War: Vietnam's Struggle for Independence.* New York: Columbia University Press, 1989. This excellent study of the war at the village level demonstrates the political strength of the communists' organization.

Lockhart, Greg. *Nation in Arms: The Origins of the People's Army of Vietnam.* Boston: Allen and Unwin, 1989. This monograph shows how the Vietminh effectively combined political and military efforts during its war against the French.

Mangold, Tom, and John Penycate. *The Tunnels of Cu Chi.* New York: Random House, 1985. The Vietcong tunnel system near Saigon, described in this book, has become a symbol of the tactics that thwarted American power.

Moïse, Edwin E. *Land Reform in China and North Vietnam: Consolidating the Revolution at the Village Level.* Chapel Hill: University of North Carolina Press, 1983. Moïse makes a balanced assessment of the methods and human costs of agricultural collectivization.

Pike, Douglas. *History of Vietnamese Communism.* Stanford, Calif.: Stanford University Press, 1978. This short book provides a reliable description of party structure.

——. *PAVN: People's Army of Vietnam.* Novato, Calif.: Presidio Press, 1986. Pike contrasts the ability of North Vietnamese leaders and the inability of South Vietnamese leaders to coordinate political and military strategy.

——. *Viet Cong: The Organization and Techniques of the National Liberation Front of South Vietnam.* Cambridge, Mass.: MIT Press, 1966. There is a wealth of information in this book, but its thesis is arguable. Pike contends that NLF cadre were less philosophical communists and more political instruments of Moscow and Beijing.

Race, Jeffrey. *War Comes to Long An: Revolutionary Conflict in a Vietnamese Province.* Berkeley: University of California Press, 1972. This older work is still one of the best accounts of the rural insurgency.

Taylor, Sandra C. *Vietnamese Women at War: Fighting for Ho Chi Minh and the Revolution.* Lawrence: University Press of Kansas, 1999. From interviews with female fighters, Taylor provides insights into significant gender and cultural issues in the war.

Thayer, Carlyle. *War by Other Means: National Liberation and Revolution in Viet-Nam, 1954–1960.* Boston: Unwin Hymar, 1989. Thayer analyzes the southern and northern origins of the insurgency against Ngo Dinh Diem.

Tran Van Tra. *History of the Bulwark B-2 Theatre.* Vol. 5., *Concluding the Thirty-Year War.* Springfield, Va.: Joint Publications Research Service, 1983. This translation of a Vietnamese military history discusses communist military strategy.

Trullinger, James W. *Village at War: An Account of Revolution in Vietnam.* New York: Longman, 1980. Trullinger reveals peasant perspectives on the political conflict.

Truong Nhu Tang, with David Chanoff and Doan Van Toai. *A Vietcong Memoir.* New York: Harcourt Brace Jovanovich, 1985. The author of this inside view of the National Liberation Front went from being a loyal supporter to fleeing communist rule.

Vietnam, Socialist Republic of. *Vietnam: The Anti-U.S. Resistance for National Salvation, 1954–1975: Military History.* Hanoi: People's Publishing House, 1980. This volume is an official government history.

5

ESCALATION OF THE AMERICAN WAR

THE GULF OF TONKIN INCIDENT

Johnson, Robert David. "The Origins of Dissent: Senate Liberals and Vietnam, 1959–1964." *Pacific Historical Review* 65 (May 1996): 249–75. This article indicates that dissent on U.S. involvement in Vietnam existed in the Senate but was too disorganized to oppose Lyndon Johnson's Tonkin Gulf decisions.

Moïse, Edwin E. *Tonkin Gulf and the Escalation of the Vietnam War.* Chapel Hill: University of North Carolina Press, 1996. This carefully researched monograph concludes that Lyndon Johnson was mistaken about events in the Tonkin Gulf and not lying to the public when he characterized the attacks he ordered against North Vietnam as retaliation.

Tourison, Sedgwick. *Secret Army, Secret War: Washington's Tragic Spy Operation in North Vietnam.* Annapolis, Md.: Naval Institute Press, 1995. This account brings to light the secret "34-Alpha" operations, including those that were behind the Gulf of Tonkin Incident.

Windchy, Eugene C. *Tonkin Gulf.* Garden City, N.Y.: Doubleday, 1971. Using public documents and interviews, Windchy concludes that the Johnson administration lied about the Gulf of Tonkin Incident.

LYNDON JOHNSON'S DECISIONS FOR WAR

Barrett, David M. *Uncertain Warriors: Lyndon Johnson and His Vietnam Advisers.* Lawrence: University Press of Kansas, 1993. According to Barrett, Johnson was open to advice on Vietnam, but the president and his inner circle persisted in viewing Vietnam as a test of containment of global communism.

Berman, Larry. *Lyndon Johnson's War.* New York: Norton, 1989. The desire to preserve his domestic political leadership shaped Johnson's Vietnam decisions.

———. *Planning a Tragedy: The Americanization of the War in Vietnam.* New York: Norton, 1982. This close examination of Johnson's escalation of the American military role in 1965 concludes that Johnson wanted a successful but limited war that would not divert attention from his Great Society program at home.

Beschloss, Michael R., ed. *Taking Charge: The Johnson White House Tapes, 1963–1964.* New York: Simon and Schuster, 1997. The transcripts of secret presidential conversations with top aides give insights into Vietnam decisions.

Blair, Anne. *Lodge in Vietnam: A Patriot Abroad.* New Haven: Yale University Press, 1995. As U.S. ambassador in Saigon, Blair argues, Lodge often failed to provide good assessments to Washington because he did not understand the Vietnamese.

Brands, H. W. *The Wages of Globalism: Lyndon Johnson and the Limits of American Power.* New York: Oxford University Press, 1995. Brands contrasts Johnson's excessive use of force in Vietnam with his caution elsewhere in the world.

Burke, John P., and Fred I. Greenstein, with Larry Berman and Richard H. Immerman. *How Presidents Test Reality: Decisions on Vietnam, 1954 and 1965.* New York: Russell Sage Foundation, 1989. These scholars contend that Eisenhower encouraged staff discussion and Johnson discouraged it, and hence on Vietnam decisions Eisenhower made were more restrained than Johnson.

Dallek, Robert. "Lyndon Johnson and Vietnam: The Making of a Tragedy." *Diplomatic History* 20 (Spring 1996): 147–62. Dallek draws a portrait of Johnson's personality and background that suggests the president acted in the only way he knew how.

DiLeo, David L. *George Ball, Vietnam, and the Rethinking of Containment.* Foreword by Arthur M. Schlesinger, Jr. Chapel Hill: University of North Carolina Press, 1991. The author explores the strengths and weaknesses of Ball's role as the principal opponent of U.S. involvement in Vietnam from within the Kennedy and Johnson administrations.

Gallucci, Robert L. *Neither Peace Nor Honor: The Politics of American Military Policy in Vietnam.* Baltimore: Johns Hopkins University Press, 1975. Gallucci finds fault with the strategic thinking of high-ranking military officers and civilian bureaucrats.

Gardner, Lloyd C. *Pay Any Price: Lyndon Johnson and the Wars for Vietnam.* Chicago: Ivan R. Dee, 1995. Gardner portrays Johnson as alternately insecure and arrogant and ultimately unimaginative on Vietnam.

Gardner, Lloyd C., and Ted Gittinger, eds. *Vietnam: The Early Decisions.* Austin: University of Texas Press, 1997. This collection of essays by leading historians of the war examines key Kennedy and Johnson decisions.

Graff, Henry. *The Tuesday Cabinet.* Englewood Cliffs, N.J.: Prentice-Hall, 1970. From Johnson's talks with key advisors, Graff gleans valuable insights into official thinking about Vietnam.

Halberstam, David. *The Best and the Brightest*. New York: Random House, 1972. Journalist Halberstam presents colorful portraits of those who advised Kennedy and Johnson, and he holds many of them personally responsible for American mistakes in Vietnam.

Helsing, Jeffrey W. *Johnson's War/Johnson's Great Society: The Guns and Butter Trap*. Westport, Conn.: Praeger, 2000. The book examines the negative economic impact on America of the way Johnson conducted the war.

Herring, George C., Jr. *LBJ and Vietnam: A Different Kind of War*. Austin: University of Texas Press, 1994. Herring demonstrates how Johnson's personality and style of leadership were ill-suited for conducting a limited war.

Humphrey, David C. "NSC Meetings During the Johnson Presidency." *Diplomatic History* 18 (Winter 1994): 29–45. According to Humphrey, Johnson used the National Security Council to validate decisions that had already been made.

Kaiser, David. *American Tragedy: Kennedy, Johnson, and the Origins of the Vietnam War*. Cambridge, Mass.: Harvard University Press, 2000. Favorably disposed toward Kennedy, Kaiser argues that the U.S. presidents had good intentions in Vietnam but made fatal errors of judgment about Vietnamese politics.

Khong, Yuen Foong. *Analogies At War: Korea, Munich, Dien Bien Phu, and the Vietnam Decisions of 1965*. Princeton: Princeton University Press, 1992. This study of decision making analyzes how policymakers used the analogy of the Korean War to guide their thinking on Vietnam.

Logevall, Fredrik. *Choosing War: The Lost Chance for Peace and the Escalation of War in Vietnam*. Berkeley: University of California Press, 1999. This multiarchival work indicts Lyndon Johnson for choosing war when, according to Logevall's research, a negotiated settlement was possible. The author speculates that, if Kennedy had lived, he would have made a different choice.

McMaster, H. R. *Dereliction of Duty: Johnson, McNamara, the Joint Chiefs of Staff, and the Lies That Led to Vietnam*. New York: HarperCollins, 1997. McMaster criticizes the military chiefs for failing to oppose the civilian leaders' plan for gradual escalation in Vietnam.

Rosen, Stephen Peter. "Vietnam and the American Theory of Limited War." *International Security* 7 (Fall 1982): 83–113. Rosen faults Johnson and McNamara for not giving military leaders a well-defined mission in Vietnam.

Schulzinger, Robert D. " 'It's Easy to Win a War on Paper': The United States and Vietnam 1961–1968." In *The Diplomacy of the Crucial Decade: American Foreign Relations During the 1960s*, edited by Diane Kunz, 183–218. New York: Columbia University Press, 1994. The more the United States did for South Vietnam, the more dependent Saigon became on Washington.

Schwab, Orrin. *Defending the Free World: John F. Kennedy, Lyndon Johnson, and the Vietnam War, 1961 1965*. Westport, Conn.: Praeger, 1998. Schwab maintains that Johnson did not want war but was unwilling to allow South Vietnam to be lost to the "Free World."

Thies, Wallace J. *When Governments Collide: Coercion and Diplomacy in the Vietnam Conflict, 1964–1968*. Berkeley: University of California Press, 1980. Thies offers an explanation of why U.S. bombing of North Vietnam did not convince Hanoi to agree to recognize the Saigon government.

Thomson, James C., Jr. "How Could Vietnam Happen? An Autopsy." *Atlantic* 221 (April 1968): 47–53. Written during the war, this article by a former State Department official remains a cogent analysis of U.S. mistakes in Vietnam.

VanDeMark, Brian. *Into the Quagmire: Lyndon Johnson and the Escalation of the Vietnam War.* New York: Oxford University Press, 1991. This meticulous examination of Johnson's 1965 decisions for war reveals a president burdened by uncertainty and doubt.

Vandiver, Frank E. *Shadows of Vietnam: Lyndon Johnson's Wars.* College Station: Texas A&M University Press, 1997. Military historian Vandiver is very critical of the advice McNamara gave Johnson.

6

THE AMERICAN WAY OF WAR

MILITARY OPERATIONS AND OVERVIEWS

Appy, Christian G. *Working-Class War: American Combat Soldiers and Vietnam.*
Chapel Hill: University of North Carolina Press, 1993. Appy provides a composite
picture of the background, combat experiences, and return home of U.S. enlisted
men in Vietnam.

Bergerud, Eric M. *The Dynamics of Defeat: The Vietnam War in Hau Nghia Province.*
Boulder, Col.: Westview Press, 1990. Focusing on U.S. combat operations and pacification efforts in one province, Bergerud finds that neither tactic could make up
for the political defects of the South Vietnamese government.

———. *Red Thunder, Tropic Lightning: The World of a Combat Division in Vietnam.*
Boulder, Col.: Westview Press, 1993. The author portrays the men of the 25th Infantry Division as good soldiers and not at all like the negative image of American
troops in some antiwar accounts.

Buckingham, William A., Jr. *Operation Ranch Hand: The Air Force and Herbicides in
Southeast Asia, 1961–1971.* Washington, D.C.: U.S. Government Printing Office,
1982. This volume is the U.S. Air Force account of the controversial defoliation program in South Vietnam.

Buzzanco, Robert. *Masters of War: Military Dissent and Politics in the Vietnam Era.*
New York: Cambridge University Press, 1996. Buzzanco describes divisions among
military leaders over Vietnam and examines the bureaucratic politics of the military chiefs.

Cable, Larry. *Unholy Grail: The U.S. and the Wars in Vietnam, 1965–68.* New York: Routledge, 1991. The author maintains that the U.S. air and ground war was ineffective against the North and weakened the South politically.

Cecil, Paul Frederick. *Herbicidal Warfare: The Ranch Hand Project in Vietnam.* Westport, Conn.: Praeger, 1986. This monograph is a somewhat technical study of defoliation as a tactic.

Clarke, Jeffrey J. *The United States Army in Vietnam: Advice and Support: The Final Years, 1965–1973.* Washington: U.S. Government Printing Office, 1988. This official U.S. Army history is a good overview of General Westmoreland's strategy and how that strategy changed under his successor General Abrams.

Clodfelter, Mark. *The Limits of Air Power: The American Bombing of North Vietnam.* New York: The Free Press, 1989. The author makes the case that U.S. bombing, even if heavier bombing had been used, could not secure the Saigon government against a guerilla enemy.

Collins, James L., Jr. *The Development and Training of the South Vietnamese Army, 1950 –1972.* Washington, D.C.: U.S. Government Printing Office, 1975. This military history is especially good on what became known as Vietnamization.

Conboy, Kenneth, and Dale Andrade. *Spies and Commandos: How America Lost the Secret War in North Vietnam.* Lawrence: University Press of Kansas, 2000. The authors expose major mistakes in U.S. covert operations against North Vietnam.

Davidson, Phillip B. *Secrets of the Vietnam War.* Novato, Calif.: Presidio Press, 1990. General Davidson was the U.S. Army's chief intelligence officer in Vietnam (1967–69) and contends that the United States could have won the war with a better strategy.

Gibson, James William. *The Perfect War: The War We Couldn't Lose and How We Did.* New York: Vintage Books, 1986. U.S. strategists had so much confidence in American technology and organizational management that they failed to recognize the communists' political strength in Vietnam and fashion an effective response.

Hooper, Edwin, Dean C. Allard, and Oscar P. Fitzgerald. *The United States Navy and the Vietnam Conflict: The Setting of the Stage to 1959.* Washington, D.C.: U.S. Government Printing Office, 1976. This book details U.S. naval assistance first to the French in Indochina and then to the South Vietnamese.

Kinnard, Douglas. *The War Managers.* Hanover, N.H.: University Press of New England, 1976. From a survey of opinions of U.S. Army generals, Kinnard discerns no consensus among them on why the American war failed.

Krepinevich, Andrew F., Jr. *The Army and Vietnam.* Baltimore: Johns Hopkins University Press, 1986. A former army officer, the author believes that pacification would have been a more successful strategy in Vietnam than attrition.

Lewy, Guenter. *America in Vietnam.* New York: Oxford University Press, 1978. Lewy faults U.S. strategy as too conventional, but he argues that the American war in Vietnam was justifiable and not immoral as antiwar critics claimed.

Littauer, Raphael, and Norman Uphoff. *The Air War in Indochina.* Rev. ed. Boston: Beacon, 1972. This book provides a wealth of information on the air war and a judicious discussion of the issues related to bombing.

McClintock, Michael. *Instruments of Statecraft: U.S. Guerrilla Warfare, Counterinsurgency, and Counterterrorism, 1940–1990.* New York: Pantheon Books, 1992. Although broad in scope, the book focuses much of its discussion on counterinsurgency warfare in Vietnam.

Moore, Harold G., and Joseph L. Galloway. *We Were Soldiers Once . . . and Young: Ia Drang: The Battle That Changed the War in Vietnam.* New York: Random House, 1992. This riveting memoir recalls the first major land battle fought by U.S. forces against North Vietnamese troops, and from this engagement Westmoreland became committed to airmobile warfare.

Mrozek, Donald J. *Air Power and the Ground War in Vietnam: Ideas and Actions.* Washington, D.C.: U.S. Government Printing Office, 1989. This U.S. Air Force history highlights the strengths and weaknesses of tactical air support.

Palmer, Bruce, Jr. *The 25-Year War: America's Military Role in Vietnam.* Lexington: University Press of Kentucky, 1984. This volume is representative of those arguments by some in the military that civilian leaders prevented them from winning the war.

Palmer, Dave Richard. *Summons of the Trumpet: U.S.-Vietnam in Perspective.* San Rafael, Calif.: Presidio Press, 1978. A good military history of the war, this book complains of civilian interference in planning military operations.

Pisor, Robert. *The End of the Line: The Siege of Khe Sanh.* New York: Norton, 1982. This account of the siege is useful, but its conclusions are debatable.

Prados, John. *The Blood Road: The Ho Chi Minh Trail and the Vietnam War.* New York: John Wiley and Sons, 1999. This book gives the history of the North's famous infiltration route into South Vietnam and describes the trail as emblematic of how Hanoi won the war.

——. *The Hidden History of the Vietnam War.* Chicago: Ivan R. Dee, 1995. Prados challenges different arguments that others have made on how the United States could have won the war.

——. *Presidents' Secret Wars: CIA and Pentagon Covert Operations Since World War II.* Revised and expanded ed. Chicago: Ivan R. Dee, 1996. U.S. covert actions in Southeast Asia are included as part of secret U.S. operations worldwide.

Prados, John, and Ray W. Stubbe. *Valley of Decision: The Siege of Khe Sanh.* Boston: Houghton Mifflin, 1991. The authors provide a full account of this significant military event.

Schell, Jonathan. *The Real War: The Classic Reporting on the Vietnam War.* New York: Pantheon, 1987. In this book, Schell reissues and updates some of the disturbing accounts that he wrote as a young journalist on the impact of the American war on Vietnamese villages.

Schlight, John. *The United States Air Force in Southeast Asia: The War in South Vietnam: The Years of the Offensive, 1965–1968.* Washington, D.C.: U.S. Government Printing Office, 1988. This official history details the heaviest U.S. bombing of the war, that on South Vietnam.

Shultz, Richard H., Jr. *The Secret War Against Hanoi: Kennedy and Johnson's Use of Spies, Saboteurs, and Covert Warriors in North Vietnam.* New York: HarperCollins, 1999. The author assembles information on some of the most secret military operations of the war.

Spector, Ronald H. *After Tet: The Bloodiest Year in Vietnam.* New York: Free Press, 1992. Spector describes the intensity of combat and the growing problems within the U.S. military in 1968.

———. *The United States Army in Vietnam: Advice and Support: The Early Years, 1941–1960.* Washington: U.S. Government Printing Office, 1983. This history published by the U.S. Army covers the initial U.S. military presence in South Vietnam.

Stanton, Shelby L. *The Rise and Fall of an American Army: U.S. Ground Forces in Vietnam, 1965–1973.* San Rafael, Calif.: Presidio Press, 1985. This book is a good source on many individual military operations and on how morale declined among U.S. soldiers.

Summers, Harry G., Jr. *On Strategy: A Critical Analysis of the Vietnam War.* Novato, Calif.: Presidio Press, 1982. Summers advances a thesis of how the United States could have won a conventional war in Vietnam, and his ideas greatly influenced U.S. military doctrine after the war.

Thompson, James C. *Rolling Thunder: Understanding Policy and Program Failure.* Chapel Hill: University of North Carolina Press, 1980. Thompson reviews why the continuous bombing of North Vietnam failed and how the operation ended.

Tilford, Earl H., Jr. *Crosswinds: The Air Force's Setup in Vietnam.* Foreword by Caroline F. Ziemke. College Station: Texas A&M University Press, 1993. The author, a U.S. Air Force veteran, explains why strategic bombing was inappropriate in Vietnam, and he corrects several fallacies about American bombing at the end of the war.

MY LAI MASSACRE

Anderson, David L., ed. *Facing My Lai: Moving Beyond the Massacre.* Lawrence: University Press of Kansas, 1998. In this work, a distinguished group of historians, journalists, veterans, and writers reflect on the massacre, the war, and their meaning.

Bilton, Michael, and Kevin Sim. *Four Hours in My Lai.* New York: Viking, 1992. British television journalists, the authors pull together a complete account of the massacre and its aftermath from interviews and military records.

Goldstein, Joseph, Burke Marshall, and Jack Schwartz. *The My Lai Massacre and Its Cover-Up: Beyond the Reach of Law?* New York: Free Press, 1976. The contents of this book include the summary of the official army investigation and discussion of the legal issues.

Olson, James S., and Randy Roberts, eds. *My Lai: A Brief History with Documents.* Boston: Bedford Books, 1997. This collection contains key historical documents and a useful introduction to the atrocity.

Peers, W. R. *The My Lai Inquiry.* New York: Norton, 1979. The author is the general who led the U.S. Army investigation of the massacre and cover-up.

PACIFICATION AND COUNTERINSURGENCY

Andrade, Dale. *Ashes to Ashes: The Phoenix Program and the Vietnamese War.* Lexington, Mass.: Lexington Books, 1990. Andrade concludes that the Phoenix Program was effective but that it and other pacification efforts were not principal U.S. strategies.

Blaufarb, Douglas S. *The Counterinsurgency Era: U.S. Doctrine and Performance, 1950 to the Present.* New York: Free Press, 1977. The Vietnam War is part of this broader study of counterinsurgency.

Colby, William, and James McCargar. *Lost Victory: A Firsthand Account of America's Sixteen-Year Involvement in Vietnam.* Chicago: Contemporary Books, 1989. Colby headed the U.S. pacification program in South Vietnam after 1968 and argues that it should have been given a greater role in U.S. strategy.

Goodman, Allan E. *Politics in War: The Bases of Political Community in South Vietnam.* Cambridge: Harvard University Press, 1973. This monograph is a detailed study of politics in the South at the peak of U.S. involvement.

Hunt, Richard A. *Pacification: The American Struggle for Vietnam's Hearts and Minds.* Boulder, Col.: Westview Press, 1995. The author concludes that U.S. expertise failed to understand and solve South Vietnam's political and social problems.

Komer, Robert W. *Bureaucracy at War: U.S. Performance in the Vietnam Conflict.* Foreword by William E. Colby. Boulder, Col.: Westview Press, 1986. Like Colby, who followed him as head of the American pacification effort, Komer believes the deficiencies of the Saigon government could have been remedied.

Marquis, Jefferson P. "American Social Science and Nation Building in Vietnam." *Diplomatic History* 24 (Winter 2000): 79–105. U.S. social scientists could not find a way to turn South Vietnam into a nation in the midst of a war.

Moyar, Mark. *Phoenix and the Birds of Prey: The CIA's Secret Campaign to Destroy the Viet Cong.* Annapolis, Md.: Naval Institute Press, 1997. This account gives a generally positive picture of the controversial Phoenix Program.

Shafer, D. Michael. *Deadly Paradigms: The Failure of U.S. Counterinsurgency Policy.* Princeton: Princeton University Press, 1988. Shafer identifies problems in U.S. counterinsurgency plans in Vietnam and elsewhere.

Valentine, Douglas. *The Phoenix Program.* New York: Morrow, 1990. This book relates the dark side of the program but is thinly researched.

INTERNATIONAL SETTING

Baldwin, Frank. "America's Rented Troops: South Koreans in Vietnam." *Bulletin of Concerned Asian Scholars* 7 (Oct.-Dec. 1975): 33–40. Korean forces in Vietnam were paid well to support the American war.

Barclay, Glen St. J. *A Very Small Insurance Policy: The Politics of Australian Involvement in Vietnam, 1954–1967.* New York: University of Queensland Press, 1988. Barclay explains why Australia forthrightly backed the United States in Vietnam.

Blackburn, Robert M. *Mercenaries and Lyndon Johnson's "More Flags": The Hiring of Korean, Filipino, and Thai Soldiers in the Vietnam War.* Jefferson, N.C.: McFarland, 1994. Appearances aside, America's Asian allies in Vietnam were there for the money.

Chen Jian. "China's Involvement in the Vietnam War, 1964–69." *China Quarterly* (June 1995): 357–87. The author documents the extensive aid China gave to North Vietnam and the tensions that developed between them.

Edwards, Peter, with Gregory Pemberton. *Crisis and Commitments: The Politics and Diplomacy of Australia's Involvement in Southeast Asian Conflicts, 1948–1965.* Sydney: Allen and Unwin, in association with the Australian War Memorial, 1992. This Australian government history reveals how Canberra's attitude figured into U.S. military escalation in Vietnam.

Gaiduk, Ilya V. *The Soviet Union and the Vietnam War.* Chicago: Ivan R. Dee, 1996. Gaiduk contends that the USSR did not want the Vietnam War to wreck détente with the United States.

Gardner, Lloyd C., and Ted Gittinger, eds. *International Perspectives on Vietnam.* College Station: Texas A&M University Press, 2000. Twelve scholars analyze how the war relates to China, the Soviet Union, Korea, Japan, Southeast Asia, Europe, and the Middle East.

Havens, Thomas R. H. *Fire Across the Sea: The Vietnam War and Japan, 1965–1975.* Princeton, N.J.: Princeton University Press, 1987. While the United States fought a war with North Vietnam, America's ally Japan carried on trade with the North Vietnamese.

Klinghoffer, Judith Apter. *Vietnam, Jews, and the Middle East: Unintended Consequences.* New York: St. Martin's Press, 1999. The author explores the political and strategic interaction of the extensive U.S. military intervention in Vietnam and the U.S. response to the 1967 war in Israel.

Levant, Victor. *Quiet Complicity: Canadian Involvement in the Vietnam War.* Toronto: University of Toronto Press, 1986. Levant cites various ways in which Canada, contrary to its government's claims, aided the U.S. war in Vietnam.

Murphy, John. *Harvest of Fear: A History of Australia's Vietnam War.* Boulder, Col.: Westview Press, 1994. Murphy writes about Australian troops in Vietnam and about the war as an issue within Australia.

Nelson, Keith L. *The Making of Détente: Soviet-American Relations in the Shadow of Vietnam.* Baltimore: Johns Hopkins University Press, 1995. Mounting political pressures on Nixon to end the war made his administration more creative in its policies toward the USSR.

Nixon, Richard M. "Asia After Vietnam." *Foreign Affairs* 46 (October 1967): 111–25. In this article, Nixon anticipates his later policies as president.

Pike, Douglas. *Vietnam and the Soviet Union: Anatomy of an Alliance.* Boulder, Col.: Westview Press, 1987. Hanoi wanted Moscow's aid but not its advice.

Ross, Douglas A. *In the Interests of Peace: Canada and Vietnam, 1954–1973.* Toronto: University of Toronto Press, 1984. Canada's domestic divisions over the Vietnam War often involved differences between Canada's interest in good relations with the United States and definition of its own international values.

Sarantakes, Nicholas Evan. "In the Service of the Pharaoh? The United States and the Deployment of Korean Troops in Vietnam, 1965–1968." *Pacific Historical Review* 68 (August 1999): 425–49. The author maintains that Seoul's concerns about South Korean security and not mercenary interests led it to support the U.S. military effort in Vietnam.

Smith, R. B. *An International History of the Vietnam War.* 3 vols. New York: St. Martin's Press, 1984–90. The author stresses the strategic importance of Vietnam to China, the Soviet Union, and the United States.

Sullivan, Marianna P. *France's Vietnam Policy: A Study in French-American Relations.* Westport, Conn.: Greenwood, 1978. Charles deGaulle's critique of U.S. policy in Vietnam reflected his broader concerns about U.S.-French relations.

Whiting, Allen. *The Chinese Calculus of Deterrence: India and Indochina.* Ann Arbor: University of Michigan Press, 1975. This book is a reliable assessment of Chinese aid to North Vietnam.

Zhai Qiang. *China and the Vietnam Wars, 1950–1975.* Chapel Hill: University of North Carolina Press, 2000. From Chinese sources, the author provides an excellent overview of Beijing's shifting attitude toward the American war in Vietnam over its long course.

Zhang Xiaoming. "The Vietnam War, 1964–1969: A Chinese Perspective." *Journal of Military History* 60 (October 1996): 731–62. The author argues that China would have engaged U.S. forces if America had invaded North Vietnam.

THE LIMITS OF AMERICAN POWER

ANTIWAR MOVEMENT

Anderson, Terry H. *The Movement and the Sixties: Protest in America from Greensboro to Wounded Knee.* New York: Oxford University Press, 1995. Along with other protest groups, the antiwar movement changed American society in the 1960s.

Baskir, Lawrence M., and William A. Strauss. *Chance and Circumstance: The Draft, the War, and the Vietnam Generation.* New York: Knopf, 1978. This work profiles that portion of young Americans who, in various ways, avoided military service in Vietnam.

Burner, David. *Making Peace with the '60s.* Princeton, N.J.: Princeton University Press, 1996. Liberals led the United States into the Vietnam War and ultimately paid the political consequences.

Caute, David. *The Year of the Barricades: A Journey Through 1968.* New York: Harper and Row, 1988. A global look at protests, this book includes discussion of the events at the 1968 Democratic National Convention.

DeBenedetti, Charles, with the assistance of Charles Chatfield. *An American Ordeal: The Antiwar Movement of the Vietnam Era.* Syracuse, N.Y.: Syracuse University Press, 1990. This significant study traces the changing nature of the antiwar movement.

Farber, David. *Chicago '68.* Chicago: University of Chicago Press, 1988. Farber gives the facts and the significance of the violent clash over the war at the Democratic National Convention.

Flynn, George Q. *The Draft, 1940–1973*. Lawrence: University Press of Kansas, 1993. This book is an authoritative history of the Vietnam-era draft.

Garfinkle, Adam M. *Telltale Hearts: The Origins and Impact of the Vietnam Antiwar Movement*. Preface by Stephen E. Ambrose. New York: St. Martin's Press, 1995. The author suggests that radical protests prolonged the war.

Gitlin, Todd. *The Sixties: Years of Hope, Days of Rage*. New York: Bantam Books, 1987. Gittlin reflects personally and historically on youthful protest.

Gottlieb, Sherry Gershon. *Hell No, We Won't Go! Resisting the Draft During the Vietnam War*. New York: Viking Penguin, 1991. Through interviews, Gottlieb relates the various ways men avoided the draft.

Hall, Mitchell K. *Because of Their Faith: CALCAV and Religious Opposition to the Vietnam War*. New York: Columbia University Press, 1991. This study finds that religious leaders who opposed the war were, as a group, moderates and not radicals.

Halstead, Fred. *Out Now! A Participant's Account of the American Movement Against the Vietnam War*. New York: Monad, 1978. This firsthand narrative is a good source on the tactics and internal tensions of the movement.

Harris, Louis. *The Anguish of Change*. New York: Norton, 1973. Pollster Harris makes a revealing analysis of public opinion on the war.

Hayden, Tom. *Reunion: A Memoir*. New York: Random House, 1988. Hayden was a prominent leader in the student and antiwar movements.

Heath, G. Louis, ed. *Mutiny Does Not Happen Lightly: The Literature of the American Resistance to the Vietnam War*. Metuchen, N.J.: Scarecrow Press, 1976. This collection reprints antiwar documents.

Heineman, Kenneth. *Campus Wars: The Peace Movement at American State Universities in the Vietnam Era*. New York: New York University Press, 1993. Included in this volume are useful case studies of campus protests, including Kent State.

Jeffreys-Jones, Rhodri. *Peace Now! American Society and the Ending of the Vietnam War*. New Haven: Yale University Press, 1999. The author notes how different segments of the American people responded to the war.

Lunch, William L., and Peter W. Sperlich. "American Public Opinion and the War in Vietnam." *Western Political Quarterly* 32 (March 1979): 21–44. This article is a useful source on public opinion patterns.

Moser, Richard. *The New Winter Soldiers: GI and Veteran Dissent During the Vietnam Era*. New Brunswick, N.J.: Rutgers University Press, 1995. Moser draws together revealing examples of American soldiers coming out in opposition to the war they fought.

Mueller, John E. *War, Presidents, and Public Opinion*. New York: Wiley and Sons, 1973. The author compares public opinion during the Korean and Vietnam wars.

Small, Melvin. *Johnson, Nixon, and the Doves*. New Brunswick, N.J.: Rutgers University Press, 1988. Small's thesis is that opponents of the war had more impact on Johnson's and Nixon's policy choices than the presidents admitted.

Small, Melvin, and William D. Hoover, eds. *Give Peace a Chance: Exploring the Vietnam Antiwar Movement*. Foreword by George McGovern. Syracuse, N.Y.:

Syracuse University Press, 1992. Chapters in this anthology address a wide variety of antiwar experiences.

Swerdlow, Amy. *Women Strike for Peace: Traditional Motherhood and Radical Politics in the 1960s.* Chicago: University of Chicago Press, 1993. This book demonstrates some unique strengths women had in taking radical antiwar stands.

Wells, Tom. *The War Within: America's Battle Over Vietnam.* Foreword by Todd Gitlin. Berkeley: University of California Press, 1994. Wells provides a good survey of the antiwar protests and official reactions to them.

Zaroulis, Nancy, and Gerald Sullivan. *Who Spoke Up? American Protest Against the War in Vietnam, 1963–1975.* New York: Doubleday, 1984. The authors present a positive image of those who participated in the war protests.

AMERICAN POLITICS AND ECONOMY

Berman, William C. J. *William Fulbright and the Vietnam War: The Dissent of a Political Realist.* Kent, Ohio: Kent State University Press, 1988. A strong figure in the U.S. Senate, Fulbright went from support of to opposition to U.S. actions in Vietnam.

Blum, John Morton. *Years of Discord: American Politics and Society, 1961–1974.* New York: Norton, 1991. This reliable but bland survey chronicles the decline of political liberalism during the Vietnam years.

Campagna, Anthony S. *The Economic Consequences of the Vietnam War.* Westport, Conn.: Greenwood, 1991. This study surveys the economic costs and consequences of the war from the 1950s to the 1970s.

Dietz, Terry. *Republicans and Vietnam, 1961–1986.* Westport, Conn.: Greenwood Press, 1986. Dietz finds that Republican leaders in Congress were divided on how to react to Democratic presidents' war decisions.

Fulbright, J. William. *The Arrogance of Power.* New York: Random House, 1966. Senator Fulbright makes a blunt warning about what the war is doing to America.

Gould, Lewis L. *1968: The Election That Changed America.* Chicago: Ivan R. Dee, 1993. According to Gould, this election, of which the issue of the war was a big part, produced lasting changes in American politics.

Matusow, Allen J. *The Unraveling of America: A History of Liberalism in the 1960s.* New York: Harper and Row, 1983. Because of the war, political liberalism was in crisis and disarray by 1968.

Olson, Gregory Allen. *Mansfield and Vietnam: A Study in Rhetorical Adaptation.* East Lansing: Michigan State University Press, 1995. Mansfield was a powerful but low-key congressional critic of the war.

Schmitz, David F., and Nancy Fousekis. "Frank Church, the Senate, and the Emergence of Dissent on the Vietnam War." *Pacific Historical Review* 63 (November 1994): 561–81. Church became one of the most vocal Senate opponents of the war.

Stevens, Robert W. *Vain Hopes, Grim Realities: The Economic Consequences of the Vietnam War.* New York: New Viewpoints, 1976. Stevens detects a direct link between the war and economic problems in the 1970s.

Tananbaum, Duane A. "Not for the First Time: Antecedents and Origins of the War Powers Resolution, 1945–1970." In *Congress and United States Foreign Policy: Con-*

trolling the Use of Force in the Nuclear Age, edited by Michael Barnhart, 39–54. Albany: State University of New York Press, 1987. This article surveys the legislative history behind the War Powers Resolution of 1973.

Unger, Irwin, and Debi Unger. *Turning Point: 1968.* New York: Scribner's, 1989. From the controversies of 1968, including the war, the authors trace the roots of the Reagan conservatism that fully emerges in the 1980s.

TELEVISION AND THE PRESS

Arlen, Michael J. *Living-Room War.* New York: Penguin Books, 1982. Arlen examines television reporting of the war, 1966–1968.

Braestrup, Peter. *Big Story: How the American Press and Television Reported and Interpreted the Crisis of Tet 1968 in Vietnam and Washington.* 2 vols. Boulder, Col.: Westview, 1977. The author faults the quality of press reporting of the Tet fighting and says the journalists produced an erroneous image that the United States had suffered a military defeat.

Browne, Malcolm W. *Muddy Boots and Red Socks: A Reporter's Life.* New York: Times Books/Random House, 1993. This memoir gives a good description of the young American reporters in Vietnam and their work.

Elegant, Robert. "How to Lose a War." *Encounter* 57 (August 1981): 73–90. This essay places virtually the entire burden of U.S. defeat in Vietnam on American television reporting.

Elwood-Akers, Virginia. *Women War Correspondents in the Vietnam War, 1961–1975.* Metuchen, N.J.: Scarecrow, 1988. The experiences of more than seventy-five female journalists are described in this volume.

Gitlin, Todd. *The Whole World Is Watching: Mass Media in the Making and Unmaking of the New Left.* Berkeley: University of California Press, 1980. The antiwar movement needed the media, but the media also utilized the movement.

Hallin, Daniel C. *The "Uncensored War": The Media and Vietnam.* New York: Oxford University Press, 1986. Hallin finds that the media generally accepted official explanations of the war and supported government policy, even during and after Tet.

Hammond, William M. *Reporting Vietnam: Media and Military at War.* Lawrence: University Press of Kansas, 1998. The author of an official U.S. Army history of media coverage of the war, Hammond effectively demonstrates that the press was not responsible for the American inability to prevail in Vietnam.

Mandelbaum, Michael. "Vietnam: The Televised War." *Daedalus* 111 (Fall 1982): 157–69. The author argues that it was the war itself, not television coverage of the war, that created antiwar sentiment.

Pach, Chester J., Jr. " 'And That's the Way It Was': The Vietnam War on the Network Nightly News." In *The Sixties: From Memory to History,* edited by David R. Farber, 90–118. Chapel Hill: University of North Carolina Press, 1994. Pach concludes that television did a fairly good job of reporting on the war and on the flaws in American strategy.

Prochnau, William. *Once Upon a Distant War: David Halberstam, Neil Sheehan, Peter Arnett—Three Young War Correspondents and Their Early Vietnam Battles.*

New York: Random House, 1995. This book is a sympathetic and useful account of these reporters.

Reporting Vietnam: American Journalism, 1959–1975. 2 vols. New York: The Library of America, 1998. This compilation includes some of the best print reporting of the war and gives biographical information about the journalists.

Rudenstine, David. *The Day the Presses Stopped: A History of the Pentagon Papers Case.* Berkeley: University of California Press, 1996. The author provides a balanced discussion of the issue of freedom of the press in this case.

Small, Melvin. *Covering Dissent: The Media and the Anti-Vietnam War Movement.* New Brunswick, N.J.: Rutgers University Press, 1994. Small contends that the national media did not favor the antiwar protestors as government officials often charged.

Turner, Kathleen J. *Lyndon Johnson's Dual War: Vietnam and the Press.* Chicago: University of Chicago Press, 1985. Turner argues that Johnson did not do a good job of explaining U.S. actions to the press and increasingly lost press support.

Ungar, Sanford J. *The Papers and the Papers: An Account of the Legal and Political Battle Over the Pentagon Papers.* New York: Columbia University Press, 1989. Ungar analyzes the two trials stemming from the publication of the Pentagon Papers.

Wyatt, Clarence R. *Paper Soldiers: The American Press and the Vietnam War.* New York: Norton, 1994. Wyatt concludes that U.S. officials did a better job of managing the press than the press did of influencing the government.

THE TET OFFENSIVE

Ford, Ronnie E. *Tet 1968: Understanding the Surprise.* Foreword by William C. Westmoreland and George W. Allen. Portland, Ore.: Frank Cass, 1995. The author contends that U.S. military response to Tet was effective but that U.S. intelligence did not understand the enemy's political strategy.

Gilbert, Marc Jason, and William Head, eds. *The Tet Offensive.* Westport, Conn.: Praeger, 1996. The essays in this volume provide a thorough discussion of many aspects of the offensive.

Hoopes, Townsend. *The Limits of Intervention: An Inside Account of How the Johnson Policy of Escalation in Vietnam Was Reversed.* New ed. New York: Norton, 1987. A Pentagon official, Hoopes reviews the policy reassessment in the two months after Tet.

Oberdorfer, Don. *Tet!* Garden City, N.Y.: Doubleday, 1971. This reporter's account remains a reliable narrative.

Schandler, Herbert Y. *The Unmaking of a President: Lyndon Johnson and Vietnam.* Princeton, N.J.: Princeton University Press, 1977. This book is a detailed examination of the impact of Tet on Johnson and his policy decisions.

Shulimson, Jack. *United States Marines in Vietnam: The Defining Year 1968.* Washington, D.C.: U.S. Government Printing Office, 1997. This official Marine Corps history recounts the Marines' role in Tet and compares U.S. Marine and Army assessments of strategy.

Wirtz, James J. *The Tet Offensive: Intelligence Failure in War.* Ithaca, N.Y.: Cornell University Press, 1992. American misconceptions about the Vietnamese enemy contributed significantly to the surprise of the Tet Offensive.

8

THE END OF THE AMERICAN WAR

RICHARD NIXON'S WAR AND DIPLOMACY

Andrade, Dale. *Trial by Fire: The 1972 Easter Offensive, America's Last Vietnam Battle.* New York: Hippocrene Books, 1995. This South Vietnamese military incursion into Laos was rescued from total defeat by U.S. air power.

Bundy, McGeorge. "Vietnam, Watergate, and Presidential Powers." *Foreign Affairs* 58 (Winter 1979/80): 397–407. Bundy disagrees with Kissinger's argument in the *White House Years* that puts the burden on Congress for U.S. failure to support South Vietnam after 1973.

Goodman, Allan E. *The Lost Peace: America's Search for a Negotiated Settlement of the Vietnam War.* Stanford, Calif.: Hoover Institution, 1978. This older account of the Johnson and Nixon administrations' diplomacy remains useful.

Griffith, Robert K. *The U.S. Army's Transition to the All-Volunteer Force, 1968–1974.* Washington, D.C.: U.S. Government Printing Office, 1997. This official U.S. Army history assesses the Vietnam War draft and the end of conscription.

Hersh, Seymour M. *The Price of Power: Kissinger in the Nixon White House.* New York: Summit, 1983. Journalist Hersh condemns the secrecy and expediency of the Kissinger-Nixon policies.

Kimball, Jeffrey. *Nixon's Vietnam War.* Lawrence: University Press of Kansas, 1998. The most authoritative study to date of Nixon's conduct of the war, this book probes his military, diplomatic, and political methods.

Kissinger, Henry A. *White House Years*. Boston: Little, Brown, 1979. Kissinger provides hundreds of pages of explanation of how he and Nixon fashioned rational policies in Vietnam.

Morris, Roger. *Uncertain Greatness: Henry Kissinger and American Foreign Policy*. New York: Harper and Row, 1977. This one-time assistant to Kissinger argues that Nixon and Kissinger's policies served their own political interests but lacked a coherent strategy for victory.

Nguyen Tien Hung and Jerrold J. Schecter. *The Palace File*. New York: Harper and Row, 1986. The book reveals secret and unfulfilled Nixon and Ford pledges of aid to South Vietnam after January 1973 and exposes the serious flaws in the Saigon government.

Porter, Gareth. *A Peace Denied: The United States, Vietnam and the Paris Agreement*. Bloomington: Indiana University Press, 1975. This book is a good source on the negotiations leading to the 1973 cease-fire and its collapse, and is also particularly useful on North Vietnam's perspective on the peace process.

Schell, Jonathan. *The Time of Illusion*. New York: Knopf, 1976. Schell criticizes Nixon's approach to the Vietnamese enemy and to his domestic foes.

Sorley, Lewis. *A Better War: The Unexamined Victories and the Final Tragedy of America's Last Years in Vietnam*. New York: Harcourt Brace, 1999. The author maintains that, after Tet, the U.S. command developed an effective military strategy but that it came too late to reverse the political momentum for a U.S. withdrawal.

Szulc, Tad. *The Illusion of Peace: Foreign Policy in the Nixon Years*. New York: Viking, 1978. Szulc provides a very critical but detailed examination of the Nixon-Kissinger actions in Cambodia and Vietnam.

THE END OF SOUTH VIETNAM

Butler, David. *The Fall of Saigon*. New York: Simon and Schuster, 1985. This account of North Vietnam's capture of the southern capital is drawn from eyewitnesses' recollections and U.S. embassy cables.

Cao Van Vien. *The Final Collapse*. Washington, D.C.: U.S. Government Printing Office, 1983. This South Vietnamese general characterizes the entire war as aggression from the North and the final offensive as a conventional military assault on the South.

Dawson, Alan. *Fifty-Five Days: The Fall of South Vietnam*. Englewood Cliffs, N.J.: Prentice-Hall, 1977. Dawson provides a gripping narrative of the chaotic final days of South Vietnam.

Haley, P. Edward. *Congress and the Fall of South Vietnam and Cambodia*. East Brunswick, N.J.: Fairleigh Dickinson University Press, 1982. During the final North Vietnamese offensive, Congress reduced or rejected various requests from the White House for funds for South Vietnam.

Herrington, Stuart A. *Peace with Honor? An American Reports on Vietnam, 1973–1975*. Novato, Calif.: Presidio Press, 1983. From his vantage point as a military intelligence officer in South Vietnam, Herrington reports on North Vietnam's preparations for and implementation of its final offensive.

Isaacs, Arnold R. *Without Honor: Defeat in Vietnam and Cambodia.* Baltimore: Johns Hopkins University Press, 1983. By an experienced journalist and researcher, this book is one of the best critiques available of the errors in U.S. policy in Vietnam and Cambodia from 1973 to 1975.

Kissinger, Henry A. *Years of Renewal.* New York: Simon and Schuster, 1999. In this memoir, Kissinger blames Congress for the inability of the United States to support South Vietnam after January 1973.

———. *Years of Upheaval.* Boston: Little, Brown, 1982. Kissinger contends that Watergate made it impossible for the Nixon administration to hold Hanoi accountable for violations of the 1973 cease-fire agreement.

Snepp, Frank. *Decent Interval: An Insider's Account of Saigon's Indecent End.* New York: Random House, 1977. Snepp witnessed the disorderly end of South Vietnam from his post as chief CIA analyst in the U.S. Embassy in Saigon.

Van Tien Dung. *Our Great Spring Victory: An Account of the Liberation of South Vietnam.* New York: Monthly Review Press, 1977. One of the senior North Vietnamese commanders describes the strategy and decisions that ended the war.

THE LEGACY OF THE VIETNAM WAR

LESSONS AND POSTMORTEMS

Allen, Douglas, and Ngô Vinh Long, eds. *Coming to Terms: Indochina, the United States, and the War*. Boulder, Col.: Westview Press, 1991. This anthology of articles originally published in the *Bulletin of Concerned Asian Scholars* primarily examines the impact of the war on Southeast Asia and on scholarship about Asia.

Capps, Walter H. *The Unfinished War: Vietnam and the American Conscience*. Boston: Beacon, 1982. Capps describes America as going through a religious and moral reevaluation after the Vietnam War.

Chanda, Nayan. *Brother Enemy: The War After the War*. New York: Harcourt Brace Jovanovich, 1986. This book reflects on regional conflicts in Southeast Asia after 1975 and on Jimmy Carter's policies toward the area.

Charlton, Michael, and Anthony Moncrief. *Many Reasons Why: The American Involvement in Vietnam*. New York: Hill and Wang, 1979. From television interviews with participants, the authors look back on why the United States was in Vietnam.

Dean, Eric T. *Shook Over Hell: Post-Traumatic Stress, Vietnam, and the Civil War*. Cambridge, Mass.: Harvard University Press, 1997. The author finds that mental problems suffered by Vietnam veterans were not historically unique.

Doyle, Robert C. *Voices from Captivity: Interpreting the American POW Narrative*. Lawrence: University Press of Kansas, 1994. Doyle places in historical perspective the American experience with its men being prisoners of war.

Ely, John Hart. *War and Responsibility: Constitutional Lessons of Vietnam and Its Aftermath.* Princeton, N.J.: Princeton University Press, 1993. The author considers the legal ambiguities in congressional war powers arising from the Vietnam War.

Emerson, Gloria. *Winners and Losers: Battles, Retreats, Gains, Losses and Ruins from the Vietnam War.* New York: Harcourt Brace Jovanovich, 1976. A journalist critical of the war, Emerson describes the impact of the war on individual persons.

Gelb, Leslie, and Richard K. Betts. *The Irony of Vietnam: The System Worked.* Washington, D.C.: Brookings Institution, 1979. Although cynical in its thesis, this book is a good study of the policy-making process.

Goodman, Allan E. "Vietnam's Post-Cold War Diplomacy and the U.S. Response." *Asian Survey* 33 (August 1993): 832–47. This article assesses the obstacles to the establishment of diplomatic relations between the United States and Vietnam after the war.

Grinter, Lawrence E., and Peter M. Dunn, eds. *The American War in Vietnam: Lessons, Legacies, and Implications for Future Conflicts.* Westport, Conn.: Greenwood Press, 1987. Many of the chapters in this anthology reexamine U.S. military strategy during the war.

Hamilton, Donald W. *The Art of Insurgency: American Military Policy and the Failure of Strategy in Southeast Asia.* Foreword by Cecil B. Currey. Westport, Conn.: Praeger, 1998. The author puts principal blame on military strategists, not civilian war opponents, for the poor U.S. performance in combating an armed insurgency.

Hass, Kristen Ann. *Carried to the Wall: American Memory and the Vietnam Veterans Memorial.* Berkeley: University of California Press, 1998. Hass finds that a wide range of cultural factors are associated with the memorial, and she also reflects on the POW-MIA issue.

Head, William, and Lawrence E. Grinter, eds. *Looking Back on the Vietnam War: A 1990s Perspective on the Decisions, Combat, and Legacies.* Westport, Conn.: Praeger, 1993. Essays in this volume by a number of distinguished authors reflect on military, domestic, and international issues.

Hearden, Patrick J., ed. *Vietnam: Four American Perspectives.* Foreword by Akira Iriye. West Lafayette, Ind.: Purdue University Press, 1990. This book brings together divergent views on the war by George McGovern, William Westmoreland, and two prominent scholars—Edward Luttwak and Thomas McCormick.

Herring, George C. "'Peoples Quite Apart': Americans, South Vietnamese, and the War in Vietnam." *Diplomatic History* 14 (Winter 1990): 1–23. Herring draws a cautionary lesson about interventionism from the tensions and lack of understanding between Americans and their South Vietnamese allies.

Holsti, Ole R., and James N. Rosenau. *American Leadership in World Affairs: Vietnam and the Breakdown of Consensus.* Winchester, Mass.: Allen and Unwin, 1984. This book studies public opinion on foreign policy after the war.

Isaacs, Arnold R. *Vietnam Shadows: The War, Its Ghosts, and Its Legacy.* Baltimore: Johns Hopkins University Press, 1997. Considering the profound impact of the war on Americans and Vietnamese, it is now very difficult to know where and why Americans should consider military intervention.

Jamieson, Neil L. *Understanding Vietnam.* Berkeley: University of California Press, 1993. This study explores different ideas among the Vietnamese about their history and visions of their future.

Jespersen, T. Christopher. "Bitter End and the Lost Chance in Vietnam: Congress, the Ford Administration, and the Battle Over Vietnam, 1975–76." *Diplomatic History* 24 (Spring 2000): 265–93. Jespersen analyzes how the POW-MIA lobby and other domestic pressures hampered efforts to establish diplomatic relations between Vietnam and the United States.

Kennan, Elizabeth. *Women at War: The Story of Fifty Military Nurses Who Served in Vietnam.* Philadelphia: University of Pennsylvania Press, 1990. This book is an academic discussion of interview data from the nurses.

Lifton, Robert Jay. *Home from the War: Learning from Vietnam Veterans.* Rev. ed. Boston: Beacon, 1992. Lifton is a psychiatrist who shares insights into veterans' readjustment problems that he derived from counseling troubled veterans.

Lind, Michael. *Vietnam: The Necessary War.* New York: The Free Press, 1999. The author attempts to defend American intervention in Vietnam as a strategic necessity, but his discussion of the costs and background of the conflict is arguable.

Lomperis, Timothy J. *From People's War to People's Rule: Insurgency, Intervention, and the Lessons of Vietnam.* Chapel Hill: University of North Carolina Press, 1996. Lomperis argues that North Vietnam won a conventional military victory after its initial People's War strategy failed.

——. *The War Everyone Lost—And Won: America's Intervention in Viet Nam's Twin Struggles.* Baton Rouge: Louisiana State University Press, 1984. The author suggests that the United States could have been successful in Vietnam because Hanoi never attained the "revolutionary legitimacy" it claimed.

Lovell, John P. "The Limits of 'Lessons Learned': From Vietnam to the Gulf War." *Peace and Change* 17 (Oct. 1992): 379–401. The Bush administration drew lessons from Vietnam that contributed to the decision to go to war against Iraq.

MacPherson, Myra. *Long Time Passing: Vietnam and the Haunted Generation.* Garden City, N.Y.: Doubleday, 1984. From extensive interviews, MacPherson describes the tensions among Americans during the decade after the war.

McNamara, Robert, James G. Blight, and Robert K. Brigham, with Thomas J. Biersteker and Herbert Y. Schandler. *Argument Without End: In Search of Answers to the Vietnam Tragedy.* New York: Public Affairs, 1999. Somewhat of a sequel to McNamara's controversial autobiography, *In Retrospect,* this book relies on the vehicle of postwar conversations between former U.S. officials (including McNamara) and Vietnamese leaders to explore the depth of misunderstanding between the two sides.

Melanson, Richard A. *American Foreign Policy Since the Vietnam War: The Search for Consensus from Nixon to Clinton.* 3d ed. Armonk, N.Y.: M. E. Sharpe, 2000. The author analyzes how each presidential administration, beginning with Nixon's, tried to restore coherence and direction to U.S. policy after the debate over culture and policy generated by the war.

Nixon, Richard M. *No More Vietnams.* New York: Arbor House, 1985. Nixon maintains that the outcome of the Vietnam War revealed, not that U.S. involvement was wrong, but that Washington's limited, incremental strategy was incorrect.

Podhoretz, Norman. *Why We Were in Vietnam.* New York: Simon and Schuster, 1983. Podhoretz contends that the United States was morally correct to try to protect South Vietnam from the oppressive regime in Hanoi.

Record, Jeffrey. *The Wrong War: Why We Lost in Vietnam.* Annapolis, Md.: Naval Institute Press, 1998. In the author's opinion, poor strategy, not domestic opposition, led to the U.S. military loss in Vietnam.

Rostow, W. W. "Vietnam and Asia." *Diplomatic History* 20 (Summer 1996): 467–71. Rostow argues that the American war in Vietnam was ultimately successful because it checked Hanoi's ambitions and gave other Southeast Asian nations time for economic development.

Rutledge, Paul James. *The Vietnamese Experience in America.* Bloomington: Indiana University Press, 1992. This work is a scholarly examination of the influx of Vietnamese refugees to the United States after 1975.

Shafer, D. Michael, ed. *The Legacy: The Vietnam War in the American Imagination.* Boston: Beacon, 1990. The articles in this collection explore a variety of cultural and social consequences of the war within America.

Shay, Jonathan. *Achilles in Vietnam: Combat Trauma and the Undoing of Character.* New York: Atheneum, 1994. A psychiatrist, Shay uses the example of ancient Athens to reflect on how the modern American democracy could have better reintroduced Vietnam combat veterans back into civil society.

Thompson, W. Scott, and Donaldson D. Frizzell, eds. *The Lessons of Vietnam.* New York: Crane, Russak, 1977. These essays deal primarily with military strategy questions.

Walzer, Michael. *Just and Unjust Wars: A Moral Argument with Historical Illustrations.* New York: Basic Books, 1977. This critical discussion of the morality of war includes several case studies from the Vietnam conflict.

Werner, Jayne S., and Luu Doan Huynh, eds. *The Vietnam War: Vietnamese and American Perspectives.* Armonk, N.Y.: M. E. Sharp, 1993. This book includes nineteen essays by prominent American and Vietnamese authorities on the war and covers a broad range of subjects.

Wilcox, Fred A. *Waiting for an Army to Die: The Tragedy of Agent Orange.* New York: Random House, 1983. Wilcox details the medical, legal, and personal dimensions of dioxin poisoning from U.S. use of chemical defoliants in Vietnam.

LITERATURE, MOVIES, AND MUSIC

Alter, Nora M. *Vietnam Protest Theatre: The Television War on Stage.* Bloomington: Indiana University Press, 1996. Alter studies protest works produced for the stage during the war years.

Anderegg, Michael, ed. *Inventing Vietnam: The War in Film and Television.* Philadelphia: Temple University Press, 1991. The essays in this volume are scholarly critiques of films and television programs about the war.

Anderson, Terry H. "American Popular Music and the War in Vietnam." *Peace and Change* 11 (February 1986): 51–65. Anderson discusses the lyrics of songs for and against the war.

Bao Ninh. *The Sorrow of War: A Novel of North Vietnam.* Translated by Phan Thanh Hao. Edited by Frank Palmos. New York: Pantheon, 1995. The author is a veteran of the North Vietnamese Army, and his novel depicts the suffering and loneliness of all soldiers.

Beidler, Philip D. *American Literature and the Experience of Vietnam.* Athens: University of Georgia Press, 1982. Beidler analyzes memory and imagination in books and poetry about the war.

———. *Re-Writing America: Vietnam Authors in Their Generation.* Athens: University of Georgia Press, 1991. The author finds that many writers seek to redefine American cultural myths in their works on the war.

Butler, Robert Olen. *A Good Scent from a Strange Mountain.* New York: Henry Holt, 1991. The stories in this book highlight Vietnamese and American cultural themes.

Clymer, Kenton J., ed. *The Vietnam War: Its History, Literature, and Music.* El Paso: Texas Western Press, 1998. Recognized authorities contribute essays on subjects reflected by the subtitle.

Dittmar, Linda, and Gene Michaud, eds. *From Hanoi to Hollywood: The Vietnam War in American Film.* New Brunswick, N.J.: Rutgers University Press, 1990. Thirty essays in this anthology analyze theatrical and documentary films and general themes in film treatments of the war.

Ehrhart, W. D., ed. *Carrying the Darkness: The Poetry of the Vietnam War.* Lubbock: Texas Tech University Press, 1989. Ehrhart has collected some of the best examples of poetry by Vietnam veterans.

Engelhardt, Tom. *The End of Victory Culture: Cold War America and the Disillusioning of a Generation.* New York: Basic Books, 1995. This analysis of popular culture, especially movies and television, describes how defeat in Vietnam and controversy over the war reshaped America's self-image.

Franklin, H. Bruce, ed. *The Vietnam War in American Stories, Songs, and Poems.* Boston: Bedford Books, 1996. This representative collection contains helpful notes on the stories, songs, and poems.

Katzman, Jason. "From Outcast to Cliché: How Film Shaped, Warped, and Developed the Image of the Vietnam Veteran, 1967–1990." *Journal of American Culture* 16 (Spring 1993): 7–24. This article critically analyzes the changing image of the Vietnam veteran in Hollywood films.

Lomperis, Timothy J. *Reading the Wind: The Literature of the Vietnam War.* Durham, N.C.: Duke University Press, 1987. This book analyzes fiction and poetry on the war through 1985.

Rowe, John Carlos, and Rick Berg, eds. *The Vietnam War and American Culture.* New York: Columbia University Press, 1991. This anthology includes essays on memory, media, gender, revisionism, and music and also has five W.D. Ehrhart poems.

Toplin, Robert Brent, ed. *Oliver Stone's U.S.A.: Film, History, and Controversy.* Commentary by Oliver Stone. Lawrence: University Press of Kansas, 2000. Essays in this book by Stone's critics and supporters, and by Stone himself, debate the relationship between history and film, analyze his films about the Vietnam War, and address how his own Vietnam experience colors all of his work.

AMERICAN CULTURAL MYTHS
AND NATIONAL IDENTITY

Baritz, Loren. *Backfire: A History of How American Culture Led Us Into Vietnam and Made Us Fight the Way We Did.* New York: Morrow, 1985. The author finds a disturbing callousness and cynicism in American military and civilian officials derived from over-reliance on technology and on concepts borrowed from business management.

Dean, Robert D. "Masculinity as Ideology: John F. Kennedy and the Domestic Politics of Foreign Policy." *Diplomatic History* 22 (Winter 1998): 29–62. Dean maintains that cultural notions of masculinity helped shape Kennedy's Vietnam policies.

Franklin, H. Bruce. *M.I.A. or Mythmaking in America.* Expanded and updated ed. New Brunswick, N.J.: Rutgers University Press, 1994. Franklin offers an explanation of the political manipulation and staying power of the belief of many Americans that Hanoi continued to hold Americans prisoner after the war.

Hellman, John. *American Myth and the Legacy of Vietnam.* New York: Columbia University Press, 1986. In Hellman's view, fiction and films about the Vietnam War address the myth of the frontier and other expressions of American culture.

Holm, Tom. *Strong Hearts, Wounded Souls: Native American Veterans of the Vietnam War.* Austin: University of Texas Press, 1996. From interviews with Native American veterans, Holm examines some of their particularized wartime and postwar experiences.

Jeffords, Susan. *The Remasculinization of America: Gender and the Vietnam War.* Bloomington: Indiana University Press, 1989. The author discovers a reinvigoration of patriarchy in the 1980s and in the rehabilitation of regard for the men who fought in the Vietnam War.

Lembcke, Jerry. *The Spitting Image: Myth, Memory, and the Legacy of Vietnam.* New York: New York University Press, 1998. Lembcke challenges the accuracy of several images associated with the war, including that of some returning soldiers being spat upon by war protestors.

Levy, David W. *The Debate Over Vietnam.* 2d ed. Baltimore: Johns Hopkins University Press, 1995. The author finds that the debate among Americans over the war arose from differing views of national interest and national identity.

Tomes, Robert R. *Apocalypse Then: American Intellectuals and the Vietnam War, 1954–1975.* New York: New York University Press, 1998. Tomes categorizes intellectual schools of thought in writings about the war.

Turner, Fred. *Echoes of Combat: The Vietnam War in American Memory.* New York: Doubleday, 1996. This book describes the difficulty in coming to terms with the war for individuals and for American society collectively.

Westheider, James E. *Fighting on Two Fronts: African Americans and the Vietnam War.* New York: New York University Press, 1997. The author places the Vietnam War experiences of African American soldiers in the context of the civil rights struggle then underway in America.

FILMS AND DOCUMENTARIES

The Anderson Platoon (1967). 64 minutes. Films Inc. This documentary film records
the patrols of a U.S. Army infantry platoon over a six-week period in 1966.

Apocalypse Now (1979). 153 minutes. Dir. Francis Ford Coppola. Stars: Martin Sheen,
Marlon Brando, Robert Duvall. Inspired by Joseph's Conrad's novel *Heart of Darkness*, Coppola uses extensive artistic license to create a grim antiwar film that cari-
catures the U.S. way of war as violent irrationality.

Born on the Fourth of July (1989). 145 minutes. Dir. Oliver Stone. Stars: Tom Cruise,
Willem Dafoe. Based upon the memoir of Ron Kovic, a disillusioned and embittered Marine paralyzed by wounds in Vietnam, the film criticizes U.S. involvement in the war and the government's treatment of disabled veterans.

Coming Home (1978). 127 minutes. Dir. Hal Ashby. Stars: Bruce Dern, Jon Voight,
Jane Fonda. The male leads are clichés of the violent veteran and the disabled veteran, but the film presents one version of the American struggle to come to terms
with the meaning of the war right after its end.

The Deer Hunter (1978). 183 minutes. Dir. Michael Cimino. Stars: Robert De Niro,
John Cazale, John Savage, Meryl Streep, Christopher Walken. Although this film
stereotypes the Vietnamese communists, its power is in its depiction of the alienation experienced at home in America by the three blue-collar friends who return
from the war to their hometown in Pennsylvania.

84 Charlie Mopic (1989). 95 minutes. Dir. Patrick Duncan. Stars: Byron Thames,
Jonathan Emerson. Many veterans consider this narrative of an army patrol as seen

by a combat cameraman one of the most realistic depictions of combat in commercial films.

Four Hours in My Lai (1989). 52 minutes. Yorkshire Television. This British-produced documentary features interviews with American soldiers who participated in the My Lai massacre and with Vietnamese survivors of that terrible incident.

Full Metal Jacket (1987). 117 minutes. Dir. Stanley Kubrick. Stars: Matthew Modine, Adam Baldwin, Lee Ermey. Following a group of Marines from boot camp through the Tet Offensive, Kubrick's movie portrays the dehumanizing violence of war and the particular frustration and senselessness of combat in Vietnam.

The Green Berets (1968). 135 minutes. Dirs. John Wayne and Ray Kellogg. Stars: John Wayne, David Janssen. This Hollywood attempt to reduce the complexities of the war to a simple morality play of American good combating Vietcong evil received much criticism from movie critics and critics of the war, but the early scenes of Green Beret training illustrate a great deal about the official U.S. rationale for military intervention.

Go Tell the Spartans (1978). 114 minutes. Dir. Ted Post. Stars: Burt Lancaster, Craig Wasson. This film depicts American military advisers to the South Vietnamese Army and reveals the difficulty for Americans to understand their Vietnamese allies and enemies.

Hamburger Hill (1987). 94 minutes. Dir. John Irvin. Stars: Don Cheadle, Michael Dolan, Tim Quill, Steven Weber. This commercial film recreates an actual battle that reveals a major issue in the conduct of the war: the American unit suffered 70 percent casualties only for the hill then to be abandoned.

Hearts and Minds (1974). 112 minutes. Dir. Peter Davis. Paramount Home Video. This award-winning but controversial antiwar documentary traces the origins of U.S. intervention in Vietnam to American culture.

Heaven and Earth (1993). 140 minutes. Dir. Oliver Stone. Stars: Tommy Lee Jones, Joan Chen, Haing S. Ngor, Hiep Thi Le. This film version of two autobiographical works by Le Ly Hayslip portrays her life as a girl and young woman in wartime Vietnam and her subsequent life in the United States.

Indochine (1992). 156 minutes. Dir. Regis Wargnier. Stars: Catherine Deneuve, Linh Dan Pham, Vincent Perez. In French with English and Spanish subtitles. This epic about French Indochina from the period of French colonialism to American involvement is a story of romance and revolution.

The Killing Fields (1984). 142 minutes. Dir. Roland Joffé. Stars: Haing S. Ngor, Sam Waterston, Craig T. Nelson. Through the dramatic story of the survival of Dith Pran, the Cambodian assistant of *New York Times* reporter Sydney Schanberg, the film depicts the U.S. bombing of Cambodia, the fall of the Lon Nol government, and the brutality of the Khmer Rouge regime.

Platoon (1986). 113 minutes. Dir. Oliver Stone. Stars: Tom Berenger, Willem Dafoe, Charlie Sheen. Drawing upon his own experience as a combat soldier in Vietnam, director Stone fashions a fairly realistic, although compressed, depiction of an infantry platoon.

The Quiet American (1958). 120 minutes. Dir. Joseph L. Mankiewicz. Stars: Audie Murphy, Michael Redgrave, Claude Dauphin, Giorgia Moll. This film version of the excellent Graham Green novel of the same name is inferior to the book but does convey the idealism of U.S. involvement in Vietnam in the 1950s.

Rambo: First Blood, Part II (1985). 95 minutes. Dir. George Pan Cosmatos. Stars: Sylvester Stallone, Richard Crenna, Julia Nickson. This simplistic Hollywood version of the "win thesis" that with a little more effort the U.S. could have won a military victory in Vietnam is famous for the line spoken by its former Green Beret hero on a one-man mission to rescue POWs: "Sir, do we get to win this time?"

The Ugly American (1962). 120 minutes. Dir. George Englund. Stars: Marlon Brando, Eiji Okada, Sandra Church, Pat Hingle, Jocelyn Brando. Based on the William J. Lederer and Eugene Burdick novel of the same name, the film dramatizes the conflicting concerns of Cold War Americans and Asian nationalists in a fictional country closely resembling Vietnam.

Vietnam: A Television History (1983). 13 episodes, 60 minutes each. PBS. The interviews with participants and the film footage in this series provide a broad and balanced coverage of the conflict in Vietnam, from the beginning of the French war in 1946 to the North's victory in 1975.

Vietnam: The Ten Thousand Day War (1980). 13 episodes, 49 minutes each. Embassy Home Entertainment. This documentary is a detailed and critical survey of the French and American wars in Vietnam and contains rare film footage and interviews with policy makers and combat soldiers conducted by journalist Peter Arnett.

Why Vietnam? (1965). 32 minutes. International Historic Films. Originally produced by the Department of Defense, this brief military training film illustrates the official U.S. position that the war in Vietnam was a case of North Vietnam's aggression against South Vietnam.

ELECTRONIC RESOURCES

The American Experience—Vietnam. URL: http://www.pbs.org/wgbh/pages/amex/viet-nam/index.html. As a companion to the PBS documentary series, *Vietnam: A Television History,* this site has biographies, maps, primary sources, bibliography, and transcripts of the television programs.

Beyond the Wall: Stories Behind the Vietnam Wall (1995). CD-ROM. Magnet Interactive. Although its historical background on the war is brief, this CD-ROM has several good video clips, a history of the Vietnam Veterans Memorial, examples of items left at the Wall, and a searchable directory of the names on the Wall.

Documents Relating to the Vietnam War. URL: http://www.mtholyoke.edu/acad/in-trel/vietnam.htm. There are many full-text primary and secondary source documents, arranged in chronological order, and links to documents found at this URL.

Edwin Moïse Bibliography of the Vietnam War. URL: http://hubcap.clemson.edu/~eemoise/bibliography.html. Created and updated regularly by a recognized scholar, this Web site provides an extensive and annotated list, divided into subject categories, of books, articles, and documents, and there are links to other Vietnam War–related sites.

Foreign Relations of the United States. URL: http://www.state.gov/r/pa/ho/frus/. Compiled by the Office of the Historian of the U.S. Department of State, this Web site contains links to the text of the volumes of *Foreign Relations of the United States* relating to the Vietnam War that have been put online. This series, known as FRUS, contains many of the nation's most important foreign policy documents—many originally classified as "top secret."

The Sixties Project. URL: http://lists.village.virginia.edu/sixties/. This Web site has a wide range of links to primary and secondary sources on the Vietnam War, antiwar movement, black power, women's liberation, and other aspects of the 1960s.

USA Wars: Vietnam (1994). CD-ROM. Quanta Press. This CD-ROM has a large amount of text from documents and secondary sources, as well as images, tables, and a section on the Vietnam War Memorial.

Vietnam: Echoes from the Wall. URL: http://www.teachvietnam.org. This interactive educational tool for high-school students, with text and video, accompanies a secondary education curriculum on teaching about the war prepared by the Vietnam Veterans Memorial Fund.

The Vietnam Era (1999). CD-ROM. Primary Source Media. Edited by George Herring, Clarence Wyatt, and Robert K. Brigham, this CD-ROM provides primary source material organized around thematic essays. There are links, timelines, maps, pictures, and full-text search capability.

Vietnam War Internet Project. URL: http://www.lbjlib.texas.edu/shwv/vwiphome.html. Available through the Lyndon Baines Johnson Library, this site has a number of links to documents, memoirs, photos, bibliographies, and the Soc.History.War.Vietnam newsgroup.

The War in Vietnam: A Multimedia Chronicle (1995). CD-ROM. Macmillan Digital. This interactive format provides text from the *New York Times*, film footage from CBS News, maps, photographs, and the Vietnam War Memorial database.

The Wars for Viet Nam: 1945 to 1975. URL: http://students.vassar.edu/~vietnam/. There is a particularly good selection of primary source documents on this site, as well as an extensive bibliography and links to other sites.

PART V

Appendices

Appendix 1

DOCUMENTS

1. POET NGUYEN THUONG HIEN ON THE FATE OF VILLAGERS WHO PLEADED WITH FRENCH COLONIAL OFFICIALS FOR LOWER TAXES AROUND 1914

In Quang Nam, a province south of our capital, the inhabitants were so heavily taxed that they came to the Resident's Headquarters to ask him to exempt them from the new tax increase. The Resident did not listen to them, but instead ordered his soldiers to charge against them. Among those driven back into the river, three drowned. The inhabitants' anger was aroused, so they brought the three corpses before the Resident's Headquarters, and for a whole week several thousand people dressed in mourning garments sat on the ground surrounding the three corpses, shouting and wailing continuously. The Resident reported the matter to the Resident General, who came and inquired of the inhabitants: "Why are you people rebelling?" The inhabitants replied: "We do not have a single stick of iron in our hands, why do you say that we are rebelling? It is only because the taxes are too high and we are not able to pay them that we must voice our opinion together." The Resident General then said: "If you people are so poor that you cannot pay taxes to the government, then you might as well all be dead." When he finished saying this, the Resident General ordered his French soldiers to fire into the crowd. Only after several hundred persons had been killed, shedding their blood in puddles, did the crowd disperse.

Ngô Vinh Long, *Before the Revolution: The Vietnamese Peasants Under the French*, 2d ed. (New York: Columbia University Press, 1991), 71–72.

2. NGUYEN AI QUOC (HO CHI MINH) DECLARATION ON THE FOUNDING OF THE COMMUNIST PARTY OF INDOCHINA, FEBRUARY 18, 1930 (EXTRACT)

Workers, peasants, soldiers, youth, pupils!
Oppressed and exploited compatriots!

The Communist Party of Indochina is founded. It is the party of the working class. It will help the proletarian class lead the revolution in order to struggle for all the oppressed and exploited people. From now on we must join the Party, help it and follow it in order to implement the following slogans:

1. To overthrow French imperialism, feudalism, and the reactionary Vietnamese capitalist class.
2. To make Indochina completely independent.
3. To establish a worker-peasant and soldier government.
4. To confiscate the banks and other enterprises belonging to the imperialists and put them under the control of the worker-peasant and soldier government.
5. To confiscate all of the plantations and property belonging to the imperialists and the Vietnamese reactionary capitalist class and distribute them to poor peasants.
6. To implement the eight hour working day.
7. To abolish public loans and poll tax. To waive unjust taxes hitting the poor people.
8. To bring back all freedoms to the masses.
9. To carry out universal education.
10. To implement equality between man and woman.

Ho Chi Minh, *Selected Works*, 4 vols.
(Hanoi: Foreign Language Publishing House, 1960–1962), 2:145–48.

3. SENATOR GEORGE F. HOAR
OPPOSES U.S. ANNEXATION OF THE PHILIPPINES,
JANUARY 9, 1899 (EXTRACT)

There are two lessons our fathers learned from the history of Greece which they hoped their children would remember—the danger of disunion and domestic strife and an indulgence in the greed and lust of empire . . . . The question is this: Have we the right, as doubtless we have the physical power, to enter upon the government of ten or twelve million subject people without constitutional restraint? . . . Is it true, or is it a falsehood, that the doctrine that governments derive their just power from the consent of the governed is to be applied in interpreting the Constitution of the United States, and controlling the action of the legislature it creates, as if the words were written between the lines of the Constitution itself? . . . Now, I claim that under the Declaration of Independence you can not govern a foreign territory, a foreign people, another people than your own, that you can not subjugate them and govern them against their will, because you think it is for their good, when they do not; because you think you are going to give them the blessings of liberty. You have no right at the cannon's mouth to impose on an unwilling people your Declaration of Independence and your Constitution and your notions of freedom and notions of what is good.

Congressional Record, 55th Cong., 3d sess., part 1, pp. 494–503.

4. SENATOR HENRY CABOT LODGE
FAVORS U.S. ANNEXATION OF THE PHILIPPINES,
MARCH 7, 1900 (EXTRACT)

All our vast growth and expansion have been due to the spirit of our race, and have been guided by the instinct of the American people, which in all great crises has proved wiser than any reasoning. This mighty movement westward, building up a nation and conquering a continent as it swept along, has not been the work of chance or accident. It was neither chance nor accident which brought us to the Pacific and which has now carried us across the great ocean even to the shores of Asia, to the very edge of the cradle of the Aryans, whence our far distant ancestors started on the march which has since girdled the world . . . .

Even now we can abandon the Monroe Doctrine, we can reject the Pacific, we can shut ourselves up between our oceans, as Switzerland is inclosed among her hills, and then it would be inevitable that we should sink out from among the great powers of the world and heap up riches that some stronger and bolder people, who do not fear their fate, might gather them. Or we may follow the true laws of our being, the laws in obedience to which we have come to be what we are, and then we shall stretch out into the Pacific; we shall stand in the front rank of the world powers; we shall give to our labor and our industry new and larger and better opportunities; we shall prosper ourselves; we shall benefit mankind. What we have done was inevitable because it was in accordance with the laws of our being as a nation, in the defiance and disregard of which lie ruin and retreat.

Congressional Record, 60th Cong., 1st sess., vol. 33, part 3, pp. 2618–30.

5. WOODROW WILSON'S FOURTEEN POINTS, JANUARY 8, 1918 (EXTRACT)

We entered this war because violations of right had occurred which touched us to the quick and made the life of our own people impossible unless they were corrected and the world secured once for all against their recurrence. What we demand in this war, therefore, is nothing peculiar to ourselves. It is that the world be made fit and safe to live in; and particularly that it be made safe for every peace-loving nation which, like our own, wished to live its own life, determine its own institutions, be assured of justice and fair dealing by the other peoples of the world as against force and selfish aggression. All the peoples of the world are in effect partners in this interest, and for our own part we see very clearly that unless justice be done to others it will not be done to us. The programme of the world's peace, therefore, is our programme; and that programme, the only possible programme, as we see it is this: . . .

V. A free, open-minded, and absolutely impartial adjustment of all colonial claims, based upon a strict observance of the principle that in determining all such questions of sovereignty the interests of the populations concerned must have equal weight with the equitable claims of the government whose title is to be determined. . . .

XIV. A general association of nations must be formed under specific covenants for the purpose of affording mutual guarantees of political independence and territorial integrity to great and small states alike. . . .

An evident principle runs through the whole programme I have outlined. It is the principle of justice to all peoples and nationalities, and their right to live on equal terms of liberty and safety with one another, whether they be strong or weak. Unless this principle be made its foundation no part of the structure of international justice can stand. The people of the United States could act upon no other principle; and to the vindication of this principle they are ready to devote their lives, their honor, and everything that they possess. The moral climax of this the culminating and final war for human liberty has come, and they are ready to put their own strength, their own highest purpose, their own integrity and devotion to the test.

Congressional Record, 65th Cong., 2d sess., vol. 56, pp. 680–81.

6. THE ATLANTIC CHARTER, AUGUST 14, 1941
(EXTRACT)

Joint declaration of the President of the United States of America and the Prime Minister, Mr. Churchill, representing His Majesty's Government in the United Kingdom, being met together, deem it right to make known certain common principles in the national policies of their respective countries on which they base their hopes for a better future for the world.

First, their countries seek no aggrandizement, territorial or other;

Second, they desire to see no territorial changes that do not accord with the freely expressed wishes of the peoples concerned;

Third, they respect the right of all peoples to choose the form of government under which they will live; and they wish to see sovereign rights and self-government restored to those who have been forcibly deprived of them;

Fourth, they will endeavor, with due respect for their existing obligations, to further the enjoyment of all states, great or small, victor or vanquished, of access, on equal terms, to the trade and to the raw materials of the world which are needed for their economic prosperity;

Fifth, they desire to bring about the fullest collaboration between all nations in the economic field with the object of securing for all improved labor standards, economic advancement, and social security . . . .

U.S. House of Representatives, *Document No. 358*, 77th Cong., 1st sess.

7. THE TRUMAN DOCTRINE, MARCH 12, 1947
(EXTRACT)

I am fully aware of the broad implications involved if the United States extends assistance to Greece and Turkey, and I shall discuss these implications with you at this time.

One of the primary objectives of the foreign policy of the United States is the creation of conditions in which we and other nations will be able to work out a way of life free from coercion. This was a fundamental issue in the war with Germany and Japan. Our victory was won over countries which sought to impose their will, and their way of life, upon other nations. . . .

The peoples of a number of countries of the world have recently had totalitarian regimes forced upon them against their will. The Government of the United States has made frequent protests against coercion and intimidation, in violation of the Yalta agreement, in Poland, Rumania, and Bulgaria. I must also state that in a number of other countries there have been similar developments.

At the present moment in world history nearly every nation must choose between alternative ways of life. The choice is too often not a free one.

One way of life is based upon the will of the majority, and is distinguished by free institutions, representative government, free elections, guarantees of individual liberty, freedom of speech and religion, and freedom from political oppression.

The second way of life is based upon the will of a minority forcibly imposed upon the majority. It relies upon terror and oppression, a controlled press and radio, fixed elections, and the suppression of personal freedoms.

I believe that it must be the policy of the United States to support free peoples who are resisting attempted subjugation by armed minorities or by outside pressures.

I believe that we must assist free peoples to work out their own destinies in their own way.

I believe that our help should be primarily through economic and financial aid which is essential to economic stability and orderly political processes.

The world is not static, and the *status quo* is not sacred. But we cannot allow changes in the *status quo* in violation of the Charter of the United Nations by such methods as coercion, or by such subterfuges as political infiltration. In helping free and independent nations to maintain their freedom, the United States will be giving effect to the principles of the Charter of the United Nations.

Public Papers of the Presidents of the United States: Harry S. Truman, 1947
(Washington, D.C.: Government Printing Office, 1963), 176–80.

8. DECLARATION OF INDEPENDENCE
OF THE DEMOCRATIC REPUBLIC OF VIETNAM,
SEPTEMBER 2, 1945 (EXTRACT)

"All men are created equal. They are endowed by their Creator with certain inalienable rights, among these are Life, Liberty, and the pursuit of Happiness."

This immortal statement was made in the Declaration of Independence of the United States of America in 1776. In a broader sense, this means: All the peoples on the earth are equal from birth, all the peoples have a right to live, to be happy and free.

The Declaration of the French Revolution made in 1791 on the Rights of Man and the Citizen also states: "All men are born free and with equal rights, and must always remain free and have equal rights."

Those are undeniable truths.

Nevertheless for more than eighty years, the French imperialists, abusing the standard of Liberty, Equality, and Fraternity, have violated our Fatherland and oppressed our fellow-citizens. They have acted contrary to ideals of humanity and justice . . . .

From the autumn of 1940, our country had in fact ceased to be a French colony and had become a Japanese possession.

After the Japanese had surrendered to the Allies, our whole people rose to regain our national sovereignty and to found the Democratic Republic of Vietnam.

The truth is that we have wrested our independence from the Japanese and not from the French.

The French have fled, the Japanese have capitulated, Emperor Bao Dai has abdicated. Our people have broken the chains which for nearly a century have fettered them and have won independence for the Fatherland. Our people at the same time have overthrown the monarchic regime that has reigned supreme for dozens of centuries. In its place has been established the present Democratic Republic . . . .

For these reasons, we, members of the Provisional Government of the Democratic Republic of Vietnam, solemnly declare to the world that Vietnam has the right to be a free and independent country— and in fact it is so already. The entire Vietnamese people are determined to mobilize all their physical and mental strength, to sacrifice their lives and property in order to safeguard their independence and liberty.

Ho Chi Minh, *Selected Works*, 3:17–21.

9. DWIGHT D. EISENHOWER'S "FALLING DOMINO" STATEMENT TO THE PRESS ON THE STRATEGIC IMPORTANCE OF INDOCHINA, APRIL 7, 1954

You have, of course, both the specific and the general when you talk about such things.

First of all, you have the specific value of a locality in its production of materials that the world needs.

Then you have the possibility that many human beings pass under a dictatorship that is inimical to the free world.

Finally, you have broader considerations that might follow what you would call the "falling domino" principle. You have a row of dominoes set up, you knock over the first one, and what will happen to the last one is the certainty that it will go over very quickly. So you could have a beginning of a disintegration that would have the most profound influences.

Now, with respect to the first one, two of the items from this particular area that the world uses are tin and tungsten. They are very important. There are others, of course, the rubber plantations and so on.

Then with respect to more people passing under this domination, Asia, after all, has already lost some 450 million of its peoples to the Communist dictatorship, and we simply can't afford greater losses.

But, when we come to the possible sequence of events, the loss of Indochina, of Burma, of Thailand, of the Peninsula, and Indonesia following, now you begin to talk about areas that not only multiply the disadvantages that you would suffer through loss of materials, sources of materials, but now you are talking about millions and millions and millions of people.

Finally, the geographical position achieved thereby does many things. It turns the so-called island defensive chain of Japan, Formosa, of the Philippines and to the southward; it moves in to threaten Australia and New Zealand.

It takes away, in its economic aspects, that region that Japan must have as a trading area or Japan, in turn, will have only one place in the world to go—that is, toward the Communist areas in order to live.

So, the possible consequences of the loss are just incalculable to the free world.

Public Papers of the Presidents of the United States: Dwight D. Eisenhower,
1954 (Washington, D.C.: Government Printing Office, 1958), 332–33.

10. FINAL DECLARATION OF THE GENEVA CONFERENCE ON INDOCHINA, JULY 21, 1954 (EXTRACT)

1. The Conference takes note of the agreements ending hostilities in Cambodia, Laos and Viet-Nam and organizing international control and the supervision of the execution of the provisions of these agreements. . . .

4. The Conference takes note of the clauses in the agreement on the cessation of hostilities in Viet-Nam prohibiting the introduction into Viet-Nam of foreign troops and military personnel as well as of all kinds of arms and munitions . . . .

5. The Conference takes note of the clauses in the agreement on the cessation of hostilities in Viet-Nam to the effect that no military base under the control of a foreign State may be established in the regrouping zones of the two parties, the latter having the obligation to see that the zones allotted to them shall not constitute part of any military alliance and shall not be utilized for the resumption of hostilities or in the service of an aggressive policy . . . .

6. The Conference recognizes that the essential purpose of the agreement relating to Viet-Nam is to settle military questions with a view to ending hostilities and that the military demarcation line is provisional and should not in any way be interpreted as constituting a political or territorial boundary . . . .

7. The Conference declares that, so far as Viet-Nam is concerned, the settlement of political problems, affected on the basis of respect for the principles of independence, unity and territorial integrity, shall permit the Viet-Namese people to enjoy the fundamental freedoms, guaranteed by democratic institutions established as a result of free general elections by secret ballot. In order to ensure that sufficient progress in the restoration of peace has been made, and that all the necessary conditions obtain for free expression of the national will, general elections shall be held in July 1956, under the supervision of an international commission . . . .

12. In their relations with Cambodia, Laos and Viet-Nam, each member of the Geneva Conference undertakes to respect the sovereignty, the independence, and unity and the territorial integrity of the above-mentioned states, and to refrain from any interference in their internal affairs.

United States-Vietnam Relations, 1945–1967: A Study Prepared by the Department of Defense, 12 vols. (Washington, D.C.: Government Printing Office, 1971), 9:671–75.

11. SOUTHEAST ASIA COLLECTIVE DEFENSE TREATY, SEPTEMBER 8, 1954 (EXTRACT)

Article IV

1. Each party recognizes that aggression by means of armed attack in the treaty area against any of the parties or against any state or territory which the parties by unanimous agreement may hereafter designate, would endanger its own peace and safety, and agrees that it will in that event act to meet the common danger in accordance with its constitutional processes. Measures taken under this paragraph shall be immediately reported to the Security Council of the United Nations.

2. If, in the opinion of any of the parties, the inviolability of the integrity of the territory or the sovereignty or political independence of any party in the treaty area or of any state or territory to which the provisions of paragraph 1 of this article from time to time apply is threatened in any way other than by armed attack or is affected or threatened by any fact or situation which might endanger the peace of the area, the Parties shall consult immediately in order to agree on the measures which should be taken for the common defense.

3. It is understood that no action on the territory of any state designated by unanimous agreement under paragraph 1 of this article or on any territory so designated shall be taken except at the invitation or with the consent of the government concerned. . . .

Designation of States and Territory as to Which Provisions of Article IV and Article III Are to Be Applicable

The parties to the Southeast Asia Collective Defense Treaty unanimously designate for the purposes of Article IV of the Treaty the states of Cambodia and Laos and the free territory under the jurisdiction of the state of Vietnam . . . .

This protocol shall enter into force simultaneously with the coming into force of the Treaty.

Department of State Bulletin (September 20, 1954), 394–96.

12. DWIGHT D. EISENHOWER'S SPEECH ON THE "NEED FOR MUTUAL SECURITY IN WAGING THE PEACE," MAY 21, 1957 (EXTRACT)

This is a policy for America that began ten years ago when a Democratic President and a Republican Congress united in an historic declaration. They then declared that the independence and survival of two countries menaced by Communist aggression—Greece and Turkey—were so important to the security of America that we would give them military and economic aid.

That policy saved those nations. And it did so without the cost of American lives.

That policy has since been extended to all critical areas of the world. It recognizes that America cannot exist as an island of freedom in a surrounding sea of Communism. It is expressed concretely by mutual security treaties embracing 42 other nations. And these treaties reflect a solemn finding by the President and the Senate that our own peace would be endangered if any of these countries were conquered by International Communism.

The lesson of the defense of Greece and Turkey ten years ago has since been repeated in the saving of other lands and peoples. A recent example is the Southeast Asian country of Viet-Nam, whose President has just visited us as our honored guest.

Two years ago it appeared that all Southeast Asia might be over-run by the forces of International Communism. The freedom and security of nations for which we had fought throughout World War II and the Korean War again stood in danger. The people of Viet-Nam responded bravely—under steadfast leadership.

But bravery alone could not have prevailed.

We gave military and economic assistance to the Republic of Viet-Nam. We entered into a treaty—the Southeast Asia Security Treaty—which plainly warned that an armed attack against this area would endanger our own peace and safety, and that we would act accordingly. Thus Viet-Nam has been saved for freedom.

Public Papers of the Presidents of the United States: Dwight D. Eisenhower,
1957 (Washington, D.C.: Government Printing Office, 1958), 387–88.

13. MANIFESTO OF THE SOUTH VIET NAM NATIONAL FRONT FOR LIBERATION, DECEMBER 1960 (EXTRACT)

At present, our people are urgently demanding an end to the cruel dictatorial rule; they are demanding independence and democracy, enough food and clothing, and peaceful reunification of the country.

To meet the aspirations of our compatriots, the *South Viet Nam National Front for Liberation* came into being, pledging itself to shoulder the historic task of liberating our people from the present yoke of slavery.

The *South Viet Nam National Front for Liberation* undertakes to unite all sections of the people, all social classes, nationalities, political parties, organizations, religious communities and patriotic personalities, without distinction of their political tendencies, in order to struggle for the overthrow of the rule of the US imperialists and their stooges—the Ngo Dinh Diem clique—and for the realization of independence, democracy, peace and neutrality pending the peaceful reunification of the fatherland.

Gareth Porter, ed., *Vietnam: A History in Documents*
(New York: New American Library, 1981), 206.

14. GENERAL MAXWELL TAYLOR'S REPORT
TO PRESIDENT JOHN F. KENNEDY,
NOVEMBER 1, 1961 (EXTRACT)

The introduction of U.S. forces may increase tensions and risk escalation into a major war in Asia.

On the other side of the argument, there can be no action so convincing of U.S. seriousness of purpose and hence so reassuring to the people and Government of SVN [South Vietnam] and to our other friends and allies in SEA [Southeast Asia] as the introduction of U.S. forces in SVN

. . . .

The size of the U.S. force introduced need not be great to provide the military presence necessary to produce the desired effect on national morale in SVN and on international opinion. A bare token, however, will not suffice; it must have a significant value . . . .

The risks of backing into a major war by way of SVN are present but are not impressive. NVN [North Vietnam] is extremely vulnerable to conventional bombing, a weakness which should be exploited diplomatically in convincing Hanoi to lay off SVN. Both the D.R.V. [Democratic Republic of Vietnam] and the Chicoms [Chinese Communists] would face severe logistical difficulties in trying to maintain strong forces in the field in SEA, difficulties which we share but by no means to the same degree . . . .

By the foregoing line of reasoning, I have reached the conclusion that the introduction of U.S. military Task Force without delay offers definitely more advantage than it creates risks and difficulties. In fact, I do not believe that our program to save SVN will succeed without it. If the concept is approved, the exact size and composition of the force should be determined by Secretary of Defense in consultation with the JCS [Joint Chiefs of Staff], the Chief MAAG [Military Assistance Advisory Group] and CINCPAC [Commander in Chief, Pacific]. My own feeling is that the initial size should not exceed about 8000, of which a preponderant number would be in logistical-type units.

United States-Vietnam Relations, 1945–1967, 11:337–42.

15. SECRETARY OF STATE DEAN RUSK TELEGRAM
TO AMBASSADOR HENRY CABOT LODGE,
OCTOBER 5, 1963

1. Following is overall instruction resulting from NSC consideration of McNamara/Taylor report and recommendations together with those you have submitted in recent weeks. These instructions have the President's

personal approval. At any time you feel it is necessary you may state to GVN [Government of Vietnam] that you are acting under the specific instructions of the President as recommended by the National Security Council.

2. Actions are designed to indicate to Diem Government our displeasure at its political policies and activities and to create significant uncertainty in that government and in key Vietnamese groups as to future intentions of United States. At same time, actions are designed to have at most slight impact on military or counterinsurgency effort against Viet Cong, at least in short run.

3. The recommendations on negotiations are concerned with what US is after, i.e., GVN action to increase effectiveness of its military effort; to ensure popular support to win war; and to eliminate strains on US Government and public confidence. The negotiating posture is designed not to lay down specific hard and fast demands or to set a deadline, but to produce movement in Vietnamese Government along these lines . . . .

12. If, as we hope, Diem seeks clarification of US policies and actions, you should present an exposition of how our actions are related to our fundamental objective of victory. There are three issues at root of strained relations between GVN and US and of our judgment that victory may be jeopardized. The first concerns military effort; GVN must take steps to make this more effective. The second is crisis of confidence among Vietnamese people which is eroding popular support for GVN that is vital for victory. The third is crisis of confidence on part of the American public and Government. Heart of problem is form of government that has been evolving in Viet-Nam. Diem's regime has trappings of democracy, but in reality it has been evolving into authoritarian government maintained by police terrorist methods. What GVN must do is to reverse this process of evolution.

Foreign Relations of the United States, 1961–1963, vol. 4, *Vietnam August-December 1963* (Washington, D.C.: Government Printing Office, 1991), 372–74.

16. JOHN F. KENNEDY INTERVIEW WITH CHET HUNTLEY AND DAVID BRINKLEY, SEPTEMBER 10, 1963

Mr. Huntley: Are we likely to reduce our aid to South Viet-Nam now?

The President: I don't think we think that would be helpful at this time. If you reduce your aid, it is possible you could have some effect upon the government structure there. On the other hand, you might have a situation which could bring about a collapse. Strongly in our mind is what happened in the case of China at the end of World War II, where China was lost—a weak government became increasingly unable to control events. We don't want that.

Mr. Brinkley: Mr. President, have you had any reason to doubt this so-called "domino theory," that if South Viet-Nam falls, the rest of Southeast Asia will go behind it?

The President: No, I believe it. I believe it. I think that the struggle is close enough. China is so large, looms so high just beyond the frontiers, that if South Viet-Nam went, it would not only give them an improved geographic position for a guerrilla assault on Malaya but would also give the impression that the wave of the future in Southeast Asia was China and the Communists. So I believe it . . . .

The fact of the matter is that with the assistance of the United States and SEATO [Southeast Asia Treaty Organization], Southeast Asia and indeed all of Asia has been maintained independent against a powerful force, the Chinese Communists. What I am concerned about is that Americans will get impatient and say, because they don't like events in Southeast Asia or they don't like the Government in Saigon, that we should withdraw. That only makes it easy for the Communists. I think we should stay. We should use our influence in as effective a way as we can, but we should not withdraw.

Public Papers of the Presidents of the United States: John F. Kennedy, 1963
(Washington, D.C.: Government Printing Office, 1964), 659–60.

17. NATIONAL SECURITY ACTION MEMORANDUM 273, NOVEMBER 26, 1963 (EXTRACT)

1. It remains the central object of the United States in South Vietnam to assist the people and Government of that country to win their contest against the externally directed and supported Communist conspiracy. The test of all U.S. decisions and actions in this area should be the effectiveness of their contribution to this purpose.

2. The objectives of the United States with respect to the withdrawal of U.S. military personnel remain as stated in the White House statement of October 2, 1963. [That statement affirmed that "by the end of the year, the U.S. program for training Vietnamese should have progressed to the point where 1,000 U.S. military personnel assigned to South Viet Nam can be withdrawn."]

3. It is a major interest of the United States Government that the present provisional government of South Vietnam should be assisted in consolidating itself and in holding and developing increased public support. All U.S. officers should conduct themselves with this objective in view.

Foreign Relations of the United States, 1961–1963, 4:638.
White House statement of October 2, 1963, ibid., 353.

18. GULF OF TONKIN RESOLUTION, AUGUST 10, 1964

Whereas naval units of the Communist regime in Vietnam, in violation of the principles of the Charter of the United Nations and of international law, have deliberately and repeatedly attacked United States naval vessels lawfully present in international waters, and have thereby created a serious threat to international peace; and

Whereas these attacks are part of a deliberate and systematic campaign of aggression that the Communist regime of North Vietnam has been waging against its neighbors and the nations joined with them in the collective defense of their freedom; and

Whereas the United States is assisting the peoples of southeast Asia to protect their freedom and has no territorial, military or political ambitions in that area, but desires only that these peoples should be left in peace to work out their own destinies in their own way; Now, therefore be it

Resolved by the Senate and the House of Representatives of the United States of America in Congress assembled.

That the Congress approves and supports the determination of the President as Commander in Chief, to take all necessary measures to repel any armed attack against the forces of the United States and to prevent further aggression.

SEC. 2. The United States regards as vital to its national interest and to world peace the maintenance of international peace and security in southeast Asia. Consonant with the Constitution of the United States and the Charter of the United Nations and in accordance with its obligations under the Southeast Asia Collective Defense Treaty, the United States is therefore, prepared, as the President determines, to take all necessary steps, including the use of armed force, to assist any member or protocol state of the Southeast Asia Collective Defense Treaty requesting assistance in defense of its freedom.

SEC. 3. This resolution shall expire when the President shall determine that the peace and security of the area is reasonably assured by international conditions created by action of the United States or otherwise, except that it may be terminated earlier by concurrent resolution of Congress.

Congressional Record, 88th Cong., 2d sess., vol. 110, part 14, p. 18,132.

19. MCGEORGE BUNDY, "A POLICY OF SUSTAINED REPRISAL," FEBRUARY 7, 1965 (EXTRACT)

We believe that the best available way of increasing our chance of success in Vietnam is the development and execution of a policy of *sustained reprisal* against North Vietnam—a policy in which air and naval action against the North is justified by and related to the whole Viet Cong campaign of violence and terror in the South. . . .

This reprisal policy should begin at a low level. Its level of force and pressure should be increased only gradually—and as indicated above it should be decreased if VC terror visibly decreases. The object would not be to "win" an air war against Hanoi, but rather to influence the course of the struggle in the South. . . .

We are convinced that the political values of reprisal require a *continuous* operation. Episodic responses geared on a one-for-one basis to "spectacular" outrages would lack the persuasive force of sustained pressure. More important still, they would leave it open to the Communists to avoid reprisals entirely by giving up only a small element of their own program. The Gulf of Tonkin affair produced a sharp upturn in morale in South Vietnam. When it remained an isolated episode, however, there was a severe relapse. It is the great merit of the proposed scheme that to stop it the Communists would have to stop enough of their activity in the South to permit the probable success of a determined pacification effort. . . .

We emphasize that our primary target in advocating a reprisal policy is the improvement of the situation in *South* Vietnam. Action against the North is usually urged as a means of affecting the will of Hanoi to direct and support the VC. We consider this an important but longer-range purpose. The immediate and critical targets are in the South—in the minds of the South Vietnamese and in the minds of the Viet Cong cadres.

Foreign Relations of the United States, 1964–1965, vol. 2, *Vietnam January-June 1965* (Washington, D.C.: Government Printing Office, 1996), 181–83.

20. GEORGE BALL MEMORANDUM TO LYNDON JOHNSON, JULY 1, 1965 (EXTRACT)

A Compromise Solution in South Vietnam

1. *A Losing War:* The South Vietnamese are losing the war to the Viet Cong. No one can assure you that we can beat the Viet Cong or even force them to the conference table on our terms, no matter how many hundred thousand *white foreign* (US) troops we deploy.

No one has demonstrated that a white ground force of whatever size can win a guerrilla war—which is at the same time a civil war between Asians—in jungle terrain in the midst of a population that refuses cooperation to the white force (and the SVN) and thus provides a great intelligence advantage to the other side. . . .

2. *The Question to Decide:* Should we limit our liabilities in South Vietnam and try to find a way out with minimal long-term costs?

The alternative—no matter what we may wish it to be—is almost certainly a protracted war involving an open-ended commitment of U.S. forces, mounting U.S. casualties, no assurance of a satisfactory solution, and a serious danger of escalation at the end of the road.

(3) *Need for a Decision Now:* So long as our forces are restricted to advising and assisting the South Vietnamese, the struggle will remain a civil war between Asian peoples. Once we deploy substantial numbers of troops in combat it will become a war between the U.S. and a large part of the population of South Viet-Nam, organized and directed from North Viet-Nam and backed by the resources of Moscow and Peiping.

The decision you face now, therefore, is crucial. Once large numbers of US troops are committed to direct combat they will begin to take heavy casualties in a war they are ill-equipped to fight in a non-cooperative if not downright hostile countryside.

Once we suffer large casualties, we will have started a well-nigh irreversible process. Our involvement will be so great that we cannot—without national humiliation—stop short of achieving our complete objectives. *Of the two possibilities I think humiliation would be more likely than the achievement of our objectives—even after we have paid terrible costs.*

(4) *A Compromise Solution:* Should we commit U.S. manpower and prestige to a terrain so unfavorable as to give a very large advantage to the enemy—or should we seek a compromise settlement which achieves less than our stated objectives and thus cut our losses while we still have the freedom of maneuver to do so?

(5) *Costs of Compromise Solution:* The answer involves a judgment as to the cost to the United States of such a compromise settlement in terms of our relations with the countries in the area of South Viet-Nam, the credibility of our commitments, and our prestige around the world. In my judgment, if we act before we commit substantial U.S. forces to combat in South Viet-Nam we can, by accepting some short-term costs, avoid what may well be a long-term catastrophe. I believe we have tended greatly to exaggerate the costs involved in a compromise settlement.

Foreign Relations of the United States, 1964–1965, vol. 3, *Vietnam June-December 1965* (Washington, D.C.: Government Printing Office, 1996), 106–8.

21. ROBERT MCNAMARA MEMORANDUM TO LYNDON JOHNSON, JULY 20, 1965 (EXTRACT)

Recommendations of additional deployments to Vietnam:

1. *Introduction.* Our object in VN is to create conditions for a favorable outcome by demonstrating to the VC/DRV that the odds are against their winning. We want to create these conditions, if possible, without causing

the war to expand into one with China or the Soviet Union and in a way which preserves support of the American people and, hopefully, of our allies and friends . . . .

4. *Options open to us.* We must choose among three courses of action with respect to Vietnam all of which involve different probabilities, outcomes, and costs:

a. Cut our losses and withdraw under the best conditions that can be arranged—almost certainly conditions humiliating the US and very damaging to our future effectiveness on the world scene.

b. Continue at about the present level, with the US forces limited to say 75,000, holding on and playing for the breaks—a course of action which, because our position would grow weaker, almost certainly would confront us later with a choice between withdrawal and an emergency expansion of forces, perhaps too late to do any good.

c. Expand promptly and substantially the US military pressure against the Viet Cong in the South and maintain the military pressure against the NVNese in the North while launching a vigorous effort on the political side to lay the groundwork for a favorable outcome by clarifying our objectives and establishing channels of communication. This alternative would stave off defeat in the short run and offer a good chance of producing a favorable settlement in the longer run; at the same time, it would imply a commitment to see a fighting war clear through at considerable cost in casualties and matériel and would make any later decision to withdraw even more difficult and even more costly than would be the case today.

My recommendations in paragraph 5 below are based on the choice of the third alternative (Option c) as the course of action involving the best odds of the best outcome with the most acceptable cost to the United States.

5. *Military recommendations.* There are now 15 US (and 1 Australian) combat battalions in Vietnam; they together with other combat and non-combat personnel, bring the total US personnel in Vietnam to approximately 75,000.

a. I recommend that the deployment of US ground troops in Vietnam be increased by October to 34 maneuver battalions (or, if the Koreans fail to provide the expected 9 battalions promptly, to 43 battalions). The battalions—together with increases in helicopter lift, air squadrons, naval units, air defense, combat support and miscellaneous log support and advisory personnel which I also recommend—would bring the total US personnel in Vietnam to approximately 175,000 (200,000 if we must make up for the Korean failure). It should be understood that the deployment of more men (an additional perhaps 100,000) may be necessary in early 1966 and that the deployment of additional forces thereafter is possible but will depend on developments.

Foreign Relations of the United States, 1964–1965, 3:171–75.

22. REPORT OF THE PRESIDENT'S COMMISSION ON AN ALL-VOLUNTEER ARMED FORCE, FEBRUARY 20, 1970 (EXTRACT)

Until the United States' commitment in Vietnam rose sharply in 1965, the draft seemed to be generally accepted as a necessary means of military manpower procurement. There was virtually no debate or opposition to the extension of the Universal Military Service and Training Act in 1955, 1959, and 1963. This was not too surprising. Following the Korean War military force levels decreased and the impact of the draft declined while the number of draft age youth increased.

During the early 1960's, 95 percent of those between the ages of 18 and 35 were excluded from the I-A and I-A-O pool [classifications indicating the registrant was available for induction]. The Selective Service System found itself faced with the problem of allocating an excess supply of eligible youth. Its solution was to create new deferments or expand the scope of existing ones. In addition, induction standards were raised and rejection rates increased during the early 1960's. Meanwhile, pay for first-term enlisted men remained below civilian levels. Even so, young men continued to volunteer and the draft call-ups remained relatively small. By 1964–65 only 5,000–10,000 men were being inducted each month, and the average age of induction was almost 23.

The escalation of the Vietnam War in 1965 once again focused attention on the draft. Monthly calls rose sharply to 20,000–30,000. Deferment criteria were tightened, and the average age of inductees declined to 19. Of the 6 million men who have served in the Armed Forces during the Vietnam war, 25 percent have been draftees. In the past few years numerous articles and books have been written about the draft and both a Congressional panel and a Presidential commission have been created to study the Selective Service System. The Marshall Commission, appointed by President Johnson in 1966, published an extensive analysis of how the draft works and concluded that the primary age of draft liability should be 19. The Marshall Commission also urged a random system of selection [a lottery] similar to the one that has since been adopted.

The Report of the President's Commission on an All-Volunteer Armed Force (Washington, D.C.: Government Printing Office, 1970), 165–66.

23. GENERAL MAXWELL D. TAYLOR, TESTIMONY TO U.S. SENATE COMMITTEE ON FOREIGN RELATIONS, FEBRUARY 17, 1966 (EXTRACT)

I am thoroughly aware of the concern of this committee over the growing requirement for American troops in South Vietnam. Is this an endless requirement in an open-ended war? I do not believe that anyone can give a completely satisfactory reply to this question but I can suggest the consideration of certain limiting factors which have a bearing on the matter.

First, on our side, we are not setting as an objective for our ground forces the occupation of all South Vietnam or the hunting down of the last armed guerrilla. We are in Vietnam to safeguard the people who are the real target of the enemy. Terrain has little meaning except insofar as it supports people. Thus the extent of control and protection of population is the true measure of progress rather than control of territory. By the former indicator we are not doing too badly. . . .

The point I wish to make is that when one expresses our military objective in terms of securing a high proportion of the population, the troops requirement loses some of its impression of open-endedness. Under this concept, the prime target of our U.S. forces becomes the main-line enemy units which constitute the greatest threat to population—not the entire guerrilla force wherever found.

Another limiting factor is the logistic difficulty of the Vietcong in supporting increased numbers of troops in combat. The combination of air attacks on their lines of supply and of increasing ground attacks on their units which must then consume supplies at an increased rate places a ceiling on the forces they can maintain in South Vietnam. . . .

The second component of our strategy relates to the use of airpower against military targets in North Vietnam. It is well to remind ourselves the reasons which impelled us to this decision. There were three which we recognized perfectly at the time of the decision and which remain valid today. The first was to give the people of South Vietnam the assurance for the first time of imposing a direct penalty on the source of the aggression. . . .

The second reason for the decision was to use airpower, insofar as it could be effective, to limit and render more difficult the infiltration of the men and supplies from North Vietnam to South Vietnam . . . .

The third reason for the decision to use our airpower was to provide a sobering reminder to the leaders in Hanoi that progressively they must pay a mounting price for the continuation of their support of the Vietcong insurgency.

In spite of their defiant statements of determination to endure these attacks forever, I for one know from experience that no one derives any enjoyment from receiving incoming shells and bombs day after day and I
have no doubt that the warning message is getting through to the leadership of Hanoi. In a very real sense, the objective of our air campaign is to
change the will of the enemy leadership.

We hope that, in due course, the combination of the Vietcong failure
to win victory on the ground in South Vietnam and the effect of continued air attacks will present to the Hanoi leadership a situation so disad-
vantageous that they will decide that it is in their interest to halt their aggression, redefine their aims, and join with us in discussing ways and
means of improving the lot of all Vietnam.

U.S. Senate Committee on Foreign Relations, *Foreign Assistance Act of 1961,*
as Amended: Hearings on S. 2793, 89th Cong., 2d sess,
January 28 and February 4, 8, 10, 17, and 18, 1966, 258–59.

24. LYNDON JOHNSON'S SPEECH AT JOHNS HOPKINS UNIVERSITY, APRIL 7, 1965 (EXTRACT)

Our objective is the independence of South Vietnam, and its freedom
from attack. We want nothing more for ourselves, only that the people of
South Vietnam be allowed to guide their own country in their own way.

We will do everything necessary to reach that objective. And we will do
only what is absolutely necessary. . . .

And we do this to convince the leaders of North Vietnam, and all who
seek to share their conquest, of a very simple fact:

We will not be defeated.

We will not grow tired.

We will not withdraw, either openly or under the cloak of a meaningless agreement. . . .

Our resources are equal to any challenge because we fight for values
and we fight for principles, rather than territory or colonies. Our patience
and determination are unending.

Once this is clear, then it should also be clear that the only path for
reasonable men is the path of peaceful settlement.

Such peace demands an independent South Vietnam securely guaranteed and able to shape its own relationships to all others, free from outside interference, tied to no alliance, a military base for no other country.

These are the essentials of any final agreement.

We will never be second in the search for such a peaceful settlement
in Vietnam.

There may be many ways to this kind of peace: in discussion or negotiation with the governments concerned; in large groups or in small ones; in the reaffirmation of old agreements or their strengthening with new ones.

We have stated this position over and over again fifty times and more, to friend and foe alike. And we remain ready, with this purpose, for unconditional discussions. . . .

These countries of Southeast Asia are homes for millions of impoverished people. Each day these people rise at dawn and struggle until the night to wrest existence from the soil. They are often wracked by disease, plagued by hunger, and death comes at the early age of 40.

Stability and peace do not come easily in such a land. Neither independence nor human dignity will ever be won by arms alone. It also requires the works of peace. . . .

I would hope that the Secretary-General of the United Nations could use the prestige of his great office, and his deep knowledge of Asia, to initiate, as soon as possible, with the countries of the area, a plan for cooperation in increased development.

For our part I will ask the Congress to join in a billion-dollar American investment in this effort as soon as it is underway.

And I hope all other industrialized countries, including the Soviet Union, will join in this effort to replace despair with hope, and terror with progress.

The task is nothing less than to enrich the hopes and existence of more than a hundred million people. And there is much to be done.

The vast Mekong River can provide food and water and power on a scale to dwarf even our own TVA [Tennessee Valley Authority]. . . .

The ordinary men and women of North Vietnam and South Vietnam—of China and India—of Russia and America—are brave people. They are filled with the same proportions of hate and fear, of love and hope. Most of them want the same things for themselves and their families. Most of them do not want their sons ever to die in battle, or see the homes of others destroyed.

Department of State Bulletin, April 26, 1965, 606–10.

25. VO NGUYEN GIAP ON THE VIETMINH'S PEOPLE'S WAR STRATEGY AGAINST FRANCE
(EXTRACT)

The Vietnamese people's war of liberation [against France] was a just war, aiming to win back the independence and unity of the country, to bring land to our peasants and guarantee them the right to it, and to defend the achievements of the August Revolution. That is why it was first and foremost a people's war. To educate, mobilize, organize and arm the whole people in order that they might take part in the Resistance was a crucial question . . . .

From the point of view of directing operations, our *strategy and tactics had to be those of a people's war and of a long-term resistance.*

Our strategy was, as we have stressed, to wage a long-lasting battle. A war of this nature in general entails several phases; in principle, starting from a stage of contention, it goes through a period of equilibrium before arriving at a general counter-offensive. In effect, the way in which it is carried on can be more subtle and more complex, depending on the particular conditions obtaining on both sides during the course of operations. Only a long-term war could enable us to utilize to the maximum our political trump cards, to overcome our material handicap and to transform our weakness into strength. To maintain and increase our forces, was the principle to which we adhered, contenting ourselves with attacking when success was certain, refusing to give battle likely to incur losses to us or to engage in hazardous actions. We had to apply the slogan: to build up our strength during the actual course of fighting . . . .

From the military point of view, *the Vietnamese people's war of liberation proved that an insufficiently equipped people's army, but an army fighting for a just cause, can, with appropriate strategy and tactics, combine the conditions needed to conquer a modern army of aggressive imperialism.*

Vo Nguyen Giap, *People's War: People's Army* (Hanoi: Foreign Languages Publishing House, 1961), 29–30.

26. SPEECH OF PAUL POTTER, PRESIDENT OF STUDENTS FOR A DEMOCRATIC SOCIETY, AT AN ANTIWAR RALLY IN WASHINGTON, D.C., ON APRIL 17, 1965 (EXTRACT)

The President says that we are defending freedom in Vietnam. Whose freedom? Not the freedom of the Vietnamese. . . .

The pattern of repression and destruction that we developed and justified in the war is so thorough that it can only be called cultural genocide. I am not talking about napalm or gas or crop destruction or torture, hurled indiscriminately on women and children, insurgent and neutral, upon the first suspicion of rebel activity. That in itself is horrendous and incredible beyond belief. But it is only part of a larger pattern of destruction to the very fabric of the country. We have uprooted the people from the land and imprisoned them in concentration camps called "sunrise villages." Through conscription and direct political intervention and control, we have destroyed local customs and traditions, trampled upon those things of value which give dignity and purpose to life. . . .

The President mocks freedom if he insists that the war in Vietnam is a defense of American freedom. Perhaps the only freedom that this war protects is the freedom of the warhawks in the Pentagon and the State Department to experiment with counter-insurgency and guerrilla warfare in Vietnam.

The Vietnam War: Opposing Viewpoints
(San Diego, Calif.: Greenhaven Press, 1998), 108.

27. MARTIN LUTHER KING JR., "A TIME TO BREAK SILENCE," APRIL 4, 1967 (EXTRACT)

I come to this magnificent house of worship tonight because my conscience leaves me no other choice. I join with you in this meeting because I am in deepest agreement with the aims and work of the organization which has brought us together: Clergy and Laymen Concerned about Vietnam. The recent statement of your executive committee are the sentiments of my own heart and I found myself in full accord when I read its opening lines: "A time comes when silence is betrayal." That time has come for us in relation to Vietnam. . . .

Perhaps the most tragic recognition of reality took place when it became clear to me that the war was doing far more than devastating the hopes of the poor at home. It was sending their sons and their brothers and their husbands to fight and to die in extraordinarily high proportions relative to the rest of the population. We were taking the black young men who had been crippled by our society and sending them eight thousand miles away to guarantee liberties in Southeast Asia which they had not found in southwest Georgia and East Harlem. So we have been repeatedly faced with the cruel irony of watching Negro and white boys on TV screens as they kill and die together for a nation that has been unable to seat them together in the same schools. . . .

As I have walked among the desperate, rejected and angry young men I have told them that Molotov cocktails and rifles would not solve their problems. I have tried to offer them my deepest compassion while maintaining my conviction that social change comes most meaningfully through nonviolent action. But they asked—and rightly so—what about Vietnam? They asked if our own nation wasn't using massive doses of violence to solve its problems, to bring about the changes it wanted. Their questions hit home, and I knew that I could never again raise my voice against the violence of the oppressed in the ghettos without having first spoken clearly to the greatest purveyor of violence in the world today—my own government. For the sake of those boys, for the sake of this government, for the sake of the hundreds of thousands trembling under our violence, I cannot be silent. . . .

Somehow this madness must cease. We must stop now. I speak as a child of God and brother to the suffering poor of Vietnam. I speak for those whose land is being laid waste, whose homes are being destroyed, whose culture is being subverted. I speak for the poor of America who are paying the double price of smashed hopes at home and death and corruption in Vietnam. I speak as a citizen of the world, for the world as it stands aghast at the path we have taken. I speak as an American to the leaders of my own nation. The great initiative in this war is ours. The initiative to stop it must be ours.

A *Testament of Hope: The Essential Writings of Martin Luther King, Jr.*, edited by James Melvin Washington (New York: Harper and Row, 1986), 231–44.

28. DAVID HALBERSTAM ON THE ROLE OF THE PRESS IN THE VIETNAM WAR

For reporters in Vietnam, our job was to ask does it work? Is it working? And it did not work. There is a wonderful story about Neil Sheehan very early in the war. He was a young kid, twenty-five-years old, and it is 1962. He is with my great predecessor, the sainted Homer Bigart, who won the Pulitzer Prize in World War II and in Korea. The first helicopters have arrived in Vietnam, and they go down to the Seventh Division in My Tho. Neil is very excited because it is going to be a big story. On the first day they have a bit of a small success, and the second day they have no success at all. It is a typical pillowpunching ARVN operation. The third day is the same thing. They drive back to Saigon together, and Neil is mumbling and grumbling and very angry. Homer Bigart, by then in his late fifties, says: "Mr. Sheehan, Mr. Sheehan what's the matter?" Neil sort of grumbles about three days of wasted time and no story. Homer says: "Mr. Sheehan, there is a story. Mr. Sheehan, there's a very good story. It doesn't work, Mr. Sheehan. That's your story." The job of the reporters was to cover whether it worked or not. American combat troops could fight bravely. . . . We could fight bravely, and then we would be gone and the VC and the NVA would keep coming.

Facing My Lai: Moving Beyond the Massacre, edited by David L. Anderson (Lawrence: University Press of Kansas, 1998), 72–73.

29. LYNDON JOHNSON'S SPEECH
OF MARCH 31, 1968 (EXTRACT)

Tonight I want to speak to you of peace in Vietnam and Southeast Asia.

No other question so preoccupies our people. No other dream so absorbs the 250 million human beings who live in that part of the world. No other goal motivates American policy in Southeast Asia . . . .

There is no need to delay the talks that could bring an end to this long and this bloody war.

Tonight, I renew the offer I made last August—to stop the bombardment of North Vietnam. We ask that talks begin promptly, that they be serious talks on the substance of peace. We assume that during those talks Hanoi will not take advantage of our restraint.

We are prepared to move immediately toward peace through negotiations.

So, tonight, in the hope that this action will lead to early talks, I am taking the first step to deescalate the conflict. We are reducing—substantially reducing—the present level of hostilities.

And we are dong so unilaterally, and at once.

Tonight, I have ordered our aircraft and our naval vessels to make no attacks on North Vietnam, except in the area north of the demilitarized zone where the continuing enemy buildup directly threatens allied forward positions and where the movements of their troops and supplies are clearly related to that threat.

The area in which we are stopping our attacks includes almost 90 percent of North Vietnam's population, and most of its territory. Thus there will be no attacks around the principal populated areas or in the food-producing areas of North Vietnam. . . .

I believed that a peaceful Asia is far nearer to reality because of what America has done in Vietnam. I believe that the men who endure the dangers of battle—fighting there for us tonight—are helping the entire world avoid far greater conflicts, far wider wars, far more destruction, than this one.

The peace that will bring them home someday will come. Tonight I have offered the first in what I hope will be a series of mutual moves toward peace. . . .

There is division in the American house now. There is divisiveness among us all tonight. And holding the trust that is mine, as President of all the people, I cannot disregard the peril to the progress of the American people and the hope and the prospect of peace for all peoples.

So, I would ask all Americans, whatever their personal interests or concern, to guard against divisiveness and all its ugly consequences. . . .

What we won when all of our people united just must not now be lost in suspicion, distrust, selfishness, and politics among any of our people.

Believing this as I do, I have concluded that I should not permit the Presidency to become involved in the partisan divisions that are developing in this political year.

With America's sons in the fields far away, with America's future under challenge right here at home, with our hopes and the world's hopes for peace in the balance every day, I do not believe that I should devote an hour or a day of my time to any personal partisan causes or to any duties other than the awesome duties of this office—the Presidency of your country.

Accordingly, I shall not seek, and I will not accept, the nomination of my party for another term as your President.

But let men everywhere know, however, that a strong, a confident, and a vigilant America stands ready tonight to seek an honorable peace—and stands ready tonight to defend an honored cause—whatever the price, whatever the burden, whatever the sacrifice that duty may require.

Public Papers of the Presidents of the United States: Lyndon B. Johnson, 1968–1969 (Washington, D.C.: Government Printing Office, 1970), 468–76.

30. EUGENE MCCARTHY, "DISSENT AND PATRIOTISM," JANUARY 16, 1968

It is certainly no more unpatriotic to criticize the foreign policy of a country than it is to criticize the domestic policy. . . . No more unpatriotic to be critical of a war in Vietnam than it is to be critical of the war on poverty. No more unpatriotic, in essence, to be concerned about the escalation of a war than it is to be concerned about the escalation of taxes or, I suppose, the escalation of prices that are reflected in inflation. And no more unpatriotic to criticize a military project overseas than it is to criticize a foreign aid program in the non-military area.

Proper criticism of a national policy certainly does not stop at the water's edge. Nor does patriotism begin at the water's edge. And criticism must not stop even at the entrance to the Central Intelligence Agency, or on the steps of the Pentagon, or any one of the other offices or buildings of the Department of Defense.

"Background Statements and Information on the Issues Facing the Nation," issued by the Massachusetts McCarthy for President Committee, Boston, Massachusetts, 1968.

31. RICHARD NIXON'S "SILENT MAJORITY" SPEECH, NOVEMBER 3,1969 (EXTRACT)

Good evening, my fellow Americans:

Tonight I want to talk to you on a subject of deep concern to all Americans and to many people in all parts of the world—the war in Vietnam. . . .

Now, many believe that President Johnson's decision to send American combat forces to South Vietnam was wrong. And many others—I among them—have been strongly critical of the way the war has been conducted.

But the question facing us today is: Now that we are in the war, what is the best way to end it? . . .

My fellow Americans, I am sure you can recognize . . . that we really only have two choices open to us if we want to end this war.

—I can order an immediate, precipitate withdrawal of all Americans from Vietnam without regard to the effects of that action.

—Or we can persist in our search for a just peace through a negotiated settlement if possible, or through continued implementation of our plan for Vietnamization if necessary—a plan in which we will withdraw all our forces from Vietnam on a schedule in accordance with our program, as the South Vietnamese become strong enough to defend their own freedom.

I have chosen this second course.

It is not the easy way.

It is the right way.

It is a plan which will end the war and serve the cause of peace—not just in Vietnam but in the Pacific and in the world. . . .

In San Francisco a few weeks ago. I saw demonstrators carrying signs reading: "Lose in Vietnam, bring the boys home."

Well, one of the strengths of our free society is that any American has a right to reach that conclusion and to advocate that point of view. But as President of the United States, I would be untrue to my oath of office if I allowed the policy of this Nation to be dictated by the minority who hold that point of view and who try to impose it on the Nation by mounting demonstrations in the street.

For almost 200 years, the policy of this Nation has been made under our Constitution by those leaders in the Congress and the White House elected by all of the people. If a vocal minority, however fervent its cause, prevails over reason and the will of the majority, this Nation has no future as a free society. . . .

Let historians not record that when America was the most powerful nation in the world we passed on the other side of the road and allowed the last hopes for peace and freedom of millions of people to be suffocated by the forces of totalitarianism.

And so tonight—to you, the great silent majority of my fellow Americans—I ask for your support.

I pledged in my campaign for the Presidency to end the war in a way that we could win the peace. I have initiated a plan of action which will enable me to keep that pledge.

The more support I can have from the American people, the sooner that pledge can be redeemed; for the more divided we are at home, the less likely the enemy is to negotiate at Paris.

Let us be united for peace. Let us also be united against defeat. Because let us understand: North Vietnam cannot defeat or humiliate the United States. Only Americans can do that.

> *Public Papers of the Presidents of the United States: Richard Nixon, 1969*
> (Washington, D.C.: Government Printing Office, 1971), 901–9.

32. THE PARIS PEACE ACCORDS, JANUARY 27, 1973 (EXTRACT)

The Parties participating in the Paris Conference on Viet-Nam,

With a view to ending the war and restoring peace in Viet-Nam on the basis of respect for the Vietnamese people's fundamental national rights and the South Vietnamese people's right to self-determination, and to contributing to the consolidation of peace in Asia and the world,

Have agreed on the following provisions and undertake to respect and to implement them: . . .

Article 1. The United States and all other countries respect the independence, sovereignty, unity, and territorial integrity of Viet-Nam as recognized by the 1954 Geneva Agreements on Viet-Nam. . . .

Article 2. A cease-fire shall be observed throughout South Viet-Nam as of 2400 hours G.M.T., on January 27, 1973.

At the same hour, the United States will stop all its military activities against the territory of the Democratic Republic of Viet-Nam by ground, air and naval forces, wherever they may be based, and end the mining of the territorial waters, ports, harbors, and waterways of the Democratic Republic of Viet-Nam. The United States will remove, permanently deactivate or destroy all the mines in the territorial waters, ports, harbors, and waterways of North Viet-Nam as soon as this Agreement goes into effect.

The complete cessation of hostilities mentioned in this Article shall be durable and without limit of time. . . .

Article 4. The United States will not continue its military involvement or intervene in the internal affairs of South Viet-Nam.

Article 5. Within sixty days of the signing of this Agreement, there will be a total withdrawal from South Viet-Nam of troops, military advisers, and military personnel, including technical military personnel and military personnel associated with the pacification program, armaments, munitions, and war material of the United States and those of the other foreign countries. . . .

Article 7. From the enforcement of the cease-fire to the formation of the government provided for in Article 9 (b) and 14 of this Agreement, the two South Vietnamese parties shall not accept the introduction of troops, military advisers, and military personnel including technical military personnel, armaments, munitions, and war materials into South Viet-Nam. . . .

Article 8

a. The return of captured military personnel and foreign civilians of the parties shall be carried out simultaneously with and completed not later than the same day as the troop withdrawal mentioned in Article 5. The parties shall exchange complete lists of the above-mentioned captured military personnel and foreign civilians on the day of the signing of this Agreement.

b. The parties shall help each other to get information about those military personnel and foreign civilians of the parties missing in action, to determine the location and take care of the graves of the dead so as to facilitate the exhumation and repatriation of the remains, and to take any such other measures as may be required to get information about those still considered missing in action. . . .

Article 9. The Government of the United States of America and the Government of the Democratic Republic of Viet-Nam undertake to respect the following principles for the exercise of the South Vietnamese people's right to self-determination: . . .

b. The South Vietnamese people shall decide themselves the political future of South Viet-Nam through genuinely free and democratic general elections under international supervision. . . .

Article 15. The reunification of Viet-Nam shall be carried out step by step through peaceful means on the basis of discussions and agreements between North and South Viet-Nam, without coercion or annexation by either party, and without foreign interference. The time for reunification will be agreed upon by North and South Viet-Nam.

United States Treaties and Other International Agreements, vol. 24, part 1, 1973
(Washington, D.C.: Government Printing Office, 1974), 1–225.

33. NORTH VIETNAMESE ACCOUNT OF THE FALL OF SAIGON, APRIL 29–30, 1975 (EXTRACT)

When "Code 2," [U.S. Ambassador Graham] Martin's code name, and "Lady 09," the name of the helicopter carrying him, left the embassy for the East Sea, it signaled the shameful defeat of U.S. imperialism after thirty years of intervention and military adventures in Vietnam. At the height of their invasion of Vietnam, the U.S. had used 60 percent of their total infantry, 58 percent of their marines, 32 percent of their tactical air force, 50 percent of their strategic air force, fifteen of their eighteen aircraft carriers, 800,000 American troops (counting those stationed in satellite countries who were taking part in the Vietnam war), and more than 1 million Saigon troops. They mobilized as many as 6 million American soldiers in rotation, dropped over 10 million tons of bombs, and spent over $300 billion, but in the end the U.S. ambassador had to crawl up to the helicopter pad looking for a way to flee. Today, looking back on the gigantic force the enemy had mobilized, recalling the malicious designs they admitted, and thinking about the extreme difficulties and complexities which our revolutionary sampan had had to pass through, we were all the more aware how immeasurably great this campaign to liberate Saigon and liberate the South was. . . .

The will and competence of our soldiers were not achieved in a day, but were the result of a continuous process of carrying out the party's ideological and organizational work in the armed forces. And throughout our thirty years of struggle, there had been no campaign in which Uncle Ho had not gone into the operation with our soldiers. Going out to battle this time, our whole army had been given singular, unprecedented strength because this strategically decisive battle bore his name: Ho Chi Minh, for every one of our cadres and fighters, was faith, strength, and life. Among the myriad troops in all the advancing wings, every one of our fighters carried toward Ho Chi Minh City [Saigon] the hopes of the nation and a love for our land. Today each fighter could see with his own eyes the resiliency which the Fatherland had built up during these many years, and given his own resiliency there was nothing, no enemy scheme that could stop him.

Van Tien Dung, *Our Great Spring Victory: An Account of the Liberation of South Vietnam*, translated by John Spragens Jr. (New York: Monthly Review Press, 1977).

34. "WHAT ARE THE LESSONS OF VIETNAM?"

Rep. John S. McCain (R-Ariz.), former Navy pilot and prisoner of war in Hanoi: It is awfully easy to look back with the benefit of history. The way the war ended up, we obviously should never have been involved. At the same time, I can understand the atmosphere and the decision-making process of the time that led us into that quagmire. We were so sure we were omnipotent that we tried to choose South Vietnam's leaders for them. When that happens, we can't expect the people to have faith in their government. I think the blame should be spread around equally — the politicians for failure to prosecute the war properly and failure to explain what we were doing to the American people; the military for failing to stand up and say "we quit" when it became obvious there was no way to win; the media, particularly television because of the limitations of the evening news, for failing to give the full picture of what was going on. I also must fault the anti-war movement, not for what they did during the war but for turning their backs on what happened later . . . .

Arthur Krause, father of Allison Krause, one of four students shot to death by Ohio National Guardsmen during a protest at Kent State University on May 4, 1970: . . . Our trial didn't end until 1979 (with an out-of-court settlement for which the Krauses and other plaintiffs got a signed apology). The end of the war meant that other people weren't getting killed, too. That was very important to me, too, but it was five years too late, five years of people being killed (in Vietnam), five years of my daughter being shot in the back by some brave guardsman. Maybe if the war had been over sooner, Allison wouldn't have been dead. . . . Is dissent a crime? Is that a reason for killing her? The war had gotten into us so badly we'd turned and were killing our own people on a campus in Ohio. . . . In other words, people were against (the war) and what did they do? They rose up in protest against it and so the next thing you know, they killed them, they reproached them. . . . The war meant shame: We killed our own children.

Los Angeles Times, April 28, 1985.

35. RONALD REAGAN'S VETERANS DAY SPEECH OF NOVEMBER 11, 1988 (EXTRACT)

Well, today, Veterans Day, as we do every year, we take that moment to embrace the gentle heroes of Vietnam and of all our wars. We remember those who were called upon to give all a person can give, and we remember those who were prepared to make that sacrifice if it were demanded of them in the line of duty, though it never was. Most of all, we remember the devotion and gallantry with which all of them ennobled their nation as they became champions of a noble cause.

I'm not speaking provocatively here. Unlike the other wars of this century, of course, there were deep divisions about the wisdom and rightness of the Vietnam war. Both sides spoke with honesty and fervor. And what more can we ask in our democracy? And yet after more than a decade of desperate boat people, after the killing fields of Cambodia, after all that has happened in that unhappy part of the world, who can doubt that the cause for which our men fought was just? It was, after all, however imperfectly pursued, the cause of freedom; and they showed uncommon courage in its service. Perhaps at this late date we can all agree that we've learned one lesson: that young Americans must never again be sent to fight and die unless we are prepared to let them win.

Public Papers of the Presidents of the United States: Ronald Reagan, 1988–1989 (Washington, D.C.: Government Printing Office, 1991), 1495–96.

36. GEORGE BUSH'S STATEMENTS ABOUT THE VIETNAM WAR DURING THE PERSIAN GULF WAR

From his address to the nation, January 16, 1991:

Just 2 hours ago, allied air forces began an attack on military targets in Iraq and Kuwait. These attacks continue as I speak. Ground forces are not engaged . . . .

Prior to ordering our forces into battle, I instructed our military commanders to take every necessary step to prevail as quickly at possible, and with the greatest degree of protection possible for American and allied service men and women. I've told the American people before that this will not be another Vietnam, and I repeat this here tonight. Our troops will have the best possible support in the entire world, and they will not be asked to fight with one hand tied behind their back. I'm hopeful that this fighting will not go on for long and that casualties will be held to an absolute minimum.

From his remarks to the American Legislative Exchange Council, March 1, 1991:

I want to conclude by thanking this group particularly but so many people across this country for the tremendous support for our men and women serving overseas. . . . I know you share this wonderful feeling that I have of joy in my heart. But it is overwhelmed by the gratitude I feel—not just to the troops overseas but to those who have assisted the United States of America, like our Secretary of Defense, like our Chairman of our Joint Chiefs, and so many other unsung heroes who have made all this possible. It's a proud day for America. And, by God, we've kicked the Vietnam syndrome once and for all.

From his radio address to United States armed forces stationed in the Persian Gulf region, March 2, 1991:

> Never have I been more proud of our troops, or more proud to be your Commander in Chief. For today, amid prayers of thanks and hope, the Kuwaiti flag once again flies high above Kuwait City. And it's there because you and your coalition allies put it there. . . .
>
> Americans today are confident of our country, confident of our future, and most of all, confident about you. We promised you'd be given the means to fight. We promised not to look over your shoulder. We promised this would not be another Vietnam. And we kept that promise. The specter of Vietnam has been buried forever in the desert sands of the Arabian Peninsula.

Public Papers of the Presidents of the United States: George Bush, 1991 (Washington, D.C.: Government Printing Office, 1992), 42–44, 196–97, and 206–7.

37. BILL CLINTON'S SPEECH ON NORMALIZATION OF DIPLOMATIC RELATIONS WITH VIETNAM, JULY 11, 1995 (EXTRACT)

Today I am announcing the normalization of diplomatic relations with Vietnam. . . .

By helping to bring Vietnam into the community of nations, normalization also serves our interest in working for a free and peaceful Vietnam in a stable and peaceful Asia. We will begin to normalize our trade relations with Vietnam, whose economy is now liberalizing and integrating into the economy of the Asia-Pacific region. . . .

I believe normalization and increased contact between Americans and Vietnamese will advance the cause of freedom in Vietnam, just as it did in Eastern Europe and the former Soviet Union. I strongly believe that engaging the Vietnamese on the broad economic front of economic reform and the broad front of democratic reform will help to honor the sacrifice of those who fought for freedom's sake in Vietnam. . . .

Whatever we may think about the political decisions of the Vietnam era, the brave Americans who fought and died there had noble motives. They fought for the freedom and independence of the Vietnamese people. Today, the Vietnamese are independent, and we believe this step will help to extend the reach of freedom in Vietnam and, in so doing, to enable these fine veterans of Vietnam to keep working for that freedom.

This step will also help our own country to move forward on an issue that has separated Americans from one another for too long now. Let the future be our destination. We have so much work ahead of us. This mo-

ment offers us the opportunity to bind up our own wounds. They have resisted time for too long. We can now move on to common ground. Whatever divided us before let us consign to the past. Let this moment, in the
words of the Scripture, be a time to heal and a time to build.

Public Papers of the Presidents of the United States: William J. Clinton, 1995
(Washington, D.C.: Government Printing Office, 1996), 1073–74.

Appendix 2

STATISTICS

TABLE 1   U.S. Military Personnel in South Vietnam

December 31, 1960	900	December 31, 1967	485,600
December 31, 1961	3,205	June 30, 1968	534,700
June 30, 1962	9,000	December 31, 1968	536,100
December 31, 1962	11,300	April 30, 1969	543,400
June 30, 1963	15,400	June 30, 1969	538,700
December 31, 1963	16,300	December 31, 1969	475,200
June 30, 1964	16,500	June 30, 1970	414,900
December 31, 1964	23,300	December 31, 1970	334,600
June 30, 1965	59,900	June 30, 1971	239,200
December 31, 1965	184,300	December 31, 1971	156,800
June 30, 1966	267,500	June 30, 1972	47,000
December 31, 1966	385,300	December 31, 1972	24,200
June 30, 1967	448,800	March 30, 1973	240

Source: U.S. Department of Defense, OASD (Comptroller), Directorate for Information.

TABLE 2   U.S. Military Personnel in
Southeast Asia Outside Vietnam

December 31, 1965	42,900
December 31, 1966	54,200
December 31, 1967	80,300
December 31, 1968	87,400
December 31, 1969	82,900
December 31, 1970	57,200
December 31, 1971	48,200
November 30, 1972	84,700

Source: U.S. Department of Defense, OASD
(Comptroller), Directorate for Information.

TABLE 3   U.S. Government Military Expenditures in Southeast Asia

Fiscal Year	Full Cost (millions)
1965	$ 103
1966	5,812
1967	20,133
1968	26,547
1969	28,805
1970	23,052
1971	14,719
1972	9,261

Full costs are for all forces and include personnel, aircraft, operations, munitions used, and equipment lost in the Southeast Asia conflict.

Source: U.S. Senate Appropriations Committee.

TABLE 4   North Vietnamese Army (NVA) Strength in South Vietnam

Infiltration from North Vietnam

1964	13,400
1965	36,300
1966	92,287
1967	101,263

NVA and Vietcong Combined Personnel in Combat Battalions

1968	250,300
1969	236,800
1970	213,800
1971	197,700

Source: Guenter Lewy, *America in Vietnam* (New York: Oxford University Press, 1978), 66, 191.

TABLE 5   Republic of Vietnam Armed Forces Strength   (in thousands)

Year	Regular Forces	Regional Forces	Popular Forces	Total
1955	177	54	48	279
1960	146	49	48	243
1964	250	96	168	514
1967	343	151	149	643
1968	427	220	173	820
1969	493	190	214	897
1970	515	207	246	968
1971–72	516	284	248	1,048

Regular Forces include Army, Navy, Air Force, and Marines. Until 1964, Regional Forces were known as the Civil Guard, and Popular Forces were known as the Self-Defense Corps.

Source: James L. Collins, Jr., *The Development and Training of the South Vietnamese Army, 1950–1972* (Washington, D.C.: U.S. Government Printing Office, 1975), 151.

TABLE 6   Total Casualties (January 1961 through January 1973)

United States

Killed in Action	45,941
Wounded	300,635
Missing	2,330
Killed or died, noncombat-related	10,420

South Vietnam

Military: Killed in action	220,357
Military: Wounded	499,026
Civilian: Killed (estimate)	415,000
Civilian: Wounded (estimate)	935,000
Vietcong/North Vietnam	
Military: Killed (estimate)	851,000
Civilian: Killed (in North Vietnam)	65,000

Third-Country Military

South Korea: Killed	4,407
Australia/New Zealand: Killed	469
Thailand: Killed	351

Sources: George Donelson Moss, *Vietnam: An American Ordeal,* 3d ed. (Upper Saddle River, N.J.: Prentice Hall, 1998), 447, and Lester H. Brune and Richard Dean Burns, *America and the Indochina Wars, 1945–1990: A Bibliographic Guide* (Claremont, Calif.: Regina Books, 1992), 146.

TABLE 7   U.S. and Republic of Vietnam Military Killed in Action by Year

Year	United States	Republic of Vietnam
1960	0	2,223
1961	11	4,004
1962	31	4,457
1963	78	5,665
1964	147	7,457
1965	1,369	11,242
1966	5,008	11,953
1967	9,377	12,716
1968	14,589	27,915
1969	9,414	21,833
1970	4,221	23,346
1971	1,381	22,738
1972	300	39,587
1973	237	27,901
1974	207	31,219

Source: Jeffrey J. Clark, *Advice and Support: The Final Years* (Washington, D.C.: U.S. Government Printing Office, 1988), 275.

TABLE 8   U.S. Deaths in Vietnam by Race

American Indian	226
Caucasian	50,120
Malayan	252
Mongolian	116
Negro	7,264
Unknown, Not Reported	215
Total	58,193

Racial category titles are those used in the creation of the documentation files circa 1967.

Source: Southeast Asia Combat Area Casualties Current File in the Records of the Office of the Secretary of Defense (Record Group 330), National Archives and Records Service, College Park, Maryland.

TABLE 9   U.S. Draftees Killed in the Vietnam War

Year	Total U.S. Deaths *All Services*	Draftees *All Services (percent)*	Draftees *Army (percent)*
1965	1,369	16	28
1966	5,008	21	34
1967	9,377	34	57
1968	14,589	34	58
1969	9,414	40	62
1970	4,221	43	57

Source: Christian G. Appy, *Working-Class War: American Combat Soldiers and Vietnam* (Chapel Hill: University of North Carolina Press, 1993), 29.

TABLE 10   Munitions Expended by U.S. Forces in World War II, Korea, and
Indochina   (in thousands of metric tons)

	Air	**Ground**	**Total**
World War II	1,957	3,572	5,529
Korea	634	1,913	2,547
Indochina			
1966	449	536	948
1967	844	1,091	1,935
1968	1,302	1,345	2,647
1969	1,257	1,274	2,531
1970	885	1,071	1,956
1971	691	755	1,446
1972	982	776	1,758
Total Indochina	6,410	6,847	13,221

Source: Brune and Burns, *America and the Indochina Wars*, 110.

TABLE 11   U.S. Vietnam Veterans

Total service personnel during Vietnam era, 1964–1975	8,700,000
Number who served in Vietnam	2,700,000
Number who served in combat (estimate*)	1,600,000
Vital Statistics 1978	
Median age	32 years
Median education	12.9 years
Median income, ages 20–39	$12,680**
Percentage using G.I. Bill benefits	65%***
Percentage Unemployed, ages 20–34	5.5%
Disabled (estimate)	512,000
In Veterans Administration hospitals	9,652

*The Vietnam War did not have conventional front and rear areas, and there are no specific combat/noncombat statistics. A survey conducted by the University of Notre Dame found that 75 percent of veterans had engaged in some type of combat. See Lawrence M. Baskir and William A. Strauss, *Chance and Circumstance: The Draft, the War, and the Vietnam Generation* (New York: Vintage Books, 1978), 53 and 283. Statistics reported in Stephen E. Ambrose and James A. Barber Jr., eds., *The Military and American Society* (New York: Free Press, 1972), 195, indicate that only 25 percent were engaged in combat at any one time.

**This average is about $2,800 higher than for nonveterans.

***This percentage is higher than the usage rate for World War II and Korean War veterans.

Source: Compilation of Veterans Administration, Department of Defense, and public reports in Brune and Burns, *America and the Indochina Wars,* 184.

INDEX

Page numbers in **bold** refer to main entry in *Guide*.